Fulfill Thy Ministry

Also available from Bloomsbury

Backcountry Slave Trader, Philip Noel Racine and Frances Melton Racine
James McDowell of Virginia, Charles A. Bodie

Fulfill Thy Ministry

Three Episcopal Clergymen, Race, and the Civil War Era

Loren B. Mead and
J. Michael Martinez

BLOOMSBURY ACADEMIC
LONDON • NEW YORK • OXFORD • NEW DELHI • SYDNEY

BLOOMSBURY ACADEMIC

Bloomsbury Publishing Inc, 1359 Broadway, New York, NY 10018, USA
Bloomsbury Publishing Plc, 50 Bedford Square, London, WC1B 3DP, UK
Bloomsbury Publishing Ireland, 29 Earlsfort Terrace, Dublin 2, D02 AY28, Ireland

BLOOMSBURY, BLOOMSBURY ACADEMIC and the Diana logo are trademarks of Bloomsbury Publishing Plc

First published in the United States of America 2026

Copyright © Bloomsbury Publishing, Inc, 2026

For legal purposes the Acknowledgments on p. xiii constitute an extension of this copyright page.

Cover design: Diana Nuhn
Cover image © iStock.com / Christine_Kohler

All rights reserved. No part of this publication may be: i) reproduced or transmitted in any form, electronic or mechanical, including photocopying, recording or by means of any information storage or retrieval system without prior permission in writing from the publishers; or ii) used or reproduced in any way for the training, development or operation of artificial intelligence (AI) technologies, including generative AI technologies. The rights holders expressly reserve this publication from the text and data mining exception as per Article 4(3) of the Digital Single Market Directive (EU) 2019/790.

Bloomsbury Publishing Inc does not have any control over, or responsibility for, any third-party websites referred to or in this book. All internet addresses given in this book were correct at the time of going to press. The author and publisher regret any inconvenience caused if addresses have changed or sites have ceased to exist, but can accept no responsibility for any such changes.

Library of Congress Cataloging-in-Publication Data

ISBN: HB: 979-8-8818-0354-4
PB: 979-8-8818-0355-1
ePDF: 979-8-8818-6800-0
eBook: 979-8-8818-0356-8

Typeset by Deanta Global Publishing Services, Chennai, India
Printed and bound in the United States of America

For product safety related questions contact productsafety@bloomsbury.com.

To find out more about our authors and books visit www.bloomsbury.com and sign up for our newsletters.

*In loving memory of Polly Ayres Mellette Mead (1931–2013)
daughter, sister, wife, mother, aunt, cousin,
grandmother, great-grandmother,
friend, confidante,
poetess, writer, educator, public servant,
hostess with the mostest,
and southern matriarch extraordinaire*

But watch thou in all things, endure afflictions, do the work of an evangelist, fulfill thy ministry.

—*2 Tim. 4:5*

CONTENTS

List of figures ix
Foreword x
Preface and Acknowledgments xiii

PART I The Antebellum Era and the War of 1861–1865 1

1 "The Rich and the Poor in the House of God Meet Together"—Three Clergymen and the Protestant Episcopal Church in the Civil War Era: An Overview 3

2 "He Was Always Entertained at the Various Plantations and Was Always Welcomed Most Warmly"—Peter Fayssoux Stevens: The Early Years (1830–1865) 37

3 "I Think I Was Born Opposed to Slavery"—Anthony Toomer Porter: The Early Years (1828–1865) 61

4 "I Redevoted Myself Wholly and Only to God"—William Porcher DuBose: The Early Years (1836–1865) 83

PART II Reconstruction and Redemption 109

5 "A World So Changed from What It Had Been Ten Years Before": South Carolina Politics During Reconstruction (1865–1877) 111

6 "Shall the Church of God Catch the Evil Infection?": The Postwar Episcopal Church in the South Carolina Diocese 137

7   "Of Bishop Stevens It May Be Well Said: 'Servant of God, Well Done!'"—Peter Fayssoux Stevens: The Later Years (1865–1910)   169

8   "He Was a True Evangelist"—Anthony Toomer Porter: The Later Years (1865–1902)   193

9   "The Only Important Creative Theologian That the Episcopal Church in the United States Has Produced"— William Porcher DuBose: The Later Years (1865–1918)   217

PART III   Conclusion   245

10   "We Have Passed Through a Season of Extraordinary Trial": Divergent Views on Race in the Lives of Stevens, Porter, and DuBose   247

References 267
Index 289
About the Authors 305

LIST OF FIGURES

This Image of Peter Fayssoux Stevens Shows Him in Uniform at the Time He Served as Superintendent of the South Carolina Military Academy 42

Oil Portrait of Colonel Peter Fayssoux Stevens in Uniform 52

Undated Photograph of Anthony Toomer Porter as a Young Man 69

A Young William Porcher Dubose in the Uniform of a Citadel Cadet 88

Thomas Frederick Davis Served as the Episcopal Bishop of South Carolina From 1853 Until 1871 138

William Bell White Howe Served as the Episcopal Bishop of South Carolina From 1871 Until 1894 150

George David Cummins Founded the Reformed Episcopal Church in 1873 155

This Undated Photograph Shows Peter Fayssoux Stevens in Middle Age 171

Peter Fayssoux Stevens Served Black Communicants in the Reformed Episcopal Church for Almost Thirty-Five Years. He Is Pictured Here in Old Age 183

This Drawing of Anthony Toomer Porter Dates From 1892 198

Anthony Toomer Porter in Middle Age 207

Anthony Toomer Porter Toward the End of His Life 211

William Porcher Dubose Is Pictured as a Young Clergyman 219

William Porcher Dubose Forged a Successful Academic Career as a Theologian at the University of the South in Sewanee, Tennessee 224

William Porcher Dubose Toward the End of His Life 227

FOREWORD

On graduating from Virginia Theological Seminary in 1955, a young and nervous deacon presented himself to the Rt. Reverend Albert Thomas, Episcopal Bishop of the diocese of South Carolina, for his first pastoral assignment. "It's a small but up and coming area soon to experience rapid industrial growth," was how Bishop Granville Bennett described Loren's first parish.

"Son, he done sent you to Hell Hole Swamp!" was how the bishop's assistant reacted, and indeed that was a common name at the time for the low-lying area of Berkeley County where my father would take the first steps in his ecclesiastical career.

The book you are about to read is a consequence of Loren Benjamin Mead's years at Trinity Church, Pinopolis. Like many South Carolinians, my father was haunted by the state's history of slavery and segregation. Born in 1930, his early childhood was spent in a world utterly dominated by the memory of what people still called "the War" and where Jim Crow race laws and customs were largely uncontested. At seminary, he would be exposed to the new theological and political ideas then challenging both the doctrinal and the social certainties of his formative years. In Pinopolis, he would irk some of the congregation by insisting that the Confederate flag no longer be carried in church processions. In Chapel Hill, North Carolina, where he served as the first rector of the newly founded Church of the Holy Family, his strong advocacy for the Civil Rights movement divided the congregation, but enabled him to know, and to work with, the Reverend Dr. Martin Luther King.

Loren went on from the parish ministry to found and lead the Alban Institute but never lost his early interest in and focus on the role of race in the life of the United States and of the Episcopal Church. For many in his generation, including his seminary classmate and lifelong friend Jack Spong (later Episcopal bishop of Newark, New Jersey), the shock of disillusionment with the white Southern society in which they grew up translated into a habit of doubting the received doctrines of the church as well as its prevailing social norms. If their parents, their church communities and the traditions of their region could be so wrong about race, what else might they be wrong about? On issues like the ordination of women to the clergy, attitudes toward abortion and gay and lesbian weddings and many other social questions, a generation of Southern white mainline clerics was more open to changed perspectives as a result of their "racial enlightenment" of the 1950s.

After retiring from the Alban Institute, Loren spent more and more time reading about Southern and Black history. And in the course of this reading, he came across the career of Peter Fayssoux Stevens. As commandant of The Citadel, South Carolina's venerable military college, Stevens was in charge of some of the cadets who fired the first shots of the Civil War. Enlisting in the Confederate Army, Stevens served in Virginia until, wounded at Antietam, he returned to take holy orders in the Episcopal Church. After the war, he ministered to both Black and white congregants in the South Carolina Low Country and ultimately asked the diocese to approve Black candidates for ordination. When the diocese refused, Stevens left the Episcopal Church to join a splinter organization, the Reformed Episcopal Church, and over the remaining decades of his career helped this largely Black church establish a presence in South Carolina that continues to the present day.

This is a compelling story that raises many questions; what made it even more compelling to Loren was that Peter Stevens had been the rector of Trinity Church Pinopolis—and that Loren had heard nothing about him or his ministry while he was there. Moreover, there were healthy and vigorous predominantly Black Reformed Episcopal churches in and around Pinopolis dating back to Stevens's time, and Loren had never heard them mentioned and had never learned anything about them while he served in Stevens's old church.

In the closing years of his life, Loren set out to understand and then to write the story of Peter Stevens and of two of his contemporaries, William Porcher DuBose and Anthony Toomer Porter, also clergymen who left a deep imprint on Loren's world. He did not finish the book; cancer intervened, though Dad was still poring through his notes as he lay in hospice care.

Loren made his family promise that we would see this project through to completion, but there was only one among us who had the background to accomplish it. Mike Martinez, Loren's nephew (Mike's mother was Loren's wife's sister), is an accomplished scholar and historian of the Postbellum South and, much to the relief of the rest of us, he agreed to take on the task of preparing the book that you are about to read.

This is Mike's book, not Loren's, as Loren's notes, often scribbled in the margins of books he was reading, could inspire but not guide a successor. But having discussed the original project with Loren many times, I am awed at Mike's ability to see what Loren found so compelling in these stories and to bring his own perspective to it. Mike has done what Loren badly wanted done and given us a portrait of three serious-minded Christian men doing their best to live good lives among a people they loved in the shadows of slavery, racism, and war. Mike has captured Loren's sense of these men and their society with all the complexity and moral balance that Loren sought to portray. He can be unsparing of their blind spots and failures; yet he grasps the constraints of the times in which they lived.

Thank you, Mike, for fulfilling my father's last wish and seeing this project through.

Walter Russell Mead
Washington, DC

PREFACE AND ACKNOWLEDGMENTS

This book tells the story of three men who came of age in antebellum South Carolina, answered the call to become ministers in the Protestant Episcopal Church, supported the Confederate cause during the war of 1861–5, and faced divisive questions over the role of Black communicants in the postwar church. Their struggles were emblematic of the struggles of all Christian clergymen in the United States who sought to fulfill their ministries in a time of unprecedented tumult.

It is also the story of Blacks and their uneasy place in white people's churches during the late nineteenth and early twentieth centuries. As enslaved persons before the Civil War, they often worshipped in whatever time, place, and manner that their slave masters dictated. After the war, Blacks freed from bondage preferred to attend churches that welcomed them with open arms. White churchmen struggled to decide if they should invite the so-called "freed people" into their churches and, if so, under what conditions.

Scripture provided no easy answers. Faced with unending ambiguity, church leaders reacted less out of ideological or religious concerns than from pragmatic considerations. The antebellum Protestant Episcopal Church proselytized Black people, but many affluent southern planters were Episcopalians. Episcopal clergymen in the South could not and would not embrace abolitionism. Black people were sometimes welcomed into the church, but they could not become full members. Moreover, the efficacy of slavery was not a topic for public debate in the antebellum Episcopal Church, but the peculiar institution influenced almost every major decision of the church before and during the war.

Owing to the mixed messages that church leaders provided in the antebellum Episcopal Church, it was left to individual ministers to decide how they would interpret and fulfill their pastoral duties. Some ministers enthusiastically pursued the mission of evangelizing people of color. Others kept their distance, embracing the traditions and customs of southern society, which considered Blacks as the "other," hence undesirable and undeserving.

After the war, Reconstruction and Jim Crow-era white churches discriminated against Blacks precisely as other institutions in society discriminated against them, although some churches allowed Blacks to join the church without affording them full membership. Accordingly, a clergyman could choose one of three options. First, if he disagreed with the church's decision to allow Blacks in the church while denying them an opportunity to choose Black leaders, the minister could petition for a change and abandon his post if the change did not occur. Second, a clergyman could petition to allow Black communicants to enjoy some rights and privileges—under the supervision of white church leaders, of course—but he would continue working within the church even if his entreaties fell on deaf ears. Finally, a clergyman could accept the church's decision to discriminate against Black communicants and defend that decision as necessary to the social order. Each of the three men profiled in this book chose a different option despite their similar backgrounds.

The book is divided into three parts. Part I explores the early lives of these men during the antebellum years as well as their activities during the Civil War. Part II begins with Chapters 5 and 6, which provide a broad overview of the political and religious issues facing the clergymen in the immediate aftermath of the war. Chapters 7, 8, and 9 discuss their later years. In Part III, Chapter 10 examines the similarities and differences in their respective views of race and the duties of the church. The book title is derived from 2 Tim. 4:5, a verse that Anthony Toomer Porter cited as among his favorites.

Fulfill Thy Ministry followed a long, circuitous road to publication. It began on February 23, 2016, when the Rev. Loren Benjamin Mead of Falls Church, Virginia, sent me a letter containing notes and an outline of a book project that he was researching. The letter arrived the old-fashioned way, appearing in my mailbox with two Forever postage stamps affixed to the top right corner of the envelope. Inside, I found five neatly typed pages, produced in a large-sized font for easy reading.

As Rev. Mead explained in his letter, "I'm going to try to do a new book on three men I call my own Three Musketeers, white men who really stood in the crossing between whites and blacks in the Episcopal Church right after the war." "The war," of course, was the conflict that ripped apart the American landscape from 1861 until 1865. Whether it was called the Civil War, the War Between the States, the War of Northern Aggression, or the Late Unpleasantness, I knew what he meant. More than fifteen decades after the surrender at Appomattox, the war continued to influence Americans' understanding of citizenship, government authority, race relations, and the role of the church in modern life.

Rev. Mead focused on the works of three emblematic Episcopal clergymen from South Carolina who confronted race during the war and Reconstruction. As he wrote in his letter,

> These three men . . . [are] Peter Stevens (celebrated in Charleston as the man who fired on Fort Sumter), Toomer Porter (who helped reestablish

education for blacks and whites after the war and whose name is kept in the name of the Porter-Gaud Academy in Charleston today), and William Porcher DuBose (later dean-founder of the seminary at Sewanee, and maybe the only American Episcopal theologian who is sometimes read outside the USA).

His research question was relatively simple, even if the answer was not: How did these three southern clergymen—each man an ardent supporter of the Confederate States of America—respond to the collapse of a slaveholding republic and the inception of the Reconstruction era and, later, the Jim Crow regime? So many ex-Confederates were unreconstructed rebels who bowed to superior northern military might but refused to accept former slaves—the freed people—as functioning members of society during the postbellum years.

The three men reacted in different ways. Peter Fayssoux Stevens became a tireless champion of the freedmen, devoting thirty-five years of his life to their religious instruction. When leaders of the South Carolina Protestant Episcopal Church refused to allow Blacks to ascend into leadership positions or establish their own congregations, Stevens left the church. Anthony Toomer Porter shared Stevens's insight that former slaves must be welcomed into the church, although the freed people would report to white bishops who made crucial decisions for them. He remained a member of the Protestant Episcopal Church his entire life. William Porcher DuBose forged a different path, embracing the traditional white perspective that Blacks were inferior and must be kept at arm's length.

Reconstructing the three ministers' views on race is not as straightforward as it appears at first blush. As discussed within these pages, attitudes on race and the appropriate level of government authority are not linear propositions. It is possible to cherish and defend competing values. To fight for a slaveholding republic on an abstract, macro level and later uplift individual freed people as a practical matter may appear contradictory to logicians, but a Christian minister may distinguish between duties to Caesar and duties to God.

As a retired Episcopal minister, Rev. Mead had long been interested in the role of race in the church during the nineteenth and twentieth centuries. His research question involved a broader query: How could men and women of God devote their lives to the Christian church, with its emphasis on helping the less fortunate, and yet discriminate against their fellow man based on race? It was a simple, almost elegant question. In choosing to examine the lives and careers of Stevens, Porter, and DuBose, Mead sought to explore the thorny questions at the heart of both religion and southern history to understand how and why these men reached their conclusions. Christ insists that we treat our fellow man with equal dignity and respect, regardless of his or her social status, but southern history often has been premised on inequality.

Alexander Stephens, vice president of the Southern Confederacy, stated in his infamous Cornerstone Speech of March 1861 that we must recognize the necessity of race-based slavery. To secure the perpetuation of slavery, Stephens argued, Americans must interpret the goal the government established in Philadelphia in 1787 as essentially unequal because "its foundations are laid, its cornerstone rests, upon the great truth that the negro is not equal to the white man; that slavery, subordination to the superior race, is his natural and normal condition. This, our new government, is the first, in the history of the world, based upon this great physical, philosophical, and moral truth."[1]

The efforts of the three clergymen profiled here were complicated not only by the ambiguities of southern history but by the realities of church dogma. The teachings of Jesus Christ, full of simple moral virtues, have been filtered through millennia of church history, with its schisms and myriad interpretations, its politics and strife. Like so much of southern history, the terrain was filled with unexpected twists and turns, a seeming contradiction here, an anomaly there. Despite the challenges, Rev. Mead believed that the motivations of these long-dead clergymen could reveal larger truths about Blacks and whites in the nineteenth century church.

It was an intriguing proposal, exactly the sort of project that a young Loren Mead would tackle with gusto, but in 2016 he fretted that the book was too much to take on. At the age of eighty-six, he concluded that the book was "bigger than me. Not only that, but I'm old. I mean OLD."

Not content to go gentle into that good night, Rev. Mead approached friends and colleagues connected with the Episcopal Church, exploring the possibility of farming out the project to a seasoned academic or scholar interested in church history. His initial inquiries fell flat. He lamented in February 2016 that "my letters don't get answered. Or, and this is true of others—their agenda is already full, and they don't want to take on something like this."

After Rev. Mead wrote his letter to me, one colleague accepted his offer, albeit in an abbreviated form. The Rev. Dr. Francis Wade penned a short biography of Peter Fayssoux Stevens for *The Historiographer*, a publication of the National Episcopal Historians and Archivists of the Historical Society of the Episcopal Church and the Episcopal Women's History Project. In a 2021 article that he adapted from a presentation he made to the 2018 annual conference of the National Episcopal Historians and Archivists, "Confederate Colonel and Priest Promotes Racial Reconciliation," Dr. Wade wrote that

> I am indebted to my friend, colleague and former parishioner the late Loren B. Mead, founder of The Alban Institute, for the original research behind this presentation. Loren's quest to understand the dynamics of

American slavery uncovered three unique stories: those of Anthony Toomer Porter (1828–1902), who contributed greatly to the education of both African Americans and Caucasians in post-war South Carolina; William Porcher DuBose (1836–1918), a founder and principal of St. Luke's Seminary at Sewanee Tennessee; and Peter Fayssoux Stevens (1830–1910), the subject of this presentation.[2]

I was unaware of Dr. Wade's decision to write an article about Stevens when Rev. Mead asked if I would finish the project. I was flattered by Mead's offer, but also perplexed. An accomplished scholar and well-respected author of numerous books on churches and congregations, he normally would not solicit my help to complete his work. I had written academic books and articles on Reconstruction and race, including projects on the Confederate battle flag as well as the Ku Klux Klan, but I was certainly not an authority on church history. Although I was carefully and painstakingly writing academic tomes that no one would read, I was under no illusions. Mine was a pedestrian career. I was not in Loren Mead's league when it came to scholarly endeavors.

In the interests of full disclosure, I should mention that Rev. Mead married my mother's sister, Polly, to whom this book is dedicated. I assumed that he approached me as much for our familial ties as for my academic expertise. Moreover, I understood that perhaps Rev. Mead turned to me out of desperation since no one else was enthusiastic about his project. In any case, it is difficult, although not impossible, for a nephew to turn aside the request of a beloved uncle.

Aside from these issues, I was one of those people who had a full agenda. When I received Rev. Mead's letter, I was working as a full-time lawyer/lobbyist for a privately held Fortune 400 corporation and a part-time teacher at Kennesaw State University in Kennesaw, Georgia. Moreover, I was involved in numerous book projects of my own. Although I had tackled the Reconstruction era earlier in my career, I had left the subject behind while I pursued numerous other projects. I found the concept interesting and worthwhile, but it was not for me. In 2016, I responded to Rev. Mead's offer with an email respectfully declining to participate.

I assumed that he eventually would find someone in the church to take up the mantle. The role of Christian churches during the war, Reconstruction, and Jim Crow, with an emphasis on the Protestant Episcopal Church, seemed to be a potentially fruitful area for scholarly inquiry. Fully confident that he would secure a co-author, I went on my way. To the extent that I thought about his letter, I equated the offer with the typical "come see me sometime" invitation that one social acquaintance extends to another.

Fast forward to December 2017. I encountered Rev. Mead at a Christmas party that month, and we chatted for a few minutes. He did not look well. I knew that he was battling cancer, and the prognosis was grim.

As we exchanged pleasantries, dancing around the delicate subject of his declining health, he mentioned his continued fascination with his Three Musketeers. He said that he had not found a co-author, and he expressed regret that he would leave the project unfinished. When he realized that I would not take a hint, Rev. Mead asked me point blank if I would reconsider taking on the project. "I'm not a church history guy," I explained. "I'm also tied up with other manuscripts for at least the next three to four years."

He nodded. "I understand," he said. "You know, this isn't a church history. It's the biography of three men who happened to work in the church. Just think it over. When you have the time, let me know your decision."

Alas, time was not something that he had. I never saw him again. Rev. Mead died on May 5, 2018, at the age of eighty-eight.

Even after his death, I was not sure that I was the right person to finish his work. Surely another scholar, someone far more accomplished than I, could see the book through to completion. I knew that he had put out feelers to other scholars. Perhaps a more intrepid soul than I would step forward.

By January 2021, I had experienced a change of heart. With my desk cleared and my interest piqued, I reconsidered my initial objections. While I am not a scholar of church history, I knew that I could handle the project. Had this been a book focusing on the theological outlook of each man or a history of the Protestant Episcopal Church of South Carolina in the nineteenth century, I would have demurred no matter how intriguing the concept. Yet, as Rev. Mead said, this was to be the story of each man's deeds as opposed to his religious thinking, although his views on religion would be part of the tale. I resolved to press forward with the work.

I immediately understood why he was drawn to these three figures. A native of Florence, South Carolina—which was my hometown as well—Rev. Mead came of age 100 years after these men lived and worked. Rev. Peter Fayssoux Stevens, born in 1830, became the rector of Trinity Church in Pinopolis as his first assignment for the Episcopal Church of South Carolina. Rev. Mead, born in 1930, also became the rector of Trinity Church in Pinopolis as his first assignment for the church. Always interested in education, Rev. Mead would certainly have felt a kinship with Anthony Toomer Porter, the great educator. As a graduate of the University of the South, Rev. Mead wished to explore the racial views of the university's most celebrated professor, William Porcher DuBose. In a final bit of synergy or irony or simple coincidence, Rev. Mead died in 2018, 100 years after the last of the three men, Rev. DuBose, died.

As I delved into the project, I discovered that Rev. Mead had outlined what he wanted to say, but his research materials were scattered about. I reached out to his family asking for books, notes, emails, and any other materials that might help reconstruct his thinking. Family members graciously provided me with a treasure trove of information. Dr. Ben Wise,

Rev. Mead's grandson, thoughtfully provided access to old computer files. Walter Russell Mead, Loren's eldest son and an eminent scholar in his own right, shipped cartons of books to my house to help me follow the research trail. This was no small task! I found five cartons of books, articles, and notes. Walter was kind enough to pen a foreword to the book. He read through the manuscript and provided a detailed critique as well. Rev. Mead's other adult children—my cousins Chris Mead, Barbara (Babs) Wise, and Phil Mead—encouraged me to persevere during the numerous delays as I worked through the materials. Babs was especially helpful in the later stages of the book as I gathered endorsements for the book jacket.

And the delays were numerous. Owing to the obscurity of these figures, especially Peter Fayssoux Stevens, I was forced to perform archival research. Finding unpublished materials, including several photographs, consumed enormous amounts of time. In the meanwhile, I had to handle mundane issues such as scratching out a living and raising the children in my household.

As a lead up to preparing a book proposal, I developed academic articles that would undergo peer review in hopes that feedback would improve the project. It worked precisely as I had hoped. Loren and I published articles in two leading journals, *Anglican and Episcopal History* and *Journal of Anglican Studies*. By the end of calendar year 2023, I had a revised proposal out the door. I was pleased when, in May 2024, Rowman & Littlefield (now Bloomsbury) agreed to publish the manuscript.[3]

As I have learned repeatedly, no one writes or publishes a book without a team of supporters working behind the scenes. First and foremost, we must extend heartfelt appreciation to our editor, Dr. Richard Brown, senior executive editor, religion & spirituality, at Rowman & Littlefield (Bloomsbury). Richard expressed unwavering faith in the project from the very beginning. As a bonus, his assistant, Victoria (Tori) Shi, proved to be a godsend when it came to handling the details involved with publishing a book.

Brad Steinecke, assistant director of local history, Spartanburg County (South Carolina) Public Libraries, went above and beyond the call of duty in introducing me to the DuPre-Moseley Family Collection in the Kennedy Room of Local History and Genealogy during my research visit in July 2021. I was especially grateful that he found a copy of Stevens's handwritten autobiography as well as images of Stevens in the archives. Unlike Porter and DuBose, Stevens did not publish an autobiography, which made the task of locating information on his background especially challenging. (DuBose penned an unpublished autobiography in addition to his published autobiography, but it was easier to find his unpublished work than it was to track down Stevens's unpublished work.) As far as I know, three of the four Stevens photographs in this book were not published before I accessed them.

I also thank Tessa Updike, archivist at The Citadel, who kindly provided background information on Peter Fayssoux Stevens. She set me on the right path by providing access to the unpublished manuscript of Marion Stevens Eberly, a detailed typewritten sketch of her family history deposited in The Citadel archives. Stevens figured prominently in the sketch.

Karen Stokes, processing archivist at the South Carolina Historical Society, kindly chased down obscure sources on all three men. She also pointed me in the right direction to locate several photographs and alerted me to the archives located in the Kennedy Room of Local History and Genealogy in the Spartanburg County (South Carolina) Public Libraries. Stokes was the co-editor of a book on William Porcher DuBose's Civil War correspondence, which helped the cause immensely.

Dr. Sheryl Kujawa-Holbrook, editor-in-chief of *Anglican and Episcopal History*, Dr. Ehren Foley of the University of South Carolina Press, and Dr. Matthew A. Lockhart, editor of *The South Carolina Historical Magazine*, were not directly involved in the book project, but each scholar read portions of the manuscript and provided feedback in the early stages. My good friend Keith W. Smith also read part of the manuscript and provided a helpful critique. These folks were extremely generous in guiding me on the path toward publication.

I also extend thanks to the following archivists and librarians (in alphabetical order) who aided my research: Abby Cole and Andrew Lankes of the South Caroliniana Library, Columbia, South Carolina; Rev. Jerry Jellico, deacon in the Church of the Holy Communion, Charleston, South Carolina; Mandi D. Johnson, director, William R. Laurie University Archives and Special Collections, the University of the South; Ellie Miller, archival assistant, the Archives of the Episcopal Church, Austin, Texas; Molly I. Silliman, librarian, South Carolina Historical Society; Matthew Turi, manuscripts research and instruction librarian, Wilson Special Collections Library, the University of North Carolina at Chapel Hill; Julie Warren, project manager, Georgetown County (South Carolina) Digital Library; and Courtnay Zeitler, information literacy librarian, Jessie Ball duPont Library, the University of the South.

Rev. Mead's children, grandchildren, great-grandchildren, and extended family—far too numerous to list here—supported this effort at each step along the journey. I could not have reconstructed his plan for the book without their assistance. Thank you one and all!

Because Rev. Mead entrusted this project to me and was not here to say, "What on earth were you thinking here?" the final book undoubtedly is different from the work that he would have written. In the Foreword, Walter Russell Mead wrote that this is my book, not Loren's. He is overly generous. Walter assigns me too much credit (or blame). The concept and the spirit of the project were Loren's. I am the wordsmith who brought it home. He was the strategist and I was the tactician. All I can say is that good, bad, or ugly, I did my best. I tried to capture the spirit of the project that Rev. Mead outlined to me in his 2016 correspondence. It should go without being said—but I will say it, anyway—any mistakes in fact or interpretation are solely my responsibility.

J. Michael Martinez
Monroe, Georgia

Notes

1. Stephens's speech is quoted in many sources. See, for example, Adolph L. Reed, Jr., *The South: Jim Crow and Its Afterlives* (Brooklyn, NY, and London: Verso, 2022), 124.
2. The Reverend Dr. Francis Wade, "Confederate Colonel and Priest Promotes Racial Reconciliation," *The Historiographer* 61, no. 3 (Summer 2021): 1.
3. Loren B. Mead and J. Michael Martinez, "A Southern White Clergyman, the Freed People, and the Nineteenth-Century Episcopal Church," *Journal of Anglican Studies* 22, no. 1 (May 2024): 290–309; Loren B. Mead and J. Michael Martinez, "Three Ministers, Black Communicants, and the Civil War Era," *Anglican & Episcopal History* 92, no. 3 (September 2023): 398–426.

PART I

The Antebellum Era and the War of 1861–1865

1

"The Rich and the Poor in the House of God Meet Together"—Three Clergymen and the Protestant Episcopal Church in the Civil War Era

An Overview

Three nineteenth-century white southern gentlemen with similar backgrounds were called to serve God through the Episcopal Church. Each man answered the call. Yet each man answered in his own way, forging a distinct path.

As they journeyed along the path, the men struggled to cope with the greatest crises in American history: an attempted dissolution of the constitutional Union; a bloody, fratricidal war; the demise of the peculiar institution of slavery; the loss of the secessionist dream of establishing a slaveholding republic; and the challenges of reconstructing a fractured nation. The pressing question for each man was how the church should respond to changing times, and how a conscientious clergyman should minister to diverse communicants. Their divergent views on the role of former slaves in the Episcopal Church illustrated the ambiguities of ecclesiastical doctrine and the difficulty of fulfilling their ministries in the postwar South.

In the beginning of their lives and careers, when the Old South still rested on a cornerstone of slavery, the commonalities among the three men far outweighed their differences. Peter Fayssoux Stevens (1830–1910),

Anthony Toomer Porter (1828–1902), and William Porcher DuBose (1836–1918) were reared in antebellum South Carolina. Two of the men, Porter and DuBose, hailed from families made wealthy by the labor of enslaved persons.[1] The three men accepted the proposition that whites were naturally superior to Blacks. Few white persons in the South—or anywhere in the United States during the nineteenth century—questioned this assumption, save a small minority of abolitionists living primarily in New England.[2]

When war erupted in 1861, each man stepped forward to do his duty. Each of the three came under enemy fire during the ensuing years. Two men, Stevens and DuBose, attended the South Carolina Military Academy, commonly called The Citadel, excelled in their studies, and served in the Holcombe Legion in the Eastern Theater of the Civil War. Stevens and DuBose suffered multiple wounds. DuBose was captured, dispatched to a prison camp, and exchanged. Porter, serving as an army chaplain, emerged physically unscathed, but, as he noted, "I do not know why I escaped death."[3]

Each man was schooled in the Protestant Episcopal Church and was called to enter the ministry. Each of the three became a father and lost at least one child to disease. Each of the men championed education as the key to a successful life. The three men shared a common understanding of their duties before the war, but their responses to emancipation and Reconstruction diverged. The reasons for this divergence and the lessons their different reactions teach about changing conceptions of race in the postwar church are the central focus of this book. The main argument is that Stevens, Porter, and DuBose were emblematic figures, each man representing an archetype of a Christian clergyman responding to war, reconstruction, and race relations in nineteenth-century America.

* * *

During their early lives, the three men bore witness to divisions that threatened to destroy the United States and prompt a schism among Protestant denominations. Americans living in the antebellum period looked to divine providence to bring stability and order to their unstable, precarious lives. Day-to-day existence in the nineteenth century was difficult. Men, women, and children often died young. The absence of necessities such as warm clothes, nutritious food, clean water, proper sanitation, adequate preventative health care, efficacious medicines and vaccines, and quality housing as well as ravages of disease, a dearth of educational opportunities, and the challenges of eking out even a subsistence living, left many citizens anxious and longing for answers to existential questions. They frequently turned to the church for solace.[4]

Providing solace in uncertain times was important but fraught with difficulty. Mainline Protestant churches offered congregants a measure of comfort, but they could not answer the central question of mid-nineteenth-century America: Did scripture condone or condemn the institution of slavery? Southerners of many denominations, largely relying on a literal interpretation of the Bible, were convinced that the Bible supported the peculiar institution, while many northerners believed that it did not.[5]

Several events influenced the theological debate and widened the divide between northern and southern denominations. As cotton production ramped up following the development of the cotton gin, the demand for slave labor increased. Southerners—sometimes consciously, sometimes not—justified their reliance on slavery primarily as an economic matter, but with religious overtones. It was God's will that allowed white men, in Abraham Lincoln's words, to wring "their bread from the sweat of other men's faces."[6]

Northern men saw things differently. After the revivalist Charles Finney converted thousands to his brand of Christianity, the new converts gleefully joined the anti-slavery crusade. Nat Turner's slave revolt in 1831 and abolitionists' assaults convinced many northern men that slavery was unsustainable. It was an abominable institution that debased master and enslaved person alike. By ensuring that slavery endured, the Founders had used the US Constitution to contaminate the nation with a sickness of the soul.[7]

Clergy on both sides shored up their arguments by citing scripture to suit their cause. Passages could be found to bolster the natural condition of slavery, while others reached the opposite conclusion. Gen. 9:25-27 appeared to favor slavery for the dark-hued sons of Ham: "And he said, Cursed be Canaan; a servant of servants shall he be unto his brethren. And he said, Blessed be the Lord God of Shem; and Canaan shall be his servant. God shall enlarge Japheth, and he shall dwell in the tents of Shem; and Canaan shall be his servant." Ham, Noah's Black son, had exposed his father's nakedness. As punishment, Ham's descendants, beginning with his son Canaan, would be slaves to Noah's other two sons. Yet Exod. 21:16 declared, in a passage that undermined slavery, "And he that stealeth a man, and selleth him, or if he be found in his hand, he shall surely be put to death."[8]

Historian Sydney E. Ahlstrom noted that many well-meaning, hard-working, God-fearing Christians stood on both sides of the slavery question. In short, the schism between northern and southern churches reflected the political, social, and economic schism between citizens on both sides of the Mason-Dixon Line from the 1830s through the 1860s. By the 1850s, the different perspectives had solidified into a seemingly unbridgeable chasm.[9]

While not altogether immune to internal disputes surrounding these and other pressing issues of the day, the antebellum Protestant Episcopal Church avoided the strife and division that plagued other Protestant denominations. Indeed, it was the only major American denomination that did not split along the North/South axis in prewar America. The relative unity owed much to the origins and characteristics of the institution. Unlike the "looser" American denominations that relied on self-proclaimed preachers and lay leaders of modest means with little or no formal education, clergy in the "refined" Protestant Episcopal Church studied assiduously for their roles. The church attracted affluent, upper-class Americans, many of whom were well educated and active in the higher echelons of business and government. Their wealth was especially obvious in the southern states, where many plantation owners were avowed Episcopalians.[10]

Because its clergy were so learned and its communicants largely devoted to rational argumentation, the Protestant Episcopal Church rejected the emotionalism common in other denominations, preferring reasoned discourse and orderly church services to spontaneous, heartfelt declarations of faith. No speaking in tongues or professions of mystical, divine interventions here. Unity was achieved because an Episcopal service in every part of the country included the Book of Common Prayer with its standard liturgy every Sunday. Clergy seldom strayed from church orthodoxy. Freelancers did not excite the passions of the unwashed masses with extemporaneous sermons on hellfire and damnation.[11]

Whereas ministers in other denominations sometimes brought their views on heated political subjects, including slavery, into the pulpit on Sunday, most (although not all) Episcopal clergymen preferred to ignore the peculiar institution, at least publicly. Church leaders emphasized the timelessness of their religion and the purity of scripture. Wallowing in the politics of the day ignited passions and accomplished little to benefit the church, especially because some Episcopalians, including bishops, owned enslaved persons, while other communicants opposed the peculiar institution. Any discussion of slavery was bound to expose deep fissures within a congregation.[12]

Most Episcopal clergymen followed well-established traditions that dated back to the church's history across the Atlantic. The Anglican Church, or Church of England, was the parent of the Protestant Episcopal Church. Englishmen who immigrated to the English-speaking colonies during the seventeenth and eighteenth centuries transported their strong religious beliefs in the sanctity of the church and its customs. No wonder that many Episcopal clergymen were loyalists during the American Revolution. Their ties to English traditions, customs, and institutions were strong.[13]

The Protestant Episcopal Church had started with much promise in South Carolina, but the eighteenth century witnessed a reversal of fortune. The eight Lords Proprietors who obtained grants from King Charles II in 1663 and 1665 for "Carolina" engaged the esteemed philosopher John Locke to develop a charter, the "Fundamental Constitutions." Under the charter, the Church of England was generally considered the established church of the colony. In 1706, the law formally established the church in South Carolina.[14]

Owing to the 1706 law, the South Carolina Episcopal Church flourished, but it grew slowly. A series of disastrous events struck South Carolina early in the eighteenth century, and the Episcopal Church, like most other institutions, suffered ill effects as a result. Yellow fever outbreaks, a series of hurricanes, and a brutal 1715 Indian massacre contributed to hard times. Nonetheless, the church persevered throughout most of the eighteenth century.[15]

In the words of one commentator, the American Revolution "delivered a crushing blow to the Church in South Carolina." Aside from being "so completely overrun by the invader from mountain to seaboard," the state experienced a deep division of opinion between citizens loyal to the crown and revolutionaries seeking independence. In 1778, even as the fighting continued, South Carolina disestablished the Episcopal Church, which led to a decline in financial support and dwindling church membership. Fighting in the Carolinas left many churches decimated, with little hope of revival. The setbacks lasted from the time of the American Revolution until 1810.[16]

Perhaps because it was so exclusive and lacking in drama and emotional rituals, the Protestant Episcopal Church struggled to attract members throughout much of the nineteenth century. Long memories of the Loyalist proclivities of church leaders might have hindered active recruitment in some quarters even decades after the colonists earned their independence. The elite characteristics of many communicants limited the pool of congregants as well. Whatever the reasons, on the eve of the Civil War in 1859, the Protestant Episcopal Church in the United States counted 139,411 communicants, many living in the Mid-Atlantic states and New England. These numbers were far below the figures for Regular Baptists (994,620), Methodists (1,700,000), and Presbyterians (700,000).[17]

Like the Protestant Episcopal Church throughout the country, the South Carolina church was divided between two groups, the High Churchmen and the Low Churchmen, or evangelicals. The groups shared a belief in the corruption of human beings, the inability of individuals to overcome sin through their own efforts, and the atonement of Jesus Christ for human sins. They parted ways in their emphasis on different aspects of Episcopalism. High church members emphasized the importance of the liturgy, the sacraments, and the ministry of bishops, priests, and deacons, while evangelicals focused on individual faith. Some Low Church clergymen argued that High Churchmen were too wedded to "Romanism" and "Popery," thereby watering down the Protestant faith and moving closer to Catholicism. High Churchmen served as church leaders in the South Carolina Diocese, but evangelicals led a grassroots push for revitalization.[18]

While the factions reached a rapprochement in the antebellum years, it was an uneasy peace. Some scholars have contended that the relationship between High Church clergy and Low Church clergy was so fragile that no one dared risk another schism, such as debating the slavery question. As Thomas Strange observed, "Given the escalating internal tension over

Evangelism, inviting a fresh division over slavery could have proved disastrous for the denomination."[19]

The South Carolina Episcopal Church began a slow rebound beginning under Bishop Theodore Dehon, who served from 1812 until 1817, and his successor, Bishop Nathaniel Bowen, who served from 1818 until 1839. Recognizing that the vitality of the church depended on aggressively growing its membership, Dehon and Bowen actively sought new congregants. They also solicited funds to improve church property and established scholarships to support education for whites as well as Blacks.[20]

In 1810, the church launched the Protestant Episcopal Society for the Advancement of Christianity in South Carolina as a mission effort. The group's first objective was to establish a church in Columbia. Episcopalism was firmly ensconced in Charleston and the Low Country, but spreading into the state's interior was an important means of increasing the church's influence. Although the Protestant Episcopal Church was known for its lack of emotionalism, church members were affected by the revivalist movement during the 1830s. The campaign to establish new churches led to a gradual increase in numbers, as did efforts to proselytize Blacks.[21]

The emphasis on attracting Black members had a religious and a practical reason. Some Episcopalians believed, in the words of Acts 17:26, that God "hath made of one blood all nations of men for to dwell on all the face of earth." The passage suggested that all people were God's creatures and equal in His eyes. Accordingly, church doctrine dictated that everyone should receive the Gospel, regardless of skin color. As Bishop Christopher Gadsden of South Carolina put it, "the rich and the poor in the house of God meet together."[22]

The practical reason was straightforward. If the South Carolina Episcopal Church hoped to grow membership substantially, it needed to recruit congregants from both races. Previously, congregants had been mostly white women, with their husbands only infrequent churchgoers. The growth of a revitalized Episcopal Church required new emphases and new ways of attracting communicants without regard to gender or race.[23]

Yet race complicated matters. In the antebellum South, the church's position on ministering to the Black race appeared to contravene the region's strict laws and customs on slavery. Church leaders had to tread carefully. Episcopalians published catechisms to teach Blacks the word of God, but a state law forbade anyone to teach enslaved persons to read. How could Black South Carolinians, free and enslaved, use a catechism or read scripture if they were illiterate? The tension between keeping enslaved persons ignorant and teaching them the values of the Christian church appeared to present an intractable problem.[24]

In May 1845, religious leaders of all denominations met in Charleston to discuss the "Religious Instruction of Our Negroes." The participants discovered that developing an egalitarian principle and putting it into practice proved to be difficult, distinct tasks. Perhaps Blacks should receive religious instruction, but should they worship in the same churches in physical proximity to whites? Southern social mores prohibited race mixing (except, of course, for the sexual assaults that some white enslavers perpetrated against Black women under the cover of night, which no one talked about). Jesus Christ promoted a message of love and harmony, but how should that message be filtered through Southern social practices and institutional norms? These were thorny questions with no easy answers.[25]

Church leaders carefully distinguished between allowing religious instruction for enslaved persons and promoting social equality of the races or hinting at emancipation. The former would be permitted, but the latter was to be avoided at all costs. In 1835, Bishop Bowen wrote a pastoral letter that walked this fine line. "The religious instruction of our slave population is one of deep and vital interest," the letter stated. "Forming as we do, a large majority of the slave holders in the low country, we . . . are bound to inquire into the duty and means of affording such instruction to our slaves, as we shall make them wise unto salvation."[26]

During the antebellum years, white southern Episcopalians recruited Blacks—some free Blacks and some enslaved persons—into their churches in impressive numbers. In some South Carolina Episcopal churches, the number of Black communicants approached the number of whites. Between 1840 and 1850, white communicants in the South Carolina Episcopal Church increased from 1,936 to 2,965, while Black communicants grew from 973 to 2,247. In 1856, 628 of the 873 persons confirmed in the church were Black. By 1857, laymen and laywomen provided catechetical instruction to enslaved congregations in forty-five places. In 1860, 2,960 of the 6,126 communicants were Black.[27]

It was common practice to find whites and Blacks worshipping together, but they were not stuffed into the same pews breaking bread and sharing fellowship. Whites rented their pews with a financial contribution to the church while Blacks occupied the galleries or were shuffled off to adjoining rooms. Blacks and whites also approached the communion rail separately. No one confused mixed worship services with social equality. In fact, white ministers who brought Black congregants to their services frequently did so owing to the eccentricities of southern culture. A "better class of whites" felt a paternalistic responsibility to assist the Black wretches lest the poor things fall victim to eternal damnation from practicing their weird, crude, animalistic African-based religions. Affluent whites could afford to bestow favors on less fortunate souls as a demonstration of superiority. *I pity you, and I lift you up as a mark of my magnanimity toward my inferiors.*[28]

The need for social control and domestic placidity played a role in biracial services. Free and enslaved Blacks left to their own devices might be tempted to plot or even launch a violent insurrection. Blacks taught to turn the other cheek and forgo earthly rewards for promises of greater satisfaction in

Heaven could be counted on to know their place and stay there. Guided by passages in scripture that justified slaveholding, ministers reinforced this code that bondsmen should remain docile and fulfill their destiny according to God's plan. Salvation depended on Black passivity. The teachings of the antebellum Christian church in the South dovetailed nicely with the planter elite's need for slave labor coupled with total, unquestioning obedience.[29]

During the 1845 conference, participants commented favorably on the effects of teaching the virtues of Christianity to enslaved peoples. They noted the "salutary influence upon them in all the domestic and social relations of life, and upon their individual characters in respect to chastity, truth, honesty, and reverence for the sabbath." Christianized Black folks were "more honest, truthful, moral and well-behaved, more neat and clean in their dress, more improved in their manners, and devoted to their owners' interests than those who have not enjoyed the same advantages." The advantages of religious instruction were clear, although whether the advantages accrued to enslaved peoples or the enslavers was open to question.[30]

Not everyone agreed. One planter who attended the 1845 conference remarked that religious instruction was valuable only when "the owner has been careful to keep them [i.e., enslaved persons] under proper government and discipline." Another participant stated that Blacks could not be counted on to internalize the lessons. In his view, they remembered what they had heard, but their conclusions were "perverted and misdirected" because Blacks were "naturally dull, and of weak intellect."[31]

Even if Christian instruction had only a negligible effect, many white southerners believed that Black folks should be evangelized. Southern society required all institutions—government entities, private sector businesses, social groups, and churches—to provide a common, united front to ensure control over enslaved Blacks, who outnumbered free whites in some places. If religious instruction provided even marginal benefits, it was worth the effort. No white person in South Carolina could forget the Primus Plot of 1720, the Stono Rebellion of 1739—the largest slave insurrection in British North America before the American Revolution—and Denmark Vesey's 1822 conspiracy, to say nothing of insurrections in other areas, such as Nat Turner's uprising in Virginia in 1831. Southern planters lived in mortal fear of Blacks rebelling, throwing off their shackles, taking up farm instruments and homemade weapons, and marching against their masters, perhaps slaughtering whites while they slept.[32]

Despite the pervasive southern fear of losing social control—or perhaps because of it—the Protestant Episcopal Church of South Carolina remained passionately committed to evangelizing Black men and women. The attitude of South Carolina Episcopalians owed much to a succession of bishops who promoted Black recruitment. When Thomas Frederick Davis of North Carolina was elected bishop of South Carolina in October 1853, he recognized a missionary opportunity. He had served as the rector of a church in Camden, South Carolina, for seven years and understood that Blacks outnumbered whites in the state. At the end of 1853, the Diocese of South Carolina had sixty-nine clergymen and fifty-six organized congregations, fifty-three of which were parish churches and three of which were mission congregations. Slightly more than half of the 5,456 communicants were enslaved people. Although the diocese was over a half-century old and relatively well-developed compared with dioceses in other slave states, Davis believed that the church could continue to grow, especially if leaders reached out to enslaved people.[33]

His predecessors, Bishops Nathaniel Bowen and Christopher Gadsden, had ministered to bondsmen as a diocesan obligation. Davis continued the tradition. Although Davis worked to increase the number of white parish churches, he devoted attention to the enslaved peoples. "There does seem to be a wider field of usefulness opening to the Church, especially among the colored population," he remarked during an 1854 diocesan address. "Here is a great field of missionary labor, and one that bears equally upon the consciences of laymen and clergymen."[34]

The question for the missionaries was how they should minister to Black folks—in white churches with Black members or in separate Black churches. A movement to establish a separate church for Blacks originated in Charleston during the 1840s. At the 1847 Convention of the Diocese of South Carolina, a committee of six laymen considered a proposal to "make all necessary arrangements for establishing and keeping up a Congregation of Black and colored persons within the city of Charleston, and the suburbs, and for meeting the expenses incident thereto." The committee set out to raise funds, although progress was slow.[35]

Fundraising proved to be difficult. Opposition to a separate Black church swiftly arose, although the reasons were not ecclesiastical. Some whites argued that when enslaved persons worshipped in white churches, the content of sermons could be controlled and steered in the proper direction. When conducted by white ministers in white churches, the services could be a calming presence in the lives of enslaved peoples. The fear was that separate Black services, whether ministered by white or Black ministers, could lead to discontent and disharmony. A discontented population might launch an insurrection.[36]

Faced with the divisions within the South Carolina Episcopal Church, Bishop Davis sought to appease all factions. He hoped to recruit Blacks, but he dared not express a position for or against establishing a separate church. Accordingly, he continued the practice of allowing Black communicants to worship in white churches—segregating them from white congregants, of course. He also agreed to minister at "slave chapels" on large plantations. Unlike an established Black church with relative autonomy, slave chapels could be tightly controlled by plantation owners and did not seem to threaten the established social order. Yet the bishop struggled to find enough ministers to serve the needs of the enslaved people. Davis visited plantations to conduct services and catechize when no one else was available. From 1854, when Davis became bishop, until the beginning of the war in 1861, the diocese steadily added Black communicants despite the draconian circumstances for people of color in white congregations.[37]

The Second Great Awakening, a religious revival stretching across the United States from approximately 1790 until 1840, further complicated the already complicated religious milieu of the Protestant Episcopal Church. With the Awakening came a tendency to permit looser biblical interpretations on all manner of questions, including slavery. Low Church Episcopalians were content to read scripture with a keen eye toward adapting the interpretation to real-world concerns, including, in some cases, an anti-slavery position. Conservative High Church Episcopalians preferred a more literal interpretation of the Bible, which southerners believed would support institutional slavery. In retrospect, it is astonishing that the differences did not spill into the public realm, exposing a perhaps irreparable denominational schism.[38]

The antebellum Protestant Episcopal Church of South Carolina was filled with paradoxes. High Churchmen and Low Churchmen ostensibly worshipped side by side, and yet their respective visions for the future of the institutional church were markedly different. Unlike other Protestant denominations, Episcopalians did not split along sectional lines, and yet the slavery issue lurked beneath the surface of church affairs. The Protestant Episcopal Church refused to embrace abolitionism, and yet a succession of South Carolina bishops encouraged the clergy to proselytize Blacks. Should Blacks be welcomed into white churches, or should they form their own separate churches? Even the efficacy of proselytization was open to debate in some quarters. Did teaching enslaved people the values of the church undermine the social order or ensure that enslaved men and women knew their place and stayed there peacefully?

The paradoxes of the Protestant Episcopal Church allowed individual clergymen the freedom to decide how they would address slavery. Although the institutional church was divided, individual ministers expressed their preferences in sermons and writings. Most ministers chose not to address the issue. A few, such as the Reverend Thomas Pyne of New York, openly promoted abolitionism. In a sermon on Thanksgiving Day in 1835, Pyne urged Americans to "liberate the slave." Adopting a decidedly contrary position, in 1832 Thomas R. Dew, a professor at the College of William & Mary, confessed that "slavery is against the spirit of Christianity," but he denied that "there is anything in the Old or New Testament, which would go to show that slavery, when once introduced, ought at all events to be abrogated, or that the master commits any offence in holding slaves."[39]

This was the social order of antebellum South Carolina society and the paradoxical state of the Protestant Episcopal Church when Peter Fayssoux

Stevens, Anthony Toomer Porter, and William Porcher DuBose came of age. On the surface, these men lived in an orderly world. White South Carolinians understood their place in the social hierarchy. Although Porter and DuBose hailed from wealthy families, while Stevens was reared in a family of less affluent means, the three men enjoyed a measure of social respectability as bright up-and-comers. Each man received an excellent education and felt called to the ministry. Each man was assured that he would be a leader in his society and his church.

In many ways, their respective lives reflected the underlying tensions within southern society as well as within the Episcopal Church. Stevens and Porter were Low Churchmen who fulfilled their duties by ministering to Black communicants. They were hardly radical advocates of upending the social order, but they took seriously the charge that they should evangelize people of color. DuBose was a man of different sensibilities than Stevens and Porter. He was a man of the Old South, and his experiences convinced him that Black people were to be kept at a distance. For a time, the Protestant Episcopal Church could accommodate these diverse perspectives. During the Reconstruction era, however, cracks appeared in the façade of denominational harmony. By the time that a group of reformers established the Reformed Episcopal Church in the 1870s, the fissures had become too pronounced to ignore.[40]

* * *

We meet Peter Fayssoux Stevens in Chapter 2, as he comes of age in South Carolina during the 1830s and 1840s. Reared in modest circumstances, at least compared with Porter and DuBose, he attended the South Carolina Military Academy (The Citadel), excelled in his classes, and became The Citadel superintendent at the young age of twenty-nine. At one time, it was his life's ambition to reach that lofty post. Despite his high-ranking position in the secular world, Stevens felt "called to the ministry of the Gospel" in the Protestant Episcopal Church.[41]

Before he took holy orders, Stevens completed his military service. He led Citadel cadets to Morris Island to fire on the *Star of the West*, a ship dispatched by the US government to reprovision troops stationed at Fort Sumter in Charleston Harbor. Later, he organized the Holcombe Legion and fought in some of the bloodiest battles of the war, including the First Battle of Rappahannock Station, the Second Battle of Manassas (Bull Run), the Battle of Boonsboro Gap (South Mountain), and Sharpsburg (Antietam).[42]

He was a brave, enthusiastic Confederate soldier, but his dedication to the cause had its limits. Stevens joined the army when the Yankees assaulted South Carolina. As superintendent of The Citadel and later a defender of Charleston, he was repelling a homeland invasion. At Sharpsburg, Confederate troops marched into Maryland. General Lee's decision to take the war to the enemy was more than Stevens, now a colonel, had bargained for when he enlisted.⁴³

Wounded twice, Stevens resigned his commission and returned to South Carolina. He was offered a promotion to brigadier general if he would remain in the army, but he declined the honor. Instead, he became a parish priest in the St. John's/Berkeley area outside of Charleston until the war's end. During these years, he ministered to white plantation owners as well as their enslaved persons. He was revered by virtually everyone with whom he conversed. A bystander recalled seeing Stevens as the clergyman rode his horse to church services, where Stevens "was always entertained at the various plantations and was always welcomed most warmly."⁴⁴

Chapter 3 recounts the early life and times of Anthony Toomer Porter, a wealthy rice planter from Georgetown, South Carolina. After losing his father at an early age, young Porter attended school at Mount Zion College in Winnsborough (Winnsboro), South Carolina, before laboring in the counting house of Robertson & Blacklock in Charleston. When his mother's health declined, he left Robertson & Blacklock to manage his family's rice plantation.

By the early 1850s, Toomer Porter had achieved everything that a man of his station could hope for. He was affluent, well-respected, ambitious, and by all accounts, an up-and-comer in his community. He might have invested his money in other enterprises to grow his wealth. He could have launched a political career. It was natural and even expected that a rich planter would seek the governor's mansion or a seat in the US Senate.

Porter was satisfied with none of these things. For many young men, becoming an elite planter would have been enough to fulfill their wildest ambitions, but Porter felt spiritually hollow. He experienced "an overwhelming sense of misery," which caused him to question the choices he had made. Once he had thought of becoming an Episcopal priest, but he had walked away from that option. At age twenty-three, he regretted the road not taken. Anxious to change his life, Porter disposed of his slaves and property, settled his debts, and prepared for the ministry.⁴⁵

During those prewar years, he was uneasy with chattel slavery, but he saw no practical alternative. The institution was too entrenched in southern society. "I think I was born opposed to slavery," he wrote in his memoirs. "I do not remember the time when I did not hate it. Yet what could I do to abolish it?" If a southern man emancipated his enslaved persons, he would be destitute. Aside from the economic self-interest of the planter elite, emancipation was detrimental to Blacks. In Porter's view, they could not fend for themselves in southern society. Prejudices were too strong. No one would hire freed people as laborers. If they could not eke out a living, they would starve or be enslaved by a far less enlightened master than he.⁴⁶

These rationalizations meant that Porter would not free his slaves when he disposed of his rice plantation. After he abandoned his life as a planter, he sold his enslaved persons to a man who promised not to break up Black families. It was the best that Porter could do given his views on the Black race. "I believe they are an inferior type of men, and the mass of them will be hewers of wood and drawers of water till the end of time—at the least, to the end of many generations," he wrote, reflecting a widespread belief among whites of his day. "Do for them as we will, a Black man will never be a white man."[47]

Freed from the encumbrances of his former life, Toomer Porter was ordained a priest in the Protestant Episcopal Church on May 16, 1854. He spent the 1850s getting married, raising a family, and building up the Church of the Holy Communion in Charleston. In keeping with his kindly, albeit paternalistic views of Blacks, he welcomed all races into his church, although people of color did not enjoy full membership. He also demonstrated an early interest in education, establishing the first industrial school for girls in South Carolina. These were happy days for Porter. Toward the end of the decade, he realized that talk of secession was in the air, but he initially ignored such ideas as foolish and shortsighted.[48]

Despite his initial reluctance to countenance secession, Porter became a firm supporter of the southern cause after the deed was done. During the ensuing war, he served as a chaplain for the Washington Light Infantry. Although he was not a combatant, Porter came under fire several times. His first taste of battle occurred during the Battle of Secessionville on June 16, 1862. The gunfire and cannon shots were so intense that he was astounded that he lived through the encounter. Porter spent the rest of the war shuttling between battlefields, ministering to the sick and wounded. He occasionally assisted in procuring soldiers' uniforms and other supplies. Later, he was on hand to witness the burning of Columbia, South Carolina, in February 1865 and encountered General Joseph E. Johnston shortly before the general surrendered his forces at Bennett Place near Durham, North Carolina, on April 26, 1865.[49]

Chapter 4 covers the early life and career of William Porcher DuBose, the most prominent of the three Episcopal priests profiled in this book. A scholar described DuBose as "the only important creative theologian that the Episcopal Church in the United States has produced." His long association with the University of the South in Sewanee, Tennessee, and his prolific scholarly writings ensured that he would gain a level of prominence denied to Peter Fayssoux Stevens and Anthony Toomer Porter.[50]

DuBose was born in Winnsboro, South Carolina, on April 11, 1836. Soon thereafter, his family moved to a plantation, Farmington, 9 miles north of Winnsboro. After his grandfather and uncle bought adjacent plantations, the family formed a tight-knit community that offered advantages unavailable to most rural inhabitants. DuBose's nephew observed that Farmington became an idyllic plantation community, "a patriarchal family and an agricultural and mechanical community and school."[51]

At the age of fifteen, DuBose entered The Citadel and, like Peter Fayssoux Stevens before him, excelled in his studies, ranking first in his class for two of his three years there. He also underwent a conversion experience. "I was born and bred in the Church, and brought up religiously in what St. Paul calls the nurture and admonition of the Lord," DuBose later wrote. By the time he was studying at The Citadel, he had begun to neglect his religious life.[52]

One evening, he and two other cadets returned from a grueling series of marches. Exhausted, the young men occupied a single hotel room. As the other cadets slumbered, DuBose, although weary, could not sleep. He said his prayers. As he recalled six decades later,

> I knelt to go through the form, when of a sudden there swept over me a feeling of the emptiness and unmeaningness of the act and of my whole life and self. I leapt to my feet trembling, and then that happened which I can only describe by saying that a light shone about me and a Presence filled the room.

His description sounds remarkably like Toomer Porter's quest to acquire meaning and purpose in his life. For both men, the church provided that meaning and purpose.[53]

After graduating with honors from The Citadel in December 1855, DuBose earned a Master of Arts from the University of Virginia before entering the Protestant Episcopal Church's diocesan seminary in Camden, South Carolina. Health reasons forced him to leave the seminary in the spring of 1860. He returned in the fall, but national events required that he depart to defend the South Carolina coastline from Union gunboats.[54]

The war was raging, and DuBose felt conflicted. He was studying for the ministry, but southern men were compelled to take up arms. The Citadel had trained him to do his part, and he was anxious to fulfill his duty as he saw it. After obtaining Bishop Davis's consent, DuBose joined the Holcombe Legion as an adjutant under the command of Colonel Peter Fayssoux Stevens. The legion spent the fall of 1861 and the winter of 1862 protecting rail lines near Charleston. Later, the troops marched off to Virginia and participated in some of the worst fighting in the Eastern Theater of the war.[55]

DuBose was injured twice at the Second Battle of Manassas and later taken prisoner. After languishing in the Union prison at Fort Delaware for a few months, he was exchanged in 1862. On December 13, 1863, Bishop Davis commissioned DuBose a chaplain in the army. He was assigned to General Joseph B. Kershaw's brigade.[56]

Kershaw's brigade fought in the Battle of the Wilderness and Spotsylvania Court House before being reassigned to support General Jubal Early's 1864 Shenandoah Valley campaign. Anticipating that Union General William T. Sherman would attack Charleston after he captured Savannah, Georgia, in

December 1864, Kershaw's brigade returned to South Carolina. They found Sherman heading toward Columbia. Too small to arrest Sherman's advance, the brigade joined Confederate General Joseph E. Johnston's troops in North Carolina.[57]

After General Johnston surrendered his army on April 26, 1865, William Porcher DuBose, discharged from Confederate service, set out for Winnsboro to check on his family's plantations and find his wife. Beyond that, his plans were uncertain. He had $1.50 to his name. The war had left him as destitute and bereft as it had left his region.[58]

* * *

Before the war, Stevens, Porter, and DuBose lived and worked within the confines of southern society and the traditions of the Protestant Episcopal Church. Despite the commonalities in their lives and careers in the antebellum era, however, their paths diverged during and after the war. As with everyone who lived through that time, the events of 1861–5 required each man to evaluate his life and prospects.

The Protestant Episcopal Church became by necessity two separate entities during the war. It wasn't a denominational or philosophical division as much as a practical reality. In the northern states, the church continued its prewar structure and operations, holding conventions but noting the absence of southern dioceses without delving into the reasons for their exclusion. In the South, church leaders had little choice but to form a separate church; however, the formation of a southern Episcopal Church was not a hardship for everyone. Some Episcopal leaders were enthusiastic supporters of the Confederacy. Leonidas Polk of Louisiana—the so-called "Bishop-General" who eschewed theological squabbles as he promoted religious solidarity among white southerners—was probably the most famous Episcopal leader to take up arms. Other Episcopalians were reluctant to support the national disunion, but they had little choice.[59]

On June 19, 1861—four months after southern delegates had met in Montgomery, Alabama, to form a provisional government, the Confederate States of America, and two months after the firing on Fort Sumter that precipitated the war—the Diocese of South Carolina met at Trinity Episcopal Church in Abbeville, South Carolina, for its annual convention. Not surprisingly, the war was the paramount consideration. Bishop Davis acknowledged that "Our brothers and our children are in the field. Our youths with whom hitherto we have only sported have sprung up into armed men." The church could not ignore the hostilities.[60]

Two weeks later, on July 3, 1861, Davis led a group of South Carolinians to a preliminary meeting of the Confederate Episcopal Church in Montgomery. In October of that same year, the attendees assembled at a convention held in Columbia, South Carolina, and developed governing documents for the

Episcopal Church of the Confederate States of America. The Diocese of South Carolina adopted the new church's constitution, canons, and prayer book, which closely resembled those of the parent Episcopal Church.[61]

The Confederate Episcopal Church operated during four long years of war. At war's end, some Episcopalians questioned whether the northern and southern churches should remain bifurcated. Leaders and communicants anxious to heal the wounds of divisiveness drowned out the discordant voices. Bishop John Henry Hopkins of Vermont wrote to all southern bishops urging them to attend the general convention in Philadelphia in October 1865. He vowed to extend a warm and friendly hand of fellowship to all who participated. Many southerners took him up on the offer, although Bishop Davis of South Carolina waited until the diocesan convention in February 1866 to participate.[62]

After flirting with the creation of a permanent Episcopal Church of the South, Davis pledged to reconcile with the parent church to prevent a schism between northern and southern dioceses. "Let us rise to our new responsibility, not sluggishly, reluctantly, or opposingly, but with clear judgments, the spirit of alacrity, and Christian confidence," he remarked. "I advise the immediate return of the diocese into union with the Church of the United States."[63]

Even as the northern and southern Episcopal churches reconciled, the race issue threatened to create a rift. Ministering to slaves before and during the war had been controversial in some camps, despite church leaders' repeated petitions to do so. Nonetheless, many good reasons existed to keep slaves inside the religious fold—with suitable accommodations made to keep Black and white communicants separated, of course. After the war, white Episcopalians wondered what role newly freed slaves would play in the church. After all, controlling the activities of enslaved persons and preventing insurrections were moot points.[64]

The mass exodus of Black communicants presented numerous problems. Approximately 90 percent of Blacks abandoned the Episcopal Church of South Carolina beginning in 1865. From a high of almost 3,000 members five years earlier, by the end of 1865, the Protestant Episcopal Church found only 300 Blacks in two Charleston churches, Calvary and St. Mark's, as well as a smattering of communicants in rural missions.[65]

The desire of formerly enslaved persons—freed people—to abandon the Protestant Episcopal Church—the church of their former enslavers—in search of other denominations should not be surprising. For generations, enslaved men and women had exercised little or no control over their lives. Even their salvation was a tool for their white enslavers to keep them in line. With the collapse of the Southern Confederacy, the freed people sought out other churches, notably the African Methodist Episcopal Church. After 1873, some Blacks, still faithful to the Episcopal creed, joined the Reformed Episcopal Church.[66]

For some white Episcopalians in South Carolina, the loss of Blacks in the church was a blessing rather than a curse. As resistance to Reconstruction grew among southern whites chafing at the carpetbaggers (transplanted northerners), scalawags (white southern Republicans), and freed people who seemed to threaten the southern way of life, the backlash carried into the church. A major division emerged in the South Carolina diocese. Some churchmen, including Peter Fayssoux Stevens and Anthony Toomer Porter, believed that the church should reach out to the freed people and minister to their needs. Others, William Porcher DuBose among them, fervently resisted such entreaties. To their way of thinking, Blacks must be kept separate from whites in all aspects of society, including religious life. With the collapse of the federal Reconstruction program and the installation of the Jim Crow regime of enforced segregation, many white Episcopal leaders believed that their church had no place for Black communicants.[67]

* * *

The growing rift was evident in the postwar lives and careers of Stevens, Porter, and DuBose. Chapter 7, which covers Stevens's postbellum life and work, finds him ministering to Blacks following the collapse of the Southern Confederacy. He exhibited a zeal surprising in a former Confederate officer, taking seriously the Protestant Episcopal Church's responsibility to Black communicants. "With them we stand or fall, and God will not permit us to be separated in interest or in fortune," the bishops of the Protestant Episcopal Church of the Confederate States of America had observed in a pastoral letter on November 22, 1862. Rev. Stevens agreed. He saw no reason to abandon the mission merely because the Confederate States of America was defunct. The responsibility of church leaders did not change based on the fortunes of war.[68]

Stevens continued preparing young Black men to become Episcopal priests. As his descendant later wrote, the "focus of his life's work . . . was the educating of young negro men to become ministers of the Gospel to their own people. Also, he encouraged the colored people to organize their own congregations, to be ready to receive their own ministers."[69]

Stevens grew disillusioned with the church over race. Following emancipation, even as Black communicants fled the church in droves, he encouraged the remaining faithful to organize their own congregations and prepare to receive their own ministers. According to Stevens's account, he thought he could accomplish these goals by having Blacks serve as adjuncts to white congregations within the Episcopal Church immediately following the war. He soon bumped up against racism among southern Episcopalians.[70]

Stevens eventually joined the Reformed Episcopal Church, an Anglican Church of evangelical Episcopal heritage created in New York City in 1873, because the southern Protestant Episcopal Church rejected his entreaties to establish Black congregations under Black leadership. It was an agonizing decision, but he believed that he had few options. As Stevens later explained in his correspondence,

> Upon the formation of the first congregation at Nazareth Chapel [a Black church], I drew up a letter of application to the Bishop for recognition. I do not now remember the distinct application for representation in the Convention but I endeavored to make the letter strictly accord with the Canon, and expected it to be laid before the Convention, as any other similar application would have been. The Bishop replied very kindly to that letter but did not lay it before the Convention for action.[71]

Stevens also sent the application of a Black churchman to the convention so the young man could be ordained, but church leaders rejected the petition. The applicant supposedly was not educated enough to serve. "I was well nigh disheartened, and so was he, feeling that Race more than want of education was the cause of his rejection," Stevens complained.[72]

When he realized that the convention would never allow Black congregations to form, Stevens reluctantly left the Protestant Episcopal Church and joined the Reformed Episcopal Church. He became a bishop in that church in 1879. For the rest of his life, until shortly before his death in 1910, Stevens worked tirelessly to promote Black congregations. He also founded the Bishop Cummins Training School to prepare Black communicants for the priesthood. As a reporter noted in December 1909, Stevens

> started out thirty-five years ago with absolutely nothing. Not a single member, nor preacher, nor church building, but today he has a well-organized denomination, with a Convocation that meets annually. Last year they reported 39 church buildings; members, 2,374; Sunday Schools, 80, with enrollment of 1,145. Each church has a pastor, and in nearly every case, the pastor is a man educated by Bishop Stevens himself.[73]

Rev. Stevens was not the only white minister to assist Black Episcopalians during Reconstruction. Chapter 8 picks up Toomer Porter's life in the postwar years. After the Southern Confederacy collapsed, the industrious clergyman believed that providing educational opportunities would help the South recover. His efforts to establish schools in Charleston were described as "Herculean." Not long after the war ended, Porter traveled to the North and solicited funds to educate formerly enslaved persons. As a result of his appeals, he gathered the funds to create a school for more than 1,800 Black children, most of whom were the children of freed people.[74]

He is best remembered for creating the forerunner of what became the Porter-Gaud School. As Porter himself told the story, he was visiting his son's grave at Magnolia Cemetery in Charleston on October 25, 1867. He stayed for four hours. While grieving for his son, who had died of yellow fever during the Civil War, Porter heard a voice say, "Stop grieving for the dead, and do something for the living." If he had successfully created a school for freedmen and their children, could he not also create a school for whites? By December 1867, he had formed the Holy Communion Church Institute, which was attached to his church.[75]

The school had modest beginnings. For fifty cents a month, or whatever farm produce a student could offer, the white children of Charleston could attend the institute and gain an "academic, moral, and spiritual education" regardless of their family's means. The school eventually moved onto the grounds of a former federal arsenal in Charleston. In 1886, the Holy Communion Church Institute became the Porter Academy (later changed to the Porter Military Academy). In 1964, long after Porter's death, the school moved to its present location, merged with the Gaud School and Watt School, and became the Porter-Gaud School.[76]

Aside from his work with the Holy Communion Church, Porter spent almost a decade as the rector at St. Mark's, a Black church in Charleston, beginning in 1878. His tenure occurred as southern states were implementing restrictive segregation laws, supported by conservative courts and federal institutions that turned a blind eye to the needs of the freed people. He became a passionate champion of Blacks joining the Protestant Episcopal Church. Unlike Stevens, however, Porter believed that white rectors and bishops would have to supervise Black churches. Even this relatively conservative position proved to be controversial in some quarters. Looking back on his long campaign to stabilize Black participation in the church, Porter confessed that "that dreadful contest waged in this diocese" was enervating, and "it almost killed me."[77]

Not every Episcopal minister shared Stevens's and Porter's commitment to nurturing Black church membership. William Porcher DuBose remained true to the social mores of the Old South during the postwar years. Despite his many virtues as a profound thinker—he became the chaplain and a professor at the University of the South beginning in the 1870s and eventually became a well-regarded Christian theologian—DuBose was not interested in ministering to Blacks. He remained an apologist for the peculiar institution and the Southern Confederacy.[78]

In a letter he sent to Mrs. Joseph Huger in 1898, DuBose defended the southern perspective on slavery before the 1860s. "It ought to be remembered that at the formation of our government no one questioned the propriety of an institution of slavery. The sentiment against it grew up after," he insisted. The comment ignored the views of a small but vocal group of anti-slavery activists in the eighteenth and nineteenth centuries, but presumably DuBose was referring to the lack of dissent in the South.

He repeated the classic defense of southern secession offered by Lost Cause proponents. Southerners, DuBose argued, "might or might not be willing to reform themselves" when it came to abolishing slavery—a dubious proposition at best—but no matter, for "the South naturally resented this invasion of their rights and the interference with their conscience." The federal government, controlled by sanctimonious northerners appealing to a "higher" law than the US Constitution, sought to undermine southern rights. These transgressions clearly were unconstitutional because "the Government which had been adopted by a compact between the sections was not going to abide by its own compact & was going to subordinate the law to which they had agreed to another 'higher' law to which they had not agreed." These northern illegalities left the South with few options. Southerners "thought they had the right, & that it was time, to withdraw from the compact and dissolve the common government. And so they withdrew from the Union." In an audacious statement of revisionist history, DuBose concluded that "No one questions now that slavery had to be abolished, but in the immediate quarrel the South was legally and constitutionally right."[79]

Four years later, DuBose and Burr James Ramage, dean of the Law Department at the University of the South, published a retrospective on the life and career of the legendary former Confederate general officer, South Carolina governor, and US Senator Wade Hampton. In their testimonial, DuBose and Ramage rhapsodized over the "great and beautiful" virtues of slavery. Acknowledging that outlawing slavery was "a necessary step in the moral progress of the world," they lamented the characterization of the institution as a sin without "loving the good that was in it." Slavery was not an evil, immoral, dehumanizing, corrupt, and corrupting form of state-sanctioned torture. The concept of human bondage remained viable; it was the practice that had fallen short. Slaveholders abused the system. In DuBose's and Ramage's view, slavery, properly employed, had a place within a modern constitutional republic.[80]

DuBose and his white contemporaries did not question the notion that Blacks were inferior beings who must be controlled lest they infect white society like a contagion. With slavery outlawed after 1865, white leaders desired a form of social control to take its place. De jure segregation was just the medicine for what ailed the white South. It was good for Blacks, too, although they did not realize it. DuBose believed that freed people, left to their own devices, would be lawless, promiscuous, and undisciplined. A well-ordered government must not allow former slaves to run wild in the streets. In the name of order, stability, consistency, and predictability in society, whites must control and direct Black folks precisely as enslavers had controlled and directed the enslaved before emancipation.

The most effective means of accomplishing this goal was to establish a color line. With the death of the peculiar institution, Blacks were free to enjoy private lives within carefully prescribed limits on the proper side of that line.

When whites needed manual laborers or domestic servants, they would call for trustworthy Blacks to cross the line and perform the necessary tasks. Afterward, Blacks were expected to scurry back to their proper station. This was the natural order of things in the South, and DuBose saw no reason to upset the southern way of life any more than it already had been upset by the war and Reconstruction.[81]

Woe to the errant freed people who crossed the line unbidden and thereby transgressed on the rights of white men. On those occasions when Blacks forgot their place, whites developed a mechanism for social and political control. "The condition of things just compelled some such organization as the Ku Klux Klan," DuBose observed. "It was an inspiration of genius—the most discreet and successful management of the situation that could have been devised." That an extralegal, paramilitary terrorist group hell bent on circumventing the US Constitution was the "inspiration of genius" for "successful management of the situation" seems not to have bothered his conscience or disturbed his notion of a just God.[82]

* * *

Three nineteenth-century white southern gentlemen with similar backgrounds were called to serve God through the Episcopal Church. Each man answered the call. Yet each man answered in his own way, forging a distinct path. This book examines those paths.

Notes

1 Porter and DuBose hailed from affluent slaveholding families. Stevens's family situation was less clear. In his autobiography, Stevens briefly commented on finances. When he was born in Florida in 1830, his father operated a sugarcane plantation called Chapofo. As a small boy, Stevens, his mother, and his siblings left Florida to live with relatives in Upstate South Carolina. Stevens never mentioned the number of enslaved persons laboring at Chapofo before their departure. Writing about his family following his father's death, he observed that "Col. James Gadsden [a family friend] became the Executor of my father's estate and the guardian of us all. Whether he was in Florida or in Charleston I do not know, but he certainly was a friend to the widow and the fatherless. At first his remittances to Mother were larger but after the first two or three years they amounted to about $300 a year. Mother lived within the narrow income teaching us all to hate debt and giving us an education nevertheless." Peter Fayssoux Stevens, "Autobiography," unpublished manuscript, n.d., handwritten copy, DuPre-Moseley Family Collection, the Kennedy Room of Local History and Genealogy, Spartanburg County Public Libraries, Spartanburg, South Carolina, 26. Earlier in his autobiography, Stevens included a passing reference to "Old Maurice the colored driver" who

assisted the family in South Carolina, but he did not mention other enslaved persons. Stevens, "Autobiography," 23. The implication was that the enslaved persons who labored at Chapofo were sold to provide funds for the estate. Other than Maurice, the family apparently did not own enslaved persons in South Carolina. Nonetheless, Stevens and his family were not averse to the peculiar institution. See also Hurley E. Badders, *Remembering South Carolina's Old Pendleton District* (Charleston, SC: History Press, 2006), 79, 82; Marion Stevens Eberly, "Our Stevens Family," unpublished manuscript, December 1979, typescript copy, Citadel Archives, 3–4.

2 Even some abolitionists did not question the underlying assumptions of white supremacy. They believed that Blacks should be afforded social and political rights as a matter of paternalistic fairness. See, for example, Aileen S. Kraditor, *Means and Ends in American Abolitionism: Garrison and His Critics on Strategy and Tactics, 1834–1850* (New York: Vintage Books, 1969). The literature on nineteenth-century ideas about race is voluminous. See, for example, Ibram X. Kendi, *Stamped from the Beginning: The Definitive History of Racist Ideas in America* (New York: Nation Books, 2016), 178–9; J. Michael Martinez, *Coming For to Carry Me Home: Race in America from Abolitionism to Jim Crow* (Lanham, MD: Rowman & Littlefield, 2012); J. Michael Martinez, *A Long Dark Night: Race in America from Jim Crow to World War II* (Lanham, MD: Rowman & Littlefield, 2016).

3 The quote is from Anthony Toomer Porter, *Led On! Step by Step Scenes from Clerical, Military, Educational, and Plantation Life in the South, 1828–1898* (New York and London: G. P. Putnam's Sons, the Knickerbocker Press, 1898), 140. For background information on Stevens, see especially Eberly, "Our Stevens Family," and Stevens, "Autobiography." For more on DuBose's background, see, for example, William Porcher DuBose, "Reminiscences, 1836–1878," typescript copy transcribed by William Haskell DuBose, Southern Historical Collection, University of North Carolina at Chapel Hill; William Porcher DuBose, *Turning Points in My Life* (New York: Longmans, Green, & Company, 1912).

4 Daniel Walker Howe, *What Hath God Wrought: The Transformation of America, 1815–1848* (New York: Oxford University Press, 2007), 19, 33–43, 175–85, 446–9, 532–40, 834–6.

5 A rich body of literature exists on this point. See especially Mark A. Noll, *The Civil War as a Theological Crisis* (Chapel Hill: The University of North Carolina Press, 2006), 1–16. See also Ted Booth, "Trapped by His Hermeneutic: An Apocalyptic Defense of Slavery," *Anglican and Episcopal History* 87, no. 2 (June 2018): 159–79; J. Albert Harrill, "The Use of the New Testament in the American Slave Controversy: A Case History in the Hermeneutical Tension between Biblical Criticism and Christian Moral Debate," *Religion and American Culture: A Journal of Interpretation* 10, no. 2 (Summer 2000): 149–86; Robert Bruce Mullin, "Biblical Critics and the Battle Over Slavery," *Journal of Presbyterian History* 61, no. 2 (Summer 1983): 210–26; Molly Oshatz, "No Ordinary Sin: Antislavery Protestants and the Discovery of the Social Nature of Morality," *Church History* 79, no. 2 (June

2010): 334–58; Caroline L. Shanks, "The Biblical Anti-Slavery Argument of the Decade 1830–1840," *The Journal of Negro History* 16, no. 2 (April 1931): 132–57.

6 Sven Beckert, *Empire of Cotton: A Global History* (New York: Vintage Books, 2015), 108–20; Kendi, *Stamped from the Beginning*, 48–9; Lincoln's Second Inaugural Address is reproduced in many sources. See, for example, Ronald C. White, Jr., *The Eloquent President: A Portrait of Lincoln Through His Words* (New York: Random House, 2005), 397–9. The quote appears on page 398.

7 Eric Foner, *Forever Free: The Story of Emancipation and Reconstruction*, Illustrations Edited with a Commentary by Joshua Brown (New York: Knopf, 2005), 25–6; Steven Hahn, *A Nation Under Our Feet: Black Political Struggles in the Rural South from Slavery to the Great Migration* (Cambridge, MA: The Belknap Press of Harvard University Press, 2005), 55; James Oliver Horton and Lois E. Horton, *Slavery and the Making of America* (Oxford: Oxford University Press, 2005), 103–4; Howe, *What Hath God Wrought*, 425; Kraditor, *Means and Ends in American Abolitionism*, 3–10.

8 The meaning of "stealeth a man" in Exod. 21:16 is open to interpretation. The passage might prohibit slavery—in which case "stealeth a man" refers to robbing a person of his liberty—or it could be read as a warning that a slave owner faced the death penalty if he stole another man's slave. The argument about dueling scriptural interpretation is developed in Noll, *The Civil War as a Theological Crisis*, 31–50. Noll argued that the "primary reason that the biblical defense of slavery remained so strong was that many biblical attacks on slavery were so weak." The passages defending slavery were relatively straightforward, while the anti-slavery passages required nuanced interpretation and context. Singling out Blacks to be enslaved was a much more difficult proposition. Noll, *The Civil War as a Theological Crisis*, 54–6. See also Peter Orr, "'Slaves, Submit to Your Masters': Understanding and Applying the Slavery Passages in the Bible," *JSTOR*, accessed June 7, 2025, https://jstor.org/stable/community.32028934. One scholar noted that Jesus never specifically condemned slavery (or even spoke about it) while the apostle Paul arguably appeared to support slavery. Harrill, "The Use of the New Testament in the American Slave Controversy," 150–2.

9 Sydney E. Ahlstrom, *A Religious History of the American People*, 2nd ed. (New Haven, CT: Yale University Press, 2004), 459–61, 659, 665, 673. See also Walter Edgar, *South Carolina: A History* (Columbia: University of South Carolina Press, 1998), 329–30; Howe, *What Hath God Wrought*, 170–6, 323–7; Mark Mohler, "The Episcopal Church and National Reconciliation, 1865," *Political Science Quarterly* 41, no. 4 (December 1926): 567–8. One scholar noted the increasingly bitter divide between northern and southern denominations throughout the antebellum era. C.C. Goen, "Broken Churches, Broken Nation: Regional Religion and North-South Alienation in Antebellum America," *Church History* 52, no. 1 (March 1983): 31–5.

10 Robert A. Bennett, "Black Episcopalians: A History from the Colonial Period to the Present," *Historical Magazine of the Protestant Episcopal Church* 43, no. 3 (September 1974): 239. See also Mohler, "The Episcopal Church

and National Reconciliation, 1865," 568. One scholar estimated that in the antebellum period of the eighteenth and nineteenth centuries, two-thirds of planters who owned one hundred or more enslaved persons in the South Carolina low country identified with the Episcopal Church. Stephanie McCurry, *Masters of Small Worlds: Yeoman Households, Gender Relations, & Political Culture of the Antebellum South Carolina Low Country* (New York: Oxford University Press, 1995), 165–6. Another scholar found that more than half of planters owning 250 or more enslaved persons in the antebellum southern region identified with the Episcopal Church. William Kaufman Scarborough, *Masters of the Big House: Elite Slaveholders in the Mid-Nineteenth Century South* (Baton Rouge: Louisiana State University Press, 2006), 2–3, 53–4. Yet another scholar described the Protestant Episcopal Church as the church for aristocrats in the antebellum South. Donald G. Mathews, *Religion in the Old South* (Chicago: The University of Chicago Press, 1977), 129–31. Figures on religious affiliation are not always accurate; the numbers should be used with caution. See also Luther P. Jackson, "Religious Instruction of Negroes, 1830–1860, with Special Reference to South Carolina," *The Journal of Negro History* 15, no. 1 (January 1930): 75, 82.

11 Ronald James Caldwell, *A History of the Episcopal Church Schism in South Carolina* (Eugene, OR: Wipf & Stock, 2017), 15; Edgar, *South Carolina*, 293; R.E. Hood, "From a Headstart to a Deadstart: The Historical Basis for Black Indifference Toward the Episcopal Church 1800–1860," *Historical Magazine of the Protestant Episcopal Church* 51, no. 3 (September 1982): 285, 290–2; Mohler, "The Episcopal Church and National Reconciliation, 1865," 568.

12 See, for example, T. Felder Dorn, *Challenges on the Emmaus Road: Episcopal Bishops Confront Slavery, Civil War, and Emancipation* (Columbia: University of South Carolina Press, 2013), 97–8. Scholars have debated the reasons why Episcopalians did not engage on the slavery issue, with some commentators arguing that it was a matter of the denomination's ideology—"the church was meant to be in this world, but not of it"—while others have contended that it was a pragmatic concern. The church was still recovering from reverses dating back to the American Revolution. Stirring up the slavery issue, especially when so many of the planter elite attended the Protestant Episcopal Church in the South, was a recipe for disaster. See, for example, Thomas Strange, "Alexander Crummell and the Anti-Slavery Dilemma of the Episcopal Church," *Journal of Ecclesiastical History* 70, no. 4 (October 2019): 768–70. See also William Wilson Manross, "The Episcopal Church and Reform," *Historical Magazine of the Protestant Episcopal Church* 12, no. 4 (December 1943): 347–9; Lowell H. Zuck, "The American Anti-Slavery Movement in the Churches Before the Civil War," *Zeitschrift für Religions-und Geistesgeschichte* 17, no. 4 (January 1965): 363.

13 Mohler, "The Episcopal Church and National Reconciliation, 1865," 569–70.

14 S. Charles Bolton, *Southern Anglicanism: The Church of England in Colonial South Carolina* (Westport, CT: Greenwood Press, 1982), 28–9; Charles H. Lippy, "Chastized by Scorpions: Christianity and Culture in Colonial South

Carolina, 1669–1740," *Church History* 79, no. 2 (June 2010): 267; Thomas J. Little, "The Origins of Southern Evangelicalism: Revivalism in South Carolina, 1700–1740," *Church History* 75, no. 4 (December 2006): 776–7; Walter B. Posey, "The Protestant Episcopal Church: An American Adaptation," *The Journal of Southern History* 25, no. 1 (February 1959): 3–30; Kimberly Pyszka, "'Built for the Publick Worship of God, according to the Church of England': Anglican Landscapes and Colonialism in South Carolina," *Historical Archaeology* 47, no. 4 (December 2013): 1; A. S. Thomas, "A Sketch of the History of the Church in South Carolina," *Historical Magazine of the Protestant Episcopal Church* 4, no. 1 (March 1935): 1–2, 6; Albert Sidney Thomas, *A Historical Account of the Protestant Episcopal Church in South Carolina, 1820–1957* (Columbia, SC: R. L. Bryan Company, 1957), 3–4, 8; Jessica L. Wallace, "Endangering the 'Peace and Safety of the Community': Anglican Religious Authority and South Carolina's Great Awakening," *The South Carolina Historical Magazine* 118, no. 2 (April 2017): 103; Bradford J. Wood, "'A Constant Attendance on God's Alter': Death, Disease, and the Anglican Church in Colonial South Carolina, 1706–1750," *The South Carolina Historical Magazine* 100, no. 3 (July 1999): 206.

15 Bolton, *Southern Anglicanism*, 36–8; Edgar, *South Carolina*, 99–102, 156–7, 161; Samuel David McConnell, D.D., *History of the American Episcopal Church from the Planting of the Colonies to the End of the Civil War* (New York: Thomas Whittaker, 1890), 93; Thomas, *A Historical Account of the Protestant Episcopal Church in South Carolina, 1820–1957*, 9–10; Thomas, "A Sketch of the History of the Church in South Carolina," 7. On Yellow fever outbreaks in the colonial era, see, for example, John Duffy, "Yellow Fever in Colonial Charleston," *The South Carolina Historical and Genealogical Magazine* 52, no. 4 (October 1951): 189–97. South Carolina was devastated by hurricanes in 1686, 1700, 1728, and 1752. See Jonathan Mercantini, "The Great Carolina Hurricane of 1752," *The South Carolina Historical Magazine* 103, no. 4 (October 2002): 352. On the 1715 Yamasee War, see William L. Ramsey, "'Something Cloudy in Their Looks': The Origins of the Yamasee War Reconsidered," *The Journal of American History* 90, no. 1 (June 2003): 44–75.

16 The quote is found in Thomas, *A Historical Account of the Protestant Episcopal Church in South Carolina, 1820–1957*, 10. See also Bolton, *Southern Anglicanism*, 63; Lawrence L. Brown, "The Americanization of the Episcopal Church," *Historical Magazine of the Protestant Episcopal Church* 44, no. 5 (December 1975): 33; David L. Holmes, "The Episcopal Church and the American Revolution," *Historical Magazine of the Protestant Episcopal Church* 47, no. 3 (September 1978): 283–4; Strange, "Alexander Crummell and the Anti-Slavery Dilemma of the Episcopal Church," 770–1; Thomas, "A Sketch of the History of the Church in South Carolina," 8–10; Lyon G. Tyler, "God and Mr. Petigru: Episcopal Attitudes Toward Faith and Doctrine in Antebellum South Carolina," *Historical Magazine of the Protestant Episcopal Church* 52, no. 3 (September 1983): 234.

17 Of that number, 25,563 communicants were in dioceses in states that joined the Confederate States of America. Information on the Protestant Episcopal

Church in the antebellum era can be found especially in Dorn, *Challenges on the Emmaus Road*, 3–8. See also Noll, *The Civil War as a Theological Crisis*, 22. According to one source, 15.7 percent of Americans identified as Episcopalian in 1776. By 1850, the number had dropped to 3.5 percent. Strange, "Alexander Crummell and the Anti-Slavery Dilemma of the Episcopal Church," 771.

18 Raymond W. Albright, *A History of the Protestant Episcopal Church* (New York: Macmillan, 1964), 272; William Stevens Perry, *The History of the American Episcopal Church, 1587–1883*, Vol. II (Boston: J.R. Osgood, 1885), 561; Strange, "Alexander Crummell and the Anti-Slavery Dilemma of the Episcopal Church," 771–2; Tyler, "God and Mr. Petigru," 235.

19 Strange, "Alexander Crummell and the Anti-Slavery Dilemma of the Episcopal Church," 772.

20 Ibid. See also Albright, *A History of the Protestant Episcopal Church*, 194–5; Hood, "From a Headstart to a Deadstart," 275; Perry, *The History of the American Episcopal Church*, 148, 204; Thomas, *A Historical Account of the Protestant Episcopal Church in South Carolina, 1820–1957*, 15, 16; Thomas, "A Sketch of the History of the Church in South Carolina," 11–12.

21 Edgar, *South Carolina*, 292–3; Hood, "From a Headstart to a Deadstart," 275; Jackson, "Religious Instruction of Negroes, 1830–1860," 80; Albert Sidney Thomas, "The Protestant Episcopal Society for the Advancement of Christianity in South Carolina," *Historical Magazine of the Protestant Episcopal Church* 21, no. 4 (December 1952): 447–60.

22 Bishop Gadsden is quoted in Dorn, *Challenges on the Emmaus Road*, 33. See also Gardiner H. Shattuck, Jr., *Episcopalians and Race: Civil War to Civil Rights* (Lexington, KY: The University Press of Kentucky, 2000), 7–8.

23 Tyler, "God and Mr. Petigru," 234.

24 Edgar, *South Carolina*, 293. See also C.W. Birnie, "Education of the Negro in Charleston, South Carolina, Prior to the Civil War," *The Journal of Negro History* 12, no. 1 (January 1927): 17–18; Denzil T. Clifton, "Anglicanism and Negro Slavery in Colonial America," *Historical Magazine of the Protestant Episcopal Church* 39, no. 1 (March 1970): 65; James Conroy Jackson, "The Religious Education of the Negro in South Carolina Prior to 1850," *Historical Magazine of the Protestant Episcopal Church* 36, no. 1 (March 1967): 49–51. According to one commentator, "To some, teaching a slave to read and write was like biting the forbidden fruit. Bestowing the gift of knowledge upon slaves, they believed, weakened subordination. Therefore, colonial legislatures passed laws prohibiting the education of slaves. Others believed religious instruction would transform slaves into a state of perpetual obedience and docility, better fitting them as members of a slaveholding society. It was mostly members of this group who introduced blacks to the rudiments of learning." In 1701, the Church of England created the Society for the Propagation of the Gospel in Foreign Parts (SPG) to build Negro schools for religious instruction in the English colonies, including South Carolina. Notably, Rev. Alexander Garden, the rector of St. Philip's Parish in Charleston, sought to instruct enslaved persons. A 1740 state law prohibited such instruction, but dedicated

parish priests such as Garden found ways to skirt the law. The quotes are from Shawn Comminey, "The Society for the Propagation of the Gospel in Foreign Parts and Black Education in South Carolina, 1702–1764," *The Journal of Negro History* 84, no. 4 (Autumn 1999): 360. See also pages 360–5.

25 Daniel E. Huger, Chairman of the Standing Committee, *Proceedings of the Meeting in Charleston, S.C., May 13–15, 1845, on the Religious Instruction of the Negroes, together with the Report of the Committee, and the Address to the Public. Pub. by Order of the Meeting* (Charleston, SC: B. Jenkins, 1845). See also Lacy K. Ford, "Christian Paternalism and the Contested Ideology of Slaveholding in Charleston and the South Carolina Low Country, 1845–1865," *The Journal of Southern History* 90, no. 1 (February 2024): 58–60; J. Carleton Hayden, "Conversion and Control: Dilemma of Episcopalians in Providing for the Religious Instructions of Slaves, Charleston, South Carolina, 1845–1860," *Historical Magazine of the Protestant Episcopal Church* 40, no. 2 (June 1971): 144–50; Jackson, "Religious Instruction of Negroes, 1830–1860," 88–9; Shattuck, *Episcopalians and Race*, 2.

26 The pastoral letter is quoted in Dorn, *Challenges on the Emmaus Road*, 32. See also Edgar, *South Carolina*, 293; Ford, "Christian Paternalism and the Contested Ideology of Slaveholding," 54–5.

27 The figures are reported in two sources: J. Carleton Hayden, "After the War: The Mission and Growth of the Episcopal Church Among Blacks in the South, 1865–1877," *Historical Magazine of the Protestant Episcopal Church* 42, no. 4 (December 1973): 403–4; Thomas, *A Historical Account of the Protestant Episcopal Church in South Carolina, 1820–1957*, 47. Their numbers match with one exception. Hayden reported the increase in white communicants from 1,936 to 2,965 between 1840 and 1850, while Thomas reported the increase from 1,936 to 2,659. Perhaps Hayden or Thomas inadvertently transposed the figures.

28 Shattuck, *Episcopalians and Race*, 7–9; Thomas, *A Historical Account of the Protestant Episcopal Church in South Carolina, 1820–1957*, 33. See also Hayden, "Conversion and Control," 147. On the pew rental system in the antebellum Protestant Episcopal Church, see, for example, Jennifer Snow, "The Altar and the Rail: 'Catholicity' and African American Inclusion in the 19th Century Episcopal Church," *Religions* 12, no. 224 (March 2021): 5. For more on Christian paternalism, see Ford, "Christian Paternalism and the Contested Ideology of Slaveholding," 52–4.

29 Edgar, *South Carolina*, 294–5; Shattuck, *Episcopalians and Race*, 7–9. Some white leaders worried that ministering to enslaved people might produce the opposite effect. By introducing new ideas to bondsmen and providing them with hope for the future, ministers might kindle a desire for freedom. In 1829, Charles Cotesworth Pinckney, speaking to the Charleston Agricultural Society of South Carolina, observed that, "There are some who object to the religious instruction of their people, on the ground it has been the cloak assumed to cover nefarious designs of insurrection." The reasoning, he explained, was simple. "We look upon the habit of Negro preaching as a wide-spreading evil; not because a Black man cannot be a good one," but rather "because

they acquire an influence independent of the owner, and not subject to his control." The answer was to prohibit Black ministers from preaching to Black communicants at separate church services. If Blacks were welcomed into the church, they would be ministered to by white ministers who could keep an eye on their spiritual salvation and their earthly obedience. Pinckney is quoted in Hayden, "Conversion and Control," 143. (This Charles Cotesworth Pinckney, who lived from 1789–1865, should not be confused with his far more famous uncle, an American Founding Father of the same name, who lived from 1746–1825.) See also Harold T. Lewis, *Yet with a Steady Beat: The African American Struggle for Recognition in the Episcopal Church* (Valley Forge, PA: Trinity Press International, 1996), 37. For more on whites' mixed motives for evangelizing Blacks, see, for example, Robert F. Durden, "The Establishment of Calvary Protestant Episcopal Church for Negroes in Charleston," *South Carolina Historical Magazine* 65, no. 2 (April 1964): 63–5.

30 The quotes are found in *Proceedings of the Meeting in Charleston, S.C., May 13–15, 1845, on the Religious Instruction of the Negroes, Together with the Report of the Committee, and the Address to the Public* (Charleston, SC: B. Jenkins, 1845), 22, 24. See also Durden, "The Establishment of Calvary Protestant Episcopal Church for Negroes in Charleston," 65; Hayden, "Conversion and Control," 145.

31 The quotes are found in *Proceedings of the Meeting in Charleston, S.C., May 13–15, 1845*, 25, 52. See also Hayden, "Conversion and Control," 145–6. A near riot in Charleston in 1849 found the Episcopal Church squarely in the crosshairs of whites worried that any form of Black worship might undercut slavery. Durden, "The Establishment of Calvary Protestant Episcopal Church for Negroes in Charleston," 72–3; Ford, "Christian Paternalism and the Contested Ideology of Slaveholding," 66–7.

32 Edgar, *South Carolina*, 72–81, 327–30; Ford, "Christian Paternalism and the Contested Ideology of Slaveholding," 55–6.

33 The 1850 census determined that 668,507 people resided in the state of South Carolina. Of that number, 274,563 were white, 384,984 were slaves, and 8,960 were free persons of color. Dorn, *Challenges on the Emmaus Road*, 31. For more on the mission to evangelize Blacks, see, for example, Posey, "The Protestant Episcopal Church," 25.

34 Bishop Davis is quoted in Dorn, *Challenges on the Emmaus Road*, 34. See also Thomas, *A Historical Account of the Protestant Episcopal Church in South Carolina, 1820–1957*, 33–5.

35 The quote is found in Hayden, "Conversion and Control," 151.

36 Ibid., 166–8.

37 Dorn, *Challenges on the Emmaus Road*, 34–5.

38 Strange, "Alexander Crummell and the Anti-Slavery Dilemma of the Episcopal Church," 772–5. See also Ford, "Christian Paternalism and the Contested Ideology of Slaveholding," 52–3; Hood, "From a Headstart to a Deadstart," 286; Jackson, "Religious Instruction of Negroes, 1830–1860," 77, 82–3.

39 The quotes are found in Strange, "Alexander Crummell and the Anti-Slavery Dilemma of the Episcopal Church," 773–4. Pyne's language was too intemperate and his message too blunt for his own good. Leaders removed him from his church. For more on differences of opinion among the Episcopal clergy, see, for example, Manross, "The Episcopal Church and Reform," 348–9.

40 Allen C. Guelzo, *For the Union of Evangelical Christendom: The Irony of the Reformed Episcopalians* (University Park: The Pennsylvania State University Press, 1994), 1–17, 187–228.

41 Eberly, "Our Stevens Family," 5.

42 Eberly, "Our Stevens Family," 6–10. See also Gary L. Baker, *Cadets in Gray: The Story of the Cadets of the South Carolina Military Academy and the Cadet Rangers in the Civil War* (Columbia, SC: Palmetto Bookworks, 1989), 12–27; Colonel O. J. Bond, *The Story of The Citadel* (Richmond, VA: Garrett and Massie, 1936), 49–52; James Lee Conrad, *The Young Lions: Confederate Cadets at War* (Mechanicsburg, PA: Stackpole Books, 1997), 31–2, 42; John Peyre Thomas, *The History of the South Carolina Military Academy, with Appendices* (Charleston, SC: Walker, Evans & Cogswell Co., 1893), 106–7.

43 Peter Fayssoux Stevens to Nell [his daughter, Helen Capers DuPre], April 14, 1902, Correspondence 1902 file, DuPre-Moseley Family Collection, the Kennedy Room of Local History and Genealogy, Spartanburg County Public Libraries, Spartanburg, South Carolina. See also Eberly, "Our Stevens Family," 8. C. Eugene Scruggs, *Tramping with the Legion: A Carolina Rebel's Story* (Victoria, BC: Trafford Publishing, 2006), 147.

44 The quote is found in Eberly, "Our Stevens Family," 8.

45 Porter, *Led On*, 75–80.

46 Ibid., 71.

47 Ibid.

48 Ibid., 106–17.

49 Porter detailed his war experiences in Ibid., 130–90. See also Anthony Toomer Porter, *The History of a Work of Faith and Love in Charleston, South Carolina* (New York: D. Appleton and Company, 1882), 5–6; Ron Field, "Clothing the Confederate Soldiers of South Carolina, 1861–1865," *Military Collector & Historian* 70, no. 1 (Spring 2018): 93.

50 W. Norman Pittenger, "The Significance of DuBose's Theology," in William Porcher DuBose, *Unity in the Faith*, ed. W. Norman Pittenger (Greenwich, CT: The Seabury Press, 1957), 21. See also Ralph E. Luker, "The Crucible of Civil War and Reconstruction in the Experience of William Porcher Dubose," *The South Carolina Historical Magazine* 83, no. 1 (January 1982): 50.

51 The quote is found in Ibid., 51. See also W. Eric Emerson and Karen Stokes, "Introduction," in William Porcher DuBose, *Faith, Valor, and Devotion: The Civil War Letters of William Porcher DuBose*, ed. W. Eric Emerson and Karen Stokes (Columbia: The University of South Carolina Press, 2010), xiv–xv.

52 DuBose, *Turning Points in My Life*, 17.

53 Ibid., 18. DuBose also recounts the experience in DuBose, "Reminiscences," 30. See also Robert B. Slocum, "The Lessons of Experience and the Theology of William Porcher DuBose," *Journal of Theological Studies* 79, no. 3 (Summer 1997): 350–3, 366.

54 Emerson and Stokes, "Introduction," xvi; Luker, "The Crucible of Civil War and Reconstruction in the Experience of William Porcher DuBose," 52–3; Slocum, "The Lessons of Experience and the Theology of William Porcher DuBose," 355. For information on the Camden seminary, see especially Thomas, *A Historical Account of the Protestant Episcopal Church in South Carolina, 1820–1957*, 687–9.

55 Scruggs, *Tramping with the Legion*, 115–84.

56 DuBose, "Reminiscences," 85–125.

57 DuBose's wartime experiences are recounted in DuBose, "Reminiscences," 69–136; DuBose, *Turning Points in My Life*, 33–52.

58 DuBose, "Reminiscences," 136–9; Emerson and Stokes, "Introduction," xvii–xxvi; Luker, "The Crucible of Civil War and Reconstruction in the Experience of William Porcher DuBose," 63–4.

59 On the establishment of the Episcopal Church in the Confederate states, see, for example, Robert E. L. Bearden, Jr., "The Episcopal Church in the Confederate States," *The Arkansas Historical Quarterly* 4, no. 4 (Winter 1945): 269–75; Caldwell, *A History of the Episcopal Church Schism in South Carolina*, 16. Joseph Blount Cheshire, D.D., *The Church in the Confederate States: A History of the Protestant Episcopal Church in the Confederate States* (New York: Longmans, Green, & Company, 1912). On Bishop Polk, see especially Cheshire, *The Church in the Confederate States*, 46–9; Glenn Robins, *The Bishop of the Old South: The Ministry and Civil War Legacy of Leonidas Polk* (Macon, GA: Mercer University Press, 2006).

60 Bishop Davis is quoted in Edgar Legare Pennington, "The Organization of the Protestant Episcopal Church in the Confederate States of America," *Historical Magazine of the Protestant Episcopal Church* 17, no. 4 (December 1948): 313. See also Albright, *A History of the Protestant Episcopal Church*, 252, 254; Caldwell, *A History of the Episcopal Church Schism in South Carolina*, 16; Cheshire, *The Church in the Confederate States*, 35–8.

61 Albright, *A History of the Protestant Episcopal Church*, 252; Caldwell, *A History of the Episcopal Church Schism in South Carolina*, 16; Cheshire, *The Church in the Confederate States*, 39–46; Lockert B. Mason, "Separation and Reunion of the Episcopal Church 1861–1865: The Role of Bishop Thomas Atkinson," *Anglican and Episcopal History* 59, no. 3 (September 1990): 345–6; Pennington, "The Organization of the Protestant Episcopal Church in the Confederate States of America," 314–23; Posey, "The Protestant Episcopal Church," 29; Harry T. Shanks, "The Reunion of the Episcopal Church, 1865," *Church History* 9, no. 2 (June 1940): 120; Mohler, "The Episcopal Church and National Reconciliation, 1865," 571–2; Shattuck, *Episcopalians and Race*, 9–10.

62 Caldwell, *A History of the Episcopal Church Schism in South Carolina*, 16; Cheshire, *The Church in the Confederate States*, 248–52; Mason, "Separation

and Reunion of the Episcopal Church 1861–1865," 360; Mohler, "The Episcopal Church and National Reconciliation, 1865," 575–9, 585–6; Shanks, "The Reunion of the Episcopal Church, 1865," 121; Francis Butler Simkins and Robert Hilliard Woody, *South Carolina During Reconstruction* (Chapel Hill: University of North Carolina Press, 1932), 380. For more details on the reconciliation, see, for example, Albright, *A History of the Protestant Episcopal Church*, 253–5.

63 Bishop Davis is quoted in Caldwell, *A History of the Episcopal Church Schism in South Carolina*, 16. See also Mohler, "The Episcopal Church and National Reconciliation, 1865," 576–7; Shanks, "The Reunion of the Episcopal Church, 1865," 126–7, 139; Shattuck, *Episcopalians and Race*, 10–11. After the war, the Protestant Episcopal Church was organized at three levels. The General Convention was a triennial national assembly that represented the entire denomination. The convention was composed of a House of Bishops that included all US Bishops as well as a House of Deputies, which included clerical and lay delegates from each diocese. Both the House of Bishops and the House of Delegates had to approve church legislation. Below this level, the diocese was the church organization of a limited geographical area, frequently a state, although sometimes the diocese contained part of a state or a metropolitan area. A bishop provided spiritual oversight and direction for each diocese and held an annual diocesan convention for lay and clerical representatives from each parish. At the last level of the hierarchy, the parish was the local Episcopal institution. The parish corresponded to the local congregation in other Protestant denominations, although sometimes, in rare instances, the parish included more than one church. For more on this point, see Gaines M. Foster, "Bishop Cheshire and Black Participation in the Episcopal Church: The Limitations of Religious Paternalism," *The North Carolina Historical Review* 54, no. 1 (January 1977): 49–50.

64 Caldwell, *A History of the Episcopal Church Schism in South Carolina*, 16–17; Mohler, "The Episcopal Church and National Reconciliation, 1865," 588–9; Shattuck, *Episcopalians and Race*, 8–9. A few Black communicants remained in those churches because of the efforts of devoted Episcopal ministers such as Rev. Peter Fayssoux Stevens. Rev. A. Toomer Porter's efforts to establish schools for Blacks and a separate school for impoverished whites also increased the goodwill that some communicants felt toward the church. Thomas, *A Historical Account of the Protestant Episcopal Church in South Carolina, 1820–1957*, 68.

65 Caldwell, *A History of the Episcopal Church Schism in South Carolina*, 16–17. See also Bennett, "Black Episcopalians," 239; George Freeman Bragg, D.D., *The Episcopal Church and the Black Man* (Baltimore, MD: Self Published, 1918); George Freeman Bragg, D.D., *History of the Afro-American Group of the Episcopal Church* (Baltimore, MD: Church Advocate Press, 1922), 128; Janet Duitsman Cornelius, *Slave Missions and the Black Church in the Antebellum South* (Columbia: University of South Carolina Press, 1999), 120–3; Thomas, *A Historical Account of the Protestant Episcopal Church in South Carolina, 1820–1957*, 385. One source reported, "The Diocese of South Carolina counted 2973 black Episcopalians in 1860—but by 1876, there were

only 262 black Episcopalians left in the diocese." John Gary Eichelberger, Jr., "Caught in an 'Evil Infection': Postbellum Conflict in the Episcopal Diocese of South Carolina over the Role of African Americans in the Life of the Church" (master's thesis, University of the South, 2020), 28. As bad as the number of losses were for the Episcopal Church, other denominations lost virtually all their Black communicants. See, for example, Foster, "Bishop Cheshire and Black Participation in the Episcopal Church," 49–50.

66 George Brown Tindall, *South Carolina Negroes, 1877–1900* (Columbia, SC: University of South Carolina Press, 1952 [2003]), 194–5. See also Caldwell, *A History of the Episcopal Church Schism in South Carolina*, 17; Shattuck, *Episcopalians and Race*, 8–9.

67 Caldwell, *A History of the Episcopal Church Schism in South Carolina*, 17–18; Foster, "Bishop Cheshire and Black Participation in the Episcopal Church," 50; Lyon G. Tyler, "Drawing the Color Line in the Episcopal Diocese of South Carolina, 1876–1890: The Role of Edward McCrady, Father and Son," *The South Carolina History Magazine* 91, no. 2 (April 1990): 107–24.

68 The pastoral letter is quoted in Hayden, "After the War," 403. See also Albright, *A History of the Protestant Episcopal Church*, 253; Eberly, "Our Stevens Family," 10–11.

69 Eberly, "Our Stevens Family," 11.

70 Eberly, "Our Stevens Family," 11–12. See also Caldwell, *A History of the Episcopal Church Schism in South Carolina*, 17; Foster, "Bishop Cheshire and Black Participation in the Episcopal Church," 49–50; Shattuck, *Episcopalians and Race*, 12–13.

71 Stevens is quoted in Eberly, "Our Stevens Family," 12. For more on the Reformed Episcopal Church, see, for example, Guelzo, *For the Union of Evangelical Christendom*, and Allen C. Guelzo, "A Sufficiently Republican Church: George David Cummins and the Reformed Episcopalians in 1873," *The Filson Club History Quarterly* 69, no. 2 (April 1995): 115–39.

72 Stevens is quoted in Eberly, "Our Stevens Family," 12.

73 The quote is found in Herbert Geer McCarriar, Jr., "A History of the Missionary Jurisdiction of the South of the Reformed Episcopal Church 1874–1970," *Historical Magazine of the Protestant Episcopal Church* 41, no. 2 (June 1972): 219. See also Badders, *Remembering South Carolina's Old Pendleton District*, 119.

74 Porter, *Led On*, 220–5. See also Porter, *The History of a Work of Faith and Love in Charleston, South Carolina*, 6.

75 Porter, *Led On*, 231–5. The quote is found on page 231. See also Thomas, *A Historical Account of the Protestant Episcopal Church in South Carolina, 1820–1957*, 763.

76 Field, "Clothing the Confederate Soldiers of South Carolina, 1861–1865," 93; Karen Greene, *Porter-Gaud School: The Next Step* (Easley, SC: Southern Historical Press, 1982), 11–12; Porter, *Led On*, 388–9.

77 Porter, *Led On*, 308–9, 332–3. The quote is on page 337. See also Eric Foner, *Reconstruction: America's Unfinished Revolution: 1863–1877* (New York: Francis Parkman Prize Edition, History Book Club, 2005 [1988]), 588–601; Tindall, *South Carolina Negroes, 1877–1900*, 195.

78 W. Eric Emerson and Karen Stokes, "Epilogue," in William Porcher DuBose, *Faith, Valor, and Devotion: The Civil War Letters of William Porcher DuBose*, ed. W. Eric Emerson and Karen Stokes (Columbia: The University of South Carolina Press, 2010), 334–5.

79 Letter from W. P. DuBose to Mrs. Joseph Huger, March 5, 1898, Habersham Elliott Papers, Southern Historical Collection, University of North Carolina at Chapel Hill.

80 In that same article, DuBose and Ramage wrote that "Slavery was no sin to the consciousness or conscience of the New Testament." Only later did slavery become anathema. "The South received and exercised slavery in good faith and without doubt or question, and, whatever we pronounce it now, it was not sin at that time to those people." William Porcher DuBose and B. J. Ramage, "Wade Hampton," *The Sewanee Review* 10, no. 3 (July 1902): 365. See also Steve Longenecker, *Pulpits of the Lost Cause: The Faith and Politics of Former Confederate Chaplains During Reconstruction* (Tuscaloosa: The University of Alabama Press, 2023), 132–3.

81 DuBose, "Reminiscences," 140. See also Edgar, *South Carolina*, 448–52; A. J. Langguth, *After Lincoln: How the North Won the Civil War and Lost the Peace* (New York: Simon & Schuster, 2014), 360–3.

82 DuBose, "Reminiscences," 140.

2

"He Was Always Entertained at the Various Plantations and Was Always Welcomed Most Warmly"—Peter Fayssoux Stevens

The Early Years (1830–1865)

Peter Fayssoux Stevens was born on his father's sugarcane plantation near Tallahassee, Florida, an area that had been under Spanish control less than a decade earlier. He was one of nine children who arrived in rapid succession: Clement (1821), Helen (1822), Henry (1824), Anne (sometimes spelled "Ann") (1826), James (1827), Martha (1829), Peter (1830), Barnard (1832), and Mary (1834). As Stevens explained in an unpublished memoir that he wrote late in his life, "Two children were born in Florida before me, Martha and James Gadsden; both died in infancy. I was born June 22, 1830. After me came my brother Barnard Bee and my sister Mary Elizabeth. I was named after my mother's brother, Peter Fayssoux. Barnard was named after Col. Barnard Elliot Bee, the husband of Mother's sister Anne."[1]

Young Pete—sometimes called "Fayssoux"—harbored only vague memories of his father, but Clement William Stevens was a fascinating character. He started life in Jamaica, lived for a while in Charleston, and eventually went to sea, where he fought against pirates. Clement Stevens married Sarah Johnston Fayssoux, the youngest daughter of Dr. Peter Fayssoux, chief physician and surgeon of the southern department in the American Revolution. Clement Stevens eventually settled in Florida with his wife and a growing family and established a sugar cane plantation that he called Chapofo.[2]

Fayssoux's earliest memories were of a tight-knit family struggling to live on the Florida frontier. His parents' lives revolved around raising cane and children. Although a sugarcane plantation could be lucrative, nothing in the boy's collection suggested even a modicum of affluence. He remembered only their shared religious faith. "Another child[hood] recollection is of Sunday and all of us seated around and my precious Mother reading the Episcopal service or teaching the Catechism. I see myself in my little chair near her side," Stevens fondly recalled.[3]

When the boy was five years old, a Seminole Indian uprising terrorized whites living near Tallahassee, including his father. Recalling another early memory, Stevens wrote,

> Now for the Indian War. I have a recollection of riding behind one of my brothers on horseback to fish in that stream past the negro quarter. I can see a pike fish distinctly under a log in the clear water. It seems to me that somebody told my brother to hurry home, and that our sport was cut short. The Indians, so I have since learned, had commenced hostilities. At night neighboring plantations were attacked and burned.[4]

Life on the frontier could be nasty, brutish, and short. Rather than risk the lives of his family in future attacks, Clement William Stevens sent his wife, Sarah, and his children to Pendleton, a small town in upstate South Carolina, to live near Sarah's sister, Anne Fayssoux. Anne had married Barnard E. Bee, Sr., a prominent attorney who later became an early settler in the Republic of Texas. "Father [stayed] to aid in defending the country. We never saw him again," Stevens remembered.[5]

The elder Stevens wisely removed his family from Tallahassee, a rough frontier town in that era. In 1827, after visiting the seedy hamlet, Ralph Waldo Emerson called Tallahassee a "grotesque place [of] land speculators and desperadoes." Another observer, Malcolm Johnson, was more pointed in his remarks, writing that Tallahassee's streets "were the scene of duels, brawls, knife fights and all the violence" of a lawless town.[6]

As if to prove his point that Florida was inhospitable to families, Clement Stevens died there in 1836. When Sarah Stevens learned that her husband had perished, she was distraught. Her reaction left an indelible impression on young Peter.

> In October of that year, my father died in Florida. When my Mother heard it I do not know but I well remember the scene as I entered her chamber and saw her weeping with her children about her. She caught one in her arms exclaiming Your father is dead! Mother's nature was a deeply emotional one. Sorrow weighed upon her but never made her morbid or neglectful of her duties. It was now [fixed] that we were not to return to Florida; therefore, we must have our own home.[7]

Sarah Stevens resolved to stay in Pendleton even as her sister, brother-in-law, and their children headed to Texas. South Carolina in the 1830s was far more stable and settled than Florida or Texas. That experience was certainly true for the Stevens family. Despite the departure of the Bee family, Peter Fayssoux Stevens grew up in a familiar small town surrounded by relatives and loved ones. Numerous aunts, uncles, and cousins lived in the area, and they saw each other almost every day. The Stevens family regularly attended St. Paul's Episcopal Church, where young Fayssoux learned to love the rituals and traditions of the church.[8]

Even at a young age, it was obvious that Peter was a bright, inquisitive child, but he was not always eager to attend school. His family sent him and his brothers to an all-male academy across the street from St. Paul's. "On the 22nd of June, my sixth birthday, I was sent to school with all the other children," Stevens recalled. "My experience could not have been very pleasant for the next day when I got out of sight of the house and in the public road, I vowed I would not go on foot further." Although as an old man Stevens could not recall what he found so distasteful about school, as a six-year-old boy he remained adamantly opposed to joining his fellow pupils in the schoolhouse. "Next day the program was repeated. Down I lay outside the gate and not a foot would I go." When this behavior persisted, the boy was switched with a stick. "I suppose that must have convinced me that it was no use fighting against fate for I do not remember giving any more trouble," Stevens wrote.[9]

It was an era when most children received little or no formal instruction. Their labor was needed in the fields or factories to augment a family's income. Young Peter Stevens was the exception that proved the rule. At fifteenth years, six months of age, he entered the Military College of South Carolina, commonly called The Citadel, in Charleston, South Carolina. He was to learn engineering principles and train as a soldier. It was a happy time, as he recalled years later. "Those were great days! December 1845 I [received] my appointment to The Citadel and went to Charleston." He departed for his new life on January 1, 1846.[10]

Established in 1842, The Citadel traced its origins to the aftermath of a planned slave revolt by the renegade ex-slave Denmark Vesey twenty years earlier. Fearful that future uprisings might endanger the white population, state legislators established a municipal guard to patrol city streets and ensure that law and order prevailed. By 1829, the state had constructed a guard house on what became Marion Square in Charleston. To secure the arms that might be necessary to quell a slave insurrection, South Carolina created an arsenal in Columbia, the state capital, and The Citadel Academy to train cadets. The academy formally became the South Carolina Military Academy and occupied the state-owned arsenal in Columbia and the guard house in Charleston.[11]

The first class of 1843 enrolled only twenty cadets, but the numbers grew each year. Peter Fayssoux Stevens was admitted on January 1, 1846, and graduated with honors in November 1849. Although he was among the youngest students, Stevens led his class from the beginning of his enrollment. During his second year, he became a sergeant major, the first cadet to hold that distinction. Within six months of his promotion, he was appointed assistant instructor of mathematics in recognition of his intellectual prowess. By the time he graduated from The Citadel on November 20, 1849, the school had fifty-five students enrolled. Stevens ranked first in his class.[12]

Following graduation, Stevens served as an engineer on the Newberry and Laurens Railroad in upstate South Carolina. A railroad construction frenzy originated in the United States during the 1830s and 1840s, and soon locomotives replaced canal travel as Americans' transportation of choice. Stevens worked on the railroad company's construction of the Yorkville line.[13]

Despite the opportunities afforded him by railroad work, Stevens returned to teaching. In January 1852, he was elected first lieutenant and professor of mathematics at the Arsenal Academy in Columbia. The following year, he transferred to The Citadel to teach mathematics and astronomy. It was a plum position for a young man of only twenty-three.[14]

In 1855, Stevens married Mary Singletary Capers, the youngest daughter of Methodist Bishop William Capers of Columbia, South Carolina.[15] The couple eventually produced nine children, four of whom survived to adulthood. The twin girls Helen (whom the family called "Nell") and Annie both suffered from cholera. In Stevens' words, "Little Annie succumbed to its power" while Helen survived. It was not uncommon in the nineteenth century for children to die of diseases that were eradicated in a later era. A family member later speculated that the other children may have died from diphtheria.[16]

Stevens decided that his life's ambition was to become the first Citadel graduate to serve as superintendent—a position later called "president"—of the institution. Even as he strove for that distinction, he "felt himself called to the ministry of the Gospel." Stevens studied scripture while he continued his work at The Citadel.[17]

His conversion occurred at a propitious moment. As Stevens recalled in his dotage, "About this time a great revival of religion took place in Charleston." Many young men felt that God had called them to the ministry. As he attended a church service with a friend, Stevens's call came during the service.

Old Dr. Manly, a Baptist minister, addressed us. In (the midst of) his discourse, he pointed to me and said, "Young man you are called to preach the gospel, and you must not resist the spirit of God." I was then a professing Christian and a member of the Church. My pastor, Mr.

Shanklin, had more than once pressed the subject of the ministry upon me, but I had rejected it. I felt now that this was God's call and that if I resisted it, he would take his spirit from me. And then and there, I surrendered myself to God.[18]

Despite his conversion, Steven could not abandon his old life. "I made my determination known to my pastor the Rev. Mr. Denison, who had succeeded Mr. Shanklin at St. Peter's, and began immediately my studies, [although] I did not resign my position in the Academy, for I had no other means of support for my family."[19]

During this time, Stevens encountered Rev. Anthony Toomer Porter. Like Stevens, Porter had forged a different career path—he was a rice planter near Georgetown, South Carolina—before changing course and becoming an Episcopal priest. Porter was a few years older than Stevens and had been ordained before they met. "I began to lay read for Mr. Porter at the Holy Communion [Church]," Stevens remembered.[20]

Even as he studied for the ministry, Stevens steadily rose through the ranks at The Citadel, earning a promotion to captain and becoming professor of belles-lettres, ethics, and French in 1856. By 1858, Stevens was overseeing the Department of Mathematics and Astronomy. He achieved his goal in 1859, when he became The Citadel superintendent at age twenty-nine. A board of visitors' resolution on September 8 of that year unanimously appointed Stevens The Citadel superintendent and promoted him to the rank of major.[21]

Stevens's promotion came at a crucial time in southern history. After decades of rhetorical conflict, people of the North and South were on the cusp of fighting. Secession, and perhaps war, seemed imminent. As an old man, Stevens reflected on the great issues that confronted the nation when he was a young man during the 1860s.

He was familiar with the ideas of the prominent South Carolina statesman John C. Calhoun, who argued that a state could nullify a federal law that contravened the interests of its white citizens. "I think Mr. Calhoun was wrong," Stevens declared.

> While a Professor in The Citadel teaching his textbook, I took the liberty to differ from the great author and teach that having entered into the Union and striven by her representatives in Congress to prevent the passage of a law, a state could not lawfully nullify it. This would practically destroy the government. It was wrong to remain a part of the government reaping all its other benefits while nullifying what others desired as right and proper. The remedy I said was secession. If the evil was too great to bear, then peacefully withdraw entirely from the Union. Such was my conception of the case.[22]

This image of Peter Fayssoux Stevens shows him in uniform at the time he served as superintendent of the South Carolina Military Academy. Courtesy of the DuPre-Moseley Family Collection, Kennedy Room of Local History and Genealogy, Spartanburg County Public Libraries, Spartanburg, South Carolina.

He would not countenance nullification, but, like many southerners, Stevens believed that a state had the legal right to secede if an obdurate federal government, controlled by northern men, enforced burdensome laws on a state without the consent of the state's white citizens. "The Union was clearly an agreement among independent states simply for mutual welfare and the right to enter into such agreement involved the right to withdraw from the Union, when that mutual welfare was not secured," he explained in his handwritten memoir penned long after the war had ended.[23]

As for slavery, Stevens believed that the institution had been forced onto southerners by historical circumstances. Northerners were not morally superior to southerners—they, too, profited from the institution—but slavery was more suitable to southern agriculture than to northern manufacturing and commerce. "Naturally, the idea of freedom, liberty, is captivating, and those who are far removed from slavery form fanciful pictures of the awful cruelties practiced by slaveholders and of the wretched misery of the poor slaves," Stevens argued.

> Of course, there were cases of cruelty among slaveholders and of misery among slaves. I would not have it back again for any consideration and I am not going to advocate its cause. But I simply say that there are cases of cruelty on the part of parents and husbands, and of wretched misery among children and wives. Whenever there is fallen humanity there will be the sad results of sin.[24]

If this was not quite a full-throated defense of slavery, it reflected the well-worn southern trope that slavery had its problems, but every human institution has its problems. Southern apologists for slavery often cited factory conditions in the North as equivalent to—and perhaps worse than— literal enslavement. According to this argument, some enslaved persons were better treated than some industrial workers. As Stevens explained, "as a general rule self-interest, if no higher motive, prompted masters to treat their slaves kindly and as a race, there were none better taken care of, and happier in the world." Northerners forgot this simple fact, according to Stevens. "As the Northern states got rid of their slaves, the same sympathy for the far off (supposed) ill-treated downtrodden slaves began to fill the northern breast. And the sin and curse (as they called it) fastened on the South by the ancestors of these Northerners came to be regarded as a shame and disgrace to the Union."[25]

Disparate views of slavery created a rift between northerners and southerners.

> Communication between the two sections was not as easy then as now and the two peoples really did not know each other. The Northerners looked upon the Southerners as a cruel proud bloodthirsty set. The Southerners from the fact of being slaveholders looked upon trade and labor as beneath their dignity. Untruthfulness they regarded the characteristic of a slave and hence despised it—consideration for cents which make a dollar, they regarded as niggardliness. Hence, they were as a rule a proud set who preferred death to dishonor and regarded "Yankees" as a lying cheating cowardly money-making set.[26]

Writing as a traditional southern polemicist, Stevens argued that slaveholders were not inherently evil. Instead, they were reacting to circumstances that arose over many decades. "The Southerners had not at first been particularly desirous of maintaining slavery," he insisted. "Very early a negro school was established in Charleston and maintained until the Revolution or very near that time. There was no law forbidding slaves to be taught to read until after 1822," the year that Denmark Vesey's slave insurrection plot was foiled.

> In 1791 the slaves of Haiti rose against their masters and destroying them, became free. This led some of the Northern people, *now clear of their slaves*, to the idea of fomenting a similar insurrection in the South, and abolition and incendiary papers were secretly circulated among the negroes. An insurrection was planned in Charleston and vicinity, on a large scale. Through the fidelity of a slave, it was discovered and several of the ringleaders executed. This alarmed the Southerners and the law forbidding the slaves to be taught to read, was thus *the fruit of fanatical abolitionists.*[27]

Stevens's defense was a cliché frequently employed by southerners to seize the moral high ground in the slavery debate. The southern people had no special love for what Calhoun called the "peculiar institution," but the fanaticism of northern extremists, which sometimes led to violence, ensured that slavery would become entrenched in southern society. His history lesson continued along this traditional line of argument:

> That Southerners were not so rabid supporters of slavery is evidenced in the fact that they strongly advocated and voted for the cessation of importation of slaves, and the prevention of the slave trade on the coast of Africa. In 1816, a Colonization Society was formed with Henry Clay a Southerner as President. Liberia in Africa was purchased and established as a country for emancipated slaves to inhabit. James Monroe, another Southerner and Ex-President of the United States, emancipated his slaves and sent them to Liberia. The Capital of that country, Monrovia, is named after him. But the fanatical acts and tirades of the North naturally aroused the Southerners to defend themselves and so their Institution. Had they been let alone they would never have advocated and maintained the Institution with the tenacity they afterwards did. When the Constitution was formed slavery was distinctly recognized as a lawful Institution. It certainly has existed from the earliest ages and is recognized [as] uncondemned in God's great ten commandments. It arose from our fallen nature no doubt having originated in the right of a man to the life of his captive in war.[28]

According to Stevens, the division of opinion on slavery influenced American religious traditions. "The Methodists of the North denounced Southern Christians as heinous sinners. On occasions at church their money was rejected from the public collection as unholy, stained with human blood.

Southern Bishops would not be [received] on Episcopal visitations. In 1846, this led to the division of the Church into North and South."[29]

The festering resentments between northerners and southerners, developed over generations, were the root causes of the Civil War, but the triggering event occurred in November 1860, when "Abraham Lincoln was elected President by [an] avowed Abolition Party bent on abolishing slavery in the South. The Southerners were convinced that the freeing of their slaves would not only destroy their property but endanger the lives of their wives and children."[30]

Political leaders in South Carolina believed that they were in an untenable position. The state formally seceded from the Union on December 20, 1860, prompting a prominent anti-secessionist lawyer, James L. Petigru, to quip, "South Carolina is too small for a republic and too large for an insane asylum."[31]

Stevens believed that the state's decision was unwise. "I saw the madness of the little State of South Carolina undertaking singlehanded to fight the Union," he confessed, but her citizens should stand with her.

> It would have been far wiser to have awaited the issue. The Christian world was certainly against slavery. England in 1838 had freed the slaves of her West India Colonies and paid the masters a fair price for the liberated slaves. I am inclined to think the same thing would have been done here. But stung by taunt and sneer and insult, we were too proud and angry to act with cool judgment.[32]

In a letter to his mother, Stevens expressed the common view that a brief war was probable, but he believed that little blood would be shed. His view reflected the oft-quoted prognostication of a former US senator from South Carolina, James Chestnut, Jr., who promised to drink all the blood that would be shed during any war that resulted from the states' desire to separate from the federal government. Both Chestnut and Stevens believed that the United States would not resist southern secession. These men were not alone in this view. US president James Buchanan had said as much. Buchanan, of course, was soon replaced by a new chief executive, Abraham Lincoln, who was not as weak-willed as his predecessor when it came to resisting secession.[33]

Matters quickly came to a head. A month before legislators signed the South Carolina secession ordinance, Major Robert Anderson of the US Army assumed command of Union forces in and around Charleston. Although he was a native Kentuckian and a former slave owner, Anderson remained loyal to the Union. Following South Carolina's decision to secede, the major worried that he and his men were vulnerable to hostile actions initiated by the increasingly abrasive South Carolinians. To forestall an expected attack, on December 26, 1860, Anderson moved his small garrison force from Fort

Moultrie, a fortress on Sullivan's Island across the harbor from Charleston, to Fort Sumter, a sea fort constructed on an artificial island in the harbor. He raised the Stars and Stripes above the fort, clearly indicating that Sumter remained federal property even as South Carolinians insisted that all federal installations belonged to the state.

It was far from impregnable, but Sumter seemed more defensible than Fort Moultrie. Anderson could see what was happening across the nation and in Charleston. With each passing day, the prospect of an armed insurrection aimed at his small force increased. He had not been ordered to vacate Fort Moultrie, but he had moved on to Sumter on his own initiative. He hoped that the move would tamp down the histrionics reverberating throughout Charleston, but he was mistaken. His relocation was not a prophylactic; it was an accelerant.

South Carolinians were incensed at the major's audacity. They believed assurances had been provided that no change in the status quo would occur. Anderson's stealthy occupation of Fort Sumter under the cover of night suggested that he would do whatever he wanted whenever he wanted. As a representative of the federal government, Anderson was the point man in Charleston. His actions carried the imprimatur of federal policy, whether in fact that was his intent. Following secession, South Carolinians believed that federal authority no longer applied on the state's soil. Now, this Union army officer dared to challenge the authority of the newly seceded state.

In a sense, Anderson had avoided an armed confrontation on Sullivan's Island, where he was especially vulnerable, but he had created another problem for himself and his men. Unlike Fort Moultrie, Sumter was surrounded by water on all sides. It could not be easily reprovisioned. Anderson would have to rely on the good faith of the agitated South Carolinians—a dubious proposition. His difficulties were exacerbated when a group of Union soldiers from Fort Sumter rowed their boats over to Charleston to purchase supplies, only to have the city policemen expropriate the goods. Without cooperation from Charlestonians, Major Anderson would need to be supplied by his superiors in Washington.[34]

Everyone knew that sooner or later, federal representatives would have to intercede on Anderson's behalf. Otherwise, the major and his garrison could be starved into submission. South Carolina Governor Francis W. Pickens and his allies discussed how they could prevent the federals from sending supplies to Fort Sumter. They could blockade the harbor, but they worried that preventing water access would harm the Charleston economy. As a compromise, the governor ordered patrol boats to watch for unidentified vessels even though it would be difficult for a large ship to navigate the dangerous shoals in Charleston Harbor, especially since the Charlestonians had removed all buoys and extinguished the lighthouses and beacons.[35]

Guns on Fort Moultrie could fire on Fort Sumter from the northern side of the harbor entrance, but Governor Pickens was not satisfied that he could prevent a supply ship from approaching on the southern side. Uninhabited Morris Island stood like a lone sentry across from Sumter. As an added precaution, the governor directed his men to place an artillery battery there. A supply ship would face an artillery barrage from two sides.

On the last day of 1860, men and materiel moved back and forth to Morris Island. An abandoned hospital on the island served as the hub of activity. Two hundred slaves labored away to ensure that the artillerymen would be well positioned to confront federal forces that attempted to enter the harbor. Approximately 300 men, mostly infantrymen, eventually arrived to man the site.[36]

A group of Citadel cadets was among the arrivals on the first day of the new year. Sources vary on the numbers. Some recollections indicate that fifty cadets and four 24-pounder siege guns arrived while other sources report that forty cadets and two 24-pounders arrived, with a third 24-pounder added later. In any case, the cadets arrived and assumed positions on the eastern edge of the island. It was an honor to participate in what everyone recognized as history in the making. Lt. Nathaniel W. Armstrong, an 1851 Citadel graduate and professor of mathematics and military engineering, selected the site and laid out the ground.[37]

As superintendent of the school, Major Peter Fayssoux Stevens accompanied the group. As he recalled years later,

> I was ordered by the Governor to take a party of Cadets to Morris Island and man a battery there. I found a small battery capable of holding 3 or 4 pieces of artillery but no guns. It was about halfway on the sea face of the island. We carried from the Citadel, three 24 pounder guns on siege carriages, that is on wheels so that they could be moved about.[38]

The cadets were young men in their teens, green and inexperienced in the realities of war. Their orders were "to fire on any vessel carrying the United States flag attempting to enter the harbor." One account noted the arrival of the cadets attired in their "neat and jaunty" uniforms. The uniforms quickly became soiled as the cadets dug gun emplacements and filled sandbags in the rain.[39]

The Citadel adolescents, imagining only the glories of war, were thrilled at the prospect of armed conflict. Older officers in the US Army were among thousands of rank-and-file soldiers who had resigned their commissions to avoid taking up arms against the Southland. Those men had experience fighting in the war against Mexico during the 1840s. They knew all too well the costs of war. The Citadel cadets were far too young to have served.[40]

The young men soon learned that a soldier's life is not filled with guns, guts, and glory. Major Stevens and his cadets spent a week mastering the drudgery of military life. The young men performed guard duty, occasionally breaking up the monotony with a "long roll" on the drums, a signal to assemble for inspection. The cadets slept in the abandoned hospital on blankets spread atop straw that littered the floor. Sand often blew in from the nearby beach, coating everything—clothes, blankets, frying pans, food, and coffee—with a layer of fine grit. In one room lay thirty empty coffins, a reminder that casualties and deaths were distinctly possible in the days ahead.[41]

As these preparations were underway, the US government resolved to send a ship filled with supplies to Fort Sumter. In early January 1861, Winfield Scott, commanding general of the US Army, dispatched an aide, Lieutenant Colonel Lorenzo Thomas, to explore the possibility of leasing a civilian vessel to transport military supplies and reinforcements to Major Anderson at Fort Sumter. Colonel Thomas found a steamship, the *Star of the West*. For $1,250 a day, the vessel would depart from New York immediately. Its captain, John McGowan, would remain at the helm. The army arranged for twenty-two recruits as well as small arms and supplies of vegetables and fresh beef to be loaded into the ship for departure on January 5. Because McGowan had never been to Charleston Harbor, Thomas hired an expert pilot although he, too, had never experienced the unique conditions in the harbor.

News of the ship's mission soon reached Charleston, but it was difficult to separate rumor from fact. It was clear, however, that the ship was tasked with resupplying the federal garrison at Fort Sumter, which was already a serious affront to the secessionists. South Carolinians were determined to prevent the vessel from docking at Fort Sumter at all costs.

The *Star of the West* moved rapidly. In fact, Captain McGowan was forced to halt near Myrtle Beach, South Carolina, on the evening of January 8 to comply with his orders. He was to arrive early in the morning so that the ship would not attract undue attention.

He finally arrived at the mouth of Charleston Harbor at 1:30 a.m. on January 9, 1861. McGowan hoped to use the harbor's lighthouses and buoys to guide his vessel into the harbor, but the Charlestonians had removed most of the navigational tools. It was a dark night, and McGowan could not risk approaching Fort Sumter without sufficient nautical guidance. Despite his desire for stealth, the captain realized that he would have to wait until daybreak to approach the fort.[42]

Shortly after 6:00 that morning, a signaling vessel, the *General Clinch*, flashed messages asking the *Star of the West* to identify itself. Because it was a civilian vessel, its purpose was unclear. Was it friend or foe? After the ship failed to respond, the vessel fired signal rockets as a warning. The captain again did not respond.[43]

A sentry on Morris Island, Cadet William Stewart Simkins of Beaufort, witnessed the episode. Shouting to Cadet Samuel Porcher Smith of Charleston, the sergeant of the guard, Simkins said that the enemy ship, spoken of with much fervor in recent days, had arrived. Moments later, the long roll echoed across the sand dunes. Thrilled at the impending confrontation, The Citadel cadets hustled to their battle stations. Their hour of glory was at hand.

Alerted to the ship's arrival, Major Stevens joined his cadets at their assigned positions. Decades later, he recalled the excitement. "Our guns were loaded and ready. The second morning after the order came, about sunrise, January 9th, 1861, I think, a vessel was spied entering the channel. The Stars and Stripes were flying. Our battery was manned." Two local volunteer companies, the Zouave Cadets and German Riflemen, joined the group to serve as infantry support. Their orders were clear. Absent positive communications from the enemy ship, his cadets were instructed to open fire.[44]

Major Stevens personally sighted the four big guns. He might have delegated the chore to a cadet, but this job was too important. His task was difficult, and he knew it. Firing artillery at a stationary target is tough enough, but striking a moving ship while lacking a sophisticated sighting instrument is almost impossible. Nonetheless, orders were orders. Major Stevens would do the best he could. Fortunately, the rain from earlier in the week had ceased, and, as one observer recalled, "the day was beautiful, the sun just peeping over the horizon."[45]

The Citadel cadets had not practiced firing artillery shells from Morris Island, but they knew the procedure. Anxious to chart the shell's trajectory, Major Stevens clambered to the top of a sand dune and plotted the direction of the approaching ship. "Commence firing," he ordered.[46]

"Number one, fire," a cadet captain, John H. Whilden, exclaimed, referring to the number one gun in the arsenal. As instructed, a cadet stepped forward and fired a warning shot in front of the ship's bow. The man who pulled the lanyard that day, Cadet George Edward "Tuck" Haynesworth of Sumter, had just fired the first shot of the American Civil War, although no one knew it at the time. He was nineteen years old.[47]

Stevens observed the shell as it descended in front of the ship, barely missing its target. Watching the action, he surmised that a friendly vessel would immediately halt her engines and make contact to avoid friendly fire. A hostile ship would speed away as rapidly as possible.[48]

On board the *Star of the West*, Captain McGowan had transported a large American flag. He had been told to display the banner if he were fired upon. When The Citadel cadets launched their shells, McGowan directed his men to hoist the Stars and Stripes up the flagpole on the ship's bow. As they did, the men dipped the flag to signal the Fort Sumter garrison that the relief vessel was in distress. Their action was interpreted differently on Morris Island. The Citadel cadets saw the American flag fluttering in the breeze and took its sudden appearance to be a defiant gesture by an unrepentant enemy.[49]

Major Stevens ordered the number two gun to fire. Moments later, the shell skipped past the *Star of the West*, as did a third shell. Eventually, two rounds struck the vessel, passing through the ship's rigging. Within a few minutes, the *Star of the West* moved out of range. Southern guns at Fort Moultrie fired as well, but they inflicted no damage.[50]

Despite the lack of physical destruction, Captain McGowan assessed the situation and grew alarmed. Soldiers on board the ship kept raising and lowering the flag, hoping that the Fort Sumter garrison would see the movement and come to their aid. When the fort did not respond, McGowan concluded that he was on his own. Unimpressed with his front-row seat at history in the making, the captain ordered that the *Star of the West* turn and exit the harbor.[51]

Inside the fort, Major Anderson witnessed the episode unfold. He was in a precarious position. His orders were to avoid an armed confrontation, if possible. Moreover, his guns probably would not reach Morris Island. He ordered that the flag flying above the fort be raised and lowered to signal the ship that its distress call had been noted, but the halyards were so tangled that the banner would not move. Before he could form a new plan, the *Star of the West* had turned around and fled the harbor.[52]

The episode was anticlimactic. After only a few minutes of bombardment, the *Star of the West* sailed off into history, leaving the men on Fort Sumter to suffer their fate. Major Anderson and his troops had adequate rations for the immediate future, but they would not last indefinitely. Sooner or later, the small band would be forced to capitulate unless their superiors discovered a new means of reprovisioning the fort.[53]

On Morris Island, Major Stevens and The Citadel cadets were elated. They had performed their duty flawlessly, meeting the enemy and, against the odds, repulsing his advance. Brimming with pride, the cadets remained on the island until they returned to school and their routine duties on February 4.[54]

The people of Charleston were overjoyed as well. One officer, imagining the conversations among the crew on the *Star of the West*, joked that the "people of Charleston pride themselves upon their hospitality, but it exceeds my expectation—they gave us several *balls* before we landed!"[55]

Major Stevens remained on duty, eventually serving as an emissary dispatched to Fort Sumter in March 1861 to discuss the condition of the fort after an errant shot had landed nearby. Later, Stevens commanded the Stevens Iron Brigade when the garrison at Fort Sumter surrendered in April 1861. He directed the batteries on Cummings Point, the northeastern edge of Morris Island, during the firing that preceded the fort's surrender. He commanded the Palmetto Guards and other volunteers during that episode. Confederate General P. G. T. Beauregard, the southern leader who led the Fort Sumter bombardment, later issued orders "To Major Stevens, of the Military Academy, in charge of the Cummings Point batteries. I feel much indebted for his valuable and scientific assistance, and the efficient batteries under his immediate charge."[56]

During the summer of 1861, as the newly established Confederate States of America scrambled to field an army, The Citadel contributed to the war effort by testing ordnance. In June, Major Stevens and his brother-in-law, Colonel Ellison Capers, tested a 24-pound smooth-bore cannon, which had been rifled to improve accuracy. After transporting the gun on the South Carolina railroad near Summerville, they fired one hundred shots before the gun burst.[57]

Later that summer, Stevens believed that his services in the military were no longer required. After achieving his ambition to serve as the superintendent of The Citadel, he felt called to the Episcopal ministry. Like many southerners, he still hoped that a war with the North would be short and lead to southern victory. Accordingly, he resigned from the academy on August 8, 1861, and traveled to Columbia to be ordained a priest in the Episcopal church. Afterward, he took charge of the Black Oak Parish in Pinopolis near Charleston.[58]

The Board of Visitors for The Citadel reluctantly accepted the superintendent's resignation. At its August 1861 meeting, the board adopted a resolution acknowledging that it "cannot sever the relation which has so long existed between them [the Board of Visitors] and Major Stevens, without bearing testimony to the marked ability and fidelity with which he had discharged his duties while connected with the Institution." Offering their best wishes, The Citadel officers believed that Stevens would never again don a military uniform.[59]

He believed it as well, but events soon changed his mind. With the fall of Fort Sumter and the coming of the Civil War, the federal army attacked sites along the coast of the newly created Confederate States of America. In November 1861, the federals launched one of the earliest amphibious operations of the war against Port Royal, South Carolina. After Port Royal fell, Rev. Stevens faced a difficult choice. Although he was a man of God, he believed that he owed a duty to the Southern Confederacy to resist the invaders who had arrived in the South Carolina Low Country. "I had hardly begun my ministerial work when Port Royal fell and the United States troops invaded [South Carolina] from that point," he later wrote. "I had been educated a beneficiary or State Cadet. My duty, I felt, was to defend my State or rather help to do so."[60]

The month after he was ordained, Stevens reluctantly offered his services to Governor Pickens, who immediately accepted. The governor commissioned the former Citadel superintendent a colonel in the Confederate States Army on November 21, 1861, directing Stevens to organize a mixed command of infantry, cavalry, and artillery. In a mark of respect, Colonel Stevens asked the governor's wife, Lucy Holcombe Pickens, if he could name his unit in her honor, the Holcombe Legion. Rumor had it that she had financed part of the operation with her personal funds. She readily assented to his request. The unit's motto was "It is for the brave to die, but not to surrender."[61]

Oil portrait of Colonel Peter Fayssoux Stevens in uniform. Charles Mason Crowson painted the portrait in 1961 from a daguerreotype. Courtesy of the South Caroliniana Library, University of South Carolina, Columbia, South Carolina.

The Holcombe Legion initially camped on the Ashley River to protect rail lines coming into Charleston. The unit saw little action during the fall and winter of 1861–2, although the men occasionally skirmished with Union gunboats. They spent most of their days drilling and preparing for battle. As discussed in more detail in Chapter 4, William Porcher DuBose, another Citadel graduate and Episcopal clergyman, joined the Legion as an adjutant.[62]

During the summer of 1862, Holcombe's Legion was dispatched to Virginia and assigned to Evans's Brigade to defend Richmond. The commanding officer, Nathan George "Shanks" Evans—his nickname reputedly came from his spindly legs—was a hard-driving, hard-drinking native South Carolinian and graduate of the US Military Academy at West Point. By all accounts, he was a brave officer and a fine tactical leader, but his prickly personality and legendary "passion for intoxicating beverages" limited his tactical usefulness and stymied his military career.[63]

The brigade arrived in Virginia at the conclusion of the Seven Days Battles, a major offensive launched by Confederate General Robert E. Lee from June 25 to July 1, 1862, marking his dramatic appearance on the main stage of American military history. The Holcombe Legion missed the major fighting, but the men engaged in small actions near Malvern Hill. At Lee's direction, the Army of Northern Virginia, which included the Holcombe Legion, moved to Gordonsville to meet Union General John Pope's advance. The Legion subsequently marched to the banks of the Rappahannock River to arrest the Union army's river crossing.[64]

Despite its relatively late arrival in Virginia, the Holcombe Legion participated in some of the bloodiest fighting in the Eastern Theater during 1862, including the First Battle of Rappahannock Station, the Second Battle of Manassas (Bull Run), the Battle of Boonsboro Gap (South Mountain), and the Battle of Sharpsburg (Antietam). Peter Stevens was in the thick of the fighting. As Mary Stevens recounted in a letter she wrote to a brother-in-law, "At Manassas a spent ball hit him in the stomach, knocking him off the pommel of his saddle and tearing through his overcoat which had been folded in front of his saddle." In addition, "a fragment of shell hit him on the knee, another scored his back." Yet the gallant Colonel Stevens refused to leave the field.[65]

Less than three weeks later, Stevens was again wounded, this time at the Battle of Sharpsburg (called Antietam in the North). The battle occurred on September 17, 1862, and was the bloodiest day in American history, with a combined total of 22,717 dead, wounded, or missing. The colonel "was wounded in he left arm but did not leave his command; a grapeshot struck his shoulder, but it was not broken." According to Mary's admittedly biased account, her husband was a hero by leaping "into the enemy's gun position and turning the gun against them."[66]

The 1862 fighting in Virginia devastated the Holcombe Legion. According to Mary, the unit "is now down to fifty men; he has lost many brave men and many strong personal friends. Ah, that God would grant us peace!"[67]

When the army retired to winter quarters, Colonel Stevens again considered his reasons for fighting. He had joined the army to repel northern invaders in South Carolina. Now that he was serving in Virginia, he resigned his commission—refusing a promotion to brigadier general—and returned to South Carolina. "My purpose, or rather, reason for resigning was this: I was a Minister of the Gospel, but educated in the Military Academy of the State," Stevens wrote in a letter forty years later.

> I felt that when the state was invaded it was my duty to defend her and therefore volunteered when Port Royal fell, and it looked as if South Carolina was to be immediately overrun. Had my command been kept in

the state I should never have resigned, but being ordered to Virginia and having finished the campaign against Maryland, when we were ordered into winter quarters, I resigned and returned to my Parish.[68]

He became the rector at St. John's/Berkeley area outside of Charleston, which included several large plantations. Years later, an eyewitness recalled seeing Stevens, noting that "he was always entertained at the various plantations and was always welcomed most warmly." Stevens "ministered not only to the masters in his congregation but to their large bodies of slaves," demonstrating that the clergyman believed his ministerial duties extended to enslaved people as well as their enslavers.[69]

Rev. Stevens became known for his willingness to minister to all of God's children, Black or white. His sermons were renowned for their powerful, eloquent insights. One observer, Confederate Major (later Brigadier General) Thomas A. Huguenin, an 1859 Citadel graduate and the last commander of Fort Sumter before the federals took possession in February 1865, remembered a noteworthy address from Stevens. Following his assignment to Fort Sumter in July 1864, Huguenin received congratulatory letters from many old friends and colleagues, including Rev. Stevens. In response, Huguenin invited Stevens, who was serving as the rector of Trinity Episcopal Church in Black Oak, to visit and preach to the Confederate garrison stationed at Fort Sumter.[70]

The minister readily agreed. Huguenin arranged for Stevens to spend the night on Sullivan's Island before traveling to the fort the following morning. "I shall never forget the day, the scene, and the sermon," Huguenin later wrote. The Union army was bombarding Fort Sumter and, in the major's opinion, it "seemed as if the fort would actually tremble when the immense mortar shells would burst under water in close proximity to the fort." Despite the risk of being maimed or killed during the onslaught, Stevens calmly stepped onto the grounds of the fort to hold church services. "No minister to my knowledge had paid the fort a visit since the siege," Huguenin remarked.

Stevens read the service contained in the Episcopal Prayer Book and preached his sermon from the text in Rom. Ch. 5, vv. 1 and 2: "Therefore being justified by faith, we have peace with God through our Lord Jesus Christ: By whom also we have access by faith into this grace wherein we stand and rejoice in hope of the glory of God."

Huguenin was stunned. "Never in the whole course of my life had I ever hear such a sermon," he recalled.

Possibly the circumstances surrounding us might have added to his words, for they seemed inspired, and I have no doubt the occasion lent force to his thoughts and fire to his language. Soldiers crowded around him and seemed to take a deep interest in the services. I myself am not ashamed to say that I could not restrain my tears. Naturally an able speaker, he seemed to be at his best, and his vivid pictures, and beautiful and convincing arguments were most lavishly given us. It was truly an impressive occasion.[71]

Stevens continued ministering to Confederate soldiers and enslaved people until the war's end. With the collapse of the Confederate States of America in April 1865, Rev. Stevens, like so many southerners, found himself at a crossroads. The ideals and institutions of the Southern Confederacy, most notably slavery, were gone. He had to forge a path forward in his life and work. He knew that he must minister to his congregation in the postbellum South, and he must decide whether his ministry would extend to formerly enslaved persons.[72]

Notes

1 Peter Fayssoux Stevens, "Autobiography," unpublished manuscript, n.d., handwritten copy, DuPre-Moseley Family Collection, the Kennedy Room of Local History and Genealogy, Spartanburg County Public Libraries, Spartanburg, South Carolina, 11. See also Hurley E. Badders, *Remembering South Carolina's Old Pendleton District* (Charleston, SC: History Press, 2006), 78; Marion Stevens Eberly, "Our Stevens Family," unpublished manuscript, December 1979, typescript copy, Citadel Archives, 3.

2 Badders, *Remembering South Carolina's Old Pendleton District*, 78, 80.

3 Stevens, "Autobiography," 18–19.

4 Ibid., 20.

5 Ibid. See also Badders, *Remembering South Carolina's Old Pendleton District*, 79; Eberly, "Our Stevens Family," 3–4. As an interesting side note, Barnard E. Bee, Jr.—Anne (sometimes spelled "Ann") Fayssoux Bee's and Barnard E. Bee, Sr.'s son—and Peter Fayssoux Stevens's cousin—became a Confederate general and was one of the earliest general officers killed in the Civil War. General Bee was credited with a quote that provided General Thomas J. Jackson with his famous nickname. Watching Jackson during the Battle of First Manassas (or Bull Run) on July 21, 1861, Bee reputedly exclaimed, "There is Jackson standing like a stone wall. Let us determine to die here, and we will conquer. Rally behind the Virginians!" Whether Bee meant this remark as a compliment for Jackson's steadfast refusal to cede the battlefield or because the general would not move his troops with dispatch is not clear. Bee was mortally wounded shortly thereafter. He died the next day. "Stonewall" Jackson went on to become one of the South's most revered generals before he died in 1863. On this point, see, for example, Douglas Southall Freeman, *Lee's Lieutenants: A Study in Command* (New York: Scribner, 1998 [1940]), 81–2; James M. McPherson, *Battle Cry of Freedom: The Civil War Era* (New York: Ballantine Books, 1988), 342; Stevens, "Autobiography," 99–100.

6 Emerson and Johnson are quoted in Gene M. Burnett, *Florida's Past: People and Events That Shaped the State* (Sarasota, FL: Pineapple Press, 1986), 228.

7 Stevens, "Autobiography," 25. The family's finances after Clement's death appear to have been precarious, but the picture is murky. In his autobiography, Stevens only briefly commented on the financial condition of his family after he, his mother, and siblings left Florida. (He never mentioned the number of enslaved persons laboring at Chapofo before their departure.) Stevens observed that "Col. James Gadsden [a family friend] became the Executor of my father's estate and the guardian of us all. Whether he was in Florida or in Charleston I do not know, but he certainly was a friend to the widow and the fatherless. At first his remittances to Mother were larger but after the first two or three years they amounted to about $300 a year. Mother lived within the narrow income teaching us all to hate debt and giving us an education nevertheless." Stevens, "Autobiography," 26. Earlier in his autobiography, Stevens referred to "Old Maurice the colored driver," but he did not mention other enslaved persons. Stevens, "Autobiography," 23. The implication was that the enslaved persons who labored at Chapofo were sold to provide funds for the estate. Other than Maurice, the family apparently did not own enslaved persons in Pendleton. Nonetheless, Stevens and his family were well acquainted with slavery and were not opposed to the institution during the antebellum years. See also Badders, *Remembering South Carolina's Old Pendleton District*, 79, 82; Eberly, "Our Stevens Family," 3–4.

8 Stevens, "Autobiography," 21–2, 37–8. See also Badders, *Remembering South Carolina's Old Pendleton District*, 81.

9 Stevens, "Autobiography," 22–4. See also Badders, *Remembering South Carolina's Old Pendleton District*, 82.

10 Stevens, "Autobiography," 39. See also Badders, *Remembering South Carolina's Old Pendleton District*, 85; Eberly, "Our Stevens Family," 4; Rev. Dr. Francis H. Wade, "Confederate Colonel and Priest Promotes Racial Reconciliation," *The Historiographer* 61, no 3 (Summer 2021): 1.

11 See, for example, Badders, *Remembering South Carolina's Old Pendleton District*, 84–5; Gary L. Baker, *Cadets in Gray: The Story of the Cadets of the South Carolina Military Academy and the Cadet Rangers in the Civil War* (Columbia, SC: Palmetto Bookworks, 1989), 1; John Peyre Thomas, *The History of the South Carolina Military Academy, with Appendices* (Charleston, SC: Walker, Evans & Cogswell Co., 1893), 12–34. On Denmark Vesey, see, for example, David Robertson, *Denmark Vesey: The Buried Story of America's Largest Slave Rebellion and the Man Who Led It* (New York: Vintage Books, 2000), 115, 149; Michael P. Johnson, "Denmark Vesey and His Co-Conspirators," *The William and Mary Quarterly* Third Series, 58, no. 4 (October 2001): 915–76.

12 *Official Register of the Officers and Cadets at the South Carolina Military Academies*, The Citadel Archives & Museum, https://citadeldigitalarchives.omeka.net/items/show/3, 1849. See also Stevens, "Autobiography," 58, 62; Thomas, *The History of the South Carolina Military Academy*, 34–64.

13 Stevens, "Autobiography," 62–3.

14 Thomas, *The History of the South Carolina Military Academy*, 66, 67.
15 Stevens, "Autobiography," 65–7; See also Eberly, "Our Stevens Family," 4–5. Colonel O. J. Bond, *The Story of The Citadel* (Richmond, VA: Garrett and Massie, 1936), 52–3. Mary's brother, Ellison Capers, later became a brigadier general in the Confederate Army as well as a college professor and Episcopal Bishop of South Carolina from 1894 until his death in 1908. For more on Ellison Capers, see Badders, *Remembering South Carolina's Old Pendleton District*, 112, 116–19; "Necrology: Ellison Capers," *The South Carolina Historical and Genealogical Magazine* 9, no. 3 (July 1908): 166–9; Albert Sidney Thomas, *A Historical Account of the Protestant Episcopal Church in South Carolina, 1820–1957* (Columbia, SC: R. L. Bryan Company, 1957), 116–29. William Porcher DuBose wrote a retrospective of the bishop's life and career shortly after Capers died. William Porcher DuBose, "Ellison Capers," *The Sewanee Review* 16, no. 3 (July 1908): 368–73.
16 The quote is found in Stevens, "Autobiography," 67. See also pages 68–9. Stevens' family life is recounted in Eberly, "Our Stevens Family," 3–5.
17 The quote is found in Eberly, "Our Stevens Family," 5.
18 Stevens, "Autobiography," 68–9.
19 Ibid., 69.
20 Ibid. See also A. Toomer Porter, *Led On! Step by Step Scenes from Clerical, Military, Educational, and Plantation Life in the South, 1828–1898* (New York: G. P. Putnam's Sons, the Knickerbocker Press, 1898), 78–83.
21 Stevens, "Autobiography," 70. See also Badders, *Remembering South Carolina's Old Pendleton District*, 90–1; Thomas, *The History of the South Carolina Military Academy*, 85, 86, 92–3, 98, 99, 100. See also Baker, *Cadets in Gray*, 5.
22 Stevens, "Autobiography," 78–9.
23 Ibid., 77.
24 Ibid., 80–1.
25 Ibid., 81.
26 Ibid., 81–2. The different perspectives between southerners and northerners have been discussed in many works. See, for example, McPherson, *Battle Cry of Freedom*, 7–8, 37–41; Eric H. Walther, *The Shattering of the Union: America in the 1850s* (Wilmington, DE: SR Books, 2004).
27 Stevens, "Autobiography," 82–3. Emphases in the original.
28 Ibid., 83–5.
29 Ibid., 86.
30 Ibid., 87.
31 Petigru is quoted in many sources. See, for example, Douglas R. Egerton, *Year of Meteors: Stephen Douglas, Abraham Lincoln, and the Election That Brought on the Civil War* (London: Bloomsbury Press, 2010), 230; Charles H. Lesser, *Relic of the Lost Cause: The Story of South Carolina's Ordinance of Secession*, 2nd ed. (Columbia: University of South Carolina Press, 2012), 3.

32. Stevens, "Autobiography," 88, 89. This stated conviction that southerners eventually would have outlawed slavery, widely avowed by southern apologists after the war's end, was either wishful thinking or revisionist history. No credible evidence exists that most slaveowners intended to surrender their economic prosperity by abolishing slavery absent a violent cataclysm.

33. Stevens's observation is discussed in Eberly, "Our Stevens Family," 5. Chestnut's observation is discussed in Egerton, *Year of Meteors*, 221. See also McPherson, *Battle Cry of Freedom*, 238.

34. The story of Major Anderson's decision to move from Fort Moultrie to Fort Sumter is discussed at length in many sources. See, for example, David Detzer, *Allegiance: Fort Sumter, Charleston, and the Beginning of the Civil War* (New York: Harcourt, 2001), 55–64; Richard W. Hatcher, III, *Thunder in the Harbor: Fort Sumter and the Civil War* (El Dorado Hills, CA: Savas Beatie, 2024), 9–22; Erik Larson, *The Demon of Unrest: A Saga of Hubris, Heartbreak, and Heroism at the Dawn of the Civil War* (New York: Crown, 2024), 135–42.

35. Bond, *The Story of The Citadel*, 49; Detzer, *Allegiance*, 100–1, 148–55.

36. Baker, *Cadets in Gray*, 12–13; Detzer, *Allegiance*, 147–8; Hatcher, *Thunder in the Harbor*, 23.

37. Baker, *Cadets in Gray*, 12–13.

38. Stevens, "Autobiography," 90–1. See also Badders, *Remembering South Carolina's Old Pendleton District*, 96; James Lee Conrad, *The Young Lions: Confederate Cadets at War* (Mechanicsburg, PA: Stackpole Books, 1997), 31–2.

39. The descriptions are found in Baker, *Cadets in Gray*, 13. See also Stevens, "Autobiography," 92.

40. Baker, *Cadets in Gray*, 13; Thomas, *The History of the South Carolina Military Academy*, 106–7.

41. Baker, *Cadets in Gray*, 13.

42. The *Star of the West* is discussed in many sources. See, for example, Detzer, *Allegiance*, 152–6.

43. Baker, *Cadets in Gray*, 17; Detzer, *Allegiance*, 156–7; Hatcher, *Thunder in the Harbor*, 23–4.

44. Stevens, "Autobiography," 93. See also W. Thomas Smith, Jr., "Big Red & The Star of the West," *Sandlapper: The Magazine of South Carolina* 22, no. 1 (Spring 2011): 28.

45. The descriptions and the quote are found in Baker, *Cadets in Gray*, 20.

46. Badders, *Remembering South Carolina's Old Pendleton District*, 96; Baker, *Cadets in Gray*, 20–1; Bond, *The Story of The Citadel*, 49–50; Conrad, *The Young Lions*, 32.

47. Baker, *Cadets in Gray*, 21; Bond, *The Story of The Citadel*, 50; Smith, "Big Red & *The Star of the West*," 29. A plaque memorializing the episode was

placed at The Citadel in 1939. Haynesworth later claimed to have fired the final shot at Bentonville, North Carolina, in April 1865, making him the last person to have fired a shot during a general engagement in the Civil War, although that claim was never verified. See, for example, Thomas, *The History of the South Carolina Military Academy*, 443. See also Wade, "Confederate Colonel and Priest Promotes Racial Reconciliation," 1, 8.

48 Detzer, *Allegiance*, 158.

49 Baker, *Cadets in Gray*, 23; Detzer, *Allegiance*, 158.

50 According to one source, Cadet Samuel Pickens fired the first shot that struck the ship and Cadet Thomas Ferguson fired the second shot that struck *The Star of the West*. Both shells inflicted only minor damage. The cadets eventually fired seventeen shots, but only three hit the target. Smith, "Big Red & *The Star of the West*," 29.

51 Baker, *Cadets in Gray*, 23–4; Larson, *The Demon of Unrest*, 180–90.

52 Baker, *Cadets in Gray*, 24; Detzer, *Allegiance*, 159.

53 Detzer, *Allegiance*, 159–60.

54 Baker, *Cadets in Gray*, 27; Stevens, "Autobiography," 93–4.

55 The quote is found in Bond, *The Story of The Citadel*, 51. Emphasis in the original.

56 Stevens's role as the emissary is recounted in Larson, *The Demon of Unrest*, 316–17. Beauregard's order is quoted in Bond, *The Story of The Citadel*, 52. See also Baker, *Cadets in Gray*, 36.

57 Bond, *The Story of The Citadel*, 52.

58 Badders, *Remembering South Carolina's Old Pendleton District*, 97; Baker, *Cadets in Gray*, 41; Stevens, "Autobiography," 100; Thomas, *The History of the South Carolina Military Academy*, 259.

59 The resolution is quoted in Baker, *Cadets in Gray*, 41. See also Thomas, *The History of the South Carolina Military Academy*, 110, 111.

60 Stevens, "Autobiography," 101. See also Eberly, "Our Stevens Family," 6–7. For more on Port Royal, see, for example, McPherson, *Battle Cry of Freedom*, 370–1.

61 Lucy Holcombe Pickens was once described as "one of the most famous women of the South, and one whose name will live in history." Family lore suggested that she financed the Legion partially with jewels that Czar Alexander II of Russia supplied to her. For more on this point, see Georganne B. Burton and Orville Vernon Burton, "Lucy Holcombe Pickens, Southern Writer," *The South Carolina Historical Magazine* 103, no. 4 (October 2002): 296, 309. See also Badders, *Remembering South Carolina's Old Pendleton District*, 108–9; Baker, *Cadets in Gray*, 41; Bond, *The Story of The Citadel*, 52; Conrad, *The Young Lions*, 42; C. Eugene Scruggs, *Tramping with the Legion: A Carolina Rebel's Story* (Victoria, BC: Trafford Publishing, 2006), 87; Stevens, "Autobiography," 101–2; Wade, "Confederate Colonel and Priest Promotes Racial Reconciliation," 8.

62 Ralph E. Luker, "The Crucible of Civil War and Reconstruction in the Experience of William Porcher Dubose," *The South Carolina Historical Magazine* 83, no. 1 (January 1982): 53; Stevens, "Autobiography," 102–3.

63 Freeman, *Lee's Lieutenants*, 83–4; McPherson, *Battle Cry of Freedom*, 341; Scruggs, *Tramping with the Legion*, 116–17.

64 Luker, "The Crucible of Civil War and Reconstruction," 54.

65 Mary Stevens is quoted in Eberly, "Our Stevens Family," 7. See also Luker, "The Crucible of Civil War and Reconstruction," 54–6; Stevens, "Autobiography," 103–6.

66 Mary Stevens is quoted in Eberly, "Our Stevens Family," 7. See also Baker, *Cadets in Gray*, 41–2; Bond, *The Story of The Citadel*, 52; Scruggs, *Tramping with the Legion*, 146; Smith, "Big Red & *The Star of the West*," 29.

67 Mary Stevens is quoted in Eberly, "Our Stevens Family," 7–8. See also Luker, "The Crucible of Civil War and Reconstruction," 55.

68 Peter Fayssoux Stevens to Nell [the family's name for Stevens' daughter, Helen Capers DuPre], April 14, 1902, Correspondence 1902 file, DuPre-Moseley Family Collection, the Kennedy Room of Local History and Genealogy, Spartanburg County Public Libraries, Spartanburg, South Carolina.

69 The quotes are found in Eberly, "Our Stevens Family," 8. See also Scruggs, *Tramping with the Legion*, 147; Baker, *Cadets in Gray*, 42.

70 On Stevens's assignment at Trinity Church, see Badders, *Remembering South Carolina's Old Pendleton District*, 97, 113.

71 The quotes are found in Ibid., 8–9. See also Hatcher, *Thunder in the Harbor*, 167.

72 Rev. Stevens paid a heavy personal price for his family's service to the Southern Confederacy. His two older brothers died during the war. Henry Kennedy Stevens, born in 1824, was shot and killed aboard the *CSS J.A. Cotton*, a Confederate sidewheel partial ironclad gunboat that came under enemy fire on January 14–15, 1863, in Bayou Teche near Brashear City, Louisiana. His eldest brother Clement Hoffman Stevens was a 42-year-old brigadier general leading a frontal assault on Yankee troops during the Battle of Peachtree Creek in the Atlanta Campaign on July 20, 1864, when he was shot in the head. He died five days later. Badders, *Remembering South Carolina's Old Pendleton District*, 10, 115, 118; Eberly, "Our Stevens Family," 3.

3

"I Think I Was Born Opposed to Slavery"— Anthony Toomer Porter

The Early Years (1828–1865)

Anthony Toomer Porter was born in Georgetown, South Carolina, on January 31, 1828. His father, John Porter, Jr., became a prominent lawyer and state legislator in South Carolina. On December 16, 1819, John Porter married Esther Ann Toomer, and the couple produced five children—two sons and three daughters—three of whom survived into adulthood.[1]

Toomer Porter never knew his father, although he admired the man when he was old enough to learn of his father's accomplishments. As he recalled in his memoirs,

> I was only nine months old when my father died. His death occurred on October 25, 1828, at the early age of thirty-three years. My father was a man of very marked character. He was elected a member of the Legislature of South Carolina, at the age of twenty-one, and served for several years. He was a member of the Episcopal Diocesan Convention at the time of his death.[2]

Widowed at the age of twenty-five with five children to care for, Esther Porter struggled to survive. Her late husband had left a "handsome estate," but she resolved to move away from the South. She had been raised in Elizabeth, New Jersey, and still had friends in the northern states. In 1832, the family left South Carolina and settled in New Haven, Connecticut.

Within a few years, Esther and her children returned to Georgetown to enjoy life at a "town residence" as well as on a plantation with eighty slaves. Porter was still a young child when they returned to the South Carolina coast. "I remember how much alarmed I was at the appearance of the black people who came around us," he recalled many decades later. He had not seen people of color during his brief time in Connecticut. "I had a white nurse, an Irish woman, who had gone with us to New Haven and returned, and remained until I was nine years old."[3]

As he learned about his lineage, Toomer Porter was confronted with the great issue of nineteenth-century America: race-based slavery. His family's connection with the peculiar institution came about because of his paternal grandfather's actions as a young man. Born in Connecticut in 1759, the grandfather, John Porter, Sr., headed south with two brothers when he was fifteen or sixteen years old. Family lore recounted John Porter's innovative work constructing the Dismal Swamp Canal, a 22-mile-long waterway on the Virginia-North Carolina border that slaves dug, mostly by hand, during a twelve-year stretch from 1793 until 1805. Unlike the slaves who supplied the bulk of the labor, John Porter, Sr., eventually earned $20,000, a princely sum at the time, for his canal work.

He eventually landed in the Georgetown District, a coastal area in the South Carolina Low Country, and settled down. Using money that he earned working on the canal, Porter purchased a large swath of land and cultivated indigo and rice. He purchased two plantations on South Carolina's Sampit River and amassed a considerable fortune from the sale of his crops. When John Porter, Sr., died at age seventy in April 1829—six months after his son, John, Jr., died—he was universally regarded as one of the wealthiest planters in his community.[4]

In his will, John, Sr., left his estate to his five grandchildren. John, Jr., had already bequeathed his holdings, including real estate, to his widow, Esther. Accordingly, much of the family's wealth was tied to the labor of enslaved persons. As a result of his grandfather's decisions, Toomer Porter came face-to-face with slavery. It was not an abstract proposition, nor was he a disinterested party. As he stated in his memoirs, his estate "consisted of rice plantations and negro slaves, some of whom he purchased from slave-ships, which were owned in Newport, Rhode Island. In 1849, I came into possession of five of these Africans, then very old. They had been, in fact, supported for many years on the plantation without earning a dollar. They were all dead by the year 1851." In an era before old-age pensions existed, southerners often justified human bondage by observing that they worked their enslaved people hard, but they cared for them in the years when the men and women were too old to earn their keep.[5]

Toomer further justified his family's reliance on slave labor with another rationalization: Slavery was not only a southern problem. Many whites, North and South, profited from trafficking in human chattel:

The bill of sale of some of these people was in my possession and was lost with other valuable papers at the burning of Columbia by General Sherman's army, in 1865. Sometime in 1866, I told Mr. Peter Cooper of New York of these facts and suggested that our Northern friends should not hold up their hands in holy horror on the slavery question. If we got the slaves those who owned the ships received the money and incurred by far the least trouble in the matter.[6]

Although Esther Porter had thrown in her lot with the South, her northern roots were strong. She sought to educate her son, John, in the North. In 1836, she sent him to study under the tutelage of the Rev. Chester in Morristown, New Jersey, where he resided for several years. When it was time for John to return home, Rev. Chester arranged for the young man to travel from New York by steamer back to South Carolina. According to an oft-repeated family story, Esther Porter dreamed that John should not return on the steamer lest an unknown calamity occur. She dashed off a letter to the clergyman urging him to remove the boy from the vessel before it departed. Upon receiving the correspondence, Chester hastened to the dock to find that the ship had just drawn in the planks. The crew was unfastening the ropes when the minister insisted that the boy decamp immediately. The ship's captain finally agreed. Young John and his trunk came back on shore. Esther's premonition was prescient; the ship encountered a gale off the coast of Hatteras and was lost, with only one soul surviving. Toomer Porter recalled his mother's agony as she learned of the ship's fate before she knew whether John was on board. When he finally turned up at home, he remembered her "rapturous joy as she recognized her son whom she had given up as lost."[7]

If Porter's brother survived a brush with death, his sister, Charlotte, did not. At age fourteen, she suffered from tremendous headaches. Charlotte had always been prone to migraines, but during the summer of 1834, they grew worse. While the family was visiting a summer retreat on North Island at the mouth of Winyah Bay, Charlotte remarked that she would be "Like that blind girl" in a book she had just read, *The Last Days of Pompeii*. Worried about the comment, Esther Porter took her daughter for a carriage ride. When Charlotte suggested that they head home because it was too dark to see, her mother assured her that, "Oh, no, it is still quite early; the sun has not gone down yet." This was the first indication that Charlotte was blind. She eventually died on February 15, 1835.[8]

"It was the first time I ever saw anyone die," Toomer Porter vividly recalled sixty-three years later. "But the peace, the joy, of that departing spirit, going, as she said, to see all the beauties of heaven, where there is no more pain; the absolute rapture of the young saint, have never passed from my memory."[9]

As Charlotte's tragic death illustrated, life in the nineteenth century was precarious. Reflecting on the fragility of life, the boy frequently thought of his dead father. He visited John Porter, Jr.'s grave in 1838, when he was ten years old, drawing inspiration from praying to the dead paterfamilias. "I believe that even a child's prayer is heard," he wrote, "and I can venture to hope that my father would not be ashamed of his son, could he know what has been the manner of my life."[10]

Toomer almost shared Charlotte's fate. He recalled the incident in his memoirs. In his view, the episode "seemed to give the colored people of the South a claim on my life service. My life indeed was actually saved by a negro who risked his own for my safety. I felt I had incurred a debt which I was bound, and afterwards endeavored, to repay."

The young man joined a group of friends on a sailboat for a fishing trip during the summer of 1839. An unexpected squall capsized the vessel. As it sank beneath the waves, Porter was convinced that he would drown "until I found myself in the arms of a colored man, being carried from the beach to our house. When I came to consciousness, he told me it was all right, not to be scared, that I was safe. We learned some time after that all the occupants of the boat got on the bottom, except myself."[11]

A skeptical reader hesitates to attribute too much significance to the dramatic disaster, but Porter contended that his rescue explained his favorable view of Black folks. It certainly demonstrated to him that relations between Blacks and whites need not be antagonistic. He remembered the lesson decades later, during the tumultuous Reconstruction era.

Family tragedies continued. His brother John Porter had survived a close call with death on board a ship, but he succumbed to bilious fever at age twenty. Once again, Toomer was present for the death of a sibling. "I was standing by his bedside, and just before he died, he clasped his hands and said, 'Conduct us, Heavenly Father, to Thy throne, and there kneeling let us praise Thee, through Jesus Christ our Lord.'" It was almost more than the family could bear. "We took his body, on the 10th of September, to Georgetown, and laid him beside our father, and the sister who had died in 1835. There were then left only two daughters and myself."[12]

He had seen much tragedy during his eleven years. After his mother departed to escort his sister to a New Jersey boarding school, young Toomer, left in the care of an aunt, began reading the Bible. He feared that he would never see the women in his life again, and he found solace in the gospels. He recalled how this practice altered his life:

> This habit begun at eleven years has been continued through life, with this improvement : soon after it was known that I was reading the Bible regularly, someone, perhaps my old aunt, took the Prayer Book, showed me the calendar, and pointed out to me that by following the Prayer Book lectionary one would read through in a year, excepting a few chapters, the Old Testament, the four accounts of the Gospel, the Acts of the Holy Apostles twice, and the Epistles four times. I immediately adopted the

plan, and through boyhood, youth, manhood, and old age have kept it up. How many times I have thus read the Bible through, and how imperceptibly it has colored my thoughts and swayed my life![13]

At age thirteen, Porter was confirmed in the church along with eleven white candidates, including his younger sister, and eight Black slaves. He felt "that something great had been done." From that moment, the boy knew what he wanted in life. "That day there began in me the desire and the purpose to study for the ministry," he later wrote.[14]

Much of his early life was less dramatic than the tragedies Porter had witnessed at a young age. He attended school at Mount Zion College in Winnsborough—later spelled "Winnsboro"—South Carolina, 25 miles north of Columbia for 16 months beginning in June 1844. He eventually left school to work in the counting house of Robertson, Blacklock, and Company in Charleston. Mr. Blacklock was known as the "king of the rice market."[15]

Young Toomer's most difficult task occurred after a man who had purchased slaves from the Porter family died, and the slaves were set for auction. Mr. Robertson directed Porter to attend to the sale. The young man reluctantly agreed. He realized that he knew some of the enslaved people on the auction block.

Recognizing Porter, the older enslaved persons begged the young man to resist the sale so their family members would not be separated. Porter was still a minor and powerless to intervene. He did all he could to console them, but the sale occurred, and the families were divided. Crying, Porter returned to tell his boss what had happened.

"Mr. Robertson, I have done as I was told to do," he confessed, "but I wish to say it is the first and it is the last of such a job. If I am again required to do such a business as that, I beg to retire from the office I hold." The firm never required the young man to handle a slave sale again.[16]

Despite Porter's antipathy for the brutal features of the institution, this was the antebellum South. Whether he saw it or not, the plantation economy depended on slave labor. Toomer Porter was a southern planter. After his mother's health failed in July 1846, he took a leave of absence from Robertson, Blacklock, and Company and traveled to Georgia to handle her affairs. He briefly returned to the counting house before permanently resigning from the firm.

Although he left the business world, Porter remained a businessman, in this case, a slaveholding rice planter. He displayed a talent for managing the plantation, but he was troubled by his role in perpetuating the peculiar institution. "I could not help it that I was a slave-holder," he later wrote. "I was born to it, and inherited it." He laid the blame for the rise of the institution on Englishmen and, later, eastern-based English-speaking colonists. "I do not believe there is anywhere on record that the [international] slave trade was carried on by Southern people."[17]

He lamented the existence of the domestic slave trade, but at least the peculiar institution resulted in many enslaved persons accepting the Christian faith. In his memoirs, Porter revealed himself to be an enlightened southerner when it came to slavery—up to a point. He expressed a paternalistic view of Blacks. "I love the African race, and think they are the most wonderful people," he confessed. Yet, he believed the Black race was inferior to whites. "I believe they are an inferior type of men, and the mass of them will be hewers of wood and drawers of water till the end of time—at the least, to the end of many generations. Do for them as we will, a black man will never be a white man."[18]

As an ambitious planter who opposed slavery, Porter explained his dilemma:

> I think I was born opposed to slavery. I do not remember the time when I did not hate it. Yet what could I do to abolish it? When I came of age, and inherited those that had been left me, when I bought my sisters' slaves, and brought them all back to the old plantation, what could I do but keep them? I could not free them, if I had wished to, and I was not such a philanthropist as to be willing to make myself a pauper by emancipating; the law forbade that. If I had so desired, I could not have taken them to many of the Western or Northern States, for the law prohibited that, but if I could have taken them to some free State, how would they have been supported?[19]

Porter's position was reminiscent of Abraham Lincoln's famous comment from the 1858 Lincoln-Douglas debates that a man could oppose the institution of slavery without defending the social equality of the races. "I do not understand that because I do not want a negro woman for a slave, I must necessarily want her for a wife. My understanding is that I can just let her alone. I am now in my fiftieth year, and I certainly never have had a black woman for either a slave or a wife."[20]

Although he was more sympathetic to the plight of enslaved persons than most planters of his era, Porter was not a civil rights advocate or a would-be emancipator. His attitude toward slavery was tinged with self-interest. He was opposed to the institution as a general proposition, but he perpetuated its existence in specific instances on his own plantation. He was a man ill at ease, torn between good conscience and economic gain. The latter concern took precedence.

Nonetheless, Porter's unease with slavery grew more pronounced with time. As the 1850s dawned, he felt stuck in his social position. He was a reluctant member of the planter elite, bored with rural life and weary of leaving his fate to the vicissitudes of wind, weather, and workmen.

Moreover, rice planting was incredibly labor-intensive and arguably the most dangerous of all agricultural work forced on enslaved laborers. To realize a satisfactory yield, Porter had to push his slaves to work almost beyond endurance. They cleared land and dredged canals on swampy acreage filled with snakes, alligators, and disease. He worried that as a "conscientious, careful, Christian master," he had to care for his workers, but as a slave owner, he was duty-bound to punish transgressions and insist on back-breaking labor from his bondsmen. He believed he was in an untenable position, but he did not see viable alternatives.[21]

Porter might have continued this way indefinitely but for a remarkable awakening that occurred in his life in 1851. One afternoon as he was riding his horse through the woods from the lower part of his plantation to the upper lands, he prayed that "God would lead me to a life more useful, and more satisfying to my nature, than the control and discipline of negroes." He later observed that the moment he offered his prayer, it was "the beginning of the end of my planter's life."[22]

In the ensuing months, he reassessed his life as a southern planter. Facing a spiritual crisis, he felt that he was wasting his life. One evening in April, as he was undressing to say his prayers and climb into bed, he was engulfed by "an overwhelming sense of misery." To all outward appearances, Toomer Porter had everything a young man could want. He was successful, wealthy, and esteemed by his neighbors. Even his spiritual life should have been satisfying. He was a vestryman of the church and a delegate to the Diocesan Convention from his parish. Yet, he asked himself, "Still, I am very unhappy, and why is it so?"[23]

He recalled his youthful desire to enter the ministry, which had left him feeling joyous. He should never have abandoned that dream. Reflecting on the choices he had made in his life, Porter wondered if he was too old to choose a different path. Could he walk away from the plantation, or sell his worldly goods as well as his enslaved persons? Was it God's will?

Porter soon announced his intentions to family and friends. To his surprise, they had expected him to enter the ministry. Encountering no serious objections to his change of heart, he set out to dispose of his plantation and tread a different path. "I had put it away from me when I was fifteen," he recalled, "and I was now twenty-three years old."[24]

The most difficult question was how to dispose of his enslaved persons. In an unusual move for a southern planter, he gathered his bondspeople and offered them a choice. He told them that he would abandon his life as a planter, but he could continue to own them. If he did so, they would labor under the supervision of an overseer. If he sold them, he promised to field only offers that would allow them to remain together. Emancipation was never an alternative.

The enslaved persons initially balked at a sale, preferring the master they knew to one they did not. Professing their love and devotion to Porter, they begged him to keep them together. "Master and slaves were in tears," Porter confessed. He eventually persuaded them to accept a sale. By the end of the year, he had reached an agreement with Dr. Allard H. Flagg of Waccamaw, whom Porter believed to be a fair man.

When the time came for the enslaved persons to board a steamer to reach their new home, Porter accompanied them to the ship and shook hands with each man, woman, and child as they boarded the vessel. It soon departed. With his mother permanently relocated to Charleston, "I was left the only living creature on the plantation."[25]

He was leaving the land settled by his grandfather almost a half-century earlier and the ancestral home of numerous relatives. His heart was heavy, but Toomer Porter knew what he must do. "It is now forty-six years since that day, and I have never had the nerve or resolution to visit it again," he wrote toward the end of his life. "And so closed forever the chapter of my Southern planter's life."[26]

Porter studied under the tutelage of Rev. Alexander Glennie of All Saints, Waccamaw, beginning in December 1851. An Englishman who had been elected rector of the parish, Glennie's primary responsibility was to hold parish church services on Sunday mornings for the local planters. The parish was more than 20 miles long, with 6,000 enslaved persons in the area. Their owners encouraged Glennie to minister to the bondspeople, which meant that the clergyman was constantly on the road. With only 150 whites in the parish, Rev. Glennie soon found himself ministering to far more Blacks than whites.

Porter took note of his mentor's activities. "I think Mr. Glennie was the first parish priest in the diocese of South Carolina who systematically ministered to the slaves as part of his parish." It was a lesson that Porter learned well.[27]

Even as he studied theology, the young man assisted Rev. Glennie in holding Sunday services on the plantations. They expanded services to four plantations every Sunday and doubled the number of weekday catechisms. By Glennie's own accounts, Porter performed services on plantations 110 times from March 15 through December 31, 1852. Glennie continued this work long after Porter had left, eventually calling a halt in 1862 as the Civil War intensified in the South Carolina Low Country.[28]

In June 1852, Porter traveled to Charleston for his first examination to enter the ministry. The examination, which lasted five or six hours, went well. Elated, Porter traveled by steamer home to Waccamaw. While onboard, he recognized Miss Susan Magdalene Atkinson, with whom he had played as a child on the beach at North Island. Her father was a wealthy rice planter at Winyah Bay, not far from Georgetown. At a young age, she had traveled to Philadelphia to complete her education, and so Porter had not seen her in years. She had now returned home. Young Toomer Porter spoke with her, rekindling their association. He was immediately smitten.

Undated photograph of Anthony Toomer Porter as a young man. Courtesy of Reading Room 2020, Alamy Stock Photo.

In the coming weeks, he visited Georgetown as often as he could, usually on the pretext of seeing his sister. As he confessed in his memoirs, Porter enjoyed seeing his sister, but he eagerly waited for a chance to steal away and court the comely young woman from Winyah Bay. She invaded his thoughts and distracted him from his theological studies.

Theirs was a whirlwind romance. On September 27, 1852, Porter asked Miss Atkinson to stroll with him in a cool afternoon breeze. Although their renewed acquaintance had lasted only three months, he professed his love. To his delight, she reciprocated. They soon announced their engagement.

At 1:00 p.m. on December 16, 1852, Anthony Toomer Porter married Susan Magdalene Atkinson, his true love, in the Prince George Winyah Episcopal Church in Georgetown, South Carolina. Rev. Robert T. Howard officiated. Porter was twenty-four years old. His bride was twenty-three.

It was a happy, fulfilling time in his life. He spent much of the year 1853 studying for the priesthood. As he prepared to be ordained in May 1854, Porter considered his options. He was offered a position in Camden, South Carolina, but a church standing committee's decision not to grant a dispensation for an expedited ordination required a change of plans. The Church of the Holy Communion in Charleston offered Porter a position as a lay reader until his ordination.[29]

The church, six years old, was in dire straits, with an unoccupied storeroom in the Charleston arsenal serving as the principal place of worship. Despite warnings from his friends and family, Porter accepted the position. Ambitious and confident, he believed that he could build the church from the ground up into a strong, healthy institution.[30]

Invigorated by the challenge, Porter returned to Georgetown on January 9, 1854, to discover that his wife had given birth to his first child, a son. The boy, John Toomer Porter, was baptized on February 24, 1854. He was called "Toomer," like his father. The happy family soon relocated to a house on Rutledge Street in Charleston. On May 16 of that year, Anthony Toomer Porter was ordained a priest in the Protestant Episcopal Church. He was twenty-six years old.[31]

He had successfully moved from a life as a wealthy planter to an Episcopal priest, and he had a young family to join him on his life's journey. Yet his path was not without its difficulties, as he soon learned. Describing his early years as "a hard apprenticeship," Porter admitted that "I was dreadfully scared at first, but as I warmed up, I know I forgot myself, and remembered that I was there to preach Christ, not myself, and at the close of the service was much encouraged by the warm greetings I had from many of my hearers."[32]

Even at this early stage in his career, Porter welcomed whites and Blacks into his church. By July 1854, by his own reckoning, "the congregation now numbered seventy-nine whites, and thirty-seven blacks." In the Sunday school, "there were thirty-one white children and thirty-five black children." Their common feature, Porter observed, was that most of his congregants were poor and in desperate need of solace. He could not help them with the former, but Porter struggled to do his best with the latter.[33]

For the next six years, Rev. Porter slowly, methodically built his church. He gathered the funds to construct a proper building, and he added new congregants. As the church became well established, a higher class of people joined the congregation.

His happiness was grounded in his work and family. In the summer of 1857, his family welcomed a second son, Theodore. His wife and second son, both frail, suffered from alarming health problems, but fortunately, they recovered.

During this time, Porter created the first industrial school for girls in South Carolina. It came about by chance. As the clergyman expanded his contacts throughout the city of Charleston, he was heartened to see how many organizations worked with the city's poor. The Fuel Society provided wood to indigents who could not afford it. The Garment Society, Hat and Shoe Society, and the Benevolent Society, which cared for the sick and homeless, met the needs of the less fortunate. The societies grew out of the charity work of the Presbyterian and Episcopal churches because, as Porter observed, "the wealth of the community were [sic] in these bodies."[34]

Porter believed that the church was obliged to provide charity, but he also encouraged the poor to work. During his travels throughout the city, he encountered girls and young women anxious to work, but lacking the skills to lift themselves out of poverty. He stumbled upon an idea. If he could buy enough sewing machines and procure garments, he could set these women to work as seamstresses. Porter employed experienced seamstresses to instruct the young women, who used their newfound skills to sew garments that they sold for profit. "The institution became entirely self-supporting," Porter proudly recalled.[35]

The industrial school eventually employed fifty-nine women and even included a children's industrial school. (In that era, poor children worked in fields, gardens, or factories rather than attend school.) Women from Porter's congregation began cooking meals to serve for lunch so the seamstresses could enjoy a home-cooked meal during the workday.

The operation was so successful that the workers presented Porter with a silver goblet and waiter in 1861. The inscription read, "From Grateful Hearts to the Founder of the First Industrial School in the City." Porter treasured the "little token."[36]

After the war erupted, the industrial school sewed uniforms for Confederate soldiers. As the war progressed, however, cloth was difficult to find, and production quotas dropped. Intent on increasing production, Colonel Lemuel M. Hatch, quartermaster of the South Carolina Militia, ordered his troops to seize the school. The Confederate army relied on the seamstresses to churn out uniforms until much of Charleston was destroyed in the war. When he returned to survey the property in 1865, Porter found that the sewing machines had been carted off and the building that housed the school was dilapidated. "Thus another great and beneficent work perished, the result of that dreadful war," he lamented. "I have never been able since to revive the work, but many persons who had come in there to help, had learned the work, and after the war supported themselves in consequence."[37]

That "dreadful war" was fast approaching by 1860. Porter remembered his fellow South Carolinians discussing "secession thunder-clouds." On a visit to the state capital in Columbia, he heard incautious threats bandied about by many citizens. "The presidential election was coming on, and everyone said that if Mr. Lincoln was elected the State would secede." Porter thought secession was insane, but many South Carolinians had caught the fever.[38]

He heard the story of James L. Petigru, a famous lawyer and former state attorney general who often voiced an anti-secessionist opinion. According to the often-repeated tale, Petigru was walking along Main Street in Columbia one day when a countryman approached him.

"Mister," the man inquired, "can you tell me where is the lunatic asylum?"

"Yes, my man," Petigru supposedly replied. "It is off down the street; they call that the asylum, but it is a mistake. Yonder is the asylum and it is full of lunatics," he said, pointing at the statehouse, where the state legislature convened.[39]

Despite his initial skepticism, Porter was swept up in the excitement. South Carolina would no longer suffer the abuses that an oppressive federal government heaped on the people of a proud, sovereign state. By the time that the state legislature called for a secession convention at year's end, the clergyman had changed his view. "I was in my thirty-third year, and became as enthusiastic as the rest," he admitted. "I look back now and wonder how it all could have been as it was."[40]

Porter recalled a postwar discussion with Christopher Memminger, the first secretary of the treasury in the Confederate States government. "Mr. Memminger," Porter remarked, "I am now as old as you were when this city and State went wild; why did not you older men take all of us young enthusiasts and hold us down?"

"Oh," Memminger replied, "it was a whirlwind, and all we could do was try to guide it."[41]

An old man looking back at a devastating war penned such lamentations. In the heat of the moment, however, he embraced secession as eagerly as anyone. In fact, Porter attended the secession convention at St. Andrew's Hall on Broad Street. He witnessed his brother-in-law, a convention member, cast a vote in favor of secession. "Yea after yea, was answered until every name was called, and the vote was unanimous," Porter later wrote. South Carolina voted to leave the Union that it had joined when the state ratified the US Constitution in May 1788.[42]

Cheers swept through the city when the vote was announced. Later, during a ratification mass meeting, politicians and state leaders boldly predicted that the state would leave the Union with little or no resistance from the government in Washington, DC. Ardent secessionists labeled "Fire-Eaters" delivered incendiary speeches about their unwavering resolve. Those in federal employ, such as federal judges, impetuously resigned their commissions. No one understood the consequences of what was to come, but everyone suffered from secessionist fever.

Porter was present when "there went up a universal yell, presage of what has gone into history as 'the rebel yell.' It died out, and rose, and died, and rose for several minutes." Porter confessed that "I, fool as I was, yelled with the rest of them, and threw up my hat, and no doubt thought we could whip creation."[43]

It was a time of passion and emotion overwhelming reason and deliberation. Everywhere southern men and women predicted a glorious outcome. "The flame of enthusiasm extended from the seaboard to the mountains, and all South Carolina was ablaze," in Porter's words. It was only when a dense smoke cloud blew over Fort Moultrie on Sullivan's Island that the reality of the situation dawned on some Charlestonians.[44]

Everyone knew that Major Robert Anderson of the US Army had been stationed at Fort Moultrie with a contingent of federal troops. After the smoke appeared, citizens wondered if the fort had accidentally caught on fire. When the South Carolinians investigated, they discovered that Fort Moultrie's guns had been spiked and the interior of the fort had been set ablaze so that it would be useless. Major Anderson and his men were nowhere to be found. It soon became clear that they had retreated to Fort Sumter, a seemingly impregnable federal fortress in Charleston Harbor.[45]

Rumors abounded. Major Anderson had fled to Fort Sumter so that he could aim big guns at the city of Charleston. The federals would soon order an attack on the city. Fighting supposedly broke out in the city streets, which quickly filled with blood. Alarmed, militia companies from across the state as well as from neighboring states such as Georgia volunteered to send arms and men to restore order and preserve Charleston. The rumors were false, but they demonstrated the fever pitch of emotion that engulfed South Carolinians in December 1860.

Now that war with the US government was a distinct possibility, militia companies organized and drilled their men. One unit, the Washington Light Infantry, dated from 1807, making it the oldest volunteer company in South Carolina. The company had elected Toomer Porter its chaplain in 1858. On December 28, 1860, the commanding officer asked Porter to come to Castle Pinckney, a fortress in Charleston Harbor, to preach a sermon to the southern troops stationed there. He agreed. Porter offered a sermon on Second Timothy, taking as his theme "a good soldier of Jesus Christ." With this appearance, Porter "had the honor of preaching the first sermon to the troops in the civil war."[46]

For all his enthusiasm, Porter believed that a war would have to be fought, and blood would be shed. Not everyone agreed. He later claimed to have encountered a former US senator, James Chestnut, Jr., and discussed the possibility of armed conflict.

"These are troublous times, Colonel," Porter remarked. "We are at the beginning of a terrible war."

"Not at all," Chestnut assured him. "There will be no war; it will be all arranged. I will drink all the blood shed in the war."

The exchange left Porter with an ill feeling because a man of the upper echelon would utter such a foolhardy, cavalier claim. "So little did our leaders realize the awful import of what we were doing."[47]

The Washington Light Infantry was dispatched to Sullivan's Island to stand guard. Porter held services at the Church of the Holy Communion in Charleston in the morning and provided worship services to the camp across the harbor on Sullivan's Island at night. His life continued in this frenetic manner for months.

The status quo changed without warning. "The fateful day of April 11, 1861, came. At four o'clock in the morning, I heard the boom of a cannon," Porter recalled. The South Carolinians were firing on Fort Sumter. "Shot after shot was following from Fort Moultrie and battery Gregg on Morris Island. But Sumter looked grim and silent."[48]

It was only in full daylight that Major Anderson and the federals garrisoned on Fort Sumter fired back. Porter and his colleagues crowded into the tower of the Moultrie House to gain a better view from the highest elevation on the island. When the tower drew fire and a shell struck the story below where the soldiers stood, the men scrambled out of the building.

A slew of batteries on Sullivan's Island fired at Fort Sumter. The barrage was deafening. The smoke of fifty big guns enveloped Fort Sumter, but Porter saw enough of the fight to render judgment thirty-seven years later. "I witnessed then a scene that I doubt was ever equaled. The gallantry of the defense struck the chivalry of the attackers, and without a command every soldier mounted the parapet of every battery of the Confederates and gave three cheers for Major Anderson."[49]

The federals soon surrendered, and Fort Sumter fell into southern hands. Shortly thereafter, orders came that the Washington Light Infantry was to return to Charleston. The city was a flurry of activities as new units were formed, some to stay in South Carolina and others to march off to Virginia in anticipation of fighting.

Porter joined several men in searching for a suitable captain to lead a company bound for Virginia. They soon tapped a prominent Charleston lawyer, James Conner. Conner's men became Company A of the Hampton Legion.[50]

Rev. Porter remained in South Carolina, but not for long. "Captain Conner promised me whenever a battle was imminent to telegraph me, 'Come at once,' and I would understand," Porter remembered. "I soon after received the telegram from him, and left as soon as I could, but reached Manassas Junction four days after the first battle of Manassas."[51]

As soon as he arrived on the battlefield, Porter rushed around ministering to the sick and wounded. I "had my hands full," he later wrote. He tried to comfort distraught Confederates and Yankees alike.[52]

Aside from his duties as a minister, Porter assisted in procuring much-needed supplies, especially uniforms, for the troops. He shuttled back and forth between South Carolina and Virginia to ensure that the men had everything they needed. He found that supplies were always in short supply—everything from clothing to food to medicines.

He was appalled at the "typical instance of Confederate mismanagement." In Porter's opinion, southern men were ready and willing to fight, but they lacked the necessary provisions. Their leaders had failed to rise to the occasion. "The want of organization and administration, I verily believe, was what neutralized the magnificent fighting, the splendid endurance of our soldiers," he bitterly remarked. "Had other departments done as well as the troops in the field, there is no telling what might have been the issue of the war."[53]

The Washington Light Infantry became a part of the 25th South Carolina Regiment, and Porter became the regimental chaplain. He reported for duty on James Island outside of Charleston. He was there for the Battle of Secessionville (sometimes called the First Battle of James Island) on June 16, 1862. It was federal forces' only serious effort to capture Charleston early in the war. Porter came under fire but somehow, miraculously, emerged unscathed. So ferocious was the gunfire that Porter admitted, "I do not know why I escaped death."[54]

Although the Union did not try to capture Charleston again until late in the war, the US Navy shelled the city from Morris Island for two years. Rev. Porter was in the city for much of this time. He came under fire on numerous occasions. He also saw Charlestonians die from yellow fever and smallpox. He called them "terrible days," and he expressed sorrow that so many noncombatants perished.[55]

He experienced death up close in 1864. In October of that year, his son Toomer, eleven years old, appeared lethargic as the family sat down to consume the evening meal. When Rev. Porter asked why the boy refused to eat, his son replied, "I do not feel very well, and if you will excuse me, papa, I will go to the fire."

A yellow fever epidemic had swept through the South Carolina Low Country, and Porter worried that his son might be its latest victim. He was right to be worried. "The shadow of a great gloom settled over me," the minister later wrote. "I pushed off from the table, and said, 'We will have family prayers and then you can go to bed, my son.'"[56]

When young Toomer knelt to say his prayers, he was fast asleep before he finished. His father was by his side immediately. "I said, 'Put your arms around papa, and give him one good hug.' He did—it was the last."[57]

Rev. Porter carried the boy upstairs to his bed. Toomer's little body was ravaged with fever. A doctor came to check on the patient, but "the boy died of yellow fever." In a melodramatic scene that may have been embellished, Porter described a young man in anguish, preternaturally old:

> The condition we were all in seemed to prey on his mind. The crash of shells falling in the city, and bursting every few minutes, the alarm of fire every now and then, the poor food we were eating, the prisoners passing our door—all seemed to weigh him down. At last, he clasped his hands,

and turning up his beautiful eyes, he said, "O Lord, save Thy people, and bless Thine heritage." Then, putting his two hands in his mother's (she was standing on the left side of the bed, and I on the right), he said, "Mamma, it is so hard, it is so hard," then turning to me, he put his hands in mine, and said, "Papa, let me go, let me go." I, consenting, said, "Go, darling, if Jesus calls you."[58]

He buried his son in Magnolia Cemetery in Charleston on October 26, 1864. In January 1870, he had the boy's remains moved to a family plot in Georgetown. Toomer's death changed his life's ambition. After the war, when Porter established schools to educate Charleston's Black and white youth, he often thought of his dead son as he labored on his life's new mission.

His son's tragic death presaged another monumental loss. By early 1865, the Southern Confederacy teetered on the brink of collapse. Life in Charleston had become unbearable. The lack of edible food and clean water, the unsanitary conditions, and the approaching Union soldiers convinced Porter that he must move his family to Anderson, South Carolina, far inland.

The Porter family boarded a westbound train, but they could not make it to Anderson. Forced to retreat to Columbia, the clergyman left his family at the home of Dr. Reynolds while he returned to Charleston. Encountering General William Hardee, commander of Confederate troops in the city, he learned that Union General William T. Sherman was headed for Columbia. Porter had moved his family from Charleston so they would be safe, only to place them in harm's way in Columbia.[59]

He raced back to the state capital and saw that "General Sherman's army had now reached the Congaree River, and fighting had begun below the city. Three days after my departure from Charleston, a portion of this army was distinctly visible on the heights outlined against the sky."[60]

The city could not hold out for long. Municipal leaders surrendered to General Sherman on February 17, 1865. As federal troops entered the city and residents fled, Columbia burned.

Against this backdrop, Porter reported that he saw General Sherman marching through the city. The general recognized Porter and admitted, "this is terrible," referring to the fire.

"Yes," Porter replied, "when you remember that women and children are your victims."

Sherman brooked no criticism. "Your Governor is responsible for this," he claimed.

"How so?"

"Whoever heard of evacuating a place and leaving it full of liquor?" Sherman asked. "My men are drunk, and this is the cause of all. Why did not your Governor destroy all the liquor before he left? There was a very great quantity of whiskey in the town when we arrived."

"The drunken men have done much," Porter observed, "but I have seen sober men fire house after house."[61]

It is difficult to envision the commanding general of the Union forces admitting to a Confederate chaplain that he, a general officer, could not control his soldiers, who were drunk and burning the city. Porter insisted that the encounter had occurred.[62]

Alcohol apparently was responsible for another episode that Porter reported. On his way back to Dr. Reynolds's house, Porter was surrounded by a drunken Union sergeant and two privates. The sergeant struck Porter and relieved him of his shawl. Only the intervention of a kindly Union soldier who forced the sergeant to return the shawl saved Porter from possibly worse treatment. "I told the speaker for the sake of humanity, I was glad to meet one man who seemed to have a human heart in his breast."[63]

Porter met another good Samaritan among the Union forces, and this time he knew the man's name. He was Lt. John A. McQueen of Company F, 15th Illinois Cavalry, and a native of Elgin, Ohio. With no apparent motive other than his desire to carry out a good deed, McQueen intervened to save Porter's family from a mob. Fearful that Union soldiers might burn the house where the family had taken refuge, McQueen ordered the soldiers off the premises. He also arranged to extinguish nearby fires so they would not consume the house.

"It was God's providence that brought us together," the clergyman observed.[64] He reciprocated by writing a letter addressed to General Wade Hampton as well as any Confederate soldier that McQueen might encounter as he departed from Columbia. "Keep this with you," Porter said as he handed the letter to his new friend. "It may be of service. Use it in any emergency, which in the changes and chances of war may come."[65]

The changes and chances came soon. Encountering a group of Confederate soldiers, McQueen displayed the letter. The men spared his life. Later, McQueen was wounded in the groin and might never have arrived home, but Porter sought him out in Camden, South Carolina.

After much maneuvering, Porter accompanied his friend into North Carolina before arranging for General Sherman's army to receive him, where he would be cared for until he returned home. "I had now travelled over seven hundred miles, by rail, on foot, in a wagon without springs, in a buggy, amidst many dangers, to set McQueen free," he wrote. "I would have travelled seven thousand to show my gratitude to that gallant man."[66]

With McQueen safely cared for, Porter arrived in Raleigh, North Carolina. The Southern Confederacy was on the brink of collapse. After meeting with Confederate General Joseph E. Johnston, the clergyman agreed "to do what I could to help the soldiers." From this perch, Toomer Porter bore witness to the closing days of the war.[67]

Notes

1. The information in this chapter is derived from A. Toomer Porter, *Led On! Step by Step Scenes from Clerical, Military, Educational, and Plantation Life in the South, 1828–1898* (New York: G. P. Putnam's Sons, the Knickerbocker Press, 1898). Instead of cluttering the chapter with endnotes, only direct quotations are cited.
2. Porter, *Led On*, 4. One source listed John Porter, Jr.'s death as 1829. "Rev. Dr. Anthony Toomer Porter," in *Cyclopedia of Eminent and Representative Men of the Carolinas of the Nineteenth Century, with a Brief Historical Introduction on South Carolina by General Edward McCrady, Jr., and on North Carolina by Hon. Samuel A. Ashe*, Vol. I (Madison, WI: Brant & Fuller, 1892), 493.
3. Porter, *Led On*, 7.
4. Owing to its proximity to water, rice cultivation was "the dominant economic activity of the County," according to 1850 data. See, for example, Sherman L. Ricards and George M. Blackburn, "A Demographic History of Slavery: Georgetown County, South Carolina, 1850," *The South Carolina Historical Magazine* 76, no. 4 (October 1975): 215. According to one commentator, "as early as 1732 the value for purposes of rice culture of swamp-land irrigated by the flow of the tide had become known" in the towns and settlements established along the South Carolina coast. See, for example, Henry A. M. Smith, "The Baronies of South Carolina," *The South Carolina Historical and Genealogical Magazine* 13, no. 1 (January 1912): 8.
5. Porter, *Led On*, 3.
6. Ibid.
7. Ibid., 8.
8. Ibid.
9. Ibid., 8–9.
10. Ibid., 12.
11. Ibid.
12. Ibid., 13.
13. Ibid., 15.
14. Ibid., 17.
15. "Rev. Dr. Anthony Toomer Porter," 493.
16. Porter, *Led On*, 58.
17. Ibid., 70. The literature on slavery apologists is too numerous to reference here. See, for example, Drew Gilpin Faust, "A Southern Stewardship: The Intellectual and the Proslavery Argument," *American Quarterly* 31, no. 1 (Spring 1979): 63–80; Gregory E. O'Malley, "Slavery's Converging Ground: Charleston's Slave Trade as the Black Heart of the Lowcountry," *The William and Mary Quarterly* 74, no. 2 (April 2017): 271–302.

18 Porter, *Led On*, 71.
19 Ibid.
20 Lincoln is quoted in Thomas L. Krannawitter, *Vindicating Lincoln: Defending the Politics of Our Greatest President* (Lanham, MD: Rowman & Littlefield, 2008), 29.
21 By the nineteenth century, rice, largely cultivated by enslaved persons, was integral to the South Carolina economy. Judith A. Carney, "From Hands to Tutors: African Expertise in the South Carolina Rice Economy," *Agricultural History* 67, no. 3 (Summer 1993): 1–30.
22 Porter, *Led On*, 74.
23 Ibid., 75.
24 Ibid., 78.
25 Ibid., 80.
26 Ibid.
27 Ibid., 83. For more on Rev. Glennie's work, see especially Joseph Blount Cheshire, D. D., *The Church in the Confederate States: A History of the Protestant Episcopal Church in the Confederate States* (New York Longmans, Green, & Company, 1912), 123–5; Janet Duitsman Cornelius, *Slave Missions and the Black Church in the Antebellum South* (Columbia: University of South Carolina Press, 1999), 124–6; Susan Markey Fickling, "Slave-Conversion in South Carolina, 1830–1860" (master's thesis, University of South Carolina, 1924), 37–9; Albert Sidney Thomas, *A Historical Account of the Protestant Episcopal Church in South Carolina, 1820–1957* (Columbia, SC: R. L. Bryan Company, 1957), 77.
28 Thomas, *A Historical Account of the Protestant Episcopal Church in South Carolina, 1820–1957*, 384–5. Glennie's accounting of Porter's services is found in Alexander Glennie, *Alexander Glennie Journal, 1831 1859*, South Carolina Historical Society, Charleston, SC, accessed June 10, 2024, https://lcdl.library.cofc.edu/lcdl/catalog/lcdl:61931.
29 Thomas, *A Historical Account of the Protestant Episcopal Church in South Carolina, 1820–1957*, 213. See also "Rev. Dr. Anthony Toomer Porter," 494.
30 "Rev. Dr. Anthony Toomer Porter," 494.
31 Thomas, *A Historical Account of the Protestant Episcopal Church in South Carolina, 1820–1957*, 763.
32 Porter, *Led On*, 97.
33 Ibid., 98.
34 Ibid., 106–7. See also Ron Field, "Clothing the Confederate Soldiers of South Carolina, 1861–1865," *Military Collector & Historian* 70, no. 1 (Spring 2018): 88.
35 Porter, *Led On*, 108.
36 Ibid., 108–9.
37 Ibid., 111. See also Field, "Clothing the Confederate Soldiers of South Carolina," 88.

38 Porter, *Led On*, 115.
39 Porter recounted the tale in Ibid., 116. For more information on Petigru, see, for example, Lacy K. Ford, "Reconsidering James Petigru: Unionist and Civic Reformer in a Radical Age," *The South Carolina Historical Magazine* 122, no. 3 (July 2021): 124–47; Lyon G. Tyler, "James Louis Petigru: Freedom's Champion in a Slave Society," *The South Carolina Historical Magazine* 83, no. 4 (October 1982): 272–86.
40 Porter, *Led On*, 116–17.
41 Ibid., 117. For more information on Memminger, see, for example, Richard C. Todd, "C.G. Memminger and the Confederate Treasury Department," *The Georgia Review* 12, no. 4 (Winter 1958): 396–410.
42 Porter, *Led On*, 117.
43 Ibid., 119. For more information on the Fire-Eaters, see, for example, William K. Scarborough, "Propagandists for Secession: Edmund Ruffin of Virginia and Robert Barnwell Rhett of South Carolina," *The South Carolina Historical Magazine* 112, no. 3/4 (July–October 2011): 126–38; Eric H. Walther, *The Fire-Eaters* (Baton Rouge: Louisiana State University Press, 1992).
44 Porter, *Led On*, 119.
45 David Detzer, *Allegiance: Fort Sumter, Charleston, and the Beginning of the Civil War* (New York: Harcourt, 2001), 55–64.
46 Porter, *Led On*, 121. See also "Rev. Dr. Anthony Toomer Porter," 494. On the origins of the Washington Light Infantry, see Jessica Johnson, "Washington Light Infantry Turns 200; Group Named for 1st President Organized in 1807 as Militia," *The Post and Courier* [Charleston, SC], February 21, 2007, B1; Newton B. Jones, "The Washington Light Infantry at the Bunker Hill Centennial," *The South Carolina Historical Magazine* 65, no. 4 (October 1964): 196.
47 The exchange is recounted in Porter, *Led On*, 122.
48 Ibid., 123.
49 Ibid., 124.
50 "Rev. Dr. Anthony Toomer Porter," 494.
51 Porter, *Led On*, 129.
52 Ibid., 130–1.
53 Ibid., 133.
54 Ibid., 140. See also Cheshire, *The Church in the Confederate States*, 80; Editors of Time-Life Books, *Voices of the Civil War: Charleston* (New York: Time-Life Books, 1997), 13–14; Field, "Clothing the Confederate Soldiers of South Carolina," 88. For more on Secessionville see, for example, James A. Morgan, *Six Miles from Charleston, Five Minutes to Hell: The Battle of Secessionville, June 16, 1862* (El Dorado Hills, CA: Savas Beatie, 2022); J. Tracy Power, "'An Affair of Outposts': The Battle of Secessionville, June 16, 1862," *Civil War History* 38, no. 2 (June 1992): 156–72.
55 Porter, *Led On*, 146–7.

56 Ibid., 149.
57 Ibid.
58 Ibid., 150.
59 "Rev. Dr. Anthony Toomer Porter," 494.
60 Porter, *Led On*, 154.
61 Ibid., 164.
62 The encounter does not ring true. General Sherman always insisted that his troops did not burn Columbia. In an 1888 article, Sherman and A. E. Wood, a captain in the Fourth Cavalry, wrote that "'Sherman's Bummers' did not set fire to Columbia, for the river prevented their passage, and knowing that we should get possession of the town in a few hours, they joined their respective companies before any of the troops passed over, and remained with them until the next day." A. E. Wood and W. T. Sherman, "The Burning of Columbia," *The North American Review* 146, no. 377 (April 1888): 404.
63 Porter, *Led On*, 166.
64 Ibid., 168.
65 Ibid., 174.
66 Ibid., 181.
67 Ibid. For more on Johnston and the North Carolina surrender, see, for example, Robert M. Hughes, "Joseph Eggleston Johnston: Soldier and Man," *The William and Mary College Quarterly Historical Magazine* Second Series 13, no. 2 (April 1933): 71–2.

4

"I Redevoted Myself Wholly and Only to God"— William Porcher DuBose

The Early Years (1836–1865)

On Friday, August 29, 1862, Holcombe's Legion crossed the Rappahannock River and marched on Manassas Junction, Virginia, arriving that evening during a respite in the Battle of Second Manassas. In his memoirs, William Porcher DuBose recalled those anxious days. "We arrived the night before and formed in line of battle, Longstreet's Corps. We lay under arms waiting for the battle to begin."[1]

The next day, after he was dispatched to order that the wagons be brought up from the rear, DuBose returned to witness a chaotic scene. Riding near a Confederate artillery battery that was opening fire on an enemy column, he recalled hearing "boom, boom, boom, boom, boom, boom, which excited me to such a pitch, that I dashed on." He saw a Yankee unit come under withering fire. "As the shells were poured into them, the column dissolved and the Confederates dashed forward, hats waving in a perfect jubilation of victory."[2]

An order to advance arrived immediately on the heels of the artillery barrage. Colonel Peter Fayssoux Stevens commanded the legion, and he led his men toward the enemy. The unit trudged through thick woods before emerging in an open field, which became "a perfect focus of firing from all sides."

DuBose was mounted on a horse, making him a convenient target for Union riflemen. As bullets whizzed past his head, he dismounted and threw himself to the ground. "A few minutes later," he remembered, "we arose to advance farther to the enemy and in less time than it takes for me to tell it our whole brigade was decimated." It was heartbreaking, devastating. He estimated that two-thirds of the soldiers went down as blistering shot and shell tore through the ranks. "How I managed to pass through that rain of bullets I don't know, but when I emerged there was not more than a dozen, if so many, to go forward with me. The command as a whole had been annihilated."[3]

Despite the annihilation of Holcombe's Legion, Confederate troops routed Union forces at Second Manassas. Surviving members of the Legion pursued the retreating Yankees from the field. DuBose picked up a fallen unit flag and hoisted it high as he ran.[4]

The fleeing Union soldiers must have realized that they could not escape. They stopped, turned, and fired. "The few men that were with me were a little to the left and were shielded somewhat from sight by some stray pine saplings," DuBose later wrote. "It so happened that I was the only one visible to them at that moment, standing with the flag in my hands." When the enemy soldiers fired, DuBose purposely fell to avoid the bullets. They hit the flag, but not the man.

As he rose to his feet, the enemy fired another volley. "At that moment a minie ball hit me, tearing my clothes and the flesh off my back and just scraping my backbone. The enemy resumed their retreat and I was left standing there—paralyzed."[5]

It was a temporary ailment. He soon found that he could move. DuBose was thankful that his wounds were not severe, but it "was an awful experience." The suffering of the dying, groaning men strewn across the battlefield was impossible to ignore. DuBose encountered a friend, mortally wounded. He desperately sought to alleviate the man's suffering, but the fellow was doomed. "The victory was a great one," DuBose lamented, "but it was a bloody one, one of the bloodiest of the war."[6]

William Porcher DuBose, twenty-six years of age, had survived one of the great battles of the American Civil War. Yet the price had been steep. He was the only field officer in Holcombe's Legion healthy enough to reorganize the regiment to march in the impending invasion of Maryland. The unit could muster but one hundred able-bodied men. With the regimental doctors dead on the battlefield, DuBose did what he could to relieve the suffering of his comrades, even securing painkillers from a nearby village.[7]

Because he was still in relatively good health, DuBose assumed command of the remnants of Holcombe's Legion, which had been reorganized into three companies. The men marched under General Lee's command for the Maryland invasion. Following a short stop in Frederick, the troops headed through Boonesboro Gap and over South Mountain to Hagerstown.[8]

DuBose recalled the long, miserable march among men who were ravaged by disease, injury, and fatigue. As they arrived in the gap during a dark night, his troops collapsed in exhaustion, settling in for the evening where they fell.

DuBose had hoped for relief, but it was not to be. Ordered to select the best men under his command to extend a picket line, he set out in a dense forest with thirty to forty soldiers under his command.

After the line was in place, DuBose received new orders to advance to the scene of an earlier skirmish. Calling the men together, he ordered them to advance as cautiously and quietly as they could considering the uneven terrain and the dark night. "In spite of the effort to be as silent and secret as possible, while moving as swiftly, we were subject to so many false alarms and necessarily made so much noise through the bushes, endangering our own discovery before we could discover the enemy," he remembered.[9]

They climbed up South Mountain almost to the top. Leaving his men, DuBose reconnoitered the hillside where a battle had occurred. He marveled at the quiet, still night until he heard a single command. "Halt!" a voice called. He wondered if this was a fellow Confederate sentry or the voice of an enemy soldier.

He could see one or two men twenty steps ahead of him, but it was too dark to distinguish their uniforms. Holding a pistol in his hand, DuBose quietly moved toward the men. When they recognized each other as enemies, the soldiers immediately reacted. The man closest to him raised his pistol just as DuBose reached out and deflected the gun. DuBose's pistol discharged.

"Instantly, the woods were alive," he later wrote. "My effort then was simply to get away. In the scuffle that ensued, I several times nearly did so, but my antagonist was a much larger and stronger man [than] I was, and I finally had to surrender to numbers." Adjutant DuBose had become a prisoner of war.[10]

He had led a charmed life until this moment. The scion of a wealthy southern family, William Porcher DuBose was born in Winnsboro, South Carolina, a small town 30 miles north of Columbia, on April 11, 1836. Shortly thereafter, his family purchased 3,000 acres of bottom land on Wateree Creek 9 miles north of Winnsboro. The family called the plantation home Farmington, and young Willie lived there for the first eight years of his life.

His father, Theodore Samuel Marion DuBose, was an affluent planter from a prominent family that could trace its roots to the Norman French Huguenots who settled near the Santee and Cooper Rivers in South Carolina during the seventeenth century. "My father was educated in the north, at Partridge's Academy first, and later at Yale," DuBose recalled. "He then came back and married his first cousin, Jane Porcher."[11]

His father inherited "large and extensive property" in the South Carolina Low Country, including a plantation on the Cooper River as well as other plantations. The Low-Country climate was not conducive to his health, however, so the elder DuBose retreated to the South Carolina interior. He eventually rented a home in Winnsboro, where his son was born. Pleased with the farmland around Winnsboro, the DuBoses stayed in the area.

Willie DuBose practically worshipped Theodore DuBose, and with little wonder. The old man cast a large shadow in his community. He was a captain in the local militia, a commissioner of free schools, and on the board of visitors for Mount Zion Schools. By 1860, he owned 204 enslaved persons in the Fairfield District as well as $40,000 worth of real estate and a personal fortune of $27,716, a considerable sum for the time.[12]

When Willie was eight years old, he remembered riding with his father in a carriage about 3 miles from Winnsboro, where they saw Roseland, the DuBose family's new plantation, for the first time. "I remember distinctly as we got to the front gate, there was an immense garden filled with trees," DuBose wrote. "At the time it was not well cared for, the place being idle, but we trimmed it up and made it beautiful. Roseland became a sort of Mecca."[13]

Life on the South Carolina plantations during the 1840s and 1850s was "a paradise for boys," assuming the boys were white and hailed from prominent families. Willie's relatives lived on adjacent acreage, and the family was close. He had his own horse, Bagatelle, and numerous playmates. He remembered his boyhood days as idyllic.

When it came time to commence his education, Willie studied at a women's school under Mrs. Atkinson. He demonstrated the first signs of intellectual prowess there, winning a schoolbook as a reward for placing first in his class. He eventually moved on to Mount Zion, a well-known school in Winnsboro. He excelled in most subjects except mathematics, which proved to be especially challenging.[14]

On January 1, 1852, shortly before his sixteenth birthday, DuBose entered the South Carolina Military Academy known as The Citadel. It was his father's wish that he attend The Citadel, and Willie almost always did what his father wished. Theodore DuBose "had determined that each of his sons should have a good education, including college and university, and after that a professional training, though all our family had for two hundred years been planters," DuBose explained. "He did a most *heroic* thing. Instead of letting me go to college, where I could have entered and for which I was prepared, my father decided to send me to a military school, The Citadel, for which I was physically unprepared, and mentally also, owing to my trouble with Mathematics."[15]

He entered school with his cousins Richard Dwight, Willie Gaillard, and Henry Gaillard. Despite his deficiencies in physical fitness and mathematics, DuBose thrived at The Citadel. He worked diligently and rose to the top of his class. He recalled "the proudest and most exalted moment of my life" came when he was elected corporal in the corps of cadets. During his second year, he was elected sergeant of cadets, another high honor.[16]

During his third year at The Citadel, DuBose lost interest in his studies. He could offer no explanation for this lethargy except perhaps for a general feeling of homesickness. His father noticed the change and wrote the young man a scathing letter. "Well, this letter was like a *lash*," DuBose admitted. "It went straight to the mark—the weakness, the folly, the unmanliness of being homesick. It woke me and stirred me up. But it was too late. I lost for that year my standing in my classes. At the end of the year, I only came out second."[17]

As a child, DuBose had been reared in the Protestant Episcopal Church and had engaged in religious reflection, but he gradually moved away from a spiritual life during his Citadel years. After receiving a letter from a friend, Tom Stoney, who attended the University of Virginia, DuBose began thinking about religion seriously for the first time in years. Stoney wrote passionately of great spiritual changes in his life, and the feeling influenced DuBose.[18]

Not long thereafter, DuBose was traveling with several Citadel cadets when the young men took a hotel room for the night. While the others slept, DuBose experienced a religious conversion.

> I declare there came into that room that night a *presence* that was so distinct and definite that—It was just as though a new world had opened to me, a new presence had come into my life and it was so absolute and positive, there was no mistaking it. I dreaded to go to sleep, lest it disappear. But when I woke, it was there.[19]

He reflected on his religious heritage. The DuBoses were descended from French Huguenots who were absorbed by the Church of England, which was the only church that DuBose knew as he grew up. Women typically were communicants while men were not. DuBose could only recall one male communicant—his uncle, Sam Porcher—in the church at Black Oak during his formative years. Men eventually joined, but it was only after a beloved community leader regretfully confessed on his deathbed that he had resisted the call of religion for much of his life. As a result of his example, many men joined the church.[20]

At the end of DuBose's third year at The Citadel, Bishop Thomas Frederick Davis confirmed the young man in St. Michael's Church in Charleston. It was a good year for Willie. He became the captain of cadets that same year as well as assistant professor of English at The Citadel. When he graduated in December 1855, he was again first in his class.[21]

The Citadel had afforded DuBose a practical education in engineering, mathematics, and what later would be called military science, but he had not read the classics. He resolved to remedy that deficiency. In 1856, he departed for Charlottesville to continue his studies at the University of Virginia.[22]

With his eyesight failing and despondent at not knowing his new classmates, DuBose suffered through depression during his early days at the university. In time, his eyesight and disposition improved. He came to regard many of his fellow students as kindred spirits, and they became dear friends.[23]

A young William Porcher DuBose in the uniform of a Citadel Cadet. Courtesy of the William R. Laurie University Archives and Special Collections, the University of the South, Sewanee, Tennessee.

He earned a Master of Arts degree in 1859 before enrolling in the Episcopal Church's diocesan seminary in Camden, South Carolina, in October of that year. DuBose was in the first class of the seminary, which admitted only seven students that fall. Founded by Bishop Davis, the seminary opened with only four professors, including Davis's son.[24]

By the spring of 1860, DuBose had developed an "obstinate cough" that caused him to leave the school prematurely. Anxious to recover his health, he departed for a camping trip to the North Carolina mountains. The trip was memorable because he met a young woman, Anne Barnwell "Nannie" Peronneau, who later became his wife.[25]

DuBose felt well enough to return to seminary in the fall of 1860. As he resumed his studies, however, political events engulfed the nation. After Abraham Lincoln won the presidency in November 1860, the southern states threatened to secede from the Union. DuBose was in Charleston, South Carolina, on December 20, 1860, when the state's convention voted to ratify a secession ordinance.[26]

Despite the momentous occasion, DuBose confessed that his primary interest lay "in the rather smaller question of whether a certain person was present in the audience." He was searching for Nannie Peronneau. He found her and enjoyed what he described as a "charming" visit. Reflecting on their short time together in Charleston, DuBose observed that his intentions were "tolerably evident."[27]

Affairs of the heart were important, but DuBose understood that he was witnessing history. War between the sections was imminent. Although he had returned to Camden before The Citadel cadets fired on the *Star of the West* in January 1861, the young man followed developments in Charleston with great interest. From the earliest days of the conflict, he embraced the southern perspective that the fighting was caused by agents of the northern states.[28]

Acknowledging that the firing on the *Star of the West* "was skillfully used as a *casus belli*," DuBose believed, as did many southerners, that northern men had provoked the fighting. Major Robert Anderson's decision to seize Fort Sumter in Charleston Harbor and the US government's decision to reprovision the fort triggered the sequence of events that caused the war.[29]

DuBose returned to Charleston on the eve of the Fort Sumter confrontation. He recalled that

> on the night of April 11 (my birthday) in company with very many others, especially that of the Misses Peronneau, I paraded the long walk of the Battery until a very late hour awaiting the shot that should open the direct attack on Fort Sumter by the South Carolina forces. The shot did not come until three or four o'clock the next morning, and the city were all asleep in their beds.

In addition to his presence at the opening salvo of the war, DuBose became engaged to Nannie Peronneau.[30]

His personal happiness became a secondary consideration when he realized that he must defend his state from Union troops, which could easily threaten the coast as well as the railroad lines connecting Charleston and Savannah, Georgia. After Governor Francis Pickens organized a legion to protect the state, the governor called on Citadel men to perform their duty. The young Citadel graduate answered the call. With Bishop Davis's blessing,

DuBose left the seminary to become adjutant in the Holcombe Legion. Colonel Peter Fayssoux Stevens, formerly The Citadel superintendent, assumed command.[31]

In the early months of the conflict, the legion camped on the Ashley River overlooking Charleston. Because the fighting had not begun in earnest, the troops drilled and occasionally engaged in skirmishes with Union gunboats. When he was away from his military duties, DuBose found time to visit his fiancée. After the city of Charleston burned, DuBose was relieved to learn that the conflagration had missed the Peronneau home.[32]

It was a strange, listless time. The southern states had seceded, but few battles had occurred in South Carolina. During this interlude, the DuBose family suffered a series of setbacks that left Willie dispirited. His father, who had loomed so large in the young man's life, died suddenly in February 1862. "He had been in perfect health," DuBose recalled years later. After ministering to sick Confederate soldiers following the Battle of First Manassas, Theodore DuBose contracted measles. He did not appear "dangerously sick" at the outset, but his condition worsened. In a letter he wrote to Nannie not long after Theodore's death, Willie DuBose explained that the "change in Father's disease was a sudden one on Thursday morning, after which he was delirious most of the time. He became conscious & said 'Goodbye to you all. May God bless & preserve you'—the very words with which he concluded his last letter to me."[33]

Willie DuBose was devastated, but he found comfort in religion.

> Oh, the unspeakable comfort of a Gospel that can so soften the terrors of death & sweeten the bitterest cup of affliction! There is no joy so deep & inexpressible as that which the Spirit of God can impart in our moments of deepest distress. Yes, it is the "love of Christ" & nothing else in the wide universe, that can give real comfort & strength.[34]

Less than four months later, his mother died. DuBose had departed for Virginia with the Holcombe Legion before he learned of her death. It was almost unbearable, coming, as it did, during a spate of deaths in his circle of friends and family. "On a certain day, the day of the Battle of Seven Pines near Richmond, my mother died, my sister Jane's husband was killed, and General Bratton, who had married sister Betsy, was missing and supposed to be killed." DuBose sought to return home, "but we were in the act of going to Virginia for immediate service and I could not get the necessary leave." The only silver lining was that Dr. Bratton had survived.[35]

Jane Porcher DuBose's health had long been poor. DuBose recalled that she was fragile and sickly for much of his childhood. "She was always delicate, but it never interfered with her efficiency and above all things with her beautiful control of the house, her children and her servants," he remembered. Although her death was not a complete surprise, DuBose was saddened by the loss. "My last years with my mother, sometimes in her worst health, (during my vacations, etc.) are very happy memories to me."[36]

By the spring of 1862, the Holcombe Legion was on the march. Dispatched to relieve Confederate troops stationed at Malvern Hill near Richmond, the legion encountered light resistance upon arrival. No sooner had the men arrived than DuBose became involved in a "little incident."[37]

A friend and fellow soldier, R. Y. Dwight, and DuBose were riding horses near their camp. They were unarmed. "As we rode along the road, we saw crossing the field in front of us a heavily armed cavalryman," DuBose later wrote. "It was too late to distinguish his uniform." Dwight and DuBose came face-to-face with the man, who asked for directions to a Yankee regiment. "Of course, I didn't know," DuBose confessed, "but I replied that he would find it just along that road that he was going. As he turned his back upon us, Dwight clapped his hand on his shoulder and said, 'You are my prisoner, sir.'"[38]

It was a moment of truth. If the cavalryman had chosen to contest the capture, he might have escaped. He could have shot his would-be captors and scampered into the brush before nearby Confederates could react. The man did not know that Dwight and DuBose were unarmed. He surrendered his weapons without bloodshed. DuBose admitted afterward that "I would have just gone on, for it was a thoroughly reckless thing to do, but Dwight did the right thing."[39]

After months of inactivity in the army, William Porcher DuBose had arrived at the scene of the action. He was destined to fight at Second Manassas and South Mountain before federal troops captured him. When he was surrounded by hostile forces at South Mountain, DuBose's first instinct was to escape at all costs, but he recognized that he was outgunned and outmanned. He had no option but to surrender or perish in a blaze of gunfire. He wisely laid down his arms and raised his hands.[40]

DuBose was fortunate to be captured while the Dix-Hill exchange cartel was in effect. In July 1862, Union and Confederate officers, led by Union General John A. Dix and Confederate Major General D. H. Hill, negotiated a formal agreement to exchange prisoners. The agreement was overdue. When war erupted between the North and South in 1861, each side had been ill-equipped to handle prisoners of war. Initially, field commanders had exchanged men through informal, ad hoc negotiations. As the war became a protracted affair, however, a formal arrangement was necessary to ensure comparable treatment of prisoners between the Federals and the Confederates. In those early days, prisoners had been held in hastily constructed stockades or barracks. Sometimes a warehouse, military facility, fort, or existing prison was retrofitted, but the increasing number of men detained meant that a permanent solution was desperately needed.[41]

The cartel was modeled on the agreement hashed out between the United States and Great Britain during the War of 1812. Prisoners were exchanged based on rank. Thus, a commanding general was worth sixty privates, a lieutenant general worth forty privates, a major general worth thirty privates, and so forth. The exchanges were supposed to occur within days or at most weeks, of capture, although administrative delays became common.[42]

The cartel eventually dissolved owing to sectional acrimony and charges of bad faith on both sides. Administrative burdens made it almost impossible to keep track of who had been captured, where the prisoners were sent, when they had been exchanged, and whether they returned to the field following the exchange. Paroled prisoners were not supposed to fight as soldiers again, but former captives on both sides routinely ignored this stipulation and entered the ranks as soon as they could be mustered into service. This was especially true in the South, which had fewer young men to draw from, and thus experienced severe personnel shortages.[43]

The question of Black soldiers also caused no small amount of strife. Southerners considered Black men in uniform to be escaped slaves and refused to exchange them as they exchanged white soldiers. This rift created tension that was never resolved, and it contributed to the ultimate failure of the Dix-Hill Cartel as the Lincoln administration insisted that the Confederates had acted in bad faith.[44]

On May 25, 1863, Union General Henry Halleck ordered a halt to all prisoner exchanges until the Confederates agreed to treat Black soldiers the same as white soldiers. These orders meant that prisoner exchanges became the exception rather than the rule, although informal exchanges occasionally occurred until war's end. The orders also meant that rather than spending a few weeks or months in captivity, prisoners of war would be held until the cessation of hostilities, or until they died.[45]

When William Porcher DuBose was captured, the cartel was in place. He was reasonably assured of a speedy exchange, which is exactly what happened. He spent his first night in captivity under guard. The next day, his captors marched him to Baltimore, where he boarded a ship bound for Fort Delaware. The fort was a harbor defense facility constructed on Pea Patch Island in the Delaware River shortly after the War of 1812.[46]

By mid-1863, Fort Delaware was notorious as "a perfect hell on earth," one of the worst Union prison camps of the Civil War. When DuBose landed there in the fall of 1862, however, it had not yet acquired that reputation. Although his experience as a prisoner of war was hardly enjoyable, the young Confederate adjutant did not share his fellow prisoners' bitterness about the period of confinement on Pea Patch Island. Naturally an optimist by disposition, DuBose confessed that "I was hoping to make the most of things."[47]

"Fort Delaware was built around a very large court or parade ground," DuBose recalled. "The whole length of the space between the interior court and the exterior river was occupied by a very long, wide room in which the officer prisoners were incarcerated, amounting to at least seventy-five of us." DuBose draped a blanket over several empty boxes to fashion a rudimentary bed. It could not be described as commodious living, but he was as comfortable as circumstances allowed.[48]

DuBose recognized friends inside the prison, including several men he had known at the University of Virginia. He reveled in their company. He also witnessed disheartening scenes among prisoners scrambling to acquire shoes shipped to the prison from Baltimore. "Any body of men thrown promiscuously together without organization or law of any kind is liable to degenerate on the part of some, at any rate, into a very offensive selfishness," he observed. In this instance, the selfishness consisted of men hoarding shoes while their fellow prisoners had none.[49]

DuBose languished in Fort Delaware, but he pronounced himself "tolerably comfortable and for a while tolerably satisfied" with prison conditions. "About this time, rumors began to circulate of our probable exchange, or parole, and there was some kind of vessel that was to take us to Richmond for that purpose," he wrote. The rumors excited him to such a degree that "I have to confess that I completely lost control of my philosophy or religion and spent most of my time gazing up the river to see the boat that was to take us away."[50]

Much to DuBose's relief, the rumors proved to be true. He and fellow prisoners shuffled onto a ship and traveled down to Aiken's Landing on the James River, a few miles below Richmond. He was pleased to be a free man, but the lack of provisions left the men starving and without a means of transportation. "It was a rather gloomy outlook," DuBose observed. "We were eight miles from Richmond and had no conception of how we were to get there. As I walked down the gangway of the boat, I must have been a sorry looking object."[51]

Fortunately, he encountered an old friend from the University of Virginia, Sam Preston, who was serving as a captain of heavy artillery and stationed at a nearby camp on the banks of the Potomac River. Captain Preston transported DuBose to the camp. To DuBose's delight, they arrived at suppertime. After enjoying a fine meal, Preston provided his friend with a tent and a cot containing clean sheets. It was a far cry from the boxes that DuBose had slept on in Fort Delaware. In his opinion, "the camp arrangements were luxurious to my eyes."[52]

The following morning, Captain Preston arranged for DuBose to be transported to Richmond. There, the young soldier found the home of family friends, the Dudleys, who were thrilled to see him. He stayed in the city, recuperating from his prison experiences, and occasionally reporting to a parole camp until he could be formally exchanged.[53]

DuBose eventually made his way to the Exchange Hotel in Richmond, a central location where many Confederates congregated to share news and learn information about the state of the war. He was surprised to learn that his commanding officer believed that DuBose had died at South Mountain.

"Colonel Stevens, commanding our brigade, assumed, as everyone else did, that I was killed," DuBose remembered. "Soon after he resigned his office, took orders in the church, and having a son born at that time, he named him after me. He felt in some way responsible for my death because it was he who had sent me on my midnight reconnaissance."[54]

Colonel Stevens had written the young man's family a letter informing them of the tragic news. "It is with a very sad heart and a deep sympathy for yourself that I address you this morning to inform you of the misfortune which has befallen my beloved friend Willie, your brother," he wrote to DuBose's sister on September 22, 1862. Acknowledging that in the fog of war no one had seen DuBose following an exchange of gunfire, Stevens feared the worst. "God assures us in his word that he chastens those whom he loves. Large must be his love for your bereaved family with whom my constant and heartfelt sympathy has been during the last few months." This last sentence referred to the loss of the DuBoses' father and mother earlier in the year.[55]

Stevens concluded the letter with a promise to inform the family of any news on DuBose's whereabouts. "God may have taken Willie to be his nurse and spiritual guide. I hope so."[56]

DuBose experienced a surreal encounter with an old friend in the streets of Richmond. As Willie hobbled along the road, he came upon a fellow Citadel man, Sam Depass. Depass spoke cordially before asking, "how is your brother?" When DuBose asked which brother, the friend replied, "Your brother William?"

"I am my brother William, myself," DuBose told him.

Depass was emphatic. "You aren't. He's dead."

When DuBose assured the man that reports of his death had been greatly exaggerated, Depass offered to prove the point. "So, he took me to a reading room and there I read an account of my death and a brief notice of myself written by Mr. Richard Yeadon of Charleston."[57]

Anxious to assuage his family's concerns, DuBose dashed off letters to his family and friends assuring them of his good health. In a letter that he dispatched to his fiancée, he confessed that "It is many weeks, Darling, since I have had the sweet satisfaction of writing to you, and in the painful interval I do not know what you have been called upon to suffer on my account." He explained the situation, including his visit to the reading room. "I was shown my obituary this morning, much to my surprise & pain. The circumstances under which I was missing might have caused serious misapprehensions, but could not have justified the statement of my death." In closing, he insisted that "I am quite well. My *wounds* never gave me much trouble."[58]

While he waited to be exchanged through official channels, DuBose had time on his hands. He traveled to Winnsboro to see his family as well as Nannie Peronneau. His visit lasted several weeks. After he was formally exchanged on November 10, 1862, DuBose traveled to Wilmington, North Carolina, to rejoin his unit.[59]

A naturally optimistic man, DuBose suffered a rare bout of depression after he entered the ranks that November. In a later age, he might have been characterized as a man suffering from post-traumatic stress disorder, but in 1862 the malady was not identified. In a letter he wrote to Nannie on November 16, 1862, DuBose confessed that "My unsettled & eventful life during the past six months has rendered me almost incapable of calm, connected & sustained thought or reflection, and I have to struggle against impatience & restlessness in sitting down to [write] a long slow letter even to you." Dispirited about his recent travails, he confessed that his faith was sorely strained, if not quite broken.

> But what is harder & more painful still, I find it hard to be still, & rest in His presence, to rejoice in dwelling quietly in the light of His countenance, as I sometimes used to do in my more favored hours. Restlessness and impatience have taken possession of me & have robbed my devotional hours of much of their joy & peace.[60]

As the troops resumed their march, DuBose's spirits lifted. By the end of November, he wrote to Nannie to assure her of his spiritual rejuvenation.

> Pray for me, my Darling, that I may improve this opportunity which has been given me of increasing my faith by prayer & meditation, of this identifying myself more & more by faith with the Son of God, acquiring his mind, his Spirit, his intimate communion face to face with the Father, & finally preparing myself to go forth in his Spirit & in his strength to do His work.[61]

Although Peter Fayssoux Stevens had resigned his commission and returned to South Carolina, DuBose remembered his former commander fondly. "I wrote to Col. Stevens a long letter yesterday," he told Nannie. "I was sorry to see the death of his eldest child, a sweet & interesting little girl, in the papers some days ago."[62]

DuBose's time for writing long letters and reflecting on his religious life soon ended; his unit was on the move again. "Some time in December of this year [1862], we were ordered up to the neighborhood of Goldsborough, North Carolina, where a very important connection of the East Coast Railway was threatened by an expedition moving up the river from Newburn." The troops occupied the town of Kinston with orders to defend a nearby bridge from imminent attack.[63]

With the ranks depleted and Colonel Stevens gone, DuBose commanded the remnants of the Holcombe Legion. Many years later, he recalled the "demoralized condition" of the men as they guarded the Kinston bridge in the wee morning hours. "I believe it is acknowledged that life is at the lowest ebb at three or four o'clock in the morning," he wrote. "Certainly, ours was that morning, when all of a sudden there was a rapid discharge of musketry in our immediate front."[64]

The enemy attacked with overwhelming force, creating a panic among the Confederates. Ordered to fall back 50 yards, DuBose admitted that "I have never in my life had to work harder" than he did as the troops retreated. He valiantly sought to restore order and was pleased at the response. DuBose was gratified that "everything was instantly restored, and they were as cool in possession of themselves as possible."[65]

Like any good field commander, DuBose paced up and down the lines, ensuring that his men remained vigilant and at their stations. As he directed his troops,

> a minie ball entered my side, fired from a distance of not more than a hundred yards. Fortunately, the ball had scraped a part of itself off on the slope just in front of us and then passed through half-a-dozen thick folds of clothing. As it was, it touched at least two mortal spots without actually penetrating. I had no feeling as I was suddenly hurried away in a stretcher to the rear.[66]

Luckily for DuBose, the wound was not fatal. The surgeons tended to him immediately, removing the minie ball without complications. Afterward, they transferred him to Raleigh to recuperate. As soon as he could travel, medical personnel sent him to Anderson, South Carolina, where Nannie Peronneau and her family were living.[67]

Considering his many close calls with mortality during his time in uniform, DuBose decided that he and Nannie should marry immediately rather than wait for the war to end. The Reverend John H. Elliott, DuBose's friend from seminary, married the couple "under conditions of great privation" on April 30, 1863. William Porcher DuBose was twenty-seven years old.[68]

During DuBose's convalescence, the Southern Confederacy was in a precarious situation. Union forces were advancing on all fronts. As spring became summer in 1863, Union and Confederate forces confronted each other at Vicksburg, Mississippi; Chattanooga, Tennessee; and Gettysburg, Pennsylvania. Although no one knew it yet, the southern nation was reeling. Soon the Confederates would be overwhelmed by the North's advantages in men and materiel.[69]

DuBose had recovered sufficiently to rejoin his brigade, which set out for Mississippi to relieve Vicksburg from a Union siege. Confederate General Joseph E. Johnston assumed command. The general directed his forces to move out of their camp on the Pearl River outside of Jackson on July 1. Their goal was to reach Vicksburg before Union General Ulysses S. Grant forced the town's surrender and attack his troops from the rear. "The weather was very warm, the dust very deep, and the enemy had preceded us all the way defiling all the sources of water with dead animals," DuBose remembered.[70]

Much to DuBose's disappointment, the men arrived too late to save the town. "It was the evening of the third of July, and we went to sleep with the expectation of crossing the river the next morning and attacking Grant from the rear, while the Vicksburg garrison attacked him from in his front." It was a good plan, but the timing was wrong. "We arose early in the morning with that expectation," DuBose later wrote, but as the men marched, they were ordered back to Jackson. "The Vicksburg garrison had surrendered to Grant."[71]

General Grant turned his forces toward the Confederates outside of Vicksburg. Fearing a bloody battle with no clear purpose, Johnston ordered his troops to retreat to Jackson, which they did. DuBose remembered constructing earthworks to defend the city. Union and Confederate forces exchanged gunfire for a few days before Johnston marched his troops away from Jackson.[72]

"We left Grant in Mississippi and moved eastward, somewhat at our leisure," DuBose recalled. They eventually arrived in Savannah, Georgia, to defend the coast from Union attack. Later, the troops marched to Charleston.[73]

From the time that he left the seminary prematurely in 1860, through two hard years of fighting, DuBose had thought of his eventual ordination in the Protestant Episcopal Church. In the waning days of 1863, he sought to return to the ministry. He had served the Southern Confederacy faithfully, and he was prepared to serve again, albeit in a different capacity.

On November 1, he resigned his commission as adjutant in the Holcombe Legion in anticipation of his ordination as a deacon in the Protestant Episcopal Church of South Carolina. In a letter to Nannie that same day, DuBose told her that "My resignation has arrived, my Darling, and I am now free to leave when I please. I will wind up my affairs in a few days & probably be with you at the end of the week."[74]

DuBose traveled back to Camden, South Carolina. On December 13, 1863, Bishop Thomas F. Davis ordained the young man a deacon in the church. Although he would not be ordained a priest until 1866, DuBose was excited to resume his ministerial duties. He would no longer bear arms. Henceforth, he would serve as an army chaplain counseling brave soldiers.[75]

Newly commissioned as a chaplain, he accompanied Lieutenant Colonel Franklin Gaillard to eastern Tennessee, where he joined Kershaw's brigade. Brigadier General Joseph B. Kershaw and his men were ensconced in winter quarters when DuBose arrived. The chaplain happily began his ministry in a small church in Greeneville, Tennessee. By his own calculations, he ministered from the church for two or three months.[76]

By the spring of 1864, Kershaw's brigade was on the move. After breaking winter quarters, the troops marched into Virginia to confront General Grant. Since Grant's victory at Vicksburg the previous summer, he had been promoted to lieutenant general and placed in command of all Union military forces. By the spring of 1864, he was preparing his Overland Campaign to destroy General Robert E. Lee's Army of Northern Virginia. Kershaw's brigade was part of Lee's forces seeking to halt Grant's advance.[77]

Kershaw's brigade arrived in May 1864. "The campaign opened with the battle of the Wilderness," DuBose recalled. "I was out of the actual fighting, though never far from it. We arrived on the battlefield just in time to take part in the battle." The fighting was desperate, and casualties on both sides were appalling.[78]

In DuBose's opinion, his traveling companion, Colonel Gaillard, had lived a charmed life, but Gaillard was uneasy going into the Wilderness, feeling "a settled presentiment . . . that he would not pass through the next battle. As he took up his position on this day, he took out a package from his pocket and entrusted it to me. In a few moments after that he was shot and instantly killed, with his faithful servant and a few others." As the unit chaplain, DuBose ensured that the man was buried. "Not only he, Col. Means of the 3rd regiment and General Micah Jenkins, both very dear friends of the Citadel days, I buried also." Not long after the burials, someone stole the package that Colonel Gaillard had entrusted to DuBose.[79]

Grant withdrew from the Wilderness, but he and Lee fought again a few days later at Spotsylvania Court House. The ferocity of the battle became the stuff of legend. "I won't attempt to say anything about the Battle of [Spotsylvania]," DuBose wrote. "Everybody who knows of it will remember the famous angle, where trees were said to have been shot down by minieballs and where General Lee was almost violently kept back from exposing himself by devoted soldiers." Although DuBose was not stationed at that part of the line, "I was not far from it, and I never in my life heard such firing."[80]

The troops enjoyed no respite from the fighting. Grant attacked again in what became known as the Battle of Cold Harbor. In DuBose's opinion, the fighting ended "with about the same result as in the two previous engagements." The horrific fighting made the Overland Campaign the bloodiest offensive movement of the war. Estimates varied, but casualties ranged from between 39,000 and 65,000 on the Union side and 32,000 to 40,000 on the Confederate side. Although the Union suffered higher losses, General Grant could look forward to receiving reinforcements in the coming days. Lee did not enjoy such luxury. His losses were irreplaceable. Forced to move back to Petersburg, an important supply center near Richmond, and unable to break out, the Confederate general understood his predicament all too well. If Grant and the Union army continued the siege, the Army of Northern Virginia would eventually capitulate.[81]

Grant also understood the strategic situation. He had Lee pinned, and he would not relent. The stalemate lasted for months, from the summer of 1864 until the following spring. In the meantime, Kershaw's brigade supported Lee's army until it became clear that Lee could not leave Petersburg. In the fall of 1864, the brigade was ordered to the Shenandoah Valley to join General Jubal Early's forces as they battled Union General Philip Sheridan.[82]

Kershaw's brigade entered the Shenandoah at Front Royal. The men joined Early's army and confronted the enemy, drawing Sheridan out of the valley. Ordered back to Petersburg, the brigade was halfway to the destination when word came that Sheridan had regained the momentum. DuBose and the men hurried back.[83]

"The crisis of the campaign came then in the affair of Cedar Creek, where Early by a surprise attack seemed to have routed the enemy when the famous sudden arrival of Sheridan (known as Sheridan's Ride) turned the tide and ended in a routing of the Confederates," DuBose wrote. It was a close thing, but once again the southerners suffered defeat on a battlefield.[84]

Everywhere the Confederates looked in the fall of 1864, the news was grim. Union forces, superior in troop numbers and war materiel, were on the move. The Confederacy was not yet on the brink of collapse, but all signs were pointing in that direction. DuBose despaired because he was emotionally unprepared for these developments. "It was a remarkable thing, but I believe it's true, that the ordinary Confederate soldier up to this time never conceived the possibility of ultimate failure," he mused. "The soldier almost always engaged in action, has no time for reflection or thought, and the Confederate soldier considered himself generally successful and victorious."[85]

As he lay down to rest after the Battle of Cedar Creek on the evening of October 19, 1864, DuBose could not sleep. He reflected on the day's events. When he recalled the scene years later, "that night's experience was the turning point of the war." He realized that the cause probably was lost. The Confederacy would soon be overwhelmed by a more powerful force.[86]

He had to face facts. "That night came over me like a shock of death that the Confederacy was beginning to break: the strain even of unbroken victory had been too long and too heavy: it would be impossible much longer to resist the force of the ever-renewed and ever-increasing pressure of new armies and inexhaustible resources." In a letter he wrote to Nannie on October 31, 1864, he confessed his continued misgivings. "The fact is that since that unfortunate reverse of the 19th I have been laboring harder to make my life & ministry what they ought to be." In short, it was time to think about a future without the Southern Confederacy.[87]

If he could not live and work under a southern government, he would turn his attention elsewhere. With "my very world at an end, I redevoted myself wholly and only to God, and to the work and life of His Kingdom, whatever and wherever that might be," DuBose vowed. It was a vow that he kept.[88]

He was still in the army, however, and his brigade was on the move. As Union General William T. Sherman's troops marched through Georgia and into South Carolina, Kershaw's brigade traveled to Charleston to resist an expected thrust into the city where secession began. Union forces unexpectedly turned toward Columbia. Slowed by winter rains as well as Confederate resistance, Sherman's South Carolina march consumed January and February, spilling into March 1865.[89]

DuBose noted that his hometown, Winnsboro, was not spared. On February 21, 1865, only a few days after Columbia was burned, Union General John W. Geary, commander of the left wing of Sherman's forces, arrived in Winnsboro. A group of "bummers" had already ransacked the town and burned several buildings. Confederates later estimated that the federals decimated between twenty and thirty buildings. When Union soldiers departed the next day, General Geary dispatched two mounted troopers to protect Winnsboro from stragglers.[90]

After departing from Winnsboro, Sherman's army turned toward Camden and Cheraw. Kershaw's brigade was still stationed in Charleston, but as Sherman reached Cheraw, "the troops from Charleston were ordered to unite with the force which General Joe Johnston was gathering upon the trail of Sherman," DuBose recalled. "As we left Charleston, we marched through some of haunts and homes of the Low Country." He spent one night with his aunt. He also visited St. Stephen's, the old Huguenot church where his grandfather was buried. "From there, we moved up to Cheraw where for the first time we came into collision with Sherman."[91]

The Confederates followed Sherman's forces into North Carolina, where they engaged with the enemy at Averasboro on March 16 and at Bentonville three days later. "At Bentonville," DuBose noted, "my brother, Robert, was painfully wounded by a fragment of shell." It was the brigade's last battle of the war.[92]

General Johnston halted at Bentonville. His troops stood ready to fight, but they awaited developments in Virginia as General Lee's forces abandoned Petersburg and General Grant chased the departing Confederates. While these events occurred, Johnston's men set up camp.

During this time, DuBose later recollected, "I had one of the most painful little duties to perform that I think was *ever* imposed upon me." Confederate soldiers from Keitt's Regiment, the 20th South Carolina Infantry Regiment, formerly under the command of Colonel Laurence M. Keitt (who had died in battle at Cold Harbor in June 1864), hailed from Orangeburg, South Carolina. As General Johnston trailed Union forces through South Carolina, a group of soldiers from Keitt's Regiment worried about their families in the aftermath of Sherman's march. They resolved to desert and check on their loved ones.[93]

Worried that his army might dissolve before the war was concluded, General Johnston ordered that the deserters be rounded up. The penalty for desertion was execution. An example had to be made of such men as a warning to others that military discipline was necessary, and dereliction of duty would not be tolerated.[94]

As the chaplain for Kershaw's brigade, DuBose ministered to deserters who faced the ultimate punishment. "It was hard because they were deserting mainly just to see how things were at home, Sherman having passed their homes," he reflected. "Some half dozen were caught, court-martialed, and sentenced to be shot, and I was told to inform and prepare them for execution. It was the most awful thing I was ever asked to do, the worst thing I ever experienced."[95]

Fortunately for the deserters, and for DuBose, the executions never occurred. General Robert E. Lee had surrendered his army to General Ulysses S. Grant at Appomattox Court House, Virginia, on April 9, 1865. Recognizing the futility of continuing the campaign, General Johnston began negotiating with General Sherman to surrender Confederate forces in North Carolina. Although the formal surrender did not occur until April 26, by mid-April it was clear that the cause was lost. The lives of the Keitt's Regiment deserters were spared.[96]

With the collapse of the Confederate army, William Porcher DuBose was released from military service. The army treasury distributed its remaining funds to former soldiers as they departed. DuBose's share came to $1.50. He had his horse shod and bought two mules for the journey to Winnsboro. He desperately wanted to check on his wife and determine whether his home had survived the Union army's advance through the area.[97]

He arrived in Winnsboro to find that "Sherman's march had swept the country clean of every facility for private travel, animals or vehicles, as well as provisions and everything else." Nannie was staying with her family in Anderson, South Carolina. He immediately set out to meet her. The distance from Winnsboro to Anderson was 89 miles as the crow flies.[98]

His journey was heartbreaking. "Widows and bereaved persons were at every turn, and worst of all, facing us everywhere was the loss of our country." Despite the hardships, DuBose found Nannie. She was well. They returned home together, their first extended time as husband and wife since their wedding. The couple had "very many sacred memories of that drive."[99]

They returned to find Winnsboro "pretty well burnt" and "*negro* troops" stationed nearby. DuBose never forgot the humiliation and dangers of that "demoralizing" time in southern history. Although he was at a crossroads in his life, he had already decided to give himself to God. His task was to become an ordained priest in the Protestant Episcopal Church.[100]

Notes

1. William Porcher DuBose, "Reminiscences, 1836–1878," typescript copy transcribed by William Haskell DuBose, Southern Historical Collection, University of North Carolina at Chapel Hill, 85. See also Ralph Luker, *A Southern Tradition in Theology and Social Criticism 1830-1930: The Religious Liberalism and Social Conservatism of James Warley Miles, William Porcher DuBose and Edgar Gardner Murphy*, Studies in American Religion 11 (New York: The Edwin Mellen Press, 1984), 117.

2. Ibid., 86.

3. DuBose mentioned that his horse was shot from under him during the battle. Ibid., 87. See also William Porcher DuBose, *Turning Points in My Life* (New York: Longmans, Green, & Company, 1912), 34; Jon Alexander, O. P., "Introduction," in William Porcher DuBose, *Selected Writings*, ed. Jon Alexander, O. P. (New York: Paulist Press, 1988), 6.

4. DuBose, "Reminiscences," 88; Moultrie Guerry, "Makers of Sewanee," *The Sewanee Review* 41, no. 4 (October-December 1933): 486; Luker, *A Southern Tradition*, 117. See also James M. McPherson, *Battle Cry of Freedom: The Civil War Era* (New York: Ballantine Books, 1988), 528–32; Russell F. Weigley, *A Great Civil War: A Military and Political History, 1861 1865* (Bloomington: Indiana University Press, 2000), 139–44.

5. DuBose, "Reminiscences," 88; Luker, *A Southern Tradition*, 117–18. See also W. Eric Emerson and Karen Stokes, "Introduction," in William Porcher DuBose, *Faith, Valor, and Devotion: The Civil War Letters of William Porcher DuBose*, ed. W. Eric Emerson and Karen Stokes (Columbia: The University of South Carolina Press, 2010), xix.

6. DuBose, "Reminiscences," 89.

7. Ralph E. Luker, "The Crucible of Civil War and Reconstruction in the Experience of William Porcher DuBose," *The South Carolina Historical Magazine* 83, no. 1 (January 1982): 55.

8. DuBose, "Reminiscences," 89–91; DuBose, *Turning Points in My Life*, 34–5; Luker, "The Crucible of Civil War and Reconstruction in the Experience of William Porcher DuBose," 55; McPherson, *Battle Cry of Freedom*, 537.

9. DuBose, "Reminiscences," 94. See also DuBose, *Turning Points in My Life*, 35.

10. DuBose, "Reminiscences," 95. See also DuBose, *Turning Points in My Life*, 35–7; Alexander, "Introduction," 6–7; Emerson and Stokes, "Introduction," xx; Luker, *A Southern Tradition*, 119–20.

11. DuBose, "Reminiscences," 2. See also Alexander, "Introduction," 5; Guerry, "Makers of Sewanee," 483; Luker, *A Southern Tradition*, 89–90.

12. Emerson and Stokes, "Introduction," xv.

13. DuBose, "Reminiscences," 5–6. See also Alexander, "Introduction," 5.

14. DuBose, "Reminiscences," 7–11. See also Emerson and Stokes, "Introduction," xiv–xv.

15 DuBose, "Reminiscences," 10–11. Emphasis in the original. See also Luker, *A Southern Tradition*, 95.
16 Ibid., 18–19, 21. See also Alexander, "Introduction," 5.
17 DuBose, "Reminiscences," 27–8.
18 Guerry, "Makers of Sewanee," 484–5.
19 Ibid., 30. See also DuBose, *Turning Points in My Life*, 17–20; Emerson and Stokes, "Introduction," xvi; Guerry, "Makers of Sewanee," 484–5; Luker, *A Southern Tradition*, 95–6; Robert B. Slocum, "The Lessons of Experience and the Theology of William Porcher DuBose," *Journal of Theological Studies* 79, no. 3 (Summer 1997): 350–3, 366.
20 DuBose, "Reminiscences," 33.
21 Ibid., 34. See also Emerson and Stokes, "Introduction," xvi; Luker, *A Southern Tradition*, 97.
22 Guerry, "Makers of Sewanee," 483–4, 485–6.
23 DuBose, "Reminiscences," 34–58; Luker, "The Crucible of Civil War and Reconstruction in the Experience of William Porcher DuBose," 52; Luker, *A Southern Tradition*, 97–102.
24 DuBose, "Reminiscences," 60. See also Luker, *A Southern Tradition*, 102; Slocum, "The Lessons of Experience and the Theology of William Porcher DuBose," 355.
25 DuBose, "Reminiscences," 65–6; Alexander, "Introduction," 6; Luker, *A Southern Tradition*, 103.
26 DuBose, "Reminiscences," 67. See also Robert B. Slocum, "A Soldier's Faith: The Civil War Experiences and Reflections of William Porcher DuBose," *Journal of Anglican Studies* 16, no. 2 (November 2018): 171–2.
27 DuBose, "Reminiscences," 68. See also Luker, *A Southern Tradition*, 109.
28 DuBose, "Reminiscences," 68–9. See also Gary L. Baker, *Cadets in Gray: The Story of the Cadets of the South Carolina Military Academy and the Cadet Rangers in the Civil War* (Columbia, SC: Palmetto Bookworks, 1989), 12–27.
29 DuBose, "Reminiscences," 68.
30 Ibid., 68–9. See also Emerson and Stokes, "Introduction," xvii; Guerry, "Makers of Sewanee," 486.
31 DuBose, "Reminiscences," 69. See also DuBose, *Turning Points in My Life*, 33; Luker, "The Crucible of Civil War and Reconstruction in the Experience of William Porcher DuBose," 53; Luker, *A Southern Tradition*, 115.
32 DuBose, "Reminiscences," 73; Luker, *A Southern Tradition*, 116.
33 The recollection is found in Ibid., 80. The letter to Nannie is reprinted in DuBose, *Faith, Valor, and Devotion*, 44.
34 DuBose, *Faith, Valor, and Devotion*, 44.
35 DuBose, "Reminiscences," 80.
36 Ibid., 81, 82.

37 Ibid., 82. See also DuBose, *Turning Points in My Life*, 33–4; Luker, *A Southern Tradition*, 116–17.
38 DuBose, "Reminiscences," 82.
39 Ibid., 83.
40 DuBose, "Reminiscences," 96. See also Emerson and Stokes, "Introduction," xx; Luker, *A Southern Tradition*, 120; Slocum, "The Lessons of Experience and the Theology of William Porcher DuBose," 345–6; Slocum, "A Soldier's Faith," 174–6.
41 See, for example, William Best Hesseltine, *Civil War Prisons: A Study in War Psychology* (Columbus: Ohio State University Press, 1930), 69–71; Lonnie R. Speer, *Portals to Hell: Military Prisons of the Civil War* (Mechanicsburg, PA: Stackpole Books, 1997), 97–105; Weigley, *A Great Civil War*, 190.
42 Hesseltine, *Civil War Prisons*, 69–94; J. Michael Martinez, *Life and Death in Civil War Prisons* (Nashville, TN: Rutledge Hill Press, 2004), 51.
43 Hesseltine, *Civil War Prisons*, 111–13; Speer, *Portals to Hell*, 14.
44 Much has been written about the mistreatment of captured Black Union soldiers in the Civil War. See especially Dudley Taylor Cornish, *The Sable Arm: Negro Troops in the Union Army, 1861–1865* (New York: Longmans, Green and Company, 1956), 177–8; Brainerd Dyer, "The Treatment of Colored Union Troops by the Confederates, 1861–1865," *Journal of Negro History* 20, no. 3 (July 1935): 273, 282; Martinez, *Life and Death in Civil War Prisons*, 52–5; Speer, *Portals to Hell*, 104–5; George W. Williams, *A History of the Negro Troops in the War of the Rebellion, 1861–1865* (New York: Harper & Brothers, 1888), 110–15.
45 Speer, *Portals to Hell*, 105.
46 DuBose, "Reminiscences," 98–102; DuBose, *Turning Points in My Life*, 37; Guerry, "Makers of Sewanee," 487–8; Information on Fort Delaware is found in Speer, *Portals to Hell*, 143–7.
47 DuBose, "Reminiscences," 103–4; Emerson and Stokes, "Introduction," xx. The quote about Fort Delaware is found in Speer, *Portals to Hell*, 143. The DuBose quote is found in DuBose, "Reminiscences," 103.
48 DuBose, "Reminiscences," 105. See also Luker, *A Southern Tradition*, 120.
49 Ibid., 104–5. The quote is found on page 104.
50 Ibid., 108. See also Luker, *A Southern Tradition*, 121–2.
51 DuBose, "Reminiscences," 110. See also Emerson and Stokes, "Introduction," xx; Luker, *A Southern Tradition*, 122–3.
52 DuBose, "Reminiscences," 110–11. The quote appears on page 111.
53 Ibid., 112.
54 Ibid.
55 The letter is reprinted in DuBose, *Faith, Valor, and Devotion*, 94–5.
56 Ibid., 95.

57 The episode is recounted in DuBose, "Reminiscences," 113–14. See also DuBose, *Turning Points in My Life*, 38; Alexander, "Introduction," 7.

58 The letter is reprinted in DuBose, *Faith, Valor, and Devotion*, 100–1. Emphasis in the original. See also Guerry, "Makers of Sewanee," 488.

59 DuBose, "Reminiscences," 117; Emerson and Stokes, "Introduction," xxi.

60 The letter is reprinted in DuBose, *Faith, Valor, and Devotion*, 113.

61 The letter is reprinted in Ibid., 117.

62 Ibid.

63 DuBose, "Reminiscences," 117–18. See also Emerson and Stokes, "Introduction," xxi.

64 DuBose, "Reminiscences," 118.

65 Ibid.

66 Ibid., 119. See also DuBose, *Turning Points in My Life*, 38; Emerson and Stokes, "Introduction," xxii; Luker, *A Southern Tradition*, 123–4.

67 DuBose, "Reminiscences," 119–20. See also Alexander, "Introduction," 7.

68 DuBose, "Reminiscences," 120–1. See also Emerson and Stokes, "Introduction," xxii; Guerry, "Makers of Sewanee," 488; Luker, "The Crucible of Civil War and Reconstruction in the Experience of William Porcher DuBose," 59; Luker, *A Southern Tradition*, 124.

69 Luker, "The Crucible of Civil War and Reconstruction in the Experience of William Porcher DuBose," 59.

70 DuBose, "Reminiscences," 121. See also Emerson and Stokes, "Introduction," xxiii; Weigley, *A Great Civil War*, 268–9.

71 DuBose, "Reminiscences," 121–2. See also McPherson, *Battle Cry of Freedom*, 637–8.

72 DuBose, "Reminiscences," 122–4. See also Emerson and Stokes, "Introduction," xxiii.

73 DuBose, "Reminiscences," 124. See also Luker, "The Crucible of Civil War and Reconstruction in the Experience of William Porcher DuBose," 60.

74 The letter is reprinted in DuBose, *Faith, Valor, and Devotion*, 231. See also DuBose, "Reminiscences," 126; Luker, "The Crucible of Civil War and Reconstruction in the Experience of William Porcher DuBose," 60.

75 Luker, "The Crucible of Civil War and Reconstruction in the Experience of William Porcher DuBose," 60; Luker, *A Southern Tradition*, 132.

76 "Influential friends in Church and State" arranged for DuBose's appointment as the chaplain for Kershaw's brigade. DuBose, "Reminiscences," 126–30; DuBose, *Turning Points in My Life*, 39. See also Alexander, "Introduction," 7; Luker, "The Crucible of Civil War and Reconstruction in the Experience of William Porcher DuBose," 61; Luker, *A Southern Tradition*, 132; Lowell Reidenbaugh, "Kershaw, Joseph B.," in *MacMillan Information Now Encyclopedia: The Confederacy*, ed. Richard N. Current (New York: MacMillan Reference USA, 1993), 313; Edgar Legare Pennington, "The

Confederate Episcopal Church and the Southern Soldiers," *Historical Magazine of the Protestant Episcopal Church* 17, no. 4 (December 1948): 359.

77 DuBose, "Reminiscences," 130–1; Alexander, "Introduction," 7. The literature on the Overland campaign is voluminous. See, for example, Robert M. Dunkerly, Donald C. Pfanz, and David R. Ruth, *No Turning Back: A Guide to the 1864 Overland Campaign, from the Wilderness to Cold Harbor, May 4–June 13, 1864*, Emerging Civil War Series (El Dorado Hills, CA: Savas Beatie, 2014); John Keegan, *The American Civil War: A Military History* (New York: Knopf, 2009), 237–58.

78 DuBose, "Reminiscences," 131. See also Emerson and Stokes, "Introduction," xxiv; Luker, *A Southern Tradition*, 133; McPherson, *Battle Cry of Freedom*, 724–8.

79 DuBose, "Reminiscences," 131. See also Emerson and Stokes, "Introduction," xxiv.

80 DuBose, "Reminiscences," 132. See also Emerson and Stokes, "Introduction," xxiv; McPherson, *Battle Cry of Freedom*, 728–33.

81 Emerson and Stokes, "Introduction," xxiv; Luker, "The Crucible of Civil War and Reconstruction in the Experience of William Porcher DuBose," 61; Luker, *A Southern Tradition*, 133–4; McPherson, *Battle Cry of Freedom*, 733–40.

82 DuBose, "Reminiscences," 133; Emerson and Stokes, "Introduction," xxiv–xxv; Luker, "The Crucible of Civil War and Reconstruction in the Experience of William Porcher DuBose," 61; Luker, *A Southern Tradition*, 147.

83 DuBose, "Reminiscences," 133; Luker, "The Crucible of Civil War and Reconstruction in the Experience of William Porcher DuBose," 61–2; Luker, *A Southern Tradition*, 147–8. See also Weigley, *A Great Civil War*, 372–4.

84 DuBose, "Reminiscences," 133. See also Emerson and Stokes, "Introduction," xxv; Luker, *A Southern Tradition*, 148; McPherson, *Battle Cry of Freedom*, 779–81; Weigley, *A Great Civil War*, 376–8.

85 DuBose, "Reminiscences," 134. See also Luker, *A Southern Tradition*, 148–9.

86 DuBose, "Reminiscences," 134. See also DuBose, *Turning Points in My Life*, 48–9.

87 The "shock of death quote" is found in DuBose, *Turning Points in My Life*, 49. The letter to Nannie is reprinted in DuBose, *Faith, Valor, and Devotion*, 321. See also Luker, *A Southern Tradition*, 148–9; Slocum, "A Soldier's Faith," 175–7.

88 DuBose, *Turning Points in My Life*, 49–50.

89 DuBose, "Reminiscences," 134; Emerson and Stokes, "Introduction," xxv; Luker, "The Crucible of Civil War and Reconstruction in the Experience of William Porcher DuBose," 63.

90 Matthew Carr, *Sherman's Ghosts: Soldiers, Civilians, and the American Way of War* (New York: The Free Press, 2015), 104, 114, 119–20, 138. See also Jacqueline G. Campbell, "'Terrible Has Been the Storm': William T. Sherman's Own Soldiers Were Shocked by the Destruction They Left Behind in South

Carolina," *Civil War Times* 51, no. 1 (February 2012): 36–43; DuBose, "Reminiscences," 134.

91 DuBose, "Reminiscences," 134–5. See also McPherson, *Battle Cry of Freedom*, 827–9.

92 DuBose, "Reminiscences," 134–5; Luker, "The Crucible of Civil War and Reconstruction in the Experience of William Porcher DuBose," 63–4; McPherson, *Battle Cry of Freedom*, 829–30.

93 DuBose, "Reminiscences," 135. Emphasis in the original. See also Emerson and Stokes, "Introduction," xxv–xxvi.

94 Luker, "The Crucible of Civil War and Reconstruction in the Experience of William Porcher DuBose," 64.

95 DuBose, "Reminiscences," 135.

96 Ibid., 135; Luker, "The Crucible of Civil War and Reconstruction in the Experience of William Porcher DuBose," 64. See also McPherson, *Battle Cry of Freedom*, 847–50; Weigley, *A Great Civil War*, 434–42; 446–50.

97 DuBose, "Reminiscences," 136–8; Luker, *A Southern Tradition*, 162.

98 DuBose, "Reminiscences," 138. See also DuBose, *Turning Points in My Life*, 39; Alexander, "Introduction," 7–8; ; Luker, *A Southern Tradition*, 162.

99 DuBose, "Reminiscences," 139.

100 Ibid., 139–40. Emphasis in the original. See also Alexander, "Introduction," 7–8.

PART II

Reconstruction and Redemption

5

"A World So Changed from What It Had Been Ten Years Before"

South Carolina Politics During Reconstruction (1865–1877)

The southern landscape that Peter Fayssoux Stevens, Anthony Toomer Porter, and William Porcher DuBose discovered when the guns fell silent in 1865 was an alien place, hardly recognizable from what it had been during the prewar years. Henry Adams, scion of a prominent Massachusetts family that included two American presidents, perfectly captured the postbellum national mood in his autobiography, *The Education of Henry Adams*. Returning to the United States in 1868 after serving as his father's private secretary in Europe for seven years, Adams recalled his and his family's sense of alienation as they disembarked from their ship in Boston Harbor. Writing about himself and his family in the third person, he remarked that "Had they been Tyrian traders of the year B.C. 1000, landing from a galley fresh from Gibraltar, they could hardly have been stranger on the shore of a world so changed from what it had been ten years before."[1]

Unlike Adams, the three Episcopal clergymen from South Carolina had not been absent from American shores during the 1860s. They had participated in a domestic insurrection to forge a slaveholding republic separate from the United States. Their efforts failed. Consequently, they and many former Confederates were left with the remnants of a southern way of life that had vanished forever. The task that lay before them, and before all Americans in 1865, was to rebuild a life and a society from the fallen pillars of the antebellum world.

The Confederate surrender left numerous unanswered questions. Lincoln's Emancipation Proclamation, which took effect on January 1, 1863, freed slaves in the rebellious states, but its applicability at the cessation of hostilities was unclear. And what would happen to enslaved people in the loyal states? Lincoln had justified the use of extraordinary executive authority as a wartime measure. How would peace and reconstruction affect the peculiar institution?

The ratification of the Thirteenth Amendment in December 1865 finally answered most questions about slavery. The amendment held that "Neither slavery nor involuntary servitude, except as a punishment for crime whereof the party shall have been duly convicted, shall exist within the United States, or any place subject to their jurisdiction." Congress was empowered to enforce the amendment by "appropriate legislation," but the nature and extent of that legislation was left vague and uncertain. It was soon apparent that assisting previously enslaved peoples in moving from bondage to a system of free labor was a fraught endeavor.[2]

The transition from bondage to freedom had already been attempted even before the Confederate surrender. In November 1861, after the Union Navy occupied the Sea Islands off the coast of South Carolina, white citizens fled, leaving some 10,000 enslaved persons suddenly free. Northern whites moved in to fill the void, establishing schools to teach the freed people to read and write. They assumed that formerly enslaved persons would transition to a world of free labor effectively if enlightened white people illuminated the path. Although the paternalism of northern elites could be off-putting, Black people were eager to learn.[3]

As the war wound to a close, the fate of previously enslaved persons was top of mind for northern military and political leaders. Union General William T. Sherman witnessed firsthand the difficulties in addressing the needs of the freed people during his infamous march through Georgia and the Carolinas in 1864 and 1865. Scores of Black refugees trailed behind his army. A change in the legal status of the refugees was many months away. Thus, a short-term solution was necessary. Sherman was hardly an enlightened thinker on race, but he recognized the pressing need to act. Accordingly, on January 16, 1865, he issued Special Field Order Number 15, which identified approximately 400,000 acres in Florida, Georgia, and South Carolina to be divided into 40-acre parcels necessary to sustain approximately 18,000 Black persons. President Andrew Johnson subsequently revoked the order, but the gesture, even if only symbolic, showed that representatives of the federal government were pondering the plight of the freed people.[4]

Aside from Sherman's ad hoc, tentative steps, victorious Union officers needed a policy and a program to address the needs of the freed people. Shortly before he died, President Lincoln signed legislation creating the Bureau of Refugees, Freedmen, and Abandoned Lands. The goal was to assist the freed people as they moved from a world of bondage to free labor.

In South Carolina, General Rufus B. Saxton, headquartered in Beaufort, became the state's Freedmen's Bureau assistant commissioner with six sub-assistant commissioners under his command.[5]

The Freedmen's Bureau was a new experiment, and for that reason, it proved to be controversial. The Bureau was supposed to assist newly emancipated slaves in negotiating labor contracts with former slaveholders working through ten districts carved from the former Confederate States of America. Because it focused on meeting the needs of impoverished Black people while ignoring the plight of destitute whites, some critics objected that the Bureau should not favor one group over another.

Arguably the most divisive provision in the Freedmen's Bureau bill concerned the disposition of land confiscated by the Union army after southern owners had fled the northern advance. The bill's authors had devoted little attention to land-use requirements, adding them at the last minute in response to General Sherman's Special Field Orders No. 15. The absence of a rich legislative history on this point left the provisions vulnerable to the vagaries of the Bureau's detractors. Freed people could use the land they occupied when the war ended for three years. After that time, their status was uncertain.[6]

The Bureau pleased no one. Whites were infuriated that Bureau agents dared to interfere in labor negotiations. Any discussion of confiscating land was sure to incense landowners. For their part, the freed people recoiled from the prospect of living and working as wage laborers, which they viewed as only a half step removed from slavery. If a former slave returned to the plantation and once again labored in the fields, it would seem as though emancipation had been a chimera. For a man who planted and harvested crops as he has always done, life was essentially unchanged. "Freedom wasn't no difference I knows of," one former slave complained. "I work for Marse John just the same."[7]

Considering its widespread unpopularity, the Bureau's accomplishments were nothing short of extraordinary. Its limited successes could be attributed largely to the Bureau's first commissioner, General Oliver O. Howard. A devout man of strong religious convictions, Howard was known as the "Christian General." Witnessing the upheaval of the Civil War, he knew that the freed people required assistance if they hoped to move into a world of free labor. He also recognized that the Johnson administration and a recalcitrant Congress had provided insufficient resources to the Bureau. General Sherman commiserated with his colleague, telling him that "I fear you have Hercules's task."[8]

The Freedmen's Bureau suffered its share of waste, fraud, cronyism, and abuse, but agents could cite a few notable successes. Some twenty-two million freed people received rations that prevented widespread starvation in the years immediately following the war. The Bureau constructed forty-five hospitals and clinics that served 148,000 former slaves. Thirty-two thousand freed people searching for loved ones lost or sold before 1865 looked to the Bureau to provide transportation. Approximately 9,500 teachers traveled south to teach Black people how to read and write. Historically black colleges and universities (HBCUs), notably Fisk University in Tennessee, Atlanta University in Georgia, and the Hampton Institute in Virginia, grew out of the Bureau's efforts. General Howard founded an HBCU that bore his name.[9]

Southerners were dismayed with Sherman's land grab and the Freedmen's Bureau's meddling in labor relations between white planters and newly emancipated slaves, but they found an unexpected ally in the Executive Mansion. Although nominally the head of the victorious Union forces, the new president, Andrew Johnson of Tennessee, was a tried-and-true southern man. Johnson did not believe that the federal government should assist the freed people; public assistance ran contrary to the free labor system and encouraged idleness. The new president was not concerned about emancipation and its problems. From his perspective, the war was fundamentally a class struggle between the rich white planter elite and poor white yeoman farmers. Johnson counted himself among the latter. He seethed with resentment toward the affluent whites who looked down on him. His feelings of resentment and hostility mirrored the emotions of many white southerners.[10]

At the outset, Johnson's overheated rhetoric suggested that he would punish the rebels, leading Ohio Senator Benjamin Wade, a prominent Radical Republican, to exclaim, "Mr. Johnson, I thank God that you are here. Lincoln had too much of the milk of human kindness to deal with these damned rebels. Now they will be dealt with according to their deserts." Wade and the other Radicals soon regretted their faith in the new man. Forty-four days into his tenure, the president revealed his intentions in stunning fashion.[11]

Nothing prepared Union supporters for Johnson's Reconstruction proclamation 134, "Granting Amnesty to Participants in the Rebellion, with Certain Exceptions," of May 29, 1865. Commonly known as the "Proclamation of Amnesty and Reconstruction," it was far more lenient than the president had promised. Johnson agreed to pardon southerners en masse and restore all property rights, except as to slaves, for everyone but high-ranking civilian and military leaders of the Southern Confederacy. He established provisional governors in states formerly in rebellion with promises that these men would not mete out harsh terms for ex-Confederates. Under this plan, if the southern states repudiated secession, abolished slavery, and set aside Confederate debt, white southerners could govern themselves with no federal interference. It was an astonishingly generous plan, and it showed the Radicals that Johnson could not be trusted.[12]

Johnson's critics were aghast. From the moment that the president issued his Proclamation of Amnesty and Reconstruction until the end of his presidency on March 4, 1869, he and the Radical Republicans in Congress battled for control of Reconstruction policy. A familiar pattern emerged. Congress passed a bill imposing harsh terms on the South, the president vetoed the bill, and two-thirds of both chambers of Congress overrode the veto. As the Radicals overrode these vetoes, control of federal Reconstruction policy passed from the president to Congress. In 1868, this battle of wills culminated in the first presidential impeachment in American history. Johnson survived the ordeal by one vote, but his presidency was hobbled. Publicly rebuked and politically castrated, he remained in office until the expiration of his term on March 4, 1869.[13]

* * *

Shortly after he issued his May 1865 proclamation, Johnson met with three white South Carolina moderates: William Waters Boyce, an antebellum US congressman and representative in the Confederate States Congress; former South Carolina Governor William Aiken, Jr., a Southern Unionist; and James Lawrence Orr, a former US congressman and speaker of the US House of Representatives. Although Johnson's comments during the meeting were not completely clear or coherent, the president intimated that he would not be as vindictive toward the South as he had suggested in the immediate aftermath of Lincoln's assassination, when bitterness toward the vanquished rebels had been at its apex. The trio returned from the meeting delighted with the president's presumed permissiveness toward the southern states. During the discussions, Johnson asked the men to send him a list of possible provisional governors for South Carolina. They honored his request, and Johnson selected Benjamin Franklin Perry, a Southern Unionist from Upstate South Carolina, from the names on the list.[14]

On June 30, President Johnson issued a proclamation restoring civil government to South Carolina on generous terms in line with his May 29 proclamation. Shortly thereafter, Governor Perry reached an accommodation with the president to allow South Carolina to schedule a constitutional convention. If the convention declared that slavery had been abolished, nullified the 1860 secession ordinance, and provided for the popular election of a governor and presidential electors, the president would acquiesce in whatever measures the southern delegates deemed appropriate for ratifying the state constitution. This accommodation was a far cry from the Radical Republicans' preference for retribution.[15]

The "Convention of the People of South Carolina" convened at noon on Wednesday, September 13, 1865, in the First Baptist Church in Columbia. Although the delegates complied with the letter of President Johnson's directive, they violated the spirit of Reconstruction. They repealed the secession ordinance, as instructed, but they did not declare it null and void, presumably suggesting that the measure retained its legitimacy. Defiant to the end, the delegates fiercely debated whether they should recognize the finality of abolition, eventually settling on this statement: "The slaves in South Carolina having been emancipated by the action of the United States authorities, neither slavery nor involuntary servitude, except as a punishment for crime, whereof the party shall have been duly convicted, shall ever be re-established in this State." In acknowledging that emancipation had been accomplished by the federal government, the statement implied that white South Carolinians had no hand in the odious business of destroying the peculiar institution. As for the repudiation of Confederate debt, the delegates never discussed the matter.[16]

Governor Perry considered himself a reformer, and he used the convention to recommend changes that would allow more whites, including those in the lower classes, to participate in government. Among his other recommendations, Perry suggested that the people, not the state legislature, should elect the governor as well as presidential electors. He argued that the traditional practice of secret voting in the state legislature be abolished and that the "parish system" of representation in the state senate be eliminated. This last recommendation was significant because South Carolina relied on a parish system dating back to the eighteenth century. Between 1706 and 1778, the state legislature enacted several laws creating twenty-four parishes. Following the Revolutionary War, the state created a series of counties even as the parish system remained in effect. This made for a confusing map of political boundaries. The 1865 state constitution reflected Perry's reforms: people were allowed to cast a ballot directly for governor, the governor acquired veto power, and low-country parishes disappeared.[17]

President Johnson approved the 1865 constitution, thereby allowing white South Carolinians to schedule state elections. In the 1865 elections, James L. Orr became governor, and the planter elite of the antebellum era won most of the seats in the state legislature. Exactly as the Radical Republicans had feared, the white leaders elected to hold statewide offices were the same men who had led the state's secession efforts. From the Radical Republican perspective, worse was yet to come.[18]

A special session of the General Assembly convened in Columbia in October 1865 to ratify the Thirteenth Amendment abolishing slavery. Legislators had no choice about ratifying the amendment if they wanted South Carolina to be readmitted to the Union. Nonetheless, whites were not content to accept this requirement without developing a new set of conventions to regulate the activities of Black folks. In December 1865, during a regular session, the General Assembly enacted three statutes, eventually dubbed "Black Codes," to ensure that persons of color were "not entitled to social and political equality with white persons." This ominous language translated into provisions prohibiting Blacks from owning property, signing legally enforceable contracts, filing lawsuits in state courts, or otherwise availing themselves of legal protections such as due process of law. Persons of color could not travel freely or own a firearm (with certain minor exceptions) without the permission of a district court judge. Defining a person of color as anyone who was seven-eighths Black, the law prohibited interracial marriage. In the words of one commentator, the "terms *master* and *servant* were used throughout the codes as the General Assembly did everything it could to re-create the institution of slavery under another guise."[19]

Moderate whites feared that the Black Codes would infuriate the Radicals and complicate the state's pending readmission into the Union. Governor Perry put the best face possible on the measures. He argued that laws were not as draconian as they initially appeared. Like many whites who claimed to be moderate, Perry infantilized Blacks. He saw them essentially as children in need of state protection. In his view, Black Codes were not punitive measures designed to hamper Black social, civil, and political rights. Instead, they were protective measures ensuring that the freed people would behave appropriately. Blacks in essence were wards of the state with legislators acting as their legal guardians.

Appalled at this brazenly transparent effort to harm the freed people, Republicans moved swiftly. The new commander of the Department of South Carolina, General Daniel Sickles, promptly declared the codes null and void. White South Carolinians had hoped that President Johnson would shield them from the Radicals' most extreme measures and leave them to enact Reconstruction measures supporting white supremacy as they saw fit, but it was not to be. The president was locked in a fierce battle with the Radical Republicans over the course and direction of Reconstruction policy, and he was losing control.[20]

Following ratification of the Thirteenth Amendment on December 18, 1865, Senator Lyman Trumbull introduced the Civil Rights Bill of 1866 to implement the amendment by eliminating the "badge of servitude" preventing the freed people from exercising the rights of full citizenship.[21] Democrats complained about the encroachment of federal authority over the states, but to no avail. The bill passed the Senate 33–12 and secured a 111–38 vote in the House of Representatives.[22]

Predictably, Johnson vetoed the measure and, just as predictably, the Radicals overrode the veto. Anxious to avoid a prolonged public spat and settle the matter permanently, congressional Republicans pushed for a constitutional amendment to protect their gains. The Joint Committee on Reconstruction, created in December 1865 as a successor to the Joint Committee on the Conduct of the War, formally proposed a constitutional amendment to define national citizenship as "all persons born or naturalized in the United States."[23]

Critics howled that the proposed amendment infringed on state rights. It was a familiar refrain. President Johnson's reaction was familiar as well. A constitutional amendment required two-thirds of both chambers of Congress to propose the measure, and three-quarters of the states for ratification. The president had no formal role in proposing or ratifying an amendment, but Johnson nonetheless expressed his grave misgivings. After gathering a group of his political supporters together, he inveighed against Congress and its leaders. Johnson's prestige was so diminished that his opinion carried no weight.[24]

Congress proposed the Fourteenth Amendment with a 128–37 vote in the House of Representatives and a 22–11 vote in the Senate. On June 16, 1866, Secretary of State William Seward transmitted the amendment to state governors for ratification. As expected, every southern state except Tennessee refused to ratify the amendment. Southern opposition did not matter—the southern states had not been readmitted to the Union—nor did attempts by New Jersey and Ohio officials to rescind their support. The amendment was ratified in July 1868.[25]

On April 2, 1866, even as the battle over the Fourteenth Amendment raged, the president issued Proclamation 153 declaring that the insurrection in all states save Texas had ended. (In August of that year, he signed a proclamation declaring the insurrection had ended in Texas as well.) It was time to move on from the war, in Johnson's view. The Radicals were determined to push their harsh Reconstruction policies, but the president was equally determined to resist.[26]

As Johnson became more isolated and politically impotent, Republicans in Congress acted to reverse the president's lenient policies. When Congress reconvened in December 1866, Thaddeus Stevens, a Pennsylvania congressman and Radical Republican firebrand, proposed that the southern states hold a new convention to revise the work of the 1865 conventions. The Radicals insisted that Negro suffrage must be guaranteed, and former Confederates must be prohibited from gaining citizenship for at least five years. To that end, Congressman James Ashley introduced a plan to remove the most permissive measures championed by the Johnson administration. Critics loudly complained that white southerners were being denigrated as subjugated peoples, but the Radicals were unconcerned. When a consensus plan could not be forged, the members of Congress sent the proposals to the Joint Committee on Reconstruction for further study.[27]

The committee eventually produced a bill that served as the basis of the first Reconstruction Act of 1867. The measure divided the eleven former states of the Confederate States of America, except Tennessee, into five military districts under the command of a military officer who would police the inhabitants and arrange elections for constitutional conventions. Congress would approve or deny state constitutions written by the convention delegates. As a condition for congressional acceptance of a new constitution, a state had to ratify the proposed Fourteenth Amendment.[28]

Johnson correctly viewed the creation of the bill as a rebuke of his leadership. The opening sections repudiated the plans for state governments that Johnson had developed before the Thirty-ninth Congress convened.

Congressional Republicans were determined to reverse Johnson's prosouthern policies and enact harsh measures to punish the rebellious states as though they were conquered provinces.[29]

Faced with growing opposition from Congress, Johnson refused to yield despite the odds stacked against him. He resented the Radicals' continued push "to protect niggers" at the expense of poor white southerners. When Congress sent the bill to his desk on March 2, 1867, Johnson vetoed the measure. The veto was expected. The Radicals knew that he would do this. After he had surprised them once, they had taken the full measure of the man. Acting swiftly, they convinced two-thirds of both chambers of Congress to override the veto. The first Reconstruction Act of 1867 became law over the president's stringent objections.[30]

The standoff continued. When the Fortieth Congress convened on March 4, 1867, legislators knew the sessions would be turbulent. Within less than three weeks, on March 23, 1867, Congress passed a second Reconstruction Act. Designed to correct ambiguities in the first Reconstruction Act, the second act directed district commanders to register eligible voters before delegates were selected for the state constitutional conventions. Johnson vetoed the measure, and Congress swiftly overrode the veto.[31]

Because the Johnson administration narrowly construed the first two Reconstruction Acts, Congress drafted a third Reconstruction Act in July 1867. The law stated that "governments then existing in the rebel States of Virginia, North Carolina, South Carolina, Georgia, Mississippi, Alabama, Louisiana, Florida, Texas, and Arkansas were not legal State governments." Consequently, they "were to be continued subject in all respects to the military commanders of the respective districts, and to the paramount authority of Congress." President Johnson, as expected, vetoed the bill. A two-thirds majority of the Fortieth Congress overrode Johnson's veto and enacted the third Reconstruction Act.[32]

Forced to convene a state constitutional convention in accordance with the new federal law, white South Carolinians attempted to elect as many delegates as possible and boycott the sessions afterward to prevent a necessary majority from crafting a new state constitution. The effort failed. The constitutional convention convened in Charleston on January 14, 1868, with 124 delegates, 73 of whom were Black.[33]

White South Carolinians watched the convention's maneuverings with a sense of horror and dread. They had depended on Johnson to ensure easy passage of laws favorable to southern whites, but the president had been politically sidelined. With increasing anger and resentment, they realized they could do nothing to stop the writing and ratification of a new state constitution. Watching events unfold from the sidelines, southern partisans took note of the fifty-one white delegates to the convention, including the fifteen delegates transplanted from the North. They denounced native-born white men as scalawags and the other men as carpetbaggers. Despite their angry objections, the new state constitution afforded voting rights and educational opportunities to all South Carolinians "without regard to race or color." The 1865 constitution had replaced parishes with a system of election districts. Less than three years later, the 1868 constitution created counties that supplanted the election districts. The changes were supposed to ensure uniformity and consistency in elections, a step toward providing equal rights for all South Carolinians. Everything, it seemed, was designed to undercut the authority that white men had exercised in South Carolina since colonial times.[34]

To say that the 1868 state constitution was progressive is an understatement. The document attempted nothing less than a remaking of South Carolina's laws and traditions. White southerners spoke of their "way of life." This constitution threatened that way of life, replacing it with a social order that was alien to most white South Carolinians. It provided a level playing field for all races, which made it especially objectionable to white supremacists. One angry white citizen insisted that he would never honor the new constitution because it was "*a negro constitution, of a negro government, establishing negro equality.*"[35]

Whether whites honored the constitution or not, the state held elections that fall. Voters chose Robert K. Scott as governor. An Ohio Republican and former head of the Freedmen's Bureau in South Carolina, he became a reviled figure in the southern white community. Even worse, Charlestonian Francis L. Cardozo became the South Carolina secretary of state. He was the first person of color to hold public office in South Carolina. In the state legislature, 75 of the 124 House members were Black. In the state Senate, ten Black men served along with fifteen white Republicans out of a total of thirty-two senators. In no other state did as many Black people hold political power as in South Carolina.[36]

The rise of Black political figures in state offices was the realization of many whites' ancestral fears of Black folks running amok. For the next nine years, white South Carolinians labored to undermine the regime created by the 1868 state constitution. Recognizing that they could not always control the election results, many whites bowed out of the electoral process, leaving the Reconstruction regime in South Carolina to succeed or fail without their participation. In public, their message was firm and unequivocal: *We want no part of state government*. The reality was very different. Whites desperately wanted to be a part of state government, but they wanted to participate on their own terms. If they could not seize control of state Reconstruction policy under the color of law, they would do so under the cover of night. Thus began a series of elaborate machinations, some involving violence and intimidation, others requiring subtle forms of electoral manipulation. Even as elections were held under the new constitution, white men devised strategies of resistance.

The most obvious strategy, and the easiest to implement, was a sustained propaganda campaign. It succeeded beyond anyone's wildest expectations. Whites argued that this period of extended "Black Republican Rule" was rife with financial mismanagement, cronyism, fraud, deceit, and government malfeasance on an unprecedented scale. According to the most charitable version of this narrative, Black people, being simpletons and inferior beings, could not be entrusted with self-rule. They simply did not possess the necessary tools and intellectual ability to run a government. Their misrule was the result of placing persons unsuited to self-governance into positions of authority for which they had no training, experience, or ability. The reality, of course, was more complicated. Although Black people as a group struggled with illiteracy—state law had made it illegal to teach enslaved persons to read—87 percent of Black legislators in South Carolina during Reconstruction were literate. Far from being poor, itinerant day laborers with no hope of supporting themselves, 75 percent of Black legislators owned property and paid taxes. Most were not former field hands, but decidedly middle-class artisans, farmers, and merchants. A quarter had never been enslaved. Considering the prejudice and animosity toward their race, Black legislators had never enjoyed an opportunity to seek and gain elective office, but inexperience did not translate into the catastrophic misrule of southern propaganda.[37]

A second version of the narrative relied on elaborate, tangled stories of dark conspiracies and nefarious behind-the-scenes maneuvering, part of the northern elites' insidious plot to disrupt southern life. According to this fanciful version, a vicious northern cabal was lurking in the shadows and pulling the strings. Black people were empty vessels controlled by spiteful, lying, manipulative northern Republicans who wielded their radical ideology like a weapon against the good white people of the South. Unprincipled northern ideologues spouted clichés about the necessity of political egalitarianism and racial harmony, but their slick, innocuous-sounding messages were little more than cynical platitudes meant to distract people from the Republicans' radical agenda. Their purpose was to grind good Christian white folks under the bootheels of northern oppression, ultimately resulting in miscegenation and the loss of a pure, superior white race. The only way to combat this skullduggery was to undermine the Reconstruction regime. Southern chicanery was an effective antidote to northern chicanery.[38]

And many opportunities existed to revel in chicanery. To make the most of those opportunities, however, Union soldiers had to be shunted aside. Fortunately for white southerners, federal officials' resolve appeared to weaken at the end of the 1860s. Following the Republican victories in the 1868 elections, the US Army withdrew all but a small contingent of soldiers from South Carolina. Left alone to act as they saw fit, politically connected white southerners sometimes gerrymandered legislative districts or practiced blatant election fraud by stuffing ballot boxes. Still others employed violence through unorganized mobs or by joining organized groups such as the Ku Klux Klan. Ironically, as it experienced its greatest triumph, the Reconstruction regime in South Carolina also faced its greatest peril.[39]

The responses of white people to Reconstruction were not monolithic or hegemonic. Reactions varied depending on where people lived and their socio-economic status. White people living in the Low Country near Charleston often employed different strategies and tactics of resistance than did the white people who resided in the Up Country, the area of South Carolina nestled in the foothills of the Blue Ridge Mountains. The terms "Low Country" (sometimes written as one word, "Lowcountry") and "Up Country" (sometimes designated the "Upcountry") dated back to colonial times. During the Reconstruction era, the terms connoted distinct social, political, and economic differences. Such sweeping statements risk overgeneralizing, but they reveal an important aspect of South Carolina politics in the 1860s and 1870s.

The Low Country encompassed the tidewater areas near and including Charleston. With a higher Black population than inland areas, the Low Country was home to a large percentage of enslaved people before the war. The area depended on a plantation-based economy; consequently, the antebellum planter elite who owned those plantations were far wealthier than most Up-Country whites. After the war, plantation owners were impoverished by the loss of their capital (i.e., enslaved people). Their crops had been destroyed, and their lands were idle. If they hoped to recover, they had to find a means of working with the freed people no matter how they personally felt about Blacks. Low-Country whites were not champions of racial equality, but they recognized the need for a nuanced view of race relations during Reconstruction. They settled on sharecropping, tenancy, and wage labor as strategies for stabilizing the postwar economy, albeit this labor system was unpopular and created almost as many problems as it solved.[40]

This portrait of the Low-Country elite depicted them as sophisticated operatives who were paternalistic toward the freed people as well as toward lower-class whites. White Low-Country leaders did not usually employ violence because it did not suit their purposes. In the early years of Reconstruction, they hoped to conciliate northerners who had access to capital (a crucial issue because plantation owners could no longer use slaves as collateral for loans) and who might persuade federal lawmakers to remove Union troops from the Southland. Later, recognizing that Blacks outnumbered them, Low-Country white elites sought to work with the freed people and Republicans to forge a new coalition that would allow affluent whites to reassert dominance over lower-class whites and Blacks alike. Affluent whites need not physically attack Blacks if their goals could be achieved through other means.[41]

Up-Country whites tended to be far less affluent than their counterparts in the Low Country. Although some slaveholders resided in Up-Country areas before the war, they usually had smaller farms and owned fewer slaves than the rich Charleston plantation owners. Many Up-Country whites were subsistence farmers who barely eked out a living. They resented rich white planters who exercised a disproportionate share of political power and profited handsomely from the economy. In their view, emancipation and anything that smacked of social, political, or economic equality threatened their status. The standard narrative suggested that even the poorest white man could take comfort in the knowledge that at least he wasn't Black. If laws enacted under the 1868 state constitution equalized the playing field and allowed the freed people to participate in the political process, enjoy the benefits of a public education, and own property free and clear, how long would it take for the lines to blur and the distinctions between poor whites and poor Blacks to become negligible? This was the haunting fear of many an Up-Country white man. Moreover, the concentration of a majority Black population in the Low Country and a majority white population in the Up Country presented a simple equation. If Black people enjoyed enhanced political power, Low-Country denizens would retain control of state government, but if whites successfully disenfranchised the freed people, political control might shift to the Up Country.[42]

The lines were drawn. As Republicans attempted to assert control over conservative whites, the Ku Klux Klan spread to the Up Country beginning in 1868. Klan violence was mostly confined to the twelve counties in Up-Country South Carolina because the Black population was not as large as in the Low Country. Therefore, Up-Country whites need not accommodate the Black population or fear reprisals. They could insist that the freed people conform to the wishes of the white citizenry without worrying whether a suitable labor force would be available to work in the fields. Moreover, because they lacked the resources of affluent Low-Country white elites, Up-Country whites may have relied on violence as a mechanism for asserting social control or for expressing their frustration at their relative powerlessness.[43]

Whatever their motivations, Up-Country men were not afraid to employ violence. When Governor Scott, fearful of outbreaks of violence in the Up Country, asked Wade Hampton III, a prominent Low-Country elite and former general officer in the Confederate Army, to intervene, the general published an address in the newspaper calling for the "preservation of order." Hampton's entreaties had the desired effect. Klan attacks diminished markedly, demonstrating the Low Country's influence over both the white Republican leaders in the state as well as over the Up-Country whites who bowed to Low-Country leaders.[44]

The peace lasted approximately eighteen months. According to this standard narrative, the Klan reappeared with a vengeance by 1870. Even

Hampton could not control the viciousness of some Kluxers, and the Up-Country whites finally went too far. Cognizant of the rising violence and the need to reassert federal control, a reluctant President Ulysses S. Grant issued a proclamation calling for armed vigilante groups to turn in their weapons and disband within five days. He also suspended the writ of habeas corpus in nine Up-Country counties found to be in active rebellion and dispatched troops to restore law and order. Some Klan leaders fled the state while others surrendered. A series of Ku Klux Klan trials resulted in few convictions, but federal intervention broke the power of the Klan in the Up Country.[45]

Although the Klan disappeared from South Carolina by 1872, whites continued to resist Black Reconstruction, albeit through different means. Wade Hampton, that model of Low Country respectability, announced in November 1872 that it was time for white South Carolinians to "dedicate themselves to the redemption of the South." The notion of redemption, so often associated with Christianity, was no accident. Following the disappearance of the Klan, Hampton's dedication to restoring a white man's government took on the fervor of a religious revival. White South Carolinians resolved to banish the Philistines and champion the values of the Old South. They would accomplish these purposes through rifle, gun, and saber clubs, which sprang up with great frequency in the 1870s.[46]

The portrayal of Low-Country white elites pitted against poor Up-Country whites had the advantage of simplicity. It accounted for many, although not all, differences in race relations across the state during Reconstruction. It also explained, to some extent, the actions of the three clergymen profiled here. Because they lived and worked in the Low Country, Peter Fayssoux Stevens and Anthony Toomer Porter did not marginalize Blacks. They were certainly not proponents of social or political equality, but they understood the need to work with people of color and encourage them to participate in the church. By contrast, before he moved to Sewanee, Tennessee, to become chaplain and professor of moral science at the University of the South, William Porcher DuBose spent much of his early life and career in the middle part of the state. His tenure at Trinity Episcopal Church in Abbeville placed him in the Up Country at precisely the time that the Ku Klux Klan appeared in South Carolina.

As with any sweeping generalization, a discussion of the Low Country versus the Up Country does not account for local conditions. The poor relationship between employers and laborers sometimes determined the propensity for violence. In some communities, Blacks had organized into militias for protection against vigilante whites apart from geographic considerations. Visions of Negro militias patrolling the streets created an arms race. Armed whites compelled Blacks to arm, which in turn compelled whites to acquire ever more arms. It did not take much prompting to trigger violence under these conditions. The year 1876 proved this point when a series of riots broke out leading up to the gubernatorial election. Bloody confrontations in Hamburg, Charleston, Ellenton, and Cainhoy, among other places, demonstrated the volatile nature of the state's politics.[47]

Unrest was everywhere across the South even as the federal government backed away from its commitments. Throughout the 1870s, federal Reconstruction policies deteriorated. President Ulysses S. Grant's administration was engulfed in myriad political scandals while the Radical Republicans in Congress retired, were defeated for reelection, or died. Many Americans simply grew weary of the time, energy, and funding devoted to policing the southern states. As the war receded into the past, citizens focused on current issues. When a financial panic gripped the United States in 1873, voters asked how their elected leaders would address their economic concerns, not whether Reconstruction policies were effective.[48]

White South Carolinians understood that times were changing. Sensing an opportunity to topple the Reconstruction regime, they stepped up their efforts to undermine the carpetbaggers who controlled the levers of state government. Daniel H. Chamberlain, elected governor in 1874, created a coalition of white and Black Republicans as well as some white Democrats when he reformed state government. For a short time, he discovered a winning combination of forces to resist the depredations of white conservatives; however, his government lasted only as long as federal officials enforced robust Reconstruction policies. By the mid-1870s, cracks appeared in the façade of a well-functioning Republican regime in the Palmetto State. Chamberlain's coalition disintegrated at the end of 1875 as "straight-out" Democrats, sensing an opportunity to eject the hated Republicans from office, urged their followers to disavow allegiance to any cause other than the white supremacy promoted by conservative white Democrats.[49]

In the bitterly fought gubernatorial election of 1876, Chamberlain faced a formidable opponent. Once again, General Wade Hampton stepped forward to champion white supremacy and the power of the old guard. Hampton remained a larger-than-life figure for most white South Carolinians. His status as a prominent antebellum planter and his record as a general officer in the Confederate States Army made him a commanding, attractive public figure. Although some Up-Country whites found his racial views too moderate for their tastes and were not always enamored of wealthy planters, Hampton attracted support because he was the candidate most likely to turn out Chamberlain and decimate the hated Reconstruction regime.[50]

The old general campaigned throughout the state, and the reaction of most whites was ecstatic. Accompanied by men wearing distinctive red shirts—usually known as the Red Shirts and viewed as the candidate's own private paramilitary group—Hampton promised to return South Carolina to its former glory. This promise meant, of course, that any nascent attempts to improve the lives of Black South Carolinians were dead. White supremacy would be the foundational principle of a Hampton regime.[51]

The Red Shirts were part of a plan instituted by former Confederate General Martin Witherspoon Gary to disrupt white Republican political rallies and voting through bribery and intimidation. A variation on the Mississippi Plan designed to disenfranchise people of color, the Gary Plan was a coordinated effort to convince Black people not to vote. Some of Gary's statements were bland admonitions along the lines of "get-out-the-vote" campaigns employed by parties for generations. Other parts of the plan urged supporters to approach Blacks and "show them you are the superior race, and that their natural position is that of subordination to the white man." Gary cautioned that "A dead Radical is very harmless," while a "threatened Radical" could be "troublesome, sometimes dangerous, always vindictive."[52]

On November 7, 1876, voters streamed to the polls in the general election. It was a chaotic scene with malfeasance practiced on both sides. At Governor Chamberlain's request, federal troops waited near county seats to visit polling places and ensure that law and order prevailed, if necessary. The troops were not needed until after the election.[53]

The results were close, with Chamberlain and Hampton exchanging the lead over several days. Irregularities occurred especially in Aiken County, Edgefield County, and Laurens County. In Edgefield County, the total vote exceeded the number of voting age citizens. In Laurens County, the number of ballots cast exceeded the number of registered voters.[54]

Both sides claimed victory. To prevent Democrats from seizing control of state government, Governor Chamberlain dispatched two companies of federal soldiers to patrol the South Carolina State House. He also ensured that his supporters discarded the returns from Edgefield and Laurens Counties. Incensed, Democrats marched away from the General Assembly and established a competing state legislature. In the meantime, on December 5, 1876, the Republican-controlled General Assembly declared Chamberlain the winner.[55]

Chamberlain's victory initially appeared to be a fait accompli, but white Democrats had come too far and sacrificed too much to give up the fight. On December 14, they declared Hampton the winner by counting the suspicious votes from Edgefield and Laurens Counties. Demonstrating his mastery of politics and his control over white citizens, Hampton called on his supporters to "starve out" the Republicans by withholding most of their tax payments. This plan had the desired effect. The Chamberlain government could not operate without adequate funding. In the past, Chamberlain had depended on federal assistance to prop up his regime, but President Grant was a lame duck and reluctant to act. Even worse for Chamberlain's fortunes, the 1876 presidential election was in limbo as the Republican, Rutherford B. Hayes, and the Democrat, Samuel J. Tilden, battled for supremacy owing to uncertain, possibly rigged results.[56]

Chamberlain held out as long as he could, but his defeat became inevitable when Hayes was declared the winner of the presidential election on March

2, 1877. Hayes understood that the only way for Chamberlain to remain in office was for the federal government to send additional troops to protect the Republican regime. Although he was nominally a Republican, the new president would not commit to such a plan. On April 3, 1877, Hayes ordered federal troops to depart from South Carolina. Recognizing that his position without military protection was untenable, Chamberlain surrendered. On April 11, 1877, the battle of the dueling governors ended with Wade Hampton stepping into office. South Carolina had been redeemed.[57]

With the collapse of the Republican regime in South Carolina in 1877, official, federally supported Reconstruction policy ended in the state. Many gains that the freed people had achieved following adoption of the 1868 state constitution were reversed. White southerners could rule as they always had except for the loss of the peculiar institution. They soon found mechanisms for establishing control over Blacks that became slavery by another name. For decades to come, whites used low-paying labor contracts, unfair sharecropping arrangements, and the creation of segregation laws to ensure that white supremacy thrived. One North Carolina Democrat noted that "When the bayonets shall depart, then look out for the reaction. Then the bottom rail will descend from the top of the fence."[58]

The Democratic Party became the predominant political operation in South Carolina for the better part of a century. As the noted historian Edward J. Blum observed in his book *Reforging the White Republic*, a new white republic emerged, based on Protestant Christian values that replaced the old North-South/slavery-abolitionist division that had shaped American history during the antebellum years. Blum argued that the nation "witnessed northern white Protestants thoroughly embracing and propagating an ethnic nationalism that privileged whiteness at the direct expense of the radical civic nationalism of the mid-1860s."[59]

Peter Fayssoux Stevens, Anthony Toomer Porter, and William Porcher DuBose faced the same unprecedented social, political, cultural, economic, and religious uncertainties as other South Carolinians living through Reconstruction and Redemption. As clergymen who were expected to provide comfort and guidance to their congregants, they needed to make sense of the changes as seamlessly as possible. To some extent, their actions depended on how they viewed the church and their roles in the diocese in the context of political developments within the state.

Like every other institution, the Episcopal Church underwent enormous changes during the war, and those changes only accelerated afterward. Some clergymen contended that political developments in South Carolina did not affect church affairs. After all, the church was supposed to be apolitical. These contentions were disingenuous. The debates over the proper role of the freed people under state and federal laws were mirrored in the debates about whether Black communicants had a place in the postwar Episcopal Church.

Notes

1. Henry Adams, *The Education of Henry Adams* (Washington, DC: Self, 1907), 206.

2. The literature on this issue is voluminous. See, for example, David Herbert Donald, *Lincoln* (New York: Simon & Schuster, 1995), 365–6; Doris Kearns Goodwin, *Team of Rivals: The Political Genius of Abraham Lincoln* (New York: Simon & Schuster, 2005), 464–5; Allen C. Guelzo, *Lincoln's Emancipation Proclamation: The End of Slavery in America* (New York: Simon & Schuster, 2006), 4–5, 126; Harold Holzer, *Lincoln: How Abraham Lincoln Ended Slavery in America* (New York: Newmarket Press, an Imprint of HarperCollins, 2012), 155–74; Harold Holzer, "A Promise Fulfilled," *Civil War Times* 48, no. 6 (December 2009): 32; David Livingstone, "The Emancipation Proclamation, the Declaration of Independence, and the Presidency: Lincoln's Model of Statesmanship," *Perspectives on Political Science* 28, no. 4 (Fall 1999): 206–7; James M. McPherson, *Battle Cry of Freedom: The Civil War Era* (New York: Ballantine Books, 1988), 840–2.

3. Eric Foner, *Forever Free: The Story of Emancipation and Reconstruction*, Illustrations Edited with a Commentary by Joshua Brown (New York: Knopf, 2005), 59–61; Eric Foner, *Reconstruction: America's Unfinished Revolution: 1863 1877* (New York: Francis Parkman Prize Edition, History Book Club, 2005 [1988]), 53–5; Joel Williamson, *After Slavery: The Negro in South Carolina During Reconstruction, 1861 1877* (Chapel Hill: University of North Carolina Press, 1965), 54–8.

4. Special Field Order Number 15 was the origin of the popular concept that newly emancipated slaves were entitled to "40 acres and a mule." See, for example, LaWanda Fenlason Cox, "The Promise of Land for the Freedmen," *Mississippi Valley Historical Review* 45, no. 3 (December 1958): 413–40; W. E. B. Du Bois, *The Souls of Black Folk: Essays and Sketches*, 8th ed. (Chicago: A. C. McClurg & Company, 1909), 22; Robert Harrison, "New Representations of a 'Misrepresented Bureau: Reflections on Recent Scholarship on the Freedmen's Bureau," *American Nineteenth Century History* 8, no. 2 (June 2007): 216.

5. Foner, *Reconstruction*, 68–70; Robert Selph Henry, *The Story of Reconstruction* (New York: Konecky & Konecky, 1999), 59–61; Francis Butler Simkins and Robert Hilliard Woody, *South Carolina During Reconstruction* (Chapel Hill: University of North Carolina Press, 1932), 29; Francis Butler Simkins and Charles Pierce Roland, *A History of the South*, 4th ed. (New York: Knopf, 1972), 261–2; Jay Winik, *April 1865: The Month That Saved America* (New York: HarperCollins, 2001), 210–11.

6. Herman Belz, "The Freedmen's Bureau Act of 1865 and the Principle of No Discrimination According to Color," *Civil War History* 21, no. 3 (September 1975): 197–217; Foner, *Reconstruction*, 68–70; Harrison, "New Representations of a 'Misrepresented Bureau'," 206; Clayton R. Newell and Charles R. Shrader, "The U.S. Army's Transition to Peace, 1865–66," *The Journal of Military History* 77, no. 3 (July 2013): 884–6; Orville Vernon

Burton, "Race and Reconstruction: Edgefield County, South Carolina," *Journal of Social History* 12, no. 1 (October 1978): 33.

7   Quoted in Richard W. Murphy, *The Nation Reunited: War's Aftermath* (Alexandria, VA: Time-Life Books, 1987), 44. See also Foner, *Reconstruction*, 409; Julie Saville, *The Work of Reconstruction: From Slave to Wage Laborer in South Carolina, 1860–1870* (Cambridge: Cambridge University Press, 1994), 138; Kenneth M. Stampp, *The Era of Reconstruction, 1865–1877* (New York: Alfred A. Knopf, 1965), 134–5.

8   Quoted in Foner, *Reconstruction*, 143. See also: Foner, *Forever Free*, 76–7; Simkins and Roland, *A History of the South*, 261–2.

9   Foner, *Forever Free*, 97–9; Harrison, "New Representations of a 'Misrepresented Bureau'," 219; Henry, *The Story of Reconstruction*, 58–61; Newell and Shrader, "The U.S. Army's Transition to Peace," 885–6; Simkins and Roland, *A History of the South*, 261–2.

10 Foner, *Reconstruction*, 144–7; Harrison, "New Representations of a 'Misrepresented Bureau'," 218–19; Brooks D. Simpson, *The Reconstruction Presidents* (Lawrence: The University Press of Kansas, 1998), 92–4. See also: Steven G. Calabresi and Christopher S. Yoo, "The Unitary Executive During the Second Half-Century," *Harvard Journal of Law & Public Policy* 26, no. 3 (Summer 2003): 741–2; David P. Currie, "The Reconstruction Congress," *University of Chicago Law Review* 75, no. 1 (2008): 392–3; George Fort Milton, *The Age of Hate: Andrew Johnson and the Radicals* (New York: Coward-McCann, Inc., 1930), 287–9.

11 Wade is quoted in Anna Laurens Dawes, *Charles Sumner* (New York: Dodd, Mead and Company, 1892), 219. See also Trefousse, *The Radical Republicans*, 307–9; Winik, *April 1865*, 226–7.

12 Johnson is quoted in John Savage, *The Life and Public Speeches of Andrew Johnson, Seventeenth President of the United States, Including His State Papers, Speeches, and Addresses* (New York: Derby & Miller, 1866), 320. See also Calabresi and Yoo, "The Unitary Executive During the Second Half-Century," 739–41; Foner, *Reconstruction*, 183–4; Henry, *The Story of Reconstruction*, 46–8; Harold M. Hyman, *The Radical Republicans and Reconstruction: 1861–1870* (Indianapolis: Bobbs-Merrill, 1967), 246–7; Howard Means, *The Avenger Takes His Place: Andrew Johnson and the 45 Days That Changed the Nation* (New York: Harcourt, Inc., 2006), 201–16; Simkins and Roland, *A History of the South*, 256–8.

13 The literature on Johnson's struggles with the Radical Republicans is voluminous. See, for example, Calabresi and Yoo, "The Unitary Executive During the Second Half-Century," 756–7; Currie, "The Reconstruction Congress," 449; Henry, *The Story of Reconstruction*, 308–9; Albert Castel, *The Presidency of Andrew Johnson* (Lawrence: The University Press of Kansas, 1979); Michael A. Genovese, *The Power of the American Presidency, 1789–2000* (New York: Oxford University Press, 2001); Robert J. Kaczorowski, "Congress' Power to Enforce Fourteenth Amendment Rights: Lessons from Federal Remedies the Framers Enacted," *Harvard Journal on Legislation* 42, no. 1 (Winter 2005): 199–205; Herman Belz, *Reconstructing the Union:*

Theory and Policy During the Civil War (Ithaca, NY: Cornell University Press, 1969); Benjamin B. Kendrick, *The Journal of the Joint Committee of Fifteen on Reconstruction, 39th Congress, 1865–1867* (Clark, NJ: The Law Book Exchange, Ltd., 2005 [1914], 115; Abel A. Bartley, "The Fourteenth Amendment: The Great Equalizer of the American People," *Akron Law Review* 36, no. 3 (2003), 474; Douglas H. Bryant, "Unorthodox and Paradox: Revisiting the Ratification of the Fourteenth Amendment," *Alabama Law Review* 53, no. 2 (Winter 2003): 564–5; Michael J. Klarman, *From Jim Crow to Civil Rights: The Supreme Court and the Struggle for Equality* (New York and Oxford: Oxford University Press, 2004), 19–20; David O. Stewart, *Impeached: The Trial of President Andrew Johnson and the Fight for Lincoln's Legacy* (New York: Simon & Schuster, 2009); Hans L. Trefousse, *Impeachment of a President: Andrew Johnson, the Blacks, and Reconstruction* (Bronx, NY: Fordham University Press, 1999 [1975]); US Senate, *Trial of Andrew Johnson, President of the United States, Before the Senate of the United States, on Impeachment by the House of Representatives from High Crimes and Misdemeanors* (Washington, DC: U.S. Government Printing Office, 1868), Vol. I; Howard K. Beale, *The Critical Year: A Study of Andrew Johnson and Reconstruction* (New York: Frederick Ungar, 1958 [1930]); Burton Folsom, Jr., "Andrew Johnson and the Constitution," *Ideas on Liberty* 53, no. 8 (September 2003): 32–3; David Miller DeWitt, *The Impeachment and Trial of Andrew Johnson: The Impeachment and Trial of Andrew Johnson, Seventeenth President of the United States: A History* (New York: The MacMillan Company, 1903), 110–26; Martin E. Mantell, *Johnson, Grant, and the Politics of Reconstruction* (New York: Columbia University Press, 1973); Eric L. McKitrick, *Andrew Johnson and Reconstruction* (New York: Oxford University Press, 1988 [1960]); David Herbert Donald, *The Politics of Reconstruction, 1863–1867* (Baton Rouge: Louisiana State University Press, 1965), 8; Brooks D. Simpson, *Let Us Have Peace: Ulysses S. Grant and the Politics of War and Reconstruction, 1861–1868* (Chapel Hill: The University of North Carolina Press, 1991), 172–3; Andrew L. Slap, *The Doom of Reconstruction: The Liberal Republicans in the Civil War Era* (New York: Fordham University Press, 2010), 223–4; John Yoo, *Crisis and Command* (New York: Kaplan Publishing, 2009), 252–3. For primary sources, see, for example, Civil Rights Act of 1866 § 1, 14 Stat at 27; *Ex Parte Milligan*, 71 the United States 2 (1866).

14 John L. Bell, Jr., "Andrew Johnson, National Politics, and Presidential Reconstruction in South Carolina," *The South Carolina Historical Magazine* 82, no. 4 (October 1981): 355–6, 359–60; Simkins and Woody, *South Carolina During Reconstruction*, 34. Johnson's remarks and actions during his first few months in office often appeared contradictory. One moment, he inveighed against the Confederates only to seemingly reverse himself shortly thereafter. See, for example, Means, *The Avenger Takes His Place*, 166; Michael Vorenberg, *Lincoln's Peace: The Struggle to End the American Civil War* (New York: Knopf, 2025), 189–90.

15 Bell, "Andrew Johnson, National Politics, and Presidential Reconstruction in South Carolina," 359–60. See also Simkins and Roland, *A History of the*

South, 257; Richard Zuczek, *State of Rebellion: Reconstruction in South Carolina* (Columbia: University of South Carolina Press, 1996), 12–14.

16 *Journal of the Convention of the People of South Carolina, Held in Columbia, South Carolina, September, 1865, Together with the Ordinances, Reports, Resolutions, Etc.* (Columbia, SC: J. A. Selby, Printer to the Convention, 1865). The quote appears on page 151. See also Simkins and Woody, *South Carolina During Reconstruction*, 39.

17 The political "parishes" are based on the notion of Anglican parishes. The years 1706 and 1778 are significant. As discussed in Chapter 1, a 1706 "church law" established the Anglican Church as the official church of South Carolina. In 1778, the state disestablished the Anglican Church. See Bell, "Andrew Johnson, National Politics, and Presidential Reconstruction in South Carolina," 363–4; Walter Edgar, *South Carolina: A History* (Columbia, SC: University of South Carolina Press, 1998), 99–102, 156–7, 161, 383; Walter B. Posey, "The Protestant Episcopal Church: An American Adaptation," *The Journal of Southern History* 25, no. 1 (February 1959): 3–30; Albert Sidney Thomas, *A Historical Account of the Protestant Episcopal Church in South Carolina, 1820–1957* (Columbia, SC: R. L. Bryan Company, 1957), 3–4, 8.

18 Simkins and Woody, *South Carolina During Reconstruction*, 43–4; Simkins and Roland, *A History of the South*, 257–58.

19 Edgar, *South Carolina*, 384. See also Bernard E. Powers, Jr., "Community Evolution and Race Relations in Reconstruction Charleston, South Carolina," *The South Carolina Historical Magazine* 101, no. 3 (July 2000): 217; Zuczek, *State of Rebellion*, 15–16.

20 Edgar, *South Carolina*, 384; J. Michael Martinez, *Carpetbaggers, Cavalry, and the Ku Klux Klan: Exposing the Invisible Empire During Reconstruction* (Lanham, MD: Rowman & Littlefield, 2007), 34–42.

21 Civil Rights Act of 1866 § 1, 14 Stat at 27; Kaczorowski, "Congress' Power to Enforce Fourteenth Amendment Rights."

22 Currie, "The Reconstruction Congress," 398–9; Simpson, *The Reconstruction Presidents*, 96–9.

23 Belz, *Reconstructing the Union*, 304; Foner, *Reconstruction*, 251–2; Henry, *The Story of Reconstruction*, 208–10; Kendrick, *The Journal of the Joint Committee of Fifteen on Reconstruction, 39th Congress, 1865–1867*, 115; Stampp, *The Era of Reconstruction*, 136–7.

24 Foner, *Reconstruction*, 260–1; Trefousse, *The Radical Republicans*, 347–51.

25 Bartley, "The Fourteenth Amendment," 474; Bryant, "Unorthodox and Paradox:," 564–5; Currie, "The Reconstruction Congress," 407; Henry, *The Story of Reconstruction*, 332–3; Klarman, *From Jim Crow to Civil Rights*, 19–20; Castel, *The Presidency of Andrew Johnson*, 73.

26 Henry, *The Story of Reconstruction*, 179, 180–1.

27 Currie, "The Reconstruction Congress," 408–9; Foner, *Reconstruction*, 273.

28 Currie, "The Reconstruction Congress," 408–14; Foner, *Reconstruction*, 275–80; Henry, *The Story of Reconstruction*, 219–21.

29 Currie, "The Reconstruction Congress," 408–9. See also: Foner, *Reconstruction*, 276–7; Henry, *The Story of Reconstruction*, 219–21.

30 Quoted in Foner, *Reconstruction*, 276. See also: Currie, "The Reconstruction Congress," 411–12; Henry, *The Story of Reconstruction*, 216; Simpson, *The Reconstruction Presidents*, 113–17; Trefousse, *The Radical Republicans*, 355–61.

31 Currie, "The Reconstruction Congress," 422–4; Henry, *The Story of Reconstruction*, 220–1; Milton, *The Age of Hate*, 425–9; Simpson, *The Reconstruction Presidents*, 116–17.

32 Quoted in Currie, "The Reconstruction Congress," 424–6. See also: Calabresi and Yoo, "The Unitary Executive During the Second Half-Century," 744–6; Milton, *The Age of Hate*, 445–7; Simpson, *The Reconstruction Presidents*, 117–18.

33 To address this issue, one last Reconstruction Act, enacted in March 1868, required that ratification of new state constitutions "shall be decided by a majority of the votes actually cast," instead of 50 percent of registered voters. The modification ensured that southerners who sought to derail the reconstruction process could not delay ratification by refusing to vote. It was a last-ditch effort to ensure congressional control over federal Reconstruction policy. See, for example, Henry, *The Story of Reconstruction*, 311; Simpson, *Let Us Have Peace*, 239; Simpson, *The Reconstruction Presidents*, 117–18; Trefousse, *The Radical Republicans*, 379.

34 Edgar, *South Carolina*, 385–8; Zuczek, *State of Rebellion*, 48–50.

35 Quoted in Edgar, *South Carolina*, 386. Emphasis in the original. See also George B. Tindall, "The Campaign for the Disfranchisement of Negroes in South Carolina," *The Journal of Southern History* 15, no. 2 (May 1949): 212.

36 Edgar, *South Carolina*, 387, 394. See also Simkins and Woody, *South Carolina During Reconstruction*, 112–14.

37 Edgar, *South Carolina*, 388–90.

38 This view of Reconstruction made its way into the history books, ensuring that the propaganda would live on well into the twentieth century. William Archibald Dunning, a Columbia University historian, became a leading figure among scholars who penned Reconstruction narratives favorable to the southern view. Owing to Dunning's influence, the myth of Black misrule and white southern victimhood found its way into numerous histories. See, for example, William Archibald Dunning, *Reconstruction, Political and Economic, 1865–1877, The American Nation: A History*, Vol. II (New York: Harper & Row, 1962 [1907]). For more on the Dunning School of historiography, see, for example, Foner, *Reconstruction*, 236–9; J. Michael Martinez, *A Long Dark Night: Race in America from Jim Crow to World War II* (Lanham, MD: Rowman & Littlefield, 2016), 67; John David Smith and J. Vincent Lowery, eds, *The Dunning School: Historians, Race, and the Meaning of Reconstruction* (Lexington: University Press of Kentucky, 2013). See also Rod Andrew, Jr., *Wade Hampton: Confederate Warrior to Southern Redeemer* (Chapel Hill: The University of North Carolina Press, 2008), 351–2.

39 Edgar, *South Carolina*, 397–8; Zuczek, *State of Rebellion*, 50–1.

40 See, for example, Louis Ferleger, "Sharecropping Contracts in the Late-Nineteenth-Century South," *Agricultural History* 67, no. 3 (Summer 1993): 31–46; Lacy K. Ford, "Rednecks and Merchants: Economic Development and Social Tensions in the South Carolina Upcountry, 1865–1900," *The Journal of American History* 71, no. 2 (September 1984): 305–6; David A. Latzko, "Mapping the Short-run Impact of the Civil War and Emancipation on the South Carolina Economy," *The South Carolina Historical Magazine* 116, no. 4 (October 2015): 261–2, 279; Tindall, "The Campaign for the Disfranchisement of Negroes in South Carolina," 212–14.

41 Low-Country planters were portrayed as a crafty lot. Recognizing the need to draw together disparate elements from several parties and movements, Low-Country elites attracted a smattering of reform-minded Republicans, Democrats, and some Black voters in a "fusion" of the parties. It was all smiles and subterfuge among Low-Country planters, but Up-Country whites resented the shenanigans. If Black voters hoped that their support would translate into less oppressive public policy than they had seen in the past, they were disappointed. See, for example, Stephen Kantrowitz, *Ben Tillman & the Reconstruction of White Supremacy* (Chapel Hill and London: The University of North Carolina Press, 2000), 64–5. See also Lacy K. Ford, *Origins of Southern Radicalism: The South Carolina Up Country, 1800–1860* (Oxford: Oxford University Press, 1988), 101; Robert Olwell, *Masters, Slaves & Subjects: The Culture of Power in the South Carolina Low Country, 1740–1790* (Ithaca, NY: Cornell University Press, 1998), 10–11.

42 See, for example, Bell, "Andrew Johnson, National Politics, and Presidential Reconstruction in South Carolina," 355; Ford, *Origins of Southern Radicalism*, 101–2.

43 Allen W. Trelease, *White Terror: The Ku Klux Klan Conspiracy and Southern Reconstruction* (Baton Rouge: Louisiana State University Press, 1999 [1971]), 72, 115–17, 349, 353. See also Richard Zuczek, "The Federal Government's Attack on the Ku Klux Klan: A Reassessment," *The South Carolina Historical Magazine* 97, no. 1 (January 1996): 48–9, 55, 59, 60.

44 Andrew, *Wade Hampton*, 349.

45 Ibid., 362–3; Edgar, *South Carolina*, 398; Martinez, *Carpetbaggers, Cavalry, and the Ku Klux Klan*, 148–50. See also Jerry L. West, *The Reconstruction Ku Klux Klan in York County, South Carolina, 1865–1877* (Jefferson, NC: McFarland & Company, Inc., 2002); Lou Falkner Williams, *The Great South Carolina Ku Klux Klan Trials, 1871–1872* (Athens: University of Georgia Press, 1996).

46 Hampton is quoted in Edgar, *South Carolina*, 401. Hampton's relationship to the Ku Klux Klan has been the subject of much debate. Many northern commentators believed that Hampton must be a Klan ringleader owing to his visibility as a champion of white supremacy as well as his association with a paramilitary group, the Red Shirts. The reality was more complex and nuanced. Although Hampton often agreed with the group's objectives, he recoiled at their tactics and never forged close ties with the Klan. See,

for example, Andrew, *Wade Hampton*, 350–1. On the redemption issue as tied to Christianity, see, for example, W. Scott Poole, "Religion, Gender, and the Lost Cause in South Carolina's 1876 Governor's Race: 'Hampton or Hell!'," *The Journal of Southern History* 68, no. 3 (August 2002): 585–6. Poole observed that "Ellison Capers, an Episcopal priest who had served as a brigadier general in the Confederate army, became one of the most active and outspoken Hampton supporters. Converted to faith in both Christianity and the Confederacy by the experience of war, Capers became a kind of high priest of the Lost Cause in South Carolina, described as one of those who 'pledged themselves to its [the state's] redemption under a white man's government.'" Poole, "Religion, Gender, and the Lost Cause in South Carolina's 1876 Governor's Race," 585–6. For more on Hampton's views on Black Republican rule, see, for example, Robert F. Durden, "The Prostrate State Revisited: James S. Pike and South Carolina Reconstruction," *The Journal of Negro History* 39, no. 2 (April 1954): 91; D.D. Wallace, "The Question of the Withdrawal of the Democratic Presidential Electors in South Carolina in 1876," *The Journal of Southern History* 8, no. 3 (August 1942): 374–5.

47 This argument is developed in detail in J. C. A. Stagg, "The Problem of Klan Violence: The South Carolina Up-Country, 1868–1871," *Journal of American Studies* 8, no. 3 (December 1974): 303–18. See also Ford, *Origins of Southern Radicalism*, 102. The Hamburg Riot marked the political emergence of a young man, Benjamin Ryan Tillman, commander of Edgefield County's Sweetwater Sabre Club, a paramilitary group that violently opposed South Carolina Republicans. Although he was a reliable Hampton supporter in the 1876 gubernatorial election, "Pitchfork Ben" subsequently launched a successful political career as governor and US senator in South Carolina based on the support of poor, rural whites. By the 1880s and 1890s, Tillman had become the quintessential Up-Country white supremacist opposed to the genteel "Bourbons" represented by Low-Country white elites such as Wade Hampton. Kantrowitz, *Ben Tillman & the Reconstruction of White Supremacy*, 5–6, 64–71, 74, 80–1, 121, 143, 145, 146, 156. See also Melinda Meek Hennessey, "Racial Violence during Reconstruction: The 1876 Riots in Charleston and Cainhoy," *The South Carolina Historical Magazine* 86, no. 2 (April 1985): 100–12; Francis Butler Simkins, "Ben Tillman's View of the Negro," *The Journal of Southern History* 3, no. 2 (May 1937): 161–74; Andrew Slap, "The Spirit of '76: The Reconstruction of History in the Redemption of South Carolina," *The Historian* 63, no. 4 (Summer 2001): 769, 777, 779; Tindall, "The Campaign for the Disfranchisement of Negroes in South Carolina," 217–19.

48 Edgar, *South Carolina*, 407–8; Martinez, *Carpetbaggers, Cavalry, and the Ku Klux Klan*, 212–14; Simkins and Roland, *A History of the South*, 286–8.

49 Edgar, *South Carolina*, 401–6; Poole, "Religion, Gender, and the Lost Cause in South Carolina's 1876 Governor's Race," 577; Wallace, "The Question of the Withdrawal of the Democratic Presidential Electors in South Carolina in 1876," 375; Zuczek, *State of Rebellion*, 167–80, 188–92.

50 William Porcher DuBose and his colleague Burr James Ramage later extolled Hampton's numerous virtues as "a great planter and a hospitable country gentleman" who possessed "statesmanlike genius and immense popularity" in his heyday. William Porcher DuBose and B. J. Ramage, "Wade Hampton," *The Sewanee Review* 10, no. 3 (July 1902): 365, 373. See also Poole, "Religion, Gender, and the Lost Cause in South Carolina's 1876 Governor's Race," 578. For some white South Carolinians, Hampton, despite his often-touted virtues, was objectionable owing to his "well-known moderation toward the Federal government and his kindly attitude toward the Negroes." The quote is from Wallace, "The Question of the Withdrawal of the Democratic Presidential Electors in South Carolina in 1876," 374.

51 Andrew, *Wade Hampton*, 371–6; Edgar, *South Carolina*, 402–5; Poole, "Religion, Gender, and the Lost Cause in South Carolina's 1876 Governor's Race," 578–9; Simkins and Woody, *South Carolina During Reconstruction*, 498–9; Richard Zuczek, "The Last Campaign of the Civil War: South Carolina and the Revolution of 1876," *Civil War History* 42, no. 1 (March 1996): 27; Zuczek, *State of Rebellion*, 167–80.

52 Quoted in Zuczek, *State of Rebellion*, 167. See also Andrew, *Wade Hampton*, 376–8, 382–91; Edgar, *South Carolina*, 403–4; Poole, "Religion, Gender, and the Lost Cause in South Carolina's 1876 Governor's Race," 581; Slap, "The Spirit of '76," 774, 776–7; Wallace, "The Question of the Withdrawal of the Democratic Presidential Electors in South Carolina in 1876," 375; Zuczek, "The Last Campaign of the Civil War," 19–20.

53 Edgar, *South Carolina*, 404–5; Martinez, *Carpetbaggers, Cavalry, and the Ku Klux Klan*, 211–12; Zuczek, *State of Rebellion*, 192–5.

54 Andrew, *Wade Hampton*, 396–7; Burton, "Race and Reconstruction," 44; Edgar, *South Carolina*, 404; Ronald F. King, "Counting the Votes: South Carolina's Stolen Election of 1876," *Journal of Interdisciplinary History* 32, no. 2 (Autumn 2001): 186–7; Simkins and Woody, *South Carolina During Reconstruction*, 453–4; Zuczek, *State of Rebellion*, 193–4.

55 Edgar, *South Carolina*, 404; Zuczek, "The Last Campaign of the Civil War," 28–9; Zuczek, *State of Rebellion*, 196.

56 Andrew, *Wade Hampton*, 405, 408, 409–15; Edgar, *South Carolina*, 404–6; Simkins and Woody, *South Carolina During Reconstruction*, 529–33.

57 Hayes's decision to remove federal troops from South Carolina, among other states, may have been the result of a "corrupt bargain" propagated by a hastily established electoral commission that decided, along party lines, to swing the election away from the Democrat, Samuel J. Tilden, to the Republican Hayes. This conclusion has been a point of contention since 1876. Andrew, *Wade Hampton*, 418–22; Cassandra Maxwell Birnie, "Race and Politics in Georgia and South Carolina," *Phylon (1940 1956)* 13, no. 3 (Third Quarter 1952): 238; Edgar, *South Carolina*, 405–6; King, "Counting the Votes," 171; Martinez, *Carpetbaggers, Cavalry, and the Ku Klux Klan*, 209–10, 12; Simkins and Roland, *A History of the South*, 287–8; Simkins and Woody, *South Carolina During Reconstruction*, 533–41; Zuczek, "The Last Campaign of the Civil War," 30–1; Zuczek, *State of Rebellion*, 201.

58 Quoted in Foner, *Reconstruction*, 588. See also Edgar, *South Carolina*, 407–29; John Hope Franklin, *Reconstruction: After the Civil War* (Chicago: The University of Chicago Press, 1961), 222–3; Lewis Gould, *Grand Old Party: A History of the Republicans* (New York: Random House, 2003), 75–6; George C. Rable, *But There Was No Peace: The Role of Violence in the Politics of Reconstruction* (Athens: University of Georgia Press, 1984), 151; Simpson, *The Reconstruction Presidents*, 199–200. The questions of precisely when the Civil War ended and when Reconstruction began and ended are open to interpretation and debate. See, for example, William A. Blair, "Finding the Ending of America's Civil War," *The American Historical Review* 120, no. 5 (December 2015): 1753–66; Aaron Sheehan-Dean, "The Long Civil War: A Historiography of the Consequences of the Civil War," *The Virginia Magazine of History and Biography* 119, no. 2 (2011): 106–53; Brooks D. Simpson, "Mission Impossible: Reconstruction Policy Reconsidered," *Journal of the Civil War Era* 6, no. 1 (March 2016): 85–102; Brook Thomas, "The Unfinished Task of Grounding Reconstruction's Promise," *Journal of the Civil War Era* 7, no. 1 (March 2017): 16–38; Vorenberg, *Lincoln's Peace*. See also "The Equal Justice Initiative (EJI)," in *Reconstruction in America: Racial Violence after the Civil War, 1865–1876* (Montgomery, AL: EJI, 2020).

59 Edward J. Blum, *Reforging the White Republic: Race, Religion, and American Nationalism, 1865–1898* (Baton Rouge: Louisiana State University Press, 2005), 7.

6

"Shall the Church of God Catch the Evil Infection?"

The Postwar Episcopal Church in the South Carolina Diocese

The story of the South Carolina Episcopal Church is partially a story of numbers. The church witnessed a notable increase in membership between 1840 and 1850, especially among the Black population. During that decade, the number of white communicants rose from 1,936 to 2,659—a 35 percent increase—but Black communicants ballooned up 130 percent, from 973 to 2,247. Although the total numbers were not large compared with other denominations, the growth was at least partly a function of church leaders' diligent efforts to recruit Black communicants. Bishop Christopher Gadsden took seriously the church's mission to minister to Blacks, especially enslaved peoples. As one commentator observed, Bishop Gadsden "constantly thought of the quarter of a million slaves in those districts in the state where there were no congregations at all."[1]

Bishop Gadsden died in 1852. Thomas Frederick Davis, rector of Grace Church in Camden, South Carolina, succeeded him. Davis was elected bishop on Friday, May 6, 1853, during balloting in St. Michael's Church in Charleston. He was consecrated in New York City on October 17 of that year. At the inception of Davis's tenure, the Protestant Episcopal Church of South Carolina had sixty-nine clergymen in the diocese and fifty-six organized congregations. For the next eighteen years, during the antebellum days, the Civil War, and much of the Reconstruction era, Davis guided his church during the most turbulent decades of the nineteenth century.[2]

The new bishop continued his predecessor's efforts to attract Black communicants. To ensure that a record of the progress was preserved, church leaders amended the diocesan canons so that "the white and colored persons shall be reported distinctively." The change allowed Davis to report on the slow, steady progress of the church in the early years of his episcopacy.³

By 1857, Bishop Davis reported that the "whole number of persons, confirmed since the last Convention, is: white 245, colored 628, in all, 873." The growth among Blacks was impressive, although Davis recognized that he could not say with certainty that the growth was as dramatic as the numbers suggested. "I have been endeavoring to collect statistics of

Thomas Frederick Davis served as the Episcopal Bishop of South Carolina from 1853 until 1871. Courtesy of Reading Room 2020, Alamy Stock Photo and the Library of Congress.

our operations among the colored people; but they are yet imperfect," he confessed. Nonetheless, based on the data he had compiled, the bishop concluded that forty-five chapels or places of worship for slaves with 150 lay persons were involved in catechetical instructions.[4]

A year later, the diocesan convention established a committee to determine whether Episcopal clergymen could unite enslaved persons in marriage. Reporting in 1859, the committee recognized that in "the Diocese of South Carolina, the relation of husband and wife has always been regarded with the highest favor." The committee listed the reasons, "municipal" and "divine," that marriage is a crucial institution. "With this high estimate of the marriage relation before us as citizens, we are now called upon as Christians, to inquire into the nature of the marriage relation between slaves," the report stated. It was a significant question, testing whether the sanctity of marriage superseded laws treating enslaved persons as property. Property, after all, cannot marry other property.[5]

Despite the obvious inconsistencies in these positions, the report found that

> it follows that the marriage relation between slaves has the same divine obligation as that between masters and mistresses. It follows, with equal clearness that the injunction, that no man shall put asunder husband and wife, is as universal in extent as the marriage relation itself. The duty of every Christian master is thus ascertained with the certainty which attaches to divine precepts. He is bound to preserve inviolate the marriage tie between his slaves, and to prevent, as far as in him lies, the separation of husband and wife.[6]

It was an extraordinary statement. Taken to its logical extreme, the committee's position undermined a fundamental justification for slavery. If slaves could marry and their union was recognized by God, a slave master would seem to be violating "divine precepts" when he sold enslaved persons and broke up a family. The church recognized "that no man shall put asunder husband and wife," and a slave owner was "bound to preserve inviolate the marriage tie between his slaves."

The committee backed away from a full-frontal assault on the peculiar institution. "The State has deemed it wise and expedient to vest in the master absolute authority over the slave," the report observed. Absolute authority was sometimes necessary in social relations, as with a parent and child or a husband and wife.

> A Christian master will, of course, exercise his authority in conformity to the law of God. But among masters who do not recognize the force of Christian obligation, there will be abuses in this as in other social relations. From these abuses as well as from other causes, separations of

husband and wife will occur; and these separations give rise to questions, the solution of which requires grave and prayerful consideration.[7]

Governments establish legal relationships, and the state of South Carolina "for wise and sufficient reasons" created the legal institution of slavery. Therefore, the church has no authority to intervene in a legal relationship between master and slave. The punishment for separating enslaved husbands and wives would occur outside the realm of government. The report concluded that "If that master should disregard the commands of God and be led by caprice or self-interest to separate those who are lawfully joined together in marriage, he incurs all the consequences of his act, and must answer for it to the Final judge."[8]

The committee's report would typically serve as the basis for one or more resolutions adopted by the diocesan convention, but the 1859 report never passed as a resolution. Like the rest of the United States, the church's activities were suspended owing to the impending split between North and South. Consequently, the report never received full consideration at a diocesan convention. Commentator Albert Sidney Thomas, a southern partisan, argued that the committee's report, even if it was never the basis of a formal resolution, "should effectually dispose of the slander that Southern men were all oblivious to considerations of Christian duty and to the dictates of mercy in dealing with their slaves."[9]

Leaders of the South Carolina Episcopal Church had done little to precipitate the Civil War—most deacons, rectors, and bishops attempted to shield the church from politics—but faced with a fait accompli, they did not hesitate to support the Confederate cause. Bishop Davis and fellow Episcopal leaders expressed enthusiasm for the Southern Confederacy in unequivocal terms at a meeting of the dioceses of Alabama, Florida, Georgia, Louisiana, Mississippi, and South Carolina in Montgomery, Alabama, on July 3, 1861. The participants recognized the creation of the Confederate government as based on "a law of alteration forced by the necessity of obedience to the law of Christ." One commentator described the gathering as a session "marked by a spirit of harmony and mutual respect."[10]

With the commencement of war, the southern Episcopal Church continued serving people of color. During a meeting of church leaders in Columbia, South Carolina, in October 1861, the Rev. Richard Hooker Wilmer of Virginia moved "that the Convention, in view of the present circumstances of the country, recognize with peculiar solemnity the duty of the Church towards the people of the African race within our borders, and earnestly urge upon the ministry and laymen of the Church increased effort for the spiritual improvement of this people." Peter Fayssoux Stevens's willingness to visit plantations and minister to enslaved persons during the war years should be considered in this light.[11]

The service commitment should not be exaggerated. Everyone understood that the "spiritual improvement" of Blacks did not require, and would not tolerate, intermingling with whites. Blacks and whites did not share pews or approach the communion rail together. White Episcopal leaders allowed, even encouraged, clergymen to provide spiritual guidance to Blacks, but improvement had its limits. People of color must never forget their place.[12]

During four years of war, church leaders did not express doctrinal differences with the northern church, but they recognized the realities of a changed political and military landscape. A schism developed owing to necessity. Church leaders living in the South established a separate church because they expected a permanent Confederate government to lead political affairs. One reporter for *The Church Intelligencer* remarked on the most extraordinary level of "cooperation between church and state ever seen in history." The observation was hyperbolic, but it illustrated the enthusiasm with which southern Episcopalians embraced their circumstances.[13]

Everything about the church's wartime ministering to Blacks reflected the Confederate view of slavery as a necessary part of the South's way of life. Church leaders spoke of the "missionary labor" involving "that class of our brethren, who in the providence of God have been committed to our sympathy and care in the national institution of slavery." This statement reflected the long-held belief that the peculiar institution was divine, not a manmade institution design to elevate one class of citizens as it subjugated another. Southern members of the Episcopal Church were obliged to assist these unfortunately enslaved persons as an act of Christian charity divorced from the question of whether the institution should be abolished. Whether any white southerner was self-aware enough to recognize the hypocrisy is a question for debate, but their written statements suggest that they were not.[14]

The devastation felt by the white people of South Carolina at war's end is beyond debate. Southern writers expressed their bitterness in defeat in numerous letters, articles, newspaper accounts, books, and sermons. According to this view, the Southern Confederacy was cut low by superior northern firepower and a willingness to throw warm bodies against ordnance, but the South remained a noble, chivalric place "where old times there are not forgotten." The Episcopal Church suffered that same devastation as other southern institutions, and many clergymen in their sermons reflected the same bitterness as other whites. They frequently wrote of their despair at the loss of a "southern way of life." One commentator summarized Episcopal writings during the immediate postwar period as typical of southerners. "There is to be found the usual defense of slavery on scriptural ground, the arguments of race superiority and the last echoes of the chivalry and pride of the landed aristocracy," he observed. William Porcher DuBose's attitude toward the institution of slavery and the freed people reflects this mindset.[15]

Faced with widespread poverty and despair, church leaders postponed the 1865 Episcopal Church Convention until May. During that spring, the Confederate States of America collapsed, with its military leaders defeated on the battlefield and its political leaders on the run. Only six churches, represented by a handful of clergymen, participated in the 1865 convention. Their reports recognized the challenges created by a prostrated South. In South Carolina, the diocese figuratively and literally lay in ruins. Rev. Peter J. Shand, rector of Trinity Church in Columbia, Shand noted that Union General William T. Sherman's troops had burned his rectory, and with it, the parochial register containing the records of his thirty-one years of service. Similarly, two ministers from Orangeburg noted that Sherman's march had disrupted the congregation to such an extent that "most of the few who were well off among [the] parishioners are now poor" and that "widows and orphans, who had saved little from the wreck of their property in the low country, are stripped of that little," with their families "living on the scraps left by those who had taken from them their supplies for domestic use."[16]

The following year, church leaders attempted to build a new foundation on the ashes of the old. The task was daunting. During the 1866 annual convention in Charleston, Bishop Davis admitted that he had much work to do. His address, which covered the time from May 13, 1864, through February 11, 1866, summarized the desperate plight of most South Carolina parishes. After acknowledging the enormous challenges facing the clergy, the bishop offered a hopeful message. He assured his audience that the "arm of the Lord is not shortened, and His word is not bound." Suffering had long been part of Christian life, but strength could come from deprivations. "I feel a cheerful confidence that the Church will rise and shine and be glorified."[17]

A child of the South, Davis could not ignore the delicate subject of the "diocese in her Confederate relations." He admitted that "I had hoped that it might be the will of our God that we should have an independent, united and self-sustaining Southern Church." It was not to be. Clergymen had to face facts. The Confederate States of America was dead, and his hopes for a southern Episcopal Church died with it. "There is no longer hope," he concluded. The "providence of God has otherwise determined; we will follow Divine determination."[18]

The bishop turned his attention to the problem of Black Episcopalians. As white churchmen scrambled to save what they could of their rectories in South Carolina, the freed people abandoned the church in large numbers. Most accounts record that the number of Black communicants decreased from a high of nearly 3,000 members shortly before the war to 300 by the end of 1865. The majority of those were members of two Charleston churches, Calvary and St. Mark's.[19]

Blacks departing from the Episcopal Church in the southern states often joined the Baptist or Methodist Church. The African Methodist Episcopal (AME) Church benefited greatly from the exodus. In 1856, the AME Church numbered about 20,000. A decade later, it counted 75,000 members. By 1876, estimates placed the number at 200,000. The desire of freed people to escape the religion of their former slave masters and enjoy a measure of control over their spiritual lives was the driving factor in the changes.[20]

Davis proposed a possible solution for the South Carolina Episcopal Church to fulfill "our Christian responsibilities to the colored population of the State." He argued that the wartime Episcopal Church had been very kind to Black congregants, providing spiritual guidance even in the darkest days of the fighting. The problem was that Blacks had heard seditious preaching and had been "carried away by their freedom" as well as the "vague and extravagant expectations they had been led to indulge in." As a result, the freed people risked "a relapse into flagrant hedonism."[21]

To stem the hemorrhaging of Black support, the national Episcopal Church created a Freedmen's Aid Commission as a department within the domestic missions of the church to assist dioceses in their work among Blacks. Davis explained that originally, he had not accepted the commission's assistance owing to the continued split between the South Carolina diocese and the northern Episcopal Church. He recommended that the matter be referred to a special committee to report back on the South Carolina diocese's history of working with persons of color along with recommendations for the future.[22]

Reviewing the declining numbers, the bishop observed that Blacks abandoned the Episcopal Church because they no longer believed that the institution served their needs. They distrusted the white leaders who had supported the Southern Confederacy. To counteract the distrust, he proposed that a Board of Missions be tasked with earning the allegiance of departing Black communicants. He cited five necessary steps. First, the Board would revive and sustain "missions to colored people." Second, the board must organize churches and congregations with mostly Black membership. To ensure adequate teaching in line with Episcopal principles, the Board must establish parochial schools. Suitable Black Episcopalians must be identified to receive the education and training to enter the ministry. Fifth, Blacks must receive appropriate funding and resources to pursue these activities, which might include providing church property no longer used by white churches.[23]

Commentator Albert Sidney Thomas admired these proposals. "When we consider the circumstances in which this action was taken by the Church in South Carolina we cannot but commend the enlightened and Christian spirit that inspired it," he wrote. Noting the "adverse conditions" under which the South Carolina Episcopal Church labored in the early days of Reconstruction, Thomas praised the church leadership, which "might well have decided to leave to those who had brought about these conditions [i.e., northerners and Unionists] the full responsibility of dealing with them." Instead, the church "showed its disposition to share that responsibility and do what lay in its power to follow the dictates of 'duty, interest, religion and humanity' towards the colored people." Considering the criticism of the church's treatment of Blacks seeking to enter the ministry in the Protestant Episcopal Church of South Carolina during the 1860s and 1870s—a criticism voiced by Peter Fayssoux Stevens, among others—Thomas's statement was a powerful if self-serving and selective defense of the postwar church.[24]

The Board of Missions offered its first report during the 1867 diocesan convention, noting that Board members had contacted the national church's Freedmen's Aid Commission for assistance. Establishing schools remained a priority. To that end, the Board had purchased a building in Charleston. The report concluded with a plea for additional resources to ensure the growth of the church in the coming hard times.[25]

At the 1868 convention, Bishop Davis reported on the progress that had occurred during the preceding year, although he acknowledged the difficulties that remained. Many parishes lacked a rector and their buildings were dilapidated. As in previous years, Davis also discussed the loss of Black communicants. "You are aware how large a proportion of the colored population have been lost to our Church; we are not, however, without hope that a more established state of things, and a more mature judgment will bring many home again to their old fold," he said. "Those who remain are chiefly to be found in the congregations of St. Mark's and Calvary in this city, and the mission now in vigorous operation in Middle St. John's and St. Stephen's Parishes, under the zealous and devoted ministry of Rev. Mr. [Peter Fayssoux] Stevens and the congregations also remaining in Upper St. John's."[26]

The 1868 report provided detailed information on the continued loss of Black church membership. "In many of our Parishes (especially in the low country, where this class was most numerous) the falling off in the number of communicants is lamentable in the extreme," the report noted. "In some Parishes where they were numbered by hundreds there are now none. In others the number of communicants has been reduced one half or one fourth." According to the report, in 1860, Black Episcopalians in South Carolina numbered 2,960. By 1868, the number had fallen to 291.[27]

The problems facing South Carolina Black parishes were not limited to declining membership. Everywhere in the state "in many instances no minister of our own church or any other denomination dispenses the word of life to these poor ones of our household of faith, now perishing for lack of knowledge." Even when ministers could be found, they were not always the most qualified or acting in good faith. In those instances, Black church members "are left to the blind guidance of ignorant, and sometimes grossly vicious preachers of their own class and color, whose only commission is a printed license to preach, issued by no authority recognized by any denomination of Christians, North or South." Numerous causes had created these untenable conditions, primarily "political and other influences [that] combine[d] to alienate them from their former pastors, and to deter them from attending their service." Moreover, "the condition of the colored people in many sections of the diocese, physical, mental and moral, is every day becoming worse." It was little wonder that the spiritual life of these men and women was deteriorating, for "in some places belief in false prophets, priests, confessors, sorcerers and other forms of African superstition, has revived, to the ruin in body and soul of its deluded victims."[28]

Although he recognized that little could be done to turn the tide of defections until more people and resources were available, Bishop Davis acknowledged the Herculean efforts of the Rev. Peter Fayssoux Stevens owing to the man's "self-denial, devotion and zeal, which are beyond all praise of men." Davis also singled out the work of a retired clergyman, the Rev. Alexander Glennie of All Saints, Waccamaw, who had done so much to mentor the young Toomer Porter in the early 1850s. Glennie had held services for enslaved persons on plantations for decades, bringing "blessed results" in growing the number of Black communicants before the war. "Alas, for the change in five or six years!" With war's end, Blacks deserted the church by the hundreds. According to Davis, the "religious deterioration" among the freed people "is painful. They have forsaken the way which they had learned and taken to themselves teachers of their own color. Fanaticism and extravagance rule in their religious assemblies to such an extent as to require the aid of the military to keep order and repress violence. There are indications of a return to African barbarism."[29]

These comments explain why leaders of the South Carolina Protestant Episcopal Church vehemently resisted entreaties to allow Blacks to prepare for the ministry. According to this perspective, Black communicants did not possess the ability to serve as church leaders; they were too primitive and backward. Left to their own devices, freed people invariably degenerated into "African barbarism."

During the 1869 convention, held in St. Philip's Church in Charleston, the Board of Missions reported that the Franklin Street School for the children of freed people was up and running, albeit a shortage of funds presented substantial problems. It was a conflicting report. On one hand, the Board of Missions had curtailed operations owing to a lack of sufficient resources. On the other hand, the Board remained optimistic that Blacks could be persuaded to return to the church, especially since the school provided opportunities for the next generation to advance.[30]

As always, Bishop Davis surveyed the landscape and presented an optimistic assessment. "In conclusion, brethren, allow me to express the hope that the light of a better day is dawning upon us. We have, I trust, reached the lowest point of depression, and are steadily advancing upwards." He claimed that the "more settled condition in the affairs of State which is propitious to religious and intellectual culture," coupled with improved finances and growing confidence in the future, suggested that the Episcopal Church would soon rebound from the difficulties created by the war and its immediate aftermath. He also saw "an increasing spirit of return among our colored people to their old homes and churches." It was an astonishing conclusion, either refreshingly optimistic or astonishingly naïve.[31]

Rev. Anthony Toomer Porter offered an encouraging report during the 1870 convention. He wrote that

> I beg leave respectfully to report that the building known as the Marine Hospital, in Franklin street, Charleston, now used as a school for colored children and freedmen, and supported by the Home Mission for colored persons and freedmen, established by the General Convention of the Church in the United States, has been paid for, and is now held in trust by Rev. A. T. Porter, Gr. A. Trenholm and S. L. Bennett, for educational purposes, without distinction of race or previous condition.

Although it was new, "the school numbers some three hundred children, and has been regularly visited by some of the clergy of Charleston, and religious instruction has been given by the same."[32]

As in previous years, Bishop Davis struck an optimistic tone, but he did not avoid unpleasant problems.

> That there is a crisis upon us cannot be doubted: we are compelled to feel it at every point. The old Church of South Carolina is gone—in those particulars, I mean, which gave especial character to its visibility; but with this there was embodied also, be it remembered, its spiritual and eternal influences. In its old forms and realizations, it is more than probable that it can never be reestablished.

The Episcopal Church of old could never be replaced; therefore, something new must take its place. Davis noted that "the reflection carries sadness to many a loving heart, and many a tear has been shed over the desolations of Zion. We are entering, then, upon a new era. It is a time to stop and inquire—'Watchman ! What of the night?' Where is the vision of the future?" Realizing that he would not share in that future and that the end of his tenure was rapidly approaching, Davis urged the convention to elect an assistant bishop who would succeed him in due course.[33]

During the 1871 convention in May, Bishop Davis's last, he reported that the "number of confirmations has been considerably more than doubled, but this does not exactly indicate a corresponding religious progress. More than a hundred of these confirmations were of the colored population, whom I had not been able to visit since the war, and, therefore, do not declare the experience simply of the year past." Considering the declining numbers since war's end, the bishop was pleased. "It was very gratifying to find their strong adherence to our Church and their very cordial welcome to its ministers," he stated. "I am persuaded that there is a returning disposition among these people towards our communion and solicit the particular aid of the Clergy in encouraging this disposition."[34]

The day after Davis delivered his final report to a diocesan convention, balloting began for an assistant bishop. Everyone understood that the assistant would likely become bishop following Davis's death. Under the rules, balloting would continue until one candidate secured a majority vote from both the clergy and lay orders. Initially, the Rev. Christopher P. Gadsden, rector of St. Luke's Episcopal Church in Charleston and nephew of former Bishop Christopher E. Gadsden, seemed to be the most likely victor. In later balloting, the Rev. William Porcher DuBose emerged as a stronger candidate. When the votes were all tallied, however, the Rev. William Bell White Howe, rector of St. Philip's Church in Charleston, had won.[35]

* * *

Bishop Davis died at his home in Camden, South Carolina, on December 2, 1871. According to plan, Howe had succeeded him earlier in the year. "By special train over the South Carolina Railroad, I attended and officiated at the funeral of the late Bishop, which took place, with every mark of respect on the part of the citizens of Camden, on the 4th of December," Howe noted in his journal.[36]

William B. W. Howe seemed to be an odd choice to serve as a bishop in the South Carolina Episcopal Church. A native of New Hampshire and a graduate of the University of Vermont, he spent his formative years far removed from the South. His father, James Blake Howe, served as the longtime rector of the Union Episcopal Church in Claremont, New Hampshire. The younger Howe was sickly as a child and adolescent. After the young man indicated a desire to follow his father into the priesthood, the elder Howe worried that his son's health would not allow him to enjoy a long career. Rev. Howe introduced his 21-year-old son to Bishop Christopher Gadsden during the 1844 General Convention. The warmer South Carolina temperatures offered a preferable climate for a frail constitution. After the bishop encouraged the young man to move to South Carolina, William B. W. Howe headed off to the Palmetto State. He lived there for the rest of his life.[37]

He started as a lay reader with Rev. Cranmore Wallace, the rector of the parish at St. John's, Berkeley, where Howe "catechized the negroes" at an area plantation. A year later, he became a candidate for holy orders while he continued visiting slave plantations. He was ordained to the diaconate on April 9, 1847, and became Wallace's assistant. On June 3, 1849, Howe was ordained priest and became the rector of St. John's for the next decade.[38]

He spent the 1850s mastering scripture and perfecting his skills as a preacher extraordinaire. It did not hurt his prospects for advancement that he married Catharine Gadsden Edwards, Bishop Gadsden's niece, in St. Philip's Church in Charleston in 1850. Bishop Gadsden officiated. The union cemented Howe's status as an up-and-comer in the South Carolina Episcopal Church. During these years, he spent much of his time ministering to slaves on Low-Country plantations.[39]

Shortly after Howe became the assistant rector of St. Philip's Church in 1861, the Civil War began. Having moved from a rural parish with many enslaved persons to serve a mostly white church in Charleston, Howe proved that he could minister to all classes of people. He also became a slave owner. Although he had once been a New Englander, by the time the war came, in the opinion of his successor, Bishop Ellison Capers, Howe was a tried-and-true southerner. Reflecting on the early days of the war, Capers observed that

> When it burst in its fury upon Charleston, it found the rector of St. Philip's in the faithful discharge of his holy office, in fullest sympathy with the cares and anxieties of his flock, a warm friend of their cause, and as true to South Carolina as if St. John's, Berkeley, had been the place of his birth, and the home of his youth. And why should he not be? He had studied the whole question for himself. He was a *just* man, with the courage of his convictions.[40]

Howe remained a loyal southerner through four hard years of war. He visited sick and wounded soldiers on the battlefield even as he continued ministering to congregants at St. Philip's. A fellow minister marveled that "Mr. Howe ministered with a calm, unswerving fidelity, a gentle tact, a good judgment, a firm hold on his people's affections." The observation was especially noteworthy because Howe stayed with his flock even as St. Philip's was badly damaged by Union shelling during the Union bombardment of Charleston.[41]

His allegiance to the Southern Confederacy was evident in the sermons he delivered during the war. One of the most memorable dated from early in the fighting, on December 15, 1861. After discussing the trials of the biblical Job, Howe urged the communicants not to lose faith in the southern cause no matter how badly the war effort appeared. In his view,

> we are being tried, not punished. God would prove what our faith is made of: whether it is a mere holiday-faith, which lasts only when the sun shines, and when all things are prosperous, or whether it is of that robust nature, which will endure a great fight of afflictions—which is the substance of things hoped for, and the evidence of things not seen. And all

that tries faith most, necessarily takes on the form of our being forsaken of God."

The Union Army had assaulted Charleston, but the South was not beaten. "And so, perchance, this, our city—our beloved city—now so depressed and stricken, shall in 'due time be exalted.' Beauty shall be given it for its ashes, and the oil of joy for mourning: and the garment of praise for the spirit of heaviness."[42]

Despite Howe's efforts to improve morale and his faith in the Confederate cause, the tide turned, and the Southern Confederacy collapsed. By 1865, St. Philip's required substantial repairs. Repeated shelling had destroyed much of the church. Following months of arduous work, however, the church reopened on March 4, 1866.[43]

In a sermon that he delivered when the church reopened, Howe expressed his support for the "justness" of the southern cause, but he was a realist. The war had ended, and the South lay prostrate. Her people had to accept the results. Perhaps most surprising to unreconstructed rebels, Howe urged his listeners to accept the end of slavery and "do all we can to make them [i.e., the freed people] equal to their new responsibilities."[44]

Howe's comment reflected the "enlightened" southern view of emancipation. It was no use to fret over the death of the peculiar institution or resist the new free labor arrangement. No one could deny the changes wrought by the war and its immediate aftermath. The institution of slavery was gone, never to return. The goal was to accept the status of the freed people and assist them in living in the postbellum world. This perspective could be labeled "benign paternalism." It placed Rev. Howe in a difficult position. As subsequent events would illustrate, he was too supportive of the freed people for many southern sensibilities, but not accepting enough of Black leadership within the church for others, such as Peter Fayssoux Stevens. In carving out a middle approach, Howe ultimately satisfied no one.

In the meantime, he was elected bishop on May 13, 1871, and consecrated in St. Paul's Church in Baltimore, Maryland, on October 8, 1871. Surveying the difficult terrain of the South Carolina Episcopal Church, Howe knew that one of his most important tasks was to attract more freed people to the church. During the general convention of 1873, he proposed that "a missionary jurisdiction" should be "erected by the General Convention with express reference to" the freed people

> and let a Missionary Bishop be Consecrated, who shall give his whole time and thought to this work; who, as the executive, not of a single Diocese, but of an entire church, shall organize congregations, provide them with Church schools and pastors, and, in due time, raise up among them the colored people themselves, and to minister to themselves,

RIGHT REVEREND WILLIAM BELL WHITE HOWE, D.D.

William Bell White Howe served as the Episcopal Bishop of South Carolina from 1871 until 1894. Reprinted from William Stevens Perry, The Bishops of the American Church, Past and Present. Sketches, Biographical and Bibliographical, of the Bishops of the American Church with a Preliminary Essay on the Historic Episcopate and Documentary Annals of the Introduction of the Anglican Line of Succession into America *(New York: The Christian Literature Company, 1897), page 208.*

deacons and priests who shall be educated men, and competent to the work of the ministry.[45]

The challenge was to find qualified clergy. A year later, Howe reported on a Black Episcopal Church that had lost its leadership. "Apparently, they were as sheep without a shepherd, and likely to become the prey of wolves," he concluded. Neighboring white leaders had stepped in to assist, but the bishop worried that it would not be enough to retain and grow Black churches in the future. He insisted that the answer lay within the Black community itself:

> The time must come when we must invoke the aid of colored men themselves to preach and minister the Sacraments to their own race, when we must look out from among them men of honest report and full of humility, whom the authorities of the Church may commission and invite into the Ministry, that so they may instruct others; and when such are found competent by education, and well reported of for good works, to teach and be examples to the flock, I will be glad, as far as in me lies, to bid such go and work in the Master's vineyard; for otherwise without their aid, and relying wholly upon a white ministry, I do not see how this Church, which we believe to be Catholic, is to make herself felt among the colored people. Under the most favorable circumstances we shall only win very slowly upon them.[46]

Later in his address, Bishop Howe offered a practical solution building on his remarks from 1873.

> In my address to you last year, I suggested for reflection simply, that possibly the Church's work among the freedmen might be more effectively discharged if undertaken by the Church at large and a Missionary Bishop appointed, rather than, as now, by Dioceses acting separately. The suggestion was not at all a new one but had been several times proposed in our Church papers.

Howe recognized that this proposal was problematic. "It has been suggested by high authority that perhaps the better way would be, and the more Churchly, to repeal the canon against suffragan Bishops, and to introduce them into the American Church, which in many ways is outgrowing the past and that they could accomplish the work," he acknowledged. "The matter, however, was referred by the Board of Missions to a Committee of Bishops, Clergymen and Laymen, who will report to the Board next October, and in this way, if deemed desirable, it can be brought to the attention of the General Convention."[47]

Toward the end of his address, Howe referenced an event that would hold enormous repercussions for the South Carolina Episcopal Church and Black communicants. "You are all familiar with the circumstances, and if I refer to them now, it is only because an omission so to do might be a failure to discharge my whole duty to the flock committed unto me," Howe explained. "God forbid that I should utter one harsh word in regard to my brother, formerly of Kentucky, for we shall stand before the judgment seat, both of his Lord and of mine, and I pray that in that day he may be pardoned for carelessly and needlessly rending the Church of Christ."[48]

* * *

Although he did not mention the man's name, Howe was referring to George David Cummins, assistant bishop of the Diocese of Kentucky in the Protestant Episcopal Church, who had led a group of eight clergymen and twenty laymen in forming the Reformed Episcopal Church (REC) in New York City in 1873. The reformers believed that the Protestant Episcopal Church had changed to such an extent that a new church must be established to correct its deficiencies. The REC would prove to be far more welcoming to Black communicants than the South Carolina Protestant Episcopal Church had been.

The creation of the Reformed Episcopal Church was a reaction to the Oxford Movement that was initiated by High Church members of the Church of England. Dating from the 1830s, the Oxford Movement was associated with the University of Oxford. Proponents sought to restore older traditions in Anglican liturgy and theology. The movement was also known as Tractarianism owing to the publications of several works titled *Tracts for the Times*, published from 1833 through 1841.[49]

Cummins was born near Smyrna, Delaware, on December 11, 1822. His father was an Episcopalian, but he died when George was four years old. The boy's mother remarried, this time to Joseph Farrow, a Methodist preacher. Young Cummins entered Dickinson College in Carlisle, Pennsylvania, at the age of fourteen, graduating as the class valedictorian in 1841. He had thought of practicing law, but a religious revival at Dickinson College changed the trajectory of his life. According to his wife, "It was at this time he gave his heart to God and joined the Methodist Episcopal Church, entering on a life of earnest love and faithful labor for Christ."[50]

During his college years, he discovered a serious health problem. After he collapsed during his senior year, a physician examined him and diagnosed an enlarged heart. Forced to delay his studies while he recovered, Cummins eventually finished college and earned an MA from Dickinson in 1844. He became an itinerant Methodist preacher under the tutelage of a presiding elder, Noriate Wilson, preaching from tree stumps by day and sleeping on trains at night. Considering his precarious health, he might have died from the strain, but he appeared to gain strength as time and his skills progressed. It was obvious to everyone that he was a young man with a gift. "Even at this early age the applause and praise were given him which reached him in so large a measure in later years," his wife explained, "but it did not seem to affect him: his one thought and aspiration seemed to be 'to work for Jesus.'"[51]

He seemed happy in the Methodist Episcopal Church, but slavery became a divisive issue among the Methodists in the 1840s. Cummins's father had owned slaves, and the young man did not seem overly concerned with the plight of enslaved persons. Nonetheless, the Methodist schism undermined the stability of the church. By March 1845, Cummins approached Alfred Lee, the Evangelical Bishop of Delaware, and applied as a candidate for orders in the Protestant Episcopal Church.[52]

Bishop Lee confirmed Cummins at St. Andrew's Church in Wilmington, Delaware, on April 20, 1845. On October 26, Cummins was ordained deacon. Afterward, for almost two decades, he moved around the country to different parishes, first at Christ Church in Baltimore and later, after he was ordained on July 6, 1845, to Christ Church in Norfolk, Virginia. In June 1853, he moved to the parish of St. James's, Richmond. The following year, he was on to Trinity Church in Washington, DC. In 1863, he moved to Chicago and became rector of Trinity Church.[53]

During these years, Cummins perfected his evangelistic style of preaching. By all accounts, he was an inspiring speaker and an intellectually curious church leader. He was not a theologian, nor did he subscribe to a specific dogma or school of thought. Cummins simply believed that the text of the Bible could resolve all major questions without theological adornments or creative interpretation.[54]

Despite his later image as an iconoclast and a rabble rouser, Cummins's reputation during the early years was quite the opposite. Many Episcopalians, clergy and laity alike, viewed him as a reconciler. When the southern dioceses cut ties with the General Convention at the advent of the Civil War, Cummins had bemoaned this decision. He supported the northern war effort, but he did not hold a grudge. Following the southern surrender, he offered a resolution welcoming the dioceses back into the fold without penalizing them for supporting a southern Episcopal Church. His willingness to offer an olive branch to southern Episcopalians was not forgotten when he was nominated to serve as the assistant bishop of Kentucky. He was consecrated on November 15, 1866.[55]

As the 1860s ended, the spread of Anglo-Catholicism disturbed Cummins. He was outraged, in his words, that "a Ritualistic service was introduced for the first time into the Diocese of Kentucky, and the unspeakable trial was placed upon me of being compelled to discharge my official duty in visiting this church and taking part in its services." Despite the "unspeakable trial," he hoped that Anglo-Catholicism could be stopped. In time, he recognized that drastic measures were required to achieve this goal.[56]

Within five years, Cummins believed that a schismatic movement was necessary to reject the gaudy ornamentation of the rising tide of Anglo-Catholic sentiment. Evangelicals must unite, he believed. Considering his ever-deepening reservations, he could no longer serve the diocese. He explained his motivations in a pamphlet, *Following the Light*. "I had watched the rise and spread of the Oxford tract movement until it had leavened, to a vast extent, the whole English American Episcopal Churches, but I firmly believed that this school was not a growth developing from seeds within the system, but a parasite fastening upon it from without and threatening its very life."⁵⁷

His wife echoed this belief in her memoir. Cummins did not abandon the Protestant Episcopal Church and help form the Reformed Episcopal Church for transient causes. "As the years rolled by, and the Gospel of our Lord and Savior became more and more supplanted by the gorgeous ritual and offensive dogmas of Rome, Bishop Cummins was led to think that there was but one way to act," she wrote. "His whole nature was averse to strife, and he came to believe that for the sake of peace, as well as consistency, he must go out from the Church in which, twenty-seven years before, he had so solemnly promised to be a faithful minister!" In his early years as a minister, Cummins had observed "the beautiful but simple ritual of the Protestant Episcopal Church," which "impressed all with its Scriptural simplicity and dignity." Much had changed in the intervening years.

> Now, the strange new "altars" and "super-altars," the "crosses" and "candlesticks," the "credence-tables," the genuflexions and crossings, the forms used in the celebration of the Lord's Supper, the Romish terms of "holy eucharist," the "holy sacrifice," "matins," "vespers," "mass," "chasubles," "maniples," "albs" and "birettas," "priests," and, worse than all, the avowed belief in the "real presence" and "baptismal regeneration," fills every true Protestant heart with sadness.⁵⁸

It wasn't simply a matter of symbols or language, but the rift represented a marked difference in the way the reformers and the mainstream Episcopalians approached faith and church affairs. The reformers sought to simplify their religion and reject "popery." Having tried all manner of conservative reform, they decided that a formal split was necessary. As they noted in the *Journal of the First General Council of the Reformed Episcopal Church*: "On this day, the second of December, one thousand eight hundred and seventy-three, after a meeting of solemn praise and prayer, certain ministers and laymen, formerly connected with The Protestant Episcopal Church in the United States of America, assembled at ten o'clock A.M. in the building of the Young Men's Christian Association, in the city of New York."⁵⁹

The founders set forth a declaration of principles. As a first article,

> The Reformed Episcopal Church, holding "the faith once delivered to the saints," declares its belief in the Holy Scriptures of the Old and New Testaments as the Word of God, and the sole rule of faith and practice; in the Creed, commonly called the Apostles' Creed'; in the Divine institution of the sacraments of baptism and the Lord's Supper; and in the doctrines of grace, substantially as they are set forth in the Thirty-nine Articles of religion.

George David Cummins founded the Reformed Episcopal Church in 1873. Courtesy of the Library of Congress.

A second article held that the "Church recognizes and adheres to Episcopacy, not as of divine right, but as a very ancient and desirable form of Church polity." In a third article, the Reformers noted that

> This Church retaining a liturgy which shall not be imperative or repressive of freedom in prayer, accepts the Book of Common Prayer, as it was revised, proposed, and recommended for use by the General Convention of the Protestant Episcopal Church A. D. 1785, reserving full liberty to alter, abridge, enlarge, and amend the same, as may seem most conducive to the edification of the people, "provided that the substance of the faith be kept entire."

In the final article, "This Church condemns and rejects the ... erroneous and strange doctrines as contrary to God's Word," followed by a list of specific beliefs that the reformers deemed repugnant.[60]

The question of whether the REC represented a schism in the church became controversial. Cummins insisted that it was not. Instead, Cummins and his followers believed that the church had been reformed against Catholic influences, providing a Protestant, Anglican identity under which there could be a "closer union of all Evangelical Christendom." Apparently, large numbers of low churchmen agreed. Within six months of its founding in 1873, the reformed church grew to about 1,500 communicants, two bishops, and fifteen other ministers. In 1875, over 400 Black Protestant Episcopal communicants in the South Carolina Low Country joined the REC as a group.[61]

The reformed church appeared in South Carolina less for doctrinal reasons than because the REC was willing to accept Black members. "It was the spiritual needs of the Colored Episcopalians in South Carolina that were ignored, shunted aside, and given the status of second-class Christians," according to one commentator, referring to the freed people's experiences in the postbellum church. "They were not looking for a free handout. They wanted only acceptance as a Christian community integrated within the Protestant Episcopal Church." Repeatedly rebuffed, Blacks searched for a suitable alternative, which the reformed church provided. Whatever faults the reformed church might have had, antipathy toward the freed people was not among them. The same could not be said of the Protestant Episcopal Church in the southern states during the postwar era.[62]

* * *

Critics of the South Carolina Protestant Episcopal Church pointed to the example of St. Mark's Episcopal Church in Charleston as evidence of the diocese's antipathy toward the freed people. With a membership almost exclusively composed of formerly enslaved persons, St. Marks could be described as a "Black Episcopal Church." In 1875, the church applied for admission to the Diocese of South Carolina. The diocesan convention initially referred the matter to a committee for study with instructions to report back the following year. When the 1876 convention convened, the leadership rejected the application, citing the southern myth that Blacks were not equal to the task of self-governance. As Albert Sidney Thomas explained it, the church elders were naturally responding to the egregious "Black rule," or misrule, that occurred immediately after the war. According to his explanation, "it must be remembered that South Carolina, in common with all the other States composing the Southern Confederacy, had been for seven years subjected to the intolerable experience of the Reconstruction era."[63]

This reaction illustrated the ways in which church matters and political affairs were inextricably linked. Church leaders could not entrust Black members with responsibilities for self-governance in the church because, in their view, Blacks had failed at self-governance in state and local governments during the late 1860s and early 1870s. "The orgy of misrule, oppression and plunder had been going on with cumulative energy and thoroughness for seven years when St. Mark's applied for admission into the union with the convention," Thomas observed.[64] It was little wonder that the St. Mark's application was denied. For "the Church is bound to recognize, in all its relations to the world, and its offices to mankind, that distinction between the races of men which God has pleased to ordain, and to conform its polity and ecclesiastical organisms to His divine ordinance."[65]

Bishop Howe had spent years working with Black communicants before and during the war. As Blacks fled the church beginning in 1865, he had carefully developed a strategy for growing new members among the freed people. It had been slow, thankless, painstaking work. By 1875, the Diocese of South Carolina listed 4,439 members, of whom 829 were Black. This was the largest number of Blacks in the diocese between the end of the war and the beginning of the twentieth century. It represented a steady increase in Black membership since 1865. After the St. Mark's application was rejected, however, the numbers once again declined.[66]

In presenting the application, Howe faced bitter opposition to anything that smacked of equal treatment for people of color. He faced a formidable duo in two lay leaders, Edward McCrady, Sr., and his son, Edward McCrady, Jr. Avowed white supremacists, the McCradys were dedicated to keeping freed people in inferior positions in all walks of life, including the church. They were the leaders, but by no means alone, in a movement to reject Black leadership in the South Carolina Diocese. The senior McCrady served on the standing committee and was a lay deputy to the General Convention. He offered the resolution referring the St. Mark's application to a committee for study. He served on the study committee to ensure that the proper outcome would be reached.[67]

The committee's report reflected the typical racism of the day. Blacks represented a threat to the purity of the white race with the lurking specter of miscegenation. Committee members wrote of the "primitive race of black men" encountered by Europeans centuries earlier. Were it not for the civilizing influence of whites, Blacks would be what they had been so long ago, "petty tribes or kingdoms, warring against, and preying upon each other, from thirst of blood, or rapine."[68]

It was an extraordinary report, laying bare the place and position of the freed people in the South Carolina Diocese. Although the committee did not speak for everyone—two of the five committee members argued in favor of accepting the application—the report was enough to sway the convention. Lest anyone miss the unbridled white supremacy in the decision to reject the application, the writers confessed that

> We believe our race to be the superior race, and do not hesitate to assert and maintain our faith in this truth and intend to conform our ecclesiastical

organization to this faith, and never can consent to give countenance and approval to such admixture . . . . We refuse to recommend to a body of Christian men that which we believe would tend to counteract God's order in Providence or creation, and to obliterate distinctions which He has seen fit to make as manifest and as conspicuous as the sun at noonday, or as the stars at midnight.[69]

To his credit, Bishop Howe argued eloquently in favor of accepting the application. Refusing to seat St. Mark's solely based on race would be uncharitable and unchristian. "You will, I say, in my judgment, do a most uncatholic act, and register the Church in this Diocese as the Church of a caste," he insisted. Establishing only a white person's church would eventually result in dwindling numbers and the loss of church influence on the spiritual life of the community. "I ask you not as Carolinians, but as representatives of the Church in convention assembled—if the two races in this State, under adverse influences, are drifting asunder, one from the other—shall the Church of God catch the evil infection, and instead of trying to put a stay to it, rather add fuel to the flame?"[70]

Howe mixed his metaphors, but his plea was passionate and heartfelt. Alas, he did not win the day. He enjoyed support from a majority of the clergy, but the lay delegations went against him. The resolution rejecting the application from St. Mark's passed. With this act, Howe's work of decades was undermined. He could only offer vague assurances that a separate missionary jurisdiction would allow for a measure of autonomy, but the offer of "Jim Crow" church membership did not appeal to many prospective Black Episcopalians.[71]

Before the 1877 convention convened, the bishop penned a letter addressed to the congregation and vestry of St. Mark's recommending that church members wait patiently for the right time to renew their application. He understood their disappointment, but

> by waiting for calmer times, you may be admitted, not only without irritation to anyone, but, I trust, with the assent of a large majority of all our Churches. My judgment, therefore, is, that for the present year you had better not renew your application for admission into union with the Convention but defer it to a more auspicious time.

This was the typical advice from paternalistic whites to Blacks seeking to exercise their rights: Be patient, wait for a better time, and don't be in such a hurry.[72]

In a reply dated March 19, 1877—three days after the date on Howe's letter—W. H. Berney, the chairman of St. Mark's vestry, agreed with the advice, telling the bishop that the letter "was received, laid before the Vestry, and met their hearty approval." The members of St. Mark's voted that "the expressions contained in the Bishop's letter of the 16th instant stand as the judgment of this congregation." He closed by thanking Howe for "your kind efforts on behalf of the congregation of St. Mark's."[73]

Howe was nothing if not tenacious. He continued his efforts even as he counseled the St. Mark's clergy and vestrymen to be patient. During his address to the convention in 1877, Howe confronted the issue after explaining that a new application was not forthcoming that year. He was characteristically blunt when he remarked that he should "speak a few words in reference to our action of last year in regard to the application of St. Mark's for union with the Synodal body of the Diocese." Indirectly criticizing the McCradys, Howe laid much of the blame for the failure of the St. Mark's application at the feet of lawyers who used their skills parsing the law to identify the obligations of the church.

> And my friends of the legal profession, whose services in behalf of the Church none appreciate more highly than I do, particularly in the Conventions, will, nevertheless, pardon me the suggestion, that their training and habits of mind, through attendance upon the duties of their profession, and in State or national legislatures, tend very strongly to assimilate the functions of a Church Council with those of a State Legislature, as if the kingdom which is *not* of this world must take its pattern here, in all things, from the State.[74]

This was Bishop Howe's version of the admonition to render unto Caesar the things which are Caesar's. The correct reasoning for enforcing legal segregation in affairs of state was not the same reasoning for welcoming freed people into the church. The church should not draw distinctions among people based on their legal or moral worth.

> Now to restrict these functions so as to exclude not ignorant persons, nor profane persons, nor unbaptized persons, but a whole class, and because of race, is in my judgment to pay obeisance to the spirit of the world, and not to the spirit of the Church, which, while it recognizes social distinctions and powers upon any revolutionary and fanatical effort to overthrow them, nevertheless acknowledges at the same time that all men are one in Christ and in His Church, which is His Body, the fullness of Him that filleth all in all.[75]

It was an eloquent plea, but, as with so much of Bishop Howe's work with respect to race, it failed to change many (or any) minds. St. Mark's did not renew its application for membership the following year, or any year thereafter for decades. It wasn't until 1954, long after Bishop Howe's death, that St. Mark's was admitted into the convention as a recognized parish.[76]

South Carolina was not the only diocese in the South struggling with questions over the appropriate place of Blacks within the Episcopal Church. Throughout the 1870s, many southern Episcopal Church leaders struggled with the issue. In 1883, a group of representatives from southern dioceses met in Sewanee, Tennessee, to debate the matter. They recommended that Black Episcopalians be governed within separate missionary districts in each diocese under the direction of white bishops. The General Convention rejected the proposal. Recognizing that Blacks objected to the plan, a majority of the General Convention attendees noted that

> in the judgment of the Committee, the Church cannot too carefully avoid the appearance of drawing lines of classification and distinction between the followers of our common Lord; and they fear that the proposed Canon, if adopted, would tend to such a result, and would produce dissensions in those portions of the Church which were chiefly meant to be benefited by it.

The decision about whether to admit Black districts to regular dioceses was left to the discretion of diocesan leadership in each state. In any event, Black districts would not be represented at the General Convention.[77]

The Sewanee conference was not the last time that Episcopalians discussed the race issue during the nineteenth century. To study the issue, in 1886 the General Convention created a committee headed by Ellison Capers, a clerical deputy from South Carolina who became the bishop of the South Carolina Diocese following William B. W. Howe's death in 1894. The committee's report repeated the stereotypes about needy Blacks who depended on white leadership to direct their efforts lest the poor wretches become misguided. The Sewanee Plan had been rejected, but the paternalistic attitudes persisted.[78]

These questions about the proper role of Blacks in the Episcopal Church confronted Peter Fayssoux Stevens, Anthony Toomer Porter, and William Porcher DuBose following the Civil War. Each man had to decide how he would confront the issue of race. Would he agree that the freed people should be denied leadership roles, or would he follow Bishop Howe's example and press for reforms? If reforms were not forthcoming, would he, like George David Cummins, turn his back on the Protestant Episcopal Church?

Considering the overt racism of the laity and many clergy within the Protestant Episcopal Church throughout the South during the postbellum era—Bishop Howe notwithstanding—it was not surprising that so many Blacks were willing to consider membership in the Reformed Episcopal Church. As recounted in Chapter 7, Peter Fayssoux Stevens became frustrated with the Episcopal Church's attitude toward Blacks. He eventually left the church to join the reformers in 1875.

Notes

1. The quote is found in Albert Sidney Thomas, *A Historical Account of the Protestant Episcopal Church in South Carolina, 1820–1957* (Columbia, SC: R. L. Bryan Company, 1957), 39. See also page 47 for the figures.
2. Ibid., 49.
3. *Journal of the Proceedings of the Sixty-Fifth Annual Convention of the Protestant Episcopal Church in South Carolina* (Charleston, SC: A. E. Miller, 1854), 32. See also John Gary Eichelberger, Jr., "Caught in an 'Evil Infection': Postbellum Conflict in the Episcopal Diocese of South Carolina over the Role of African Americans in the Life of the Church" (master's thesis, University of the South, 2020), 21.
4. *Journal of the Proceedings of the Sixty-Eighth Annual Convention of the Protestant Episcopal Church in South Carolina* (Charleston, SC: A. E. Miller, 1857), 30–1.
5. *Journal of the Proceedings of the Seventieth Annual Convention of the Protestant Episcopal Church in South Carolina* (Charleston, SC: A. E. Miller, 1859), 30. See also Eichelberger "Caught in an 'Evil Infection'," 22.
6. *Journal of the Proceedings of the Seventieth Annual Convention of the Protestant Episcopal Church in South Carolina*, 31.
7. Ibid.
8. Ibid., 33.
9. Thomas, *A Historical Account of the Protestant Episcopal Church in South Carolina, 1820–1957*, 50.
10. The "law of alteration" quote is found in Robert E. L. Bearden, Jr., "The Episcopal Church in the Confederate States," *The Arkansas Historical Quarterly* 4, no. 4 (Winter 1945): 271. The quote "marked by a spirit of harmony and mutual respect" is from Thomas, *A Historical Account of the Protestant Episcopal Church in South Carolina, 1820–1957*, 59.
11. Wilmer's resolution is quoted in Edgar Legare Pennington, "The Organization of the Protestant Episcopal Church in the Confederate States of America," *Historical Magazine of the Protestant Episcopal Church* 17, no. 4 (December 1948): 322. See also pages 309, 313.
12. Gardiner H. Shattuck, Jr., *Episcopalians and Race: Civil War to Civil Rights* (Lexington, KY: The University Press of Kentucky, 2000), 7–9; Thomas, *A Historical Account of the Protestant Episcopal Church in South Carolina, 1820–1957*, 33. See also J. Carleton Hayden, "Conversion and Control: Dilemma of Episcopalians in Providing for the Religious Instructions of Slaves, Charleston, South Carolina, 1845–1860," *Historical Magazine of the Protestant Episcopal Church* 40, no. 2 (June 1971): 147; David M. Reimers, "Negro Bishops and Diocesan Segregation in the Protestant Episcopal Church: 1870–1954," *Historical Magazine of the Protestant Episcopal Church* 31, no. 3 (September 1962): 231.

13 *The Church Intelligencer* is quoted in Bearden, "The Episcopal Church in the Confederate States," 272. See also Lawrence F. London, "The Literature of the Church in the Confederate States," *Historical Magazine of the Protestant Episcopal Church* 17, no. 4 (December 1948): 350–2.

14 The quote is found in Thomas, *A Historical Account of the Protestant Episcopal Church in South Carolina, 1820–1957*, 60.

15 Bearden, "The Episcopal Church in the Confederate States," 274.

16 Quoted in Thomas, *A Historical Account of the Protestant Episcopal Church in South Carolina, 1820–1957*, 63.

17 Davis is quoted in Thomas, *A Historical Account of the Protestant Episcopal Church in South Carolina, 1820–1957*, 64. See also Bearden, "The Episcopal Church in the Confederate States," 273–5.

18 Davis is quoted in Thomas, *A Historical Account of the Protestant Episcopal Church in South Carolina, 1820–1957*, 64.

19 Robert A. Bennett, "Black Episcopalians: A History from the Colonial Period to the Present," *Historical Magazine of the Protestant Episcopal Church* 43, no. 3 (September 1974): 239; George Freeman Bragg, D.D., *History of the Afro-American Group of the Episcopal Church* (Baltimore, MD: Church Advocate Press, 1922), 128; Ronald James Caldwell, *A History of the Episcopal Church Schism in South Carolina* (Eugene, OR: Wipf & Stock, 2017), 16–17.

20 J. Carleton Hayden, "After the War: The Mission and Growth of the Episcopal Church Among Blacks in the South, 1865–1877," *Historical Magazine of the Protestant Episcopal Church* 42, no. 4 (December 1973): 413. The Episcopal Church was not the only denomination to lose Black members. See, for example, Kenneth K. Bailey, "The Post Civil War Racial Separations in Southern Protestantism: Another Look," *Church History* 46, no. 4 (December 1977): 456–61.

21 The quotes are found in Thomas, *A Historical Account of the Protestant Episcopal Church in South Carolina, 1820–1957*, 65.

22 *Journal of the Proceedings of the Seventy-Sixth Annual Convention of the Protestant Episcopal Church in South Carolina* (Charleston, SC: Joseph Walker, 1866), 28–30. See also Eichelberger "Caught in an 'Evil Infection'," 30–1; Thomas, *A Historical Account of the Protestant Episcopal Church in South Carolina, 1820 1957*, 64–5.

23 *Journal of the Proceedings of the Seventy-Sixth Annual Convention of the Protestant Episcopal Church in South Carolina*, 48–9; Thomas, *A Historical Account of the Protestant Episcopal Church in South Carolina, 1820 1957*, 66–7.

24 Thomas, *A Historical Account of the Protestant Episcopal Church in South Carolina, 1820–1957*, 67.

25 *Journal of the Proceedings of the Seventy-Seventh Annual Convention of the Protestant Episcopal Church in South Carolina* (Charleston, SC: W. W. Deane, 1867), 22. See also H. Peers Brewer, "The Protestant Episcopal Freedman's

Commission, 1865–1878," *Historical Magazine of the Protestant Episcopal Church* 26, no. 4 (December 1957): 374; Eichelberger, "Caught in an 'Evil Infection'," 32–3; Thomas, *A Historical Account of the Protestant Episcopal Church in South Carolina, 1820–1957*, 68.

26 *Journal of the Proceedings of the Seventy-Eighth Annual Convention of the Protestant Episcopal Church in South Carolina* (Charleston, SC: Joseph Walker, 1868), 50. See also Eichelberger, "Caught in an 'Evil Infection'," 35.

27 *Journal of the Proceedings of the Seventy-Eighth Annual Convention of the Protestant Episcopal Church in South Carolina*, 96–7.

28 Ibid., 97.

29 Ibid. The quote about Stevens is found on page 98. The discussion of Glennie is on page 89. For more on Rev. Glennie's work, see Susan Markey Fickling, "Slave-Conversion in South Carolina, 1830–1860" (master's thesis, University of South Carolina, 1924), 37–9. The 1868 report also praised the "Parochial School connected with the Church of the Holy Communion, together with the Orphan Home established by the Rev. A. T. Porter," a "noble Christian enterprise, for the relief of suffering, and to afford education to those with whom it would otherwise be impossible." The comments on Porter are found on page 50.

30 The diocese also adopted a resolution proposed by Rev. A. Toomer Porter to merge the Board of Missions into a general Missionary Board of the diocese. *Journal of the Proceedings of the Seventy-Ninth Annual Convention of the Protestant Episcopal Church in South Carolina* (Charleston, SC: Wm. G. Mazyck, 1869), 38–9. See also Eichelberger, "Caught in an 'Evil Infection'," 39–40.

31 *Journal of the Proceedings of the Seventy-Ninth Annual Convention of the Protestant Episcopal Church in South Carolina*, 52–3.

32 *Journal of the Proceedings of the Eightieth Annual Convention of the Protestant Episcopal Church in South Carolina* (Charleston, SC: Walker, Evans & Cogswell, 1870), 33.

33 Ibid., 69.

34 *Journal of the Proceedings of the Eighty-First Annual Convention of the Protestant Episcopal Church in South Carolina* (Charleston, SC: Walker, Evans & Cogswell, 1871), 55.

35 Ibid., 28–39. John Gary Eichelberger, Jr., recounted the circumstances surrounding Howe's election. The new assistant bishop later claimed that when Gadsden realized that he could not win, he withdrew his name from consideration and urged his friends to support Howe. As discussed in Chapter 9 of this book, DuBose considered his loss "one of the fortunate escapes of my life." He eventually left South Carolina to become chaplain and professor of moral science at the University of the South in Sewanee, Tennessee. Eichelberger, "Caught in an 'Evil Infection'," 43–6. DuBose's quote is found in William Porcher DuBose, "Reminiscences, 1836–1878," typescript copy transcribed by William Haskell DuBose, Southern Historical Collection, University of North Carolina at Chapel Hill, 151.

36 Howe is quoted in Thomas, *A Historical Account of the Protestant Episcopal Church in South Carolina, 1820–1957*, 82.

37 Ellison Capers, *A Sermon Preached in Commemoration of the Episcopate of Rt. Rev. William Bell White Howe, D.D., the Sixth Bishop of the Diocese of South Carolina* (Greenville, SC: Shannon & Co., Printers and Binders, 1895), 5–6. See also Eichelberger, "Caught in an 'Evil Infection'," 48–9; *A Historical Account of the Protestant Episcopal Church in South Carolina, 1820–1957*, 83.

38 Ellison Capers, *A Sermon Preached in Commemoration of the Episcopate of Rt. Rev. William Bell White Howe*, 6; *Journal of the One Hundred and Fifth Annual Council of the Protestant Episcopal Church in the Diocese of South Carolina a Held in Grace Church, Camden, on the 8th, 9th, and 10th of May 1895* (Greenville, SC: Shannon & Co., Printers and Binders, 1895), 218. See also Eichelberger, "Caught in an 'Evil Infection'," 50–1.

39 Eichelberger, "Caught in an 'Evil Infection'," 51. In 1856, Bishop Davis traveled with Rev. Howe around plantations and observed his work. "There was here to be observed a manifest improvement in the religious condition of the blacks, this parish, and the last visited show plainly the necessity and benefit of constant and laborious attention to their spiritual interests," Davis noted. Howe was responsible for the "constant and laborious attention." *Journal of the Proceedings of the Sixty-Seventh Annual Convention of the Protestant Episcopal Church in South Carolina* (Charleston, SC: A. E. Miller, 1856), 29–30.

40 Capers, *A Sermon Preached in Commemoration of the Episcopate of Rt. Rev. William Bell White Howe*, 9. Emphasis in the original.

41 The quote is found in Ibid. See also Eichelberger, "Caught in an 'Evil Infection'," 54.

42 Rev. W. B. W. Howe, *Cast Down, But Not Forsaken! A Sermon Delivered in St. Philip's Church, Charleston, December 15, 1861, Being the Sunday After the Great Fire* (Charleston, SC: Steam-Power Presses of Evans & Cogswell, 1861), 13–15.

43 *Journal of the Proceedings of the Seventy-Seventh Annual Convention of the Protestant Episcopal Church in South Carolina*, 49.

44 Howe is quoted in Eichelberger, "Caught in an 'Evil Infection'," 57.

45 *Journal of the Eighty-Third Annual Convention of the Protestant Episcopal Church in the Diocese of South Carolina* (Charleston, SC: Walker, Evans & Cogswell, 1873), 42.

46 *Journal of the Eighty-Fourth Annual Convention of the Protestant Episcopal Church in the Diocese of South Carolina* (Charleston, SC: Walker, Evans & Cogswell, 1874), 46.

47 Ibid., 57.

48 Ibid., 58. See also Eichelberger, "Caught in an 'Evil Infection'," 58.

49 Allen C. Guelzo, *For the Union of Evangelical Christendom: The Irony of the Reformed Episcopalians* (University Park: The Pennsylvania State University

Press, 1994), 13–14, 53–9, 70–1. See also Warren C. Platt, "The Reformed Episcopal Church: The Origins and Early Development of Its Ideological Expression," *Historical Magazine of the Protestant Episcopal Church* 52, no. 3 (September 1983): 5–73; Richard G. Salomon, "Mother Church—Daughter Church—Sister Church: The Relations of the Protestant Episcopal Church and the Church of England in the 19th Century," *Historical Magazine of the Protestant Episcopal Church* 21, no. 4 (December 1952): 427–8.

50 A. M. Cummins, *Memoir of George David Cummins, DD., First Bishop of the Reformed Episcopal Church, By His Wife* (New York: Dodd, Mead & Company, 1878), 13–18. The quote appears on page 16.

51 Ibid., 23. See also Guelzo, *For the Union of Evangelical Christendom*, 89–90.

52 Allen C. Guelzo, "A Sufficiently Republican Church: George David Cummins and the Reformed Episcopalians in 1873," *The Filson Club History Quarterly* 69, no. 2 (April 1995): 119.

53 Cummins, *Memoir of George David Cummins, DD.*, 36–7; Guelzo, "A Sufficiently Republican Church," 119–20.

54 Guelzo, *For the Union of Evangelical Christendom*, 97–8.

55 Cummins, *Memoir of George David Cummins, DD.*, 238, 265–6; Guelzo, "A Sufficiently Republican Church," 122–3.

56 Cummins is quoted in Guelzo, "A Sufficiently Republican Church," 124.

57 George D. Cummins, *Following the Light: A Statement of the Author's Experiences Resulting in a Change of Views Respecting the Prayer-Book of the Protestant Episcopal Church, and of the Reasons for Changing the Direction of Ministerial Labors in the Gospel of Christ* (Philadelphia, PA: James A. Moore, 1876), 8.

58 Cummins, *Memoir of George David Cummins, DD.*, 360.

59 Quoted in Ibid., 432–3. See also Mrs. Annie Darling Price, *A History of the Formation and Growth of the Reformed Episcopal Church, 1873–1902* (Philadelphia, PA: James M. Armstrong, 1902), 119.

60 Quoted in Cummins, *Memoir of George David Cummins, DD.*, 433–4.

61 Cummins is quoted in Guelzo, *For the Union of Evangelical Christendom*, 160. The figures are found in Price, *A History of the Formation and Growth of the Reformed Episcopal Church, 1873–1902*, 154, 241.

62 Herbert Geer McCarriar, Jr., "A History of the Missionary Jurisdiction of the South of the Reformed Episcopal Church 1874–1970," *Historical Magazine of the Protestant Episcopal Church* 41, no. 2 (June 1972): 198.

63 Thomas, *A Historical Account of the Protestant Episcopal Church in South Carolina, 1820–1957*, 88. See also Brewer, "The Protestant Episcopal Freedman's Commission, 1865–1878," 378–9; George F. Bragg, Jr., "The Episcopal Church and the Negro Race," *Historical Magazine of the Protestant Episcopal Church* 4, no. 1 (March 1935): 50; Harold T. Lewis, *Yet with a Steady Beat: The African American Struggle for Recognition in the Episcopal Church* (Valley Forge, PA: Trinity Press International, 1996), 56–7; George

Brown Tindall, *South Carolina Negroes, 1877–1900* (Columbia: University of South Carolina Press, 1952 [2003]), 196–7.

64 Thomas, *A Historical Account of the Protestant Episcopal Church in South Carolina, 1820-1957*, 88.

65 The quote is found in Thomas, *A Historical Account of the Protestant Episcopal Church in South Carolina, 1820–1957*, 89. See also *Journal of the Eighty-Third Annual Convention of the Protestant Episcopal Church in the Diocese of South Carolina* (Charleston, SC: Walker, Evans & Cogswell, 1873), 88, 89; Guelzo, *For the Union of Evangelical Christendom*, 220.

66 *Journal of the Eighty-Fifth Annual Convention of the Protestant Episcopal Church in the Diocese of South Carolina* (Charleston, SC: Walker, Evans & Cogswell, 1875), 150. See also Eichelberger, "Caught in an 'Evil Infection'," 70–1.

67 *Journal of the Eighty-Fifth Annual Convention of the Protestant Episcopal Church in the Diocese of South Carolina*, 19. See also Lyon G. Tyler, "Drawing the Color Line in the Episcopal Diocese of South Carolina, 1876–1890: The Role of Edward McCrady, Father and Son," *The South Carolina Historical Magazine* 91, no. 2 (April 1990): 107–24.

68 *Journal of the Eighty-Sixth Annual Convention of the Protestant Episcopal Church in the Diocese of South Carolina* (Charleston, SC: Walker, Evans & Cogswell, 1876), 33.

69 Ibid., 36. See also Eichelberger, "Caught in an 'Evil Infection'," 76–7.

70 *Journal of the Eighty-Sixth Annual Convention of the Protestant Episcopal Church in the Diocese of South Carolina*, 63.

71 Guelzo, *For the Union of Evangelical Christendom*, 220–1.

72 Howe's letter is reprinted in *Journal of the Eighty-Seventh Annual Convention of the Protestant Episcopal Church in the Diocese of South Carolina* (Charleston, SC: Walker, Evans & Cogswell, 1877), 47.

73 Berney's letter is reprinted in *Journal of the Eighty-Seventh Annual Convention of the Protestant Episcopal Church in the Diocese of South Carolina*, 48.

74 Ibid., 39, 40. Emphasis in the original. McCrady Sr. and his supporters were upset about Howe's comments. Later, they published a statement explaining why they voted to reject the St. Mark's application. McCrady insisted that the Protestant Episcopal Church "is a Race Church. Its policy is constructed upon race ideas, history and sentiment." Quoted in Tyler, "Drawing the Color Line in the Episcopal Diocese of South Carolina, 1876–1890," 112.

75 *Journal of the Eighty-Seventh Annual Convention of the Protestant Episcopal Church in the Diocese of South Carolina*, 42.

76 Caldwell, *A History of the Episcopal Church Schism in South Carolina*, 22; Eichelberger, "Caught in an 'Evil Infection'," 85–6; Thomas, *A Historical Account of the Protestant Episcopal Church in South Carolina, 1820–1957*, 92, 159.

77 *Journal of the Proceedings of the Bishops, Clergy, and Laity of the Protestant Episcopal Church in the United States of America* (Philadelphia, PA: The

Protestant Episcopal Church, 1883), 251. See also Gardiner H. Shattuck, Jr., "'One Fold and One Chief Shepherd': The Sewanee Conference of 1883 and the Beginnings of Racial Segregation in the Episcopal Church," in *Vale of Tears: New Essays on Religion and Reconstruction*, ed. Edward J. Blum and W. Scott Poole (Macon, GA: Mercer University Press, 2005), 53–72; Reimers, "Negro Bishops and Diocesan Segregation in the Protestant Episcopal Church," 232; Rhondda Robinson Thomas, "*The First Negro Priest on Southern Soil*: George Freeman Bragg, Jr., and the Struggle of Black Episcopalians in the South, 1824–1900," *Southern Quarterly* 50, no. 1 (Fall 2012): 80; Tyler, "Drawing the Color Line in the Episcopal Diocese of South Carolina, 1876–1890," 111–13.

78 Shattuck, "'One Fold and One Chief Shepherd'," 67. Capers was Peter Fayssoux Stevens's brother-in-law. See, for example, Peter Fayssoux Stevens, "Autobiography," unpublished manuscript, n.d., handwritten copy, DuPre-Moseley Family Collection, the Kennedy Room of Local History and Genealogy, Spartanburg County Public Libraries, Spartanburg, South Carolina, 65–7. See also Thomas, "*The First Negro Priest on Southern Soil*," 86.

7

"Of Bishop Stevens It May Be Well Said: 'Servant of God, Well Done!'"—Peter Fayssoux Stevens

The Later Years (1865–1910)

By 1865, Peter Fayssoux Stevens had spent much of his ministerial career serving Black Episcopalians in South Carolina, some of whom were free and some of whom were enslaved. Everything changed when the war ended. In that year, 90 percent of the Black communicants left the Protestant Episcopal Church of South Carolina. The church boasted of almost 3,000 Black members in 1860, but one tenth remained in the diocese by war's end. Those who remained were mostly members of two Charleston parishes, Calvary and St. Mark's.[1]

Their decision to depart was not surprising. The Protestant Episcopal Church had been the spiritual home of their slave masters. Now that they were free from bondage, Black people refused to remain loyal to an institution that had served their captors so well. Their lives were difficult enough without remaining members of a church they no longer supported and that did not welcome them. With the demise of the peculiar institution, the freed people faced numerous obstacles, including poverty, racism, and illiteracy, but at least they could seize control of their spiritual lives. It was not a large victory, but it was something.[2]

Despite the declining numbers, or perhaps because of them, Rev. Stevens believed that it was his duty to serve the needs of the freed people. If he could welcome them into the church and encourage them to become leaders in their own parishes, he might arrest the decline and even rebuild a new church from the vestiges of the old. As his descendant Marion Stevens

Eberly explained in an unpublished manuscript written seven decades after his death, Peter Fayssoux Stevens believed that the freed people should be educated in academic subjects as well as in the Christian Gospel. He repeatedly expressed his faith that Blacks would embrace the Protestant Episcopal Church if they could "become ministers of the Gospel to their own people." To that end, Stevens encouraged the freed people to prepare for the ministry.[3]

First and foremost, it was a matter of simple decency. He believed that the leaders of the South Carolina Diocese had made promises to Black church members about the possibility of full membership, but the promises had not been kept. They had been assured that they could become church leaders if they formed congregations and presented "suitable persons for the ministry," as he wrote in an 1875 letter. Yet, to his dismay, they were repeatedly rebuffed.[4]

Stevens's protégés, formerly enslaved persons Frank C. Ferguson and Lawrence [sometimes spelled "Laurens"] Dawson, were determined to become Episcopal ministers and lead Black churches. Stevens assisted them in every way that he could. When Ferguson was short on funds, Stevens paid for the man's education at St. Augustine's College. Recognizing that Blacks would need systematic training to assume leadership roles in the church, he also established two "colored" chapels, Nazareth and Emmanuel, while he served as the rector of Trinity Church in Pinopolis.[5]

In Stevens's opinion, it wasn't simply a fairness issue. Cultivating Black churches and leaders would help the South Carolina Diocese prosper. In his 1868 report at the annual convention, Stevens observed, "If it please God to prosper me and give me the means I will build a Church expressly for this people [i.e., the freed people] when, I make no doubt, many more of the numbers who once were connected with us will again be drawn to us." He had made significant and noteworthy progress. "My labors among the colored people of my other Parish still go on, notwithstanding the moving to and fro; I have at 'Nazareth Church' full congregations with, I trust, an increasing interest on the part of regular attendance and a widening influence on the surrounding population. My communicants there number nearly ninety. My other Church, 'Emmanuel,' is slowly progressing."[6]

A year later, he reported that he had made even more progress. "Since my last report I have been enabled to complete two Chapels for the Colored people," he wrote. "These Chapels were finished about the beginning of October last. The congregations in each have been very encouraging and are constantly increasing."[7]

He compiled an impressive record. By the end of the 1860s, Stevens had established five South Carolina parishes. Bishop Davis certainly was impressed. He described Stevens as a man who worked "with a self-denial, devotion and zeal which all beyond all praise of man." Seldom dissuaded from honoring his commitments, Stevens "sometimes [kept] his appointments on foot" when he could not find a horse to ride.⁸

In 1870, he voluntarily left his position as rector of the Trinity and Black Oak churches in Pinopolis to reopen "old" St. Stephen's, a Black church in Summerville. Through his slow, methodical, patient labors, he nurtured a pool of Black men who could train to become leaders in the diocese. In time, he understood that the Diocese of South Carolina was not prepared to allow Black leadership within the churches, but for close to a decade, Stevens worked to change attitudes among his white brethren.⁹

As discussed in Chapter 6, Bishop William B. W. Howe, who succeeded Bishop Davis in 1871, agreed with Stevens's sentiments; however, Howe could not persuade the lay leaders within the South Carolina Diocese to support him. The heavy hand of Jim Crow was too strong. Try as he might, the bishop could not alter the prevalent racism among the laity in the South

This undated photograph shows Peter Fayssoux Stevens in middle age. Courtesy of the DuPre-Moseley Family Collection, Kennedy Room of Local History and Genealogy, Spartanburg County Public Libraries, Spartanburg, South Carolina.

Carolina Episcopal Church. Howe was devastated when St. Mark's Church applied for full membership in the Diocese of South Carolina but was denied owing to "that distinction between the races of men which God has been pleased to ordain."[10]

The father-son duo of Edward McCrady, Sr., and Edward McCrady, Jr., typified the position of white supremacists in the Palmetto State. Blacks were inherently inferior to whites, and the point need not be argued. Associating with inferior peoples degraded everyone. McCrady, Sr., observed that the "Black man with his kinky hair and the impenetrable veil which conceals his emotions" was useful as a servant, but he must never be afforded an equal station in life. The McCradys practiced law and served in the state legislature in addition to serving as active lay leaders in the South Carolina Episcopal Church. They attended the diocesan conventions for decades and wielded enormous power and influence. Edward McCrady, Jr., donned the uniform of a Confederate military officer during the war.[11]

The McCradys believed, as did many white southerners, that the freed people had proved themselves incapable of self-rule during the era of "Black Reconstruction" in the late 1860s and early 1870s. Allowing them to prepare for the ministry would be calamitous. This debate over race engulfed the Episcopal Diocese of South Carolina well into the 1880s.[12]

As discussed in Chapter 5, the debate over the role of the freed people in the South Carolina Episcopal Church occurred precisely at a time when southern states were "redeemed" in the 1870s. Federal troops departed from the former states of the Southern Confederacy, leaving white southerners, many of whom were unreconstructed Confederate veterans, in positions of power in state and local governments. They used that power to separate people of color from whites, denying formerly enslaved persons the rights and privileges available to Caucasians. Segregation laws kept freed people politically powerless by denying them their basic constitutional rights. Any "uppity" freed people faced the strong possibility of violence inflicted on them and their families.[13]

If segregation worked in political institutions, schools, hospitals, hotels, and restaurants, it could work in churches as well, or so the McCradys and men of their ilk believed. It was only a matter of time before matters came to a head. Stevens had moved to Anderson, in upstate South Carolina, where he encouraged Blacks to seek leadership positions within the church. In a March 1874 letter, Stevens wrote to Frank Ferguson after the diocesan standing committee refused to ordain Blacks in the church. "I am not greatly surprised by the decision of the Standing Committee," he confessed. "It is not your fault. You have shown yourselves anxious for the church and ready to receive it. The fault must lie with those in authority."[14]

In an unpublished memoir, Ferguson recalled that "Rev. Mr. Stevens recommended Mr. Dawson and me to the Bishop, as candidates for the diaconate. The Bishop called us to appear before examining Chaplains of the

Diocese of South Carolina." Although they passed the required examinations, their application "found no favor before the Standing Committee. We were rejected and notified of the same. We waited eighteen months and made a second application and were again rejected. We made also a third application and were rejected a third time." By the end of 1874, Ferguson and Dawson had resolved to leave the Protestant Episcopal Church in favor of the reformed church.[15]

Stevens understood their decision. "Without ministers of their own, only a very few congregations could be served by the two or three white ministers who were trying to preach to the colored people," he recalled in correspondence written in 1892. Repeatedly rejected, the freed people had few options but to find a more hospitable spiritual home.[16]

Late in 1874, Ferguson assembled representatives from Calvary Church in Charleston; Redeemer Church in Pineville; Nazareth Church in Pinopolis; and Bethlehem Church in Oakley to discuss their future, or lack thereof, in the Episcopal Diocese of South Carolina. "Brethren, our object here tonight is a most peculiar one," he told the delegates. "We are here to consider our situation in the Episcopal Church of which we claim to be members. Has not the Protestant Episcopal Church given the Negro a Church or not? I answer, 'No.'"[17]

The indignities that Blacks suffered in the church mirrored the indignities they suffered in all walks of life under the Jim Crow regime. The church was supposed to be special. It was supposed to be a place where people were nurtured, and their spiritual lives were enriched by their worship of the Lord. To stay within a church that treated them as second-class citizens was unacceptable. "Four colored men have been turned away from the doors of her ministry," Ferguson continued. "Where this will end, we do not know. Have we an organization as a church? I contend that we need one for ourselves and our children."[18]

As Ferguson's situation illustrated, Black Episcopalians had few options until the Reformed Episcopal Church (REC) formed in New York City in 1873. The REC grew out of an ongoing controversy about ecumenical activity. Separate from debates among northern Episcopalians concerning the Tractarian Movement, the REC was attractive to southern Blacks. Most Blacks in the church had been raised as Low Church Episcopalians who engaged in liturgical worship and relied on the Book of Common Prayer. The REC would allow them to continue these practices, and most importantly, Bishop George Cummins, one of the REC founders, was amenable to allowing Blacks to assume leadership positions within the church.[19]

Considering the REC's liberal views on race relations, several reformed Episcopalians approached Stevens to gauge his interest in joining a new church. It was easy to recognize the reformed church's appeal for Peter Stevens. Aside from the REC's enlightened approach to race, it lived up to its name as an institution devoted to reform. In time, it became a refuge for lower-middle-class Episcopalians who resented elites steeped in the staid traditions of the Protestant Episcopal Church. One commentator noted that "the Reformed Episcopal Church was turning into a largely lower-middle-class denomination" of "working people." Aside from this ethos, the REC issued statements espousing "social moralism" that served as "a form of protest against the economic misery of the Gilded Age."[20]

Stevens's decision to leave the Protestant Episcopal Church was agonizing. He pondered the move for the first half of 1875. In January of that year, several congregants from Calvary Mission traveled to Pinopolis to confer with Stevens and determine if he would join the REC. Six months later, in June 1875, Rev. Benjamin Johnson, a former Protestant Episcopal clergyman who had joined the reformed church as a traveling missionary-evangelist, visited South Carolina on a recruiting mission. He was aware of Stevens's frustrations regarding the proper role of the freed people in the Protestant Episcopal Church as well as his dissatisfaction with the South Carolina Diocese's racial prejudices. As Johnson later reported, "On the 17th of June I visited Columbia, S.C., by request of Bishop Cummins, to meet and confer with Rev. P. F. Stevens, who has made overtures for work in our Church."

It was a pivotal meeting. "This conference resulted in the decision of Mr. Stevens to return to his old field of labor in St. Stephen's and St. John's, and to take charge of the congregations gathered, as a Reformed Episcopal Minister," Johnson reported. Stevens agreed to assume his new duties in July 1875, which delighted Johnson. "The acquisition of so able and zealous a worker was indeed a valuable advantage to our church," he reported.[21]

Johnson was pleased with his recruiting mission, but Stevens was more conflicted about the matter than Johnson's comments suggested. Despite his disagreements with the Protestant Episcopal Church, Stevens fretted over his decision to leave. The Episcopal Church had nurtured him since he was a child. He had grown up with its customs and traditions. Departing would require him to turn his back on decades of friendships and professional affiliations. He debated the move for much of the year, even after he had pledged formally to join the REC.

Months before Stevens left the Protestant Episcopal Church, the word spread that he was considering a change. His refusal to follow the dictates of the South Carolina Episcopal Church concerning the lack of Black leadership led to a rebuke from his bishop, which surely hastened his departure from the diocese. In a letter dated January 17, 1875, William Porcher DuBose, formerly a minister in the South Carolina Protestant Church but then serving as the chaplain of the University of the South in Sewanee, Tennessee, warned Stevens of the possibility of sanctions. DuBose had served under Stevens in the Holcombe Legion during the war, and the two men remained affectionate friends. Stevens had even named a son after DuBose.[22]

Visiting South Carolina to lay a cornerstone at St. Mark's Church, DuBose penned a letter to his former commander. "My Dear Friend and

Brother," he began, "I have thought much of you since reaching the state, and although there is a chasm between us now much broader than that of mere geographical distances," it was important to maintain a "bond of personal affections" which "have so long bound me to you. However little I may be able to understand and sympathize with the causes you have felt impelled to pursue, be assured that I know you too well to attribute to you any but the purest and sincerest motives." The chasm, of course, developed over their different approaches to dealing with freed people within the church.

Dispensing with the pleasantries, he came to the point. After acknowledging that "my motive in writing is not a purely personal one," DuBose recalled a meeting with Howe where the bishop discussed the possibility of levying "sanctions of deposition" against Stevens. "He spoke with much feeling of the pain it gave him to sever you from our fellowship and asked whether any one of us could show cause which could fortify him in delaying" the sanctions. "The [bishop's] reluctance was echoed by all and much that was affectionate." DuBose insisted that "not one word that was harsh was said about you." Howe asked DuBose and another gentleman "to confer with you one more time before final action shall be taken and we promised to do so."

DuBose came to the heart of the matter. "The only question [I] should ask is one much as this: Is our parting irrevocable and final? I know it will pain you to answer 'Yes' but we are loath to give you up until you force us to do so. And *must* it be so?"

Considering DuBose's lack of sympathy for the plight of the freed people, he could not fathom Stevens's reasoning. "So far as I understand your position (I mean your ones with those of [Bishop] Cummins' Church) the thing which has forced you out of the church is the attitude of this Diocese with regard to the Negroes." DuBose reckoned that "there is a vast amount of work to be done for the Negroes" in the long run, but that was a question for another time and place. For the present, "the Diocese is with the church," and they "command accordingly" that Stevens obey the decisions of the General Convention, no matter how much he disagreed.[23]

DuBose's letter was too little, too late. An exchange of letters between Bishop Howe and Stevens underscored how far Stevens had moved since the beginning of the year. The correspondence began on July 9, 1875, when Howe wrote to discuss Stevens's "Renunciation of the Ministry." Referring to the growth of the REC in the Diocese of South Carolina, Howe told Stevens that "Your friend B. Johnson and others who preceded you in going over to the Cummings [sic] movement" had caused no small measure of consternation. "I naturally thought you intended to do the same," Howe explained. "It becomes my duty to notify you that unless you shall, within six months' time, make [a] declaration that the facts [in the standing committee's report indicating that Stevens had abandoned the PEC] are false, you will be deposed from the ministry of this church."[24]

In a reply dated July 28, 1875, Stevens did not mince words. "Your letter of the 9th would have been answered earlier, but for that I was waiting for certain information," Steven explained. "You forwarded me [the] Resolution of the Standing Committee which state[s] that satisfactory evidence has been laid before them that I have 'abandoned the Commission of the Protestant Episcopal Church' and you notify me that if in six months' time I do not declare the charge false, you will proceed to depose me from the ministry of the church."

By this time, Stevens had already left the Protestant Episcopal Church. Nonetheless, he took issue with Howe's reasons for deposing him. "If by 'Commission' the Standing Committee mean[s] 'Ecclesiastical organization,' then I declare the charge to be true, for I have abandoned the Ecclesiastical organization of the Protestant Episcopal Church." He viewed his churchly duties in a different light. "If by 'Commission' the Standing Committee means 'community of faith and the fellowship flowing therefrom,' I declare I am still under your jurisdiction and should obey your admonitions." Stevens argued that he had not violated any canons of the church. He remained a man of faith devoted to God and Christian principles. He had not failed the church. The church had failed him when it rejected his candidates for ordination based solely on the race of the candidates. No longer concerned with niceties, he sarcastically asked his bishop, "how will you ever depose me? You dare not do it under the canon." In a final bit of insolence, he closed with a caustic comment. "I leave you, Sir, to study the difficulty."[25]

In other correspondence with Howe, he was less abrasive in his language, but his message was no less pointed. "The evidence was too clear to my mind," he explained. Still reflecting on the church's rejection of Ferguson and Dawson for the ministry, Stevens was blunt in his complaint. "That these men were rejected because of their race was . . . apparent." In his opinion,

> my success, and that of others, in winning these people to the Church, despite . . . the Church's position towards them, had convinced me of the impossibility of the two races working harmoniously and effectively in the same diocesan organization. The colored element if fairly dealt with would be in the majority or at least constitute so large a proportion as to excite jealousy and strife.[26]

Stevens felt compelled to join the REC because the reformers allowed freed people to become leaders and form their own churches. In Stevens's view, turning his back on the Protestant Episcopal Church of South Carolina, which had been his home since the 1850s, and abandoning the people and institutions that had nurtured him was necessary, albeit painful. He acted owing to his firm conviction that Blacks, regardless of their status in the postwar South, should be welcomed into the church. "Some day our people will find that the colored man does not wait for his 'white friend' to do all this thinking," he wrote in correspondence from 1875.[27]

"Born and reared in the Episcopal Church, I have ever loved it and will love it to the day of my death," he confessed toward the end of one letter to Bishop Howe. Yet, he must act as a matter of conscience. "Believe me, Reverend Sir, that it costs me no little pain to sever the ties of a life time. If I have erred I need your prayers and ask the forgiveness of you and my brethren for brethren they still are tho[ugh] they may not acknowledge it."[28]

As the correspondence indicated, the rift between Rev. Stevens and the Protestant Episcopal Church could not be repaired. In its 1876 report, the standing committee reported, "After due examination, they [the committee members] have certified to the Bishop the fact that Rev. P. F. Stevens, Presbyter of the Diocese, had abandoned the communion of this Church, without complying with the requirements of Canon V., Section 2." St. Luke's Church in Newberry also reported that on "the 22nd of June, 1875, the Rev. P. F. Stevens resigned his charge of this Church, since which date it has been without a minister."[29]

Peter Fayssoux Stevens officially assumed his duties in the Reformed Episcopal Church, as promised, in July 1875. Four months later, Bishop Cummins visited Charleston and Pinopolis, preaching alongside Johnson and Stevens. Cummins also ordained Frank C. Ferguson, Lawrence Dawson, and another Black man, Edward A. Forrest, deacons in the church.[30]

Bishop Cummins's visit was the highlight of a long, stressful year in Peter Fayssoux Stevens's life. As Cummins's wife recounted the episode in a later memoir,

> November 18th, Bishop Cummins left his home in Lutherville for an extended visit to Charleston, S.C. The year previous a number of congregations, formed of colored people who had been members of the Protestant Episcopal Church, had been received into the Reformed Episcopal Church, and the General Council had appointed the Rev. P. F. Stevens pastor over them all, aided by the colored preachers who had been ministering to them.

Stevens subsequently created the Bishop Cummins Training School "for the purpose of educating the colored preachers more thoroughly, and to prepare them for Holy Orders in the Reformed Episcopal Church." For his part, "Bishop Cummins had always felt a deep interest in this neglected race, and it was with great pleasure he undertook this journey, that he might be with them for several weeks."[31]

Cummins found a receptive audience. "As the representative of our dear Church I have received in this city the most cordial and hearty welcome," he told one crowd of well-wishers.

Clergymen of all Evangelical churches have come forward to greet me and bid me God-speed. Many churches have been opened to me, and I have been urged to preach in their pulpits. On the morning of Sunday, November 21st, I preached in the Central Methodist Church, and at night to our own colored congregation at Trinity Church. The congregation numbered over a thousand colored people, and I never spoke to a more attentive audience.[32]

Cummins recorded that "Sunday last I ordained the first clergyman of the Reformed Episcopal Church from among the ranks of the freedmen of the South." He was referring to Frank Ferguson. The date of Ferguson's ordination was December 5, 1875, just over a year after the freedman had met with the four Black missions of the Protestant Episcopal Church.[33]

"Sunday morning dawned with cloudy, threatening weather, but the church was filled by our colored friends," Cummins later recorded.

Mr. Stevens read the service, and I preached. The candidate for deacon's orders was presented by Rev. Mr. Johnson. The newly ordained deacon, Mr. Frank C. [Ferguson], was an earnest and faithful worker in the Protestant Episcopal Church among his race and is highly esteemed by both the white and colored people among whom he resides. He has been preparing himself by study for the ministry, while teaching a large school for colored children.

Cummins was pleased at the progress that Stevens and Johnson had achieved, but he reserved special praise for the freed people. "It was a pleasant sight to me to see these people worshipping in their new church, built by themselves after they had been driven from their former place of worship for uniting with us."[34]

Following his visit, Bishop Cummins commented that "[o]ur interest in the colored people of the South could not have fallen into better hands than those of our dear brothers, Johnson and Stevens. They were not carpetbaggers, but native Southerners so thoroughly identified with the South as to have been in the Confederate Army." In Cummins's opinion, Johnson's and Stevens's commitment to the spiritual needs of the freed people demonstrated that the reformed church "pays no regards to politics."[35]

Within six months of assuming his duties, Stevens became the "Pastor of all the Colored churches" within the Special Missionary District of the South—the REC designation for Black churches—with the departure of Rev. Johnson. In the words of one commentator, "A new era began for the Freedmen of South Carolina." They still faced innumerable challenges in their daily lives, but their participation in the Reformed Episcopal Church was guaranteed. "Now they were free to preach the Gospel, to prosper, and to grow unhindered."[36]

Because the REC originated in the northern states, the church remained strongest above the Mason-Dixon Line. Nonetheless, church leaders anxiously followed the growth of congregations in the South. Recognizing the REC's expansion in South Carolina, Stewart L. Woodford, a prominent layman, donated $3,000 to continue mission work in Georgia and South Carolina. In 1877, Stevens received $1,500 from the church for his continued work with the freed people.[37]

Bishop Samuel Fallows visited Stevens frequently, and his praise typically was effusive. "I found the Churches under the care of Rev. P. F. Stevens enjoying marked prosperity," he reported following an 1877 visit.

> Nearly all of the fourteen parishes and congregations of which he has the oversight have church edifices, erected by the means or labor of their own communicants. Under the competent leadership of our honored brother, these Churches, with their own ordained Deacons and Presbyters, will increase in number and usefulness, without imposing any additional burden upon the Missionary Treasury of the Church.[38]

The following year, Fallows returned. "The Rev. P. F. Stevens has the charge of sixteen congregations," he later wrote. "As I accompanied him to the rice plantations and through the pine woods of South Carolina, I learned of the high regard in which he is held, both by the white planters and the people of color." Everyone in the church "recognized the great services Mr. Stevens was rendering them personally by his laborious, self-denying efforts among the freedmen." Fallows lavished numerous compliments on Stevens, culminating with a comment reflecting the flowery language of the day.

> If there were more men like Mr. Stevens in every Southern State, men of birth, culture and high social standing, men Southern born, and filled with the spirit of the Gospel of love and reconciliation, toiling patiently for the elevation of these wards of the nation, there would be no exodus of the colored race from the States where they are most needed and the land which is their most congenial home.[39]

The approbation with which the white and Black people of South Carolina held Stevens was ever more remarkable when considered in the context of the times. Jim Crow laws and customs usually limited interactions between the races. Even when they did mix, it was an uneasy alliance. The Low Country was not as torn by racial strife as some areas of interior South Carolina—places where the Ku Klux Klan had run rampant once upon a time—but Black people seldom emerged from the interaction better off than they were before. With his commitment toward improving the lives of the freed people, however, Stevens established a level of trust usually missing in Black-white relations.[40]

As a reward for Stevens's steady leadership, in May 1879, the General Council elected him the missionary bishop to the Special Jurisdiction of the South. Bishop W. R. Nicholson, with Bishop Samuel Fallows assisting, consecrated Stevens at the Second Reformed Episcopal Church in Philadelphia on June 22, 1879. At the time, Stevens had forty stations in South Carolina under his care, which included thirteen ordained ministers and 1,500 communicants.[41]

Never satisfied to rest on his laurels, the missionary bishop traveled constantly for decades, including numerous fundraising trips north of the Mason-Dixon Line. Although he appreciated contributions from northern churches, Stevens recognized the importance of building self-sustaining churches that were not overly beholden to their northern brethren. He also realized that fast-growing Black churches required new leadership. In 1876, he helped to establish the Bishop Cummins Training School, a seminary for Black Episcopalians who were barred from attending white seminaries. During its early years, the school moved from place to place as Stevens headed to new ministries.[42]

Bishop Stevens spent the next three decades ministering in the South Carolina Low Country in and around Charleston except for brief interludes. Self-effacing and quiet, he went about his work with little fanfare. His reports listed slow, steady progress as he gradually attracted Blacks to the reformed church. The 1883 report was typical of his matter-of-fact statements highlighting his accomplishments. "The condition of the Special Jurisdiction of the South is as follows," he wrote: "bishop; 5 presbyters; 7 deacons; 3 students looking to the ministry; 2 applicants to be admitted into the Training School next fall; 19 lay preachers; 20 congregations; 11 missions, 27 church buildings; 1500 communicants; 37 Sunday-school teachers, and 506 Sunday-school scholars."[43]

From 1885 until 1889, he served as the temporary bishop in charge of the Synod of Canada. "The Jurisdiction of Canada is very extensive, and the expense of traveling from the extreme churches, so great, that the Synod had not met since its organization," he reported. "After consultation with the brethren, it was deemed necessary that a meeting of the Synod should be held, and it was called for the latter part of September 1885. The meeting had a very happy and encouraging influence." By the following year, every congregation save one had improved markedly.[44]

As for the Special Jurisdiction of the South, Stevens reported to his brethren that the "work of this Jurisdiction, as you will remember, is entirely missionary among the colored people of the South; most of those whom we have reached being in very humble circumstances. The growth of the work has been slow, but I trust healthful." He acknowledged that the "older parishes have not gained much in numbers, but are more stable, and in most instances have improved their church property. The area of our operations is gradually extending. Through increased means placed at my disposal, sites have been purchased and buildings erected at new points, and we look for a larger development the coming year."⁴⁵

His annual reports delivered during the REC general councils continually reflected his zeal for the mission. Stevens traveled almost nonstop, lecturing and preaching in South Carolina as well as in neighboring southern states. He was especially proud when he ordained his son, William D. Stevens, to the diaconate on August 5, 1888. During the 1880s and 1890s, he also devoted much of his energy to his family, reveling in his grandchildren.⁴⁶

Stevens persevered despite numerous setbacks. The 1886 Charleston earthquake did not damage many REC church buildings, but an 1893 hurricane caused extensive damage, as did a nationwide financial panic that same year. He reported that "last fall, just as the harvests were about to begin, two of the most destructive storms that have ever visited our coast swept over a large part of the State." In surveying the damage, he concluded that some areas "suffered more severely than others, all have been more or less seriously injured and depressed. Several of our church buildings have been blown down or injured, only two or three of which have been repaired. In addition to this special cause, the general financial depression of the country has affected our people also." Despite these challenges, Stevens refused to succumb to despair. He was a man of faith, and he hoped "for God's favor in the coming harvests of this year and look for evidence of the people's gratitude in a liberal support of the cause."⁴⁷

Although slowed by advancing age and a variety of ailments, Bishop Stevens never ceased working with Black congregations. One commentator noted that in "1892, Rev. J. S. Mobley, an Elder of the African Methodist Church, in Charleston, S. C, came into our communion, with eighty members, under the name of the Mt. Pisgah Reformed Episcopal Church. The work among the colored brethren under Bishop P. F. Stevens, D. D., steadily increased, the total number of communicants in 1894 being 1900."⁴⁸

Despite his devotion to Black communicants, Stevens apparently could not sustain his legendary work ethic. One commentator lamented that it "is unfortunate that Bishop Stevens, in later years, appeared to lose the fire and zeal of the early period." The change was hardly surprising, for Stevens's health declined during the 1890s. To compound his misery, his wife, Mary, died in 1894. The following year, he married again, and his second wife, Harriet Rebecca Palmer, tended to him in his dotage.⁴⁹

He soldiered on even as his health and energy diminished. In his 1897 report to the General Council, which covered the period from May 16, 1894, through May 12, 1897, Stevens wrote that he had "preached, lectured, and held official services in my Jurisdiction 275 times," confirming 249 people. "There are 16 Congregations entitled to representation in this Council, and 24 Missions numbering 1,295 Communicants in good standing, and about 2,000 adherents in all."

He claimed that declining church membership was not necessarily negative. "This number of Communicants is smaller than that of my last report and would seem to indicate a loss of strength in the work," he admitted. The numbers were deceptive. "I think it really indicates an increase of strength, for the number of our adherents is no less than before; but we have been endeavoring to cut off from our list of working members all who are negligent and non-contributing."[50]

As the years passed and Stevens aged, he suffered numerous losses. Perhaps the greatest loss of all occurred when his longtime protégé Frank C. Ferguson died. Depressed and feeling his age, Stevens reported that his friend and colleague "departed this life on the 7th of April 1901, from the City of Charleston, at the age of fifty-four years." The loss was almost more than he could bear. "The Convocation owes its existence to him more than any other man," he reflected. By this time, Stevens was suffering another major loss, namely his eyesight. He eventually became completely blind.[51]

Aside from his church duties, Stevens always championed education. In 1877, he led a movement to revive his alma mater, The Citadel, which had been shuttered since the war. Stevens assembled a group of nine alumni who petitioned the state legislature to reopen the school. After much lobbying and political maneuvering, the new Citadel opened in 1882. Beginning in 1878, Stevens also served as the commissioner of Charleston County Schools. In 1890, he became a professor of mathematics at the all-Black Claflin College, a position that he held until 1896. Claflin's president later remarked of Stevens that "[h]e has devoted the best years of his life to the work of educating the colored youth and fully sympathizes with them in their efforts to improve themselves."[52]

Throughout his tenure as a REC missionary bishop, Stevens was a vocal supporter of parochial schools. His plans were realized in 1889, when the Reformed Episcopal Parochial School opened on Nassau Street in Charleston. Public education for Black children was virtually nonexistent during the nineteenth century, but the Nassau Street school was created to change this trend. According to one commentator, "Bishop Stevens was socially ostracized from the white community for his founding of this school."[53]

Suffering from ill health in the early years of the twentieth century, he eventually stepped away from his duties in 1909. A year earlier, Stevens reported that his routine continued "as usual until May 22nd, when I experienced a fall from a staircase at my home, which gave a severe shock to my whole system." He recovered from the fall but "on Sunday, June 2nd, I was partially stricken with paralysis and was confined to my bedroom the whole week." The time had come to retire. "I notified the Presiding Bishop [Samuel Fallows] in June that I felt myself unable to continue the discharge of my duties and sent in my resignation. The Bishop advised me to hold on

Peter Fayssoux Stevens served Black communicants in the Reformed Episcopal Church for almost thirty-five years. He is pictured here in old age. Courtesy of the DuPre-Moseley Family Collection, Kennedy Room of Local History and Genealogy, Spartanburg County Public Libraries, Spartanburg, South Carolina.

until next May, when the meeting of the General Council will take place; I did so and have so far been doing what I could."[54]

Somehow, Stevens limped on for almost a year. Finally, on May 21, 1909, the General Council voted to accept his resignation. In recognition of his stellar service, members voted to designate him a bishop emeritus so that he could continue drawing his $1,200 annual salary.[55]

Unable to attend the 1909 meeting, Stevens was nonetheless in the hearts and prayers of his colleagues. The General Council passed a resolution stating:

> WHEREAS, Our beloved Bishop P. F. Stevens, D. D., is unable to meet with us in this General Council of our Church on account of physical infirmity; be it therefore RESOLVED, That this, the Nineteenth General Council of the Reformed Episcopal Church, hereby expresses its great regret that we shall miss from the Council one who is so dear to all our hearts. We shall miss his words in behalf of the work to which God has for many years called him, and in which He has so abundantly blessed him, for he has made him "a workman who needeth not to be ashamed." May God bless him and prosper the work which will ever stand as a monument of the power of God working through a consecrated life.[56]

To no one's surprise, the bishop emeritus did not live long following his resignation. Stevens died on January 9, 1910, at age seventy-nine. During the 1912 meeting of the General Council, the Reformed Episcopal Church memorialized the late bishop. The encomiums ended with an eloquent recognition of his work among the freed people:

> The unique work of Bishop Stevens, all his other multifarious and efficient labors being incidental, was the planting and nurturing of churches of Jesus Christ among the Freedmen, in which our orderly forms of worship should be used. He was evangelist, teacher, counsellor, friend, pastor, bishop, of a handful at first, increasing to a host, comprising over one-fourth of the communicant membership of the Reformed Episcopal Church. In our Church paper he was rightly called "Bishop, Hero and Saint." True as steel, fearless, untiring, enthusiastic, uncomplaining in his later years of blindness, apostolic in faith and zeal to the end of the well-nigh four score years of his noble life, Bishop Stevens left his generation better when he departed to be with Jesus.[57]

Newspaper reporter I. E. Lowery lauded the "Rt. Rev. Bishop P. F. Stevens, D.D." as unforgettable. "What South Carolinian is there who lives within the bounds of this State that has not heard of this good and great man? Bishop Stevens is a white man who has devoted his best days of his life to the education and elevation of the negro." Whatever else could be said about Stevens, Lowery cited "an undisputable fact" that the bishop had performed "great work in South Carolina, Georgia, and Florida for the negro race. And because of this noble work, which he, through the Providence of God, has been enabled to do among them, they love him, they idolize him."[58]

Stevens's successor, Robert Livingston Rudolph, recalled in his 1912 report that "I received word that Bishop Stevens had been called to his eternal reward. When I saw him, on the occasion of my first visit to the Jurisdiction [in December 1909], Bishop Stevens was in very feeble health. Notwithstanding his extreme weakness, he was consumed with a desire to return to the work he loved so much." Despite his declining health and blindness, Stevens remained engaged with the church until the end of his life. Rudolph concluded, "Of Bishop Stevens it may be well said: 'Servant of God, well done! Rest from thy loved employ. The battle fought, the victory won, Enter thy Master's joy.'"[59]

In recognition of the bishop's long, devoted years of service, the church agreed to provide his widow with financial assistance. "The Rt. Rev. P. F. Stevens, D. D., of honored memory, passed to his reward in the early part of the Council period," the Council minutes noted in 1912. "Following the precedent set in the case of the death of Bishop Latane, the salary of Bishop Stevens was paid to his widow, Mrs. H. R. Stevens, until the first of January 1911." She received $1,200 for the year following Bishop Stevens's death and $500 a year thereafter until the General Council assembled again in 1915.[60]

During Stevens's funeral, Black members of the Reformed Episcopal Church honored the man who had done so much for them. "The pallbearers will be negro ministers in the church, whose doctrines he taught for so many years to the negroes of South Carolina," the *State* newspaper reported. Stevens was laid to rest in Magnolia Cemetery in Charleston after a memorial service populated with Blacks and whites congregating together in a rare display of racial harmony. Bishop Rudolph conducted the funeral service, with Rev. Arthur L. Pengelly assisting. Rudolph recalled that a "very large congregation of white and colored people were present, some of them of great prominence in Church and State."[61]

His unwavering faith in the necessity of the church welcoming Black folks into the pews transformed Peter Fayssoux Stevens into an extraordinary religious figure for his time. His behavior initially appears puzzling when considered in the context of his life before and during the Civil War. His casual acceptance of the values and traditions of the white antebellum South and his support for the Southern Confederacy were consistent with his life as a young man growing up in South Carolina. He studied at—and briefly led—The Citadel, an institution specifically designed to defend whites in South Carolina from marauding Blacks. It was only natural that Stevens, as superintendent of The Citadel, would defend the Southland from what he saw as a northern invasion.

Stevens's postwar stance toward people of color might appear anomalous, but it was not. He empathized with the plight of Blacks. He spent much of his life watching their lives and interacting with them. Their concerns and problems were his concerns and problems.

For all his efforts on behalf of the freed people, however, Stevens did not see them as social equals. He was not a proponent of egalitarian ideals. He was a man of his time. The church must welcome all of God's creatures into the fold, but Christian charity had its limits.

Stevens was a man of faith who was not satisfied to preach from a pulpit far removed from the congregation. He practiced what he preached. His life was a testament to his faith. He even left the Protestant Episcopal Church, an institution that he loved and had supported all his life, for the Reformed Episcopal Church over the issue of race.[62]

Notes

1. Ronald James Caldwell, *A History of the Episcopal Church Schism in South Carolina* (Eugene, OR: Wipf & Stock, 2017), 16–17. See also George Freeman Bragg, D.D., *The Episcopal Church and the Black Man* (Baltimore, MD: Self Published, 1918); George Freeman Bragg, D.D., *History of the Afro-American Group of the Episcopal Church* (Baltimore, MD: Church Advocate Press, 1922), 128; Herbert Geer McCarriar, Jr., "A History of the Missionary Jurisdiction of the South of the Reformed Episcopal Church 1874–1970," *Historical Magazine of the Protestant Episcopal Church* 41, no. 2 (June 1972): 197–220; Albert Sidney Thomas, *A Historical Account of the Protestant Episcopal Church in South Carolina, 1820–1957* (Columbia, SC: R. L. Bryan Company, 1957), 385; John Gary Eichelberger, Jr., "Caught in an 'Evil Infection': Postbellum Conflict in the Episcopal Diocese of South Carolina over the Role of African Americans in the Life of the Church" (master's thesis, University of the South, 2020), 28.

2. Allen C. Guelzo, *For the Union of Evangelical Christendom: The Irony of the Reformed Episcopalians* (University Park: The Pennsylvania State University Press, 1994), 219–20.

3. Marion Stevens Eberly, "Our Stevens Family," unpublished manuscript, December 1979, typescript copy, Citadel Archives, 10–11.

4. Stevens is quoted in Ibid., 12.

5. *Journal of the Proceedings of the Seventy-Eighth Annual Convention of the Protestant Episcopal Church in South Carolina* (Charleston, SC: Joseph Walker, 1868), 68. See also Eichelberger, "Caught in an 'Evil Infection'," 88–9; Guelzo, *For the Union of Evangelical Christendom*, 221; McCarriar, "A History of the Missionary Jurisdiction of the South of the Reformed Episcopal Church 1874–1970," 200–1. In his 1868 report, Stevens strongly promoted Ferguson's decision to enter the ministry. "In connection with this work," he wrote, "I report the arrangements I have made respecting a candidate for Orders. Frank C. Ferguson, freedman, having notified me of his desire to enter the ministry, and the same having been approved by yourself, in conformity with your instructions I endeavored to devise some plan for his proper education. On application to the Evangelical Educational Society, they at once consented to aid in his education, and recommended his being sent to the Training School in Raleigh, N. C. Upon writing to Dr. Smith, the Principal of that School, I found his terms so liberal that I determined to accept them immediately, and accordingly Frank started for Raleigh on the 6th of April. The Evangelical Society has engaged to pay $150 per annum for his board and clothing so long as he shall continue a satisfactory student, and upon testimonials of your approval of him and the arrangement. A second young

man of very high character, and I hope of true piety, has expressed his desire of entering the ministry, if possible." Lawrence Dawson was the second young man. *Journal of the Proceedings of the Seventy-Eighth Annual Convention of the Protestant Episcopal Church in South Carolina*, 68–9.

6 *Journal of the Proceedings of the Seventy-Eighth Annual Convention of the Protestant Episcopal Church in South Carolina*, 67–8.

7 *Journal of the Seventy-Ninth Annual Convention of the Protestant Episcopal Church in the Diocese of South Carolina* (Charleston, SC: Wm. G. Mazyck, 1869), 82.

8 Bishop Davis is quoted in Thomas, *A Historical Account of the Protestant Episcopal Church in South Carolina, 1820–1957*, 448.

9 Ibid., 404. See also *Journal of the Proceedings of the Eightieth Annual Convention of the Protestant Episcopal Church in South Carolina* (Charleston, SC: Walker, Evans & Cogswell, 1870), 53.

10 The quote is found in Thomas, *A Historical Account of the Protestant Episcopal Church in South Carolina, 1820–1957*, 89. See also *Journal of the Eighty-Third Annual Convention of the Protestant Episcopal Church in the Diocese of South Carolina* (Charleston, SC: Walker, Evans & Cogswell, 1873), 88, 89; Guelzo, *For the Union of Evangelical Christendom*, 220.

11 The quote is found in Lyon G. Tyler, "Drawing the Color Line in the Episcopal Diocese of South Carolina, 1876–1890: The Role of Edward McCrady, Father and Son," *The South Carolina Historical Magazine* 91, no. 2 (April 1990): 108.

12 Ibid., 107–24. See also David M. Reimers, "Negro Bishops and Diocesan Segregation in the Protestant Episcopal Church: 1870–1954," *Historical Magazine of the Protestant Episcopal Church* 31, no. 3 (September 1962): 232.

13 The literature on this point is voluminous. See, for example, Edward L. Ayers, *The Promise of the New South: Life After Reconstruction*, Fifteenth Anniversary ed. (New York: Oxford University Press, 2007), 434; Leon F. Litwack, *Trouble in Mind: Black Southerners in the Age of Jim Crow* (New York: Knopf, 1998), 233; C. Vann Woodward, *Origins of the New South, 1877–1913* (Baton Rouge: Louisiana State University Press, 1951), 104–6; C. Vann Woodward, *The Strange Career of Jim*, 2nd ed. (Oxford: Oxford University Press, 1966), 54–8.

14 Peter Fayssoux Stevens to Frank C. Ferguson, March 2, 1874, Correspondence 1874 file, DuPre-Moseley Family Collection, the Kennedy Room of Local History and Genealogy, Spartanburg County Public Libraries, Spartanburg, South Carolina. See also Guelzo, *For the Union of Evangelical Christendom*, 221.

15 Ferguson is quoted in McCarriar, "A History of the Missionary Jurisdiction of the South of the Reformed Episcopal Church 1874–1970," 200. See also Eichelberger, "Caught in an 'Evil Infection'," 88–9.

16 Stevens is quoted in Guelzo, *For the Union of Evangelical Christendom*, 221.

17 Ferguson is quoted in McCarriar, "A History of the Missionary Jurisdiction of the South of the Reformed Episcopal Church 1874–1970," 201. See also Guelzo, *For the Union of Evangelical Christendom*, 222.

18 Ferguson is quoted in McCarriar, "A History of the Missionary Jurisdiction of the South of the Reformed Episcopal Church 1874–1970," 201.

19 Annie Price Darling, *A History of the Formation and Growth of the Reformed Episcopal Church, 1873–1902* (Philadelphia, PA: James M. Armstrong, 1902), 56–62. See also Paul A. Carter, "The Reformed Episcopal Schism of 1873: An Ecumenical Perspective," *Historical Magazine of the Protestant Episcopal Church* 33, no. 3 (September 1964): 229–30; McCarriar, "A History of the Missionary Jurisdiction of the South of the Reformed Episcopal Church 1874–1970," 198.

20 Guelzo, *For the Union of Evangelical Christendom*, 274, 275.

21 Rev. Benjamin Johnson in *Journal of the Proceedings of the Fourth General Council of the Reformed Episcopal Church, Held in Emmanuel Church, Ottawa, Ontario, Canada, Commencing Wednesday, July 12, and Ending Monday, July 17, 1876, Published by Order of the General Council* (Philadelphia, PA: James A. Moore, 1876), 55. See also Guelzo, *For the Union of Evangelical Christendom*, 223; McCarriar, "A History of the Missionary Jurisdiction of the South of the Reformed Episcopal Church 1874–1970," 202;

22 For more on the warm relationship between Stevens and DuBose during the war, see, for example, William Porcher DuBose, "Reminiscences, 1836–1878," typescript copy transcribed by William Haskell DuBose, Southern Historical Collection, University of North Carolina at Chapel Hill, 112.

23 William Porcher DuBose to Peter Fayssoux Stevens, January 17, 1875, Correspondence 1875 file, DuPre-Moseley Family Collection, the Kennedy Room of Local History and Genealogy, Spartanburg County Public Libraries, Spartanburg, South Carolina. Emphasis in the original.

24 Rev. William Bell White Howe to Peter Fayssoux Stevens, July 9, 1875, Correspondence 1875 file, DuPre-Moseley Family Collection, the Kennedy Room of Local History and Genealogy, Spartanburg County Public Libraries, Spartanburg, South Carolina.

25 Peter Fayssoux Stevens to Rev. William Bell White Howe, July 28, 1875, Correspondence 1875 file, DuPre-Moseley Family Collection, the Kennedy Room of Local History and Genealogy, Spartanburg County Public Libraries, Spartanburg, South Carolina.

26 Stevens is quoted in Eberly, "Our Stevens Family," 13. Bishop Howe and many Episcopal clergy in South Carolina supported allowing Black laymen and clergy to join the church and participate, for example, in the diocesan convention. Howe set forth his position in Rt. Rev. W. B. W. Howe, "Paper," in *Authorized Report of the Proceedings of the Eighth Church Congress in the Protestant Episcopal Church in the United States, Held in the City of Richmond, Virginia, Tuesday, Wednesday, Thursday, and Friday, October 24th, 25th, 26th, and 27th, 1882*, ed. by the Committee on the Publication Appointed by the Executive Committee (New York: Thomas Whittaker,

Publisher, Nos. 2 and 3, Bible House, 1882), 83–90. As discussed previously, many of the laity did not agree with this position, which severely limited church leaders' options. Tyler, "Drawing the Color Line in the Episcopal Diocese of South Carolina, 1876–1890," 107. See also Rev. Dr. Francis H. Wade, "Confederate Colonel and Priest Promotes Racial Reconciliation," *The Historiographer* 61, no 3 (Summer 2021): 8.

27 Peter Fayssoux Stevens to editors of *The Record*, August 23, 1875, Correspondence 1875 file, DuPre-Moseley Family Collection, the Kennedy Room of Local History and Genealogy, Spartanburg County Public Libraries, Spartanburg, South Carolina.

28 Stevens is quoted in Eberly, "Our Stevens Family," 14, 16.

29 *Journal of the Eighty-Sixth Annual Convention of the Protestant Episcopal Church in the Diocese of South Carolina* (Charleston, SC: Walker, Evans & Cogswell, 1876, 89, 131.

30 *Journal of the Proceedings of the Fifth General Council of the Reformed Episcopal Church, Held in the Chapel of the Second Reformed Episcopal Church, Philadelphia, PA, Commencing Wednesday, May 9, and Ending Tuesday, May 15, 1877, Published by Order of the General Council* (Philadelphia, PA: James A. Moore, 1876), 22, 31. See also Benjamin Aycrigg, *Memoirs of the Reformed Episcopal Church and the Protestant Episcopal Church in the Contemporary Reports Respecting these and The Church of England, Extracted from the Public Press, Analysed and Compared with Proven History* (New York: Edward O. Jenkins, 1880), 190; Guelzo, *For the Union of Evangelical Christendom*, 223; McCarriar, "A History of the Missionary Jurisdiction of the South of the Reformed Episcopal Church 1874–1970," 203–4; Darling, *A History of the Formation and Growth of the Reformed Episcopal Church, 1873 1902*, 240.

31 A. M. Cummins, *Memoir of George David Cummins, DD., First Bishop of the Reformed Episcopal Church, By His Wife* (New York: Dodd, Mead & Company, 1878), 482, 483. See also Darling, *A History of the Formation and Growth of the Reformed Episcopal Church, 1873–1902*, 240.

32 Cummins, *Memoir of George David Cummins*, 484. See also McCarriar, "A History of the Missionary Jurisdiction of the South of the Reformed Episcopal Church 1874–1970," 203–4.

33 Cummins, *Memoir of George David Cummins*, 486–7. See also McCarriar, "A History of the Missionary Jurisdiction of the South of the Reformed Episcopal Church 1874–1970," 203–4; Guelzo, *For the Union of Evangelical Christendom*, 223.

34 Cummins, *Memoir of George David Cummins*, 486–7.

35 The quote was provided by Benjamin Aycrigg, a REC founding layman and historiographer of the church, who claimed to be quoting Bishop Cummins. The quote is reproduced in McCarriar, "A History of the Missionary Jurisdiction of the South of the Reformed Episcopal Church 1874–1970," 205.

36 Ibid., 203, 205.

37 Aycrigg, *Memoirs of the Reformed Episcopal Church and the Protestant Episcopal Church*, 290.

38 Bishop Fallows's report is found in *Journal of the Proceedings of the Sixth General Council of the Reformed Episcopal Church, Held in Emmanuel Church, Newark, New Jersey, Commencing Wednesday, May 8, and Ending Monday, May 13, 1878, Published by Order of the General Council* (Philadelphia, PA: James A. Moore, 1878), 45.

39 Bishop Fallows's remarks are found in *Journal of the Proceedings of the Seventh General Council of the Reformed Episcopal Church, Held in Christ Church, Chicago, Illinois, Commencing Wednesday, May 28th, and Ending Wednesday, June 4th, 1879, Published by Order of the General Council* (Philadelphia, PA: James A. Moore, 1879), 36.

40 Ralph E. Luker, "The Crucible of Civil War and Reconstruction in the Experience of William Porcher DuBose," *The South Carolina Historical Magazine* 83, no. 1 (January 1982): 66–8; McCarriar, "A History of the Missionary Jurisdiction of the South of the Reformed Episcopal Church 1874–1970," 199–203; Allen W. Trelease, *White Terror: The Ku Klux Klan Conspiracy and Southern Reconstruction* (Baton Rouge: Louisiana State University Press, 1999 [1971]), 72, 115–17, 349, 353; Richard Zuczek, *State of Rebellion: Reconstruction in South Carolina* (Columbia: University of South Carolina Press, 1996), 55–9.

41 Bishop William Rufus Nicholson to Peter Fayssoux Stevens, June 7, 1879, Correspondence 1879 file, DuPre-Moseley Family Collection, the Kennedy Room of Local History and Genealogy, Spartanburg County Public Libraries, Spartanburg, South Carolina. See also *Journal of the Proceedings of the Eighth General Council of the Reformed Episcopal Church, Held in the First Reformed Episcopal Church in New York City, Commencing Wednesday, May 25th, and Ending Monday, May 30, 1881, Published by Order of the General Council* (Philadelphia, PA: James A. Moore, 1881), 30, 41; Eberly, "Our Stevens Family," 18; McCarriar, "A History of the Missionary Jurisdiction of the South of the Reformed Episcopal Church 1874–1970," 207–8; Darling, *A History of the Formation and Growth of the Reformed Episcopal Church, 1873 1902*, 174, 241–2; Wade, "Confederate Colonel and Priest Promotes Racial Reconciliation," 9.

42 *Journal of the Proceedings of the Eighth General Council of the Reformed Episcopal Church*, 41–3; McCarriar, "A History of the Missionary Jurisdiction of the South of the Reformed Episcopal Church 1874–1970," 209–10.

43 *Journal of the Proceedings of the Ninth General Council of the Reformed Episcopal Church, Held in Bishop Cummins' Memorial Church, Baltimore, Maryland, Commencing Wednesday, May 23rd, and Ending Monday, May 28, 1883, Published by Order of the General Council* (Philadelphia, PA: William Syckelmoore, 1883), 45.

44 *Journal of the Proceedings of the Eleventh General Council of the Reformed Episcopal Church, Held in the Second Reformed Episcopal Church, Philadelphia, Commencing Wednesday, May 25th, and Ending Monday, May 30, 1887, Published by Order of the General Council* (Philadelphia,

PA: Reformed Episcopal Publication Society, Limited, 1887), 47, 48. See also *Journal of the Proceedings of the Twentieth General Council of the Reformed Episcopal Church, Held in Christ Memorial Church, Philadelphia, Pennsylvania, Commencing Wednesday, May 15th, and Ending Saturday, May 18, 1912, Published by Order of the General Council* (Philadelphia, PA: James M. Armstrong, 1912), 152.

45 *Journal of the Proceedings of the Eleventh General Council of the Reformed Episcopal Church*, 41–2.

46 *Journal of the Proceedings of the Twelfth General Council of the Reformed Episcopal Church, Held in the First Reformed Episcopal Church, Boston, Commencing Wednesday, May 22nd, and Ending Monday, May 27, 1889, Published by Order of the General Council* (Philadelphia, PA: James A. Moore, 1889), 72, 73. See also Peter Fayssoux Stevens to Nell [his daughter, Helen Capers DuPre], April 27, 1892, Correspondence 1892 file, DuPre-Moseley Family Collection, the Kennedy Room of Local History and Genealogy, Spartanburg County Public Libraries, Spartanburg, South Carolina.

47 *Journal of the Proceedings of the Fourteenth General Council of the Reformed Episcopal Church, Held in Christ Church, Chicago, Illinois, Commencing Wednesday, June 6th, and Ending Monday, June 11th, 1894, Published by Order of the General Council* (Philadelphia, PA: James A. Moore, 1894), 121.

48 Darling, *A History of the Formation and Growth of the Reformed Episcopal Church, 1873–1902*, 189.

49 Eberly, "Our Stevens Family," 19. The commentator is McCarriar, "A History of the Missionary Jurisdiction of the South of the Reformed Episcopal Church 1874–1970," 214.

50 *Journal of the Proceedings of the Fifteenth General Council of the Reformed Episcopal Church, Held in First Church, New York City, Commencing Wednesday, June 9th, and Ending Monday, June 14th, 1897, Published by Order of the General Council* (Philadelphia, PA: Reformed Episcopal Publication Society, 1897), 60.

51 Stevens is quoted in McCarriar, "A History of the Missionary Jurisdiction of the South of the Reformed Episcopal Church 1874–1970," 215. See also Eberly, "Our Stevens Family," 19; *Journal of the Proceedings of the Seventeenth General Council of the Reformed Episcopal Church, Held in St. Paul's Church, Chicago, Illinois, Commencing Wednesday, May 20th, and Ending Monday, May 25, 1903, Published by Order of the General Council* (Philadelphia: James M. Armstrong, 1903), 58–9; Herbert Geer McCarriar, Jr., "A History of the Missionary Jurisdiction of the South of the Reformed Episcopal Church 1874–1970, Part II," *Historical Magazine of the Protestant Episcopal Church* 41, no. 3 (September 1972): 287.

52 The quote is found in Eberly, "Our Stevens Family," 19. See also *Journal of the Proceedings of the Thirteenth General Council of the Reformed Episcopal Church, Held in the Church of the Epiphany, Cleveland, Ohio, Commencing Wednesday, May 27th, and Ending Monday, June 1, 1891, Published by Order*

of the General Council (Philadelphia: James A. Moore, 1891), 80; *Journal of the Proceedings of the Twentieth General Council of the Reformed Episcopal Church*, 152; "Colored Ministers Will Act at Rev. P. F. Stevens Burial," n.p.; Blinzy L. Gore, *On a Hilltop High: The Origin and History of Claflin College to 1984* (Spartanburg, SC: The Reprint Company, 1994), 112; Thomas, *The History of the South Carolina Military Academy*, 303–28; George Brown Tindall, *South Carolina Negroes, 1877–1900* (Columbia, SC: University of South Carolina Press, 1952 [2003]), 219. On the effort to reopen The Citadel, see especially James Lee Conrad, *The Young Lions: Confederate Cadets at War* (Mechanicsburg, PA: Stackpole Books, 1997), 164.

53 McCarriar, "A History of the Missionary Jurisdiction of the South of the Reformed Episcopal Church 1874–1970," 216.

54 Stevens is quoted in Ibid., 218. See also *Journal of the Proceedings of the Nineteenth General Council of the Reformed Episcopal Church, Held in St. Paul's Church, Philadelphia, Penna., Commencing Wednesday, May 19th, and Ending Saturday, May 22nd, 1909, Published by Order of the General Council* (Philadelphia, PA: James A. Armstrong, 1909), 112–13.

55 *Journal of the Proceedings of the Nineteenth General Council of the Reformed Episcopal Church*, 114. See also McCarriar, "A History of the Missionary Jurisdiction of the South of the Reformed Episcopal Church 1874–1970, Part II," 287.

56 *Journal of the Proceedings of the Nineteenth General Council of the Reformed Episcopal Church*, 143.

57 *Journal of the Proceedings of the Twentieth General Council of the Reformed Episcopal Church*, 152. See also McCarriar, "A History of the Missionary Jurisdiction of the South of the Reformed Episcopal Church 1874–1970, Part II," 289.

58 Lowery is quoted in McCarriar, "A History of the Missionary Jurisdiction of the South of the Reformed Episcopal Church 1874–1970," 219.

59 *Journal of the Proceedings of the Twentieth General Council of the Reformed Episcopal Church*, 116–17.

60 Ibid., 43, 174.

61 "Colored Ministers Will Act at Rev. P. F. Stevens Burial," n.p. Bishop Rudolph is quoted in *Journal of the Proceedings of the Twentieth General Council of the Reformed Episcopal Church*, 116–17. See also Wade, "Confederate Colonel and Priest Promotes Racial Reconciliation," 9.

62 "Colored Ministers Will Act at Rev. P. F. Stevens Burial," n.p.; Eberly, "Our Stevens Family," 19–20.

8

"He Was a True Evangelist"— Anthony Toomer Porter

The Later Years (1865–1902)

Like virtually every American of his generation, Anthony Toomer Porter viewed the war of 1861–5 as the defining event of his life. He had spent four hard years laboring to secure medicines and uniforms for Confederate troops and ministering to sick and wounded soldiers. Living and working in Charleston, he had survived federal bombardments, infectious diseases, severe shortages of basic goods, and the loss of a way of life that he held dear. Only his religious faith sustained him in the war's closing days.

He was traveling from Cheraw, South Carolina, to the state capital in Columbia when he heard the news that the Confederate States of America had collapsed. He had known the end was near. By his own reckoning, he had spent time with Confederate General Joseph E. Johnston near Raleigh, North Carolina, as General Sherman's troops marched across South Carolina. With the Southern Confederacy's resources dwindling, the army could not long endure.[1]

Despite the grim reality facing southerners, "the news was not to be believed." No telegraph lines stretched from Cheraw to Columbia; therefore, he could not verify the reports of the southern surrender. Soon enough, he learned the truth. Despondent, he loaded a horse-drawn wagon and made his way to Anderson, South Carolina, to reunite with his wife. After he arrived, "I at once called my servants together, and told them they were free, and could leave me if they so desired, but no one left."[2]

Porter recounted a story, perhaps apocryphal, of federal deserters showing up at his house soon after his return. The treasure hunters had heard rumors of Confederate gold stashed somewhere nearby, but they were foraging for anything of value. A faithful servant, Ann, on her own initiative, hid the family's silver dinnerware away from the premises. After the deserters departed, she returned the valuables. Porter marveled that she "was a faithful servant, and died in my service some ten years afterwards, faithful to the end." Ann was the living embodiment of the "faithful slave" narrative so common in southern accounts of the peculiar institution.[3]

At war's end, Porter felt as many southerners did: the Confederate cause had been noble and just. The South was defeated not because of a lack of valor or devotion, but because the federal army possessed more resources—more materiel, more ordnance, more bodies—and the Butcher Ulysses S. Grant had thrown everything he could at the Confederates. "The thought that a cause in which Robert E. Lee and Stonewall Jackson, such men, such eminent Christian men, had drawn their swords, should fail, made life worthless, and I folded my hands and wished to die," he later wrote.[4]

Had the story ended there, Porter's declaration would have been a standard southern expression of longing and regret over the loss of a slaveholding republic. Yet, upon further reflection, he acknowledged that "my religious and intellectual outlook was changed." He poured through the pages of history books, realizing that even failure offered advantages. "Had we succeeded, slavery, which we hated, would have been perpetuated with the sentiment of the world against us," he observed. "It would have been a cankering sore in our body politics." Sooner or later, the existence of a slaveholding nation side by side with a free nation would become untenable. Additional wars would be fought. Instead, "freed from the incubus of slavery, I believe there is a future for this dear Southland yet, and I am going to do all I can to make it." He continued: "I was, and am still, true to the lost cause; but I am not going to hug a corpse and carry it about with me; I am too young for that; I am just thirty-seven years old." This realistic appraisal of circumstances was liberating. "What a burden I rolled off that precious heart that night!"[5]

The admission comes as close as anything that Porter ever wrote to explain why he defended the Southern Confederacy during the war years but evinced no animosity toward the freed people in the postbellum era. He was a realist. Slavery, which he opposed, was dead, and the Southern Confederacy, which he supported, was also dead. The latter must be mourned, and the former forgotten. Both must be buried.

Despite his clear-eyed view of the death of slavery and the loss of an independent southern government, Porter was not an egalitarian. He would not terrorize Blacks, but neither would he lift them up from the bottom of the social strata. In his memoirs, he recalled his entry into postwar Charleston where he encountered "a burly black, dressed in United States uniform, with a gun on his shoulder, passing in front of my door." When Porter attempted to pass by the soldier, the man stopped him, informing Porter that the house belonged to the Freedmen's Bureau.

Having never heard of the Bureau and surprised at a Black man's effrontery, Porter was indignant. "Look here, darkey," he responded in a huff, "that is my house, and if you do not get out of the way, I will make you."

It was an audacious threat to utter to a man bearing arms, but Porter was confident that he would be obeyed. "I saw that he was one of the island negroes, dressed up in a uniform," he explained, "so I thought I would try him to see if he had lost his sense of obedience." As Porter expected, the man "dropped his gun from his shoulder, caught hold of his woolly head by a front curl, scraped his feet, and said, 'Yes, boss, go in.'" These were not the sentiments of a man committed to uplifting people of color. Anthony Toomer Porter was a white man of the Old South, and he expected Black people to obey him without question or hesitation.[6]

When he learned details about the establishment and operation of the Freedmen's Bureau—as discussed in Chapter 5, a federal agency created to assist formerly enslaved persons in making the transition from slavery to a free labor economy—Porter was unimpressed. He believed that the Bureau did more harm than good, and he deplored the creation of "that institution which did the negroes so much harm." As Porter saw it, the Freedmen's Bureau "defrauded them of their savings in the bank it established, and by feeding them in idleness, and putting the worst ideas in their heads, caused such an annoyance to us white people, and it became such an abomination that the United States abolished it as soon as it discovered its mistake in creating it." Porter's summary of the Bureau's mission and history was far from accurate, but it was the typical interpretation of a white southerner.[7]

Despite his impoverished circumstances, Porter found an encouraging sign of better days to come. He encountered George Shrewsbury, "a colored butcher" who "belonged to that respectable class of free colored citizens, who were so numerous in the city of Charleston before the war, and who had always commanded the respect and esteem of the white population." When Shrewsbury learned that Porter was essentially destitute, the man "offered me a roll of money, one hundred dollars in greenbacks." Porter was touched—"I confess my eyes were not dry," he wrote—because he needed the money. He gratefully accepted the loan although he confessed that he was concerned "that I should be in the condition to need such aid, and next that it should come from one not in my own sphere, and not even of my own race." Shrewsbury even refused to accept interest on the loan.[8]

Shrewsbury's generosity might have been the grounds for Porter to reassess his opinions about the character of Black people. The standard myth suggested that people of color were simpletons who did not possess the same moral qualities as whites; therefore, they must be guided and instructed by their betters—that is, white people—so they could learn how to behave in polite society. The notion that a free Black man of means would voluntarily offer a helping hand to a less affluent white man appears to contradict the myth and might serve as an abject lesson in human nature. Rather than engage in self-reflection or a reassessment of his views on persons of color, however, Porter dismissed the episode as the singular action of an unusual free Black man who in no way represented his race. Had Porter stopped to consider the possible ramifications of Shrewsbury's behavior, it might have affected the clergyman's views on the appropriate role of Blacks in the Episcopal Church in later years.

The available evidence does not suggest that Porter's views on race and the church changed because of his chance encounter with George Shrewsbury. Porter's memoirs do attest to the continued importance of the Episcopal Church in his life. The horrors that he witnessed had not shaken his faith or undermined his desire to participate in the affairs of the South Carolina Episcopal Church. Invited to preach at the Church of the Holy Communion, his former church, Porter carried his good feelings about George Shrewsbury into the pulpit. He urged the parishioners to "turn their backs on the past and look to the future; not to waste energies on vain regrets, but to realize that they were on a wreck and to save life they must build, out of materials at hand, a raft to bear them to the shore." As part of this raft-building, it

> was their duty to accept as a fact the freedom of the slaves, and to act accordingly; the negroes had not freed themselves, and had acted well, and needed our aid; if we would, we could keep them as friends, and not drive them over to the Northerners, whom they would look upon as their deliverers, and would become subservient to them.

Porter resolved to do all he could to educate the freed people "that they might learn that liberty was not licentiousness." One day, they might earn the right to cast a ballot, and "we should offer it to them when they could read, write, and cipher, and owned five hundred dollars of freehold property, etc."[9]

The suggestion that Blacks might someday vote in an election and take part in civic life outraged some listeners, including Porter's cousin Laurens, who groused, "Why, you have gone over to the enemy; you have turned abolitionist!"

Porter demurred, insisting that he was taking a practical view. Having affirmed an oath of allegiance to the US government, Porter felt honor-bound to live up to his oath. "Turned abolitionist!" he exclaimed. "What have we to abolish? The victorious arms of the Federal Government abolished slavery, and I, for one, thank God it is done." Perhaps emancipation had been accomplished too quickly, which led to "suffering, and wholesale death to the poor blacks," but it was too late to change the situation. "If more judgment, and less passion, had been shown, the negroes could have been freed, and the South not left so destitute, and the whole country would have been the better for it. But it is done, and now, if we have any sense left, let us make the most and best of it." Setting aside the question of whether the federals were the parties inflamed by passion, the statement served as Porter's perspective on Reconstruction. White southerners must accept a fait accompli and move on with their lives.[10]

The question, of course, was *how* he should move on. What actions qualified as moving on and making progress? As he usually did when he set his mind to a problem, Porter threw himself into the task of making the most of a dire situation. With the war over and the Southern Confederacy an unrealized dream, he turned his attention toward bettering the condition of whites and Blacks alike. He believed that providing new educational opportunities would aid them as well as the entire South in recovering from the war. His task, therefore, was to build schools that would provide opportunities for advancement to everyone.

Porter's efforts to establish schools in Charleston were described as "Herculean." The first step was to secure funding, but almost no capital was available in the former states of the Confederacy. Consequently, in April 1866, he traveled to the North and solicited funds to educate the freed people. As a result of his numerous and wide-ranging appeals, he gathered the funds necessary to create a school for more than 1,800 Black children, most of whom were the offspring of freed people.[11]

In a memoir that he wrote late in his life, Porter recalled a fundraising trip to Washington, DC. He met with General O. O. Howard, who was serving as the head of the Freedmen's Bureau, the organization that Porter learned about when he tried to enter his home in Charleston. After Porter told the general of his plans to buy the Marine Hospital in Charleston as the site for a school to educate Black children, Howard readily agreed to help acquire the property. He even escorted Porter to the White House for an audience with President Andrew Johnson.

As discussed in Chapter 5, Johnson was no friend of the freed people, nor did he approve of the Freedmen's Bureau any more than Porter did, but he understood the desperate situation in the southern states. After listening to Porter's appeal, Johnson agreed to help. According to Porter, the president turned to General Howard and said, "This is the pleasantest thing I have heard from the South." Recognizing that it would take an act of Congress to transfer title to the hospital, Johnson instructed Howard to "get a bill through Congress authorizing the sale of the Marine Hospital and I will sign it." Without hesitation, the president opened his checkbook and produced a check. "This is my subscription toward its purchase," he said as he handed Porter a check for $1,000. After the bill subsequently passed both chambers of Congress, Johnson was true to his word, signing into law the authorization to sell the building to Porter.[12]

Now that he could finance the operations, Porter's school made steady progress, and he was pleased with its growth.

This drawing of Anthony Toomer Porter dates from 1892. Reprinted from Cyclopedia of Eminent and Representative Men of the Carolinas of the Nineteenth Century, *Vol. I, (Madison, WI: Brant & Fuller, 1892), facing page 493.*

> I beg leave respectfully to report that the building known as the Marine Hospital, in Franklin Street, Charleston, now used as a school for colored children and freedmen, and supported by the Home Mission for colored persons and freedmen, established by the General Convention of the Church in the United States, has been paid for, and is now held in trust by Rev. A. T. Porter, Gr. A. Trenholm and S. L. Bennett, for educational purposes, without distinction of race or previous condition,

he reported at the annual convention in 1870. "That the school numbers some three hundred children and has been regularly visited by some of the clergy of Charleston, and religious instruction has been given by the same."[13]

Considering his success educating the children of the freed people, Porter eventually created a school for white children. To that end, he founded the Holy Communion Church Institute in 1867. He explained the school's origins using a dramatic, tragic anecdote. While he was visiting his son's grave at Magnolia Cemetery in Charleston for four hours on October 25, 1867, he had an epiphany. Grieving for his son, who had died from yellow fever during the war, Porter heard a voice say, "Stop grieving for the dead, and do something for the living."[14]

He admitted that "there was no audible sound, yet I heard it as distinctly as if someone had spoken." He asked aloud, "What can I do for the living?" Porter was financially destitute. He did not know how he could accomplish anything in his sad, sorry state.

"I heard the same voice saying, 'Your child is enjoying what you are only hoping for; but see his young companions who are mostly poor orphans without churches or schools. Take them and educate them.'"

"I knelt upon my child's grave, and used these words," he recalled, "'Heavenly Father, if this is from Thee, give me wisdom, give me zeal, give me continuity of purpose, and open the hearts of people to me, and I will do it; but if it is only a fleeting enthusiasm, let it pass away as a morning cloud, for Jesus' sake.'"[15]

It was not a fleeting enthusiasm. It was a revelation. He had found his life's work. In addition to his work with the church, Anthony Toomer Porter would devote his life to educating the young people of Charleston.

He saw a path forward despite his impecunious circumstances. If he had successfully created a school for freed people and their children, could he not also create a school for white children by leveraging the goodwill he had amassed during his ministry? He believed that he could. Within only a few months, Porter formed his school for white children, which was attached to his church. The school opened its doors on December 9, 1867.[16]

The school had modest beginnings. For fifty cents a month, or whatever farm produce a student could offer, the white children of Charleston could attend the institute and gain an "academic, moral, and spiritual education" regardless of their family's means. It was a noble undertaking, but it almost failed at the outset. "The school was opened in December, but up to the middle of March in the following year I had received little or no money. My expenses were running on, and no salaries or bills had been paid. Things looked desperate, but neither my faith nor my courage failed me," Porter later wrote.[17]

The school continued to grow as its founder scrambled to secure funding. By May 1868, 300 children attended classes under the tutelage of three male and seven female teachers. Porter traveled continuously, and his efforts paid rich dividends. According to one report, "From May 1869 to May 1870, Mr. Porter raised $20,810.75 for the school—$13,502.00 was collected in Newark, New York, Philadelphia, Baltimore, and Washington, with $6,709.03 from South Carolina tuition fees and donations." He eventually traveled to England searching for donors as well.[18]

In his report to the General Council in 1868, Bishop Thomas F. Davis lauded Porter's work. "The Parochial School connected with the Church of the Holy Communion, together with the Orphan Home established by the Rev. A. T. Porter, is a noble Christian enterprise, for the relief of suffering, and to afford education to those with whom it would otherwise be impossible," the bishop gushed.

> No one can understand the real value of this school—and especially the Home—to our own church, without passing through the country, looking into the real condition of things, and being informed how many parents' hearts have been relieved, and awakened to hope and life by the opportunities thus afforded to their children. I cordially commend it to your kindness and patronage.[19]

As he collected money and the school grew and prospered, Porter knew that he needed a new location. In 1879, he sought to acquire the US Arsenal on Ashley Avenue in Charleston as the new site for his school. When he learned that federal authorities were departing from the arsenal, leaving it vacant, Porter took pen in hand and wrote to George W. McCray, President Rutherford B. Hayes's secretary of war and the officer who had withdrawn the last federal troops from South Carolina to end Reconstruction early in 1877. "Sir," he began,

> I have been informed that it is the purpose of the Government to withdraw the troops from the arsenal property in Charleston, South Carolina, and leave it practically vacant, for the present, at least." Porter had a suggestion that would benefit the federal government and the Holy Communion Church Institute, as he called the school in 1879. "I have the honor to make application for the lease of the property upon such terms as will secure its preservation and protect the interests of the Government.[20]

He lobbied South Carolina's two US senators, former Confederate generals Matthew Butler and Wade Hampton, to sponsor legislation authorizing the transfer. Two former general officers from opposite sides of the war, Joseph E. Johnston of the Confederacy and William T. Sherman of the Union, argued on Porter's behalf as well.

Sherman was especially solicitous. "He and I had frequently met in the intervening years, and he always spoke of that trip that I made with McQueen, and what he thought of the act on my part; and again, and again he had asked me what the Government had done for me in return for my saving that young man," Porter remembered. Sherman advised him to "go to General Hampton and General Butler, and get them to draw a bill, and let them go to the Democrats, and me to the Republicans, and we will see if we cannot get it done." With Sherman's strong support, the bill eventually passed both houses of Congress and President Rutherford B. Hayes signed it into law. The property transfer conveying the land to Porter for use as his school occurred on December 19, 1879. On January 8, 1880, the school officially took possession of the land and buildings. In the ensuing months, Porter and his staff spent $10,000 retrofitting the buildings to suit the needs of the school.[21]

Porter and his family eventually moved onto the grounds of the school and continued repairing the premises. Each year saw steady improvement. By 1882, the school had established a $16,000 endowment. Two hundred and seventy-six students attended, with 166 of them boarding at the school. One hundred students paid no tuition.[22]

In 1886, school officials changed the school's name. According to a resolution unanimously adopted by the board of trustees,

> the time has arrived for the change of its corporate name to that of the Porter Academy. They [the trustees] deem this a just tribute to a great Christian philanthropist, who from its origin, and amid all its trials and struggles, has borne the burden and heat of the day. His name should in the coming years be indissolubly connected with it, for he has devoted to it the best years of a long and honorable life; in its darkest days his faith never wavered, his heroic courage never failed.[23]

As the trustees hoped, Porter's name was indissolubly linked with the school. The academy continued long after his death. C. J. Colcock, Porter's "unfaltering assistant," headed the school for a time, as did Bishop William Alexander Guerry. Guerry's tenure ended dramatically when he died on June 9, 1928, five days after he was shot by a priest who was upset with Guerry's proposal to install a Black suffragan bishop in the diocese. Before his death, Bishop Guerry had characterized the Porter Academy as "the most valuable, the most important and the most far-reaching in its influence of any institution connected with the Church in this Diocese."[24]

The school changed its name again, this time to the Porter Military Academy. Much later, in July 1964, more than six decades after Porter's death, the school moved to its present location on Albemarle Road in Charleston, joined with the Gaud School and Watt School, and became the Porter-Gaud School. By the end of the twentieth century, it was a prestigious college preparatory school serving many of South Carolina's finest young students.[25]

Aside from his work educating young people, Porter was active in church affairs. In 1868, he became a trustee of the University of the South, a position he held until he chose not to seek reelection eighteen years later. In 1869, he was elected to the standing committee of the Diocese of South Carolina. A year later, he became deputy to the General Convention.[26]

In May 1878, Bishop William B. W. Howe asked Porter to serve as the rector of St. Mark's Church, a congregation of Blacks and mulattoes in Charleston, in addition to Porter's work at the Church of the Holy Communion. The church's rector, Rev. J. B. Seabrook, had died a year earlier and left the church without a rector. Worse, St. Mark's was financially destitute and mismanaged.[27]

Recall from Chapter 6 that St. Mark's had applied for admission to the Diocese of South Carolina in 1875. After much controversy and debate, the diocese denied the application, largely on the strength of the laity's antipathy toward Black congregants seeking leadership positions within the church. Porter was aware of this controversy when he balked at Howe's request that he serve as the church rector.[28]

"Bishop, I cannot do it," he explained after he learned of the appointment. "I am overwhelmed with work now."

Howe agreed. "I know it. You have more to do than six men ordinarily have, and I think this will kill you, yet it is a good cause to die in." After this joking, flippant remark, Howe assured Porter that "you have always taken an interest in the colored work, they are fond of you, and you are the only one of the clergy who knows anything about finance, and there will have to be a great deal of financial work done there, and you can do it."

Porter understood that this was more than a simple request. "Is it W. B. W. Howe who says this to me, or the Rt. Rev. W. B. W. Howe? If the former, I answer at once, 'No, I will not touch it.'; if it is my Bishop, I am under orders and I will obey."

As Porter recalled, the "Bishop laughed, and said, 'Well, it is the Bishop.'"

Porter reluctantly agreed to take on St. Mark's in addition to his other duties. Relieved, Bishop Howe told him, "You have rolled away a weight that was on my heart."[29]

Porter's tenure as the St. Mark's rector commenced on June 6, 1878. The church had been in limbo since Rev. Seabrook's death twenty-one months earlier. Work on a new church building had halted while St. Mark's waited on new leadership. As his first order of business, Porter directed that the labors continue. Five months later, on November 7, 1878, the building was consecrated. At the time, the church listed 181 active communicants.[30]

Porter experienced enormous satisfaction with the consecration. It was an early triumph for a church in need of revitalization. He also agreed to take on much of the church debt personally—otherwise, the church probably would not have secured financing—but he never paid out of his own pocket. The members of St. Mark's "paid it all themselves, and we never renewed without taking off a good slice of the debt." Even after the church was damaged by a cyclone in 1885 and an earthquake in 1886, church members remained optimistic that they could weather the bad times and persevere in the long run.³¹

Porter's position at St. Mark's placed him squarely in the middle of the debate about the role of Black people in the postwar Protestant Episcopal Church in South Carolina. He came to believe that all parishes, white and Black, should be united. He knew that some Black communicants, as well as white ministers such as Peter Fayssoux Stevens, had joined the Reformed Episcopal Church, but Porter thought that the Protestant Episcopal Church of South Carolina was large enough and generous enough to accommodate everyone.³²

The case of Thaddaeus Saltus became the first test of the role of Blacks within the Protestant Episcopal Church of South Carolina since Frank Ferguson and Lawrence [Laurens] Dawson had left the church. The case initially seemed promising. Saltus became the first Black man ordained in the South Carolina Diocese. He was offered opportunities that had been denied to people of color in the church, becoming an assistant at St. Mark's. Yet his situation proved to be unique. Around the time that Saltus died, the Jim Crow regime took a brutal turn in the southern states, and that turn was reflected in the church.³³

The Saltus case started out on a positive note. In his 1879 report, Rev. Porter, referring to St. Mark's, noted that "Taking it altogether, there is no more flourishing and encouraging Parish in the Diocese. Mr. Saltus is a candidate for Holy Orders from this Parish." With this reference to Thaddaeus Saltus, Porter was raising an issue that had divided the diocese earlier in the decade. Once again, the church would be forced to confront the issue of race.³⁴

Subsequent reports noted Saltus's progress. Porter reported in 1881 that the "ordination of Mr. Saltus and his assistance as Deacon in charge, has given an impetus to the Parish, and he is making good proof of his ministry." The standing committee agreed, noting that its members "have recommended that Mr. Thaddaeus Saltus be admitted to the Sacred Order of Deacons."³⁵

This matter-of-fact report of Saltus's admission to the diaconate might seem surprising at first blush, perhaps revealing a newfound racial tolerance in the South Carolina Diocese, but the generosity of spirit was limited. The standing committee also included six resolutions "intended to promote harmonious religious relations between the two races in this Diocese." The resolutions insulted people of color, questioning their ability to govern themselves. The first resolution observed that "Divine Providence" had "brought together two races in this Diocese to occupy the same territory, differing in all those essential characteristics which constitute different peoples, and most especially in Christian knowledge and culture." As a result of this plan, "this Diocese has become a missionary field, in which the race in possession of the higher gifts should endeavor to advance the

Christian condition of their deficient neighbors and are invested with proper authority to promote that end."

In short, anyone who ignored the natural hierarchy of knowledge between whites and Blacks would do more harm than good. According to the standing committee, allowing Black members to ascend into leadership positions within the church "would reverse the order of missionary operations and even of nature itself, and could tend to the advantage of neither race, that the race having the lesser Christian knowledge and culture should be advanced to the position of teachers and rulers of the other race." In other words, "it is not expedient to invest individuals of the less advanced race with official authority over the other race." Thaddaeus Saltus's advancement should not serve as a precedent for other cases because

> the case now presented to the Committee is exceptional in so many particulars that when it is understood to be the intention of the applicant to confine the ministrations of his office to St. Mark's and similar congregations, the objections to his admission may be considered as sufficiently obviated to allow his testimonials to be signed by the whole Committee.[36]

With Saltus safely confined to St. Mark's and standing as an exception to the general rule of not allowing Blacks to be church leaders, on February 3, 1882, the standing committee recommended that he be admitted to the priest's orders. On March 3, Porter presented Saltus as a candidate. In due course, the candidate was ordained.[37]

In his 1882 report, Porter noted that St. Mark's had improved to such an extent since he became rector that he might step away from his duties and leave it to his successor, Saltus, to serve. "All the obligations of the Parish are promptly met, and [it] is in a prosperous condition," he wrote. "Having accomplished the end for which I accepted the Rectorship, namely, to build their Church, I have gradually withdrawn from the actual charge of the Church, leaving it almost entirely in the hands of my assistant. The time is not far distant when I will retire entirely, as other work fully taxes my energies." In this manner, much like Peter Fayssoux Stevens, Porter advanced the career of an aspiring Black clergyman.[38]

Although Porter remained the official rector of St. Mark's the following year, with Saltus serving as his assistant, the reality was, in his words, that the "Rev. Mr. Saltus has had the entire charge of this work during the year, and with what faithfulness, this report shows." Unfortunately, Saltus's health was declining, and his condition was grave. "We thank God for these good results but have to express our sorrow that the efficient minister has broken down under his labors and has been compelled to seek rest in Summerville." If Porter hoped to leave his duties at St. Mark's and allow his protégé to become rector, Saltus would have to recover his health. "We are very anxious as to the result and pray God to spare his life and restore his health, for he would be a loss indeed, if taken from his labors," Porter wrote. "We ask the prayers of the Brethren for this their faithful brother and fellow servant of Christ."[39]

By 1884, Saltus's health was so poor that he was forced to retire from the ministry. This was a blow to Porter both because he wished to see his faithful assistant advance, but also because he sought to lay the burden of St. Mark's leadership onto another man's shoulders. "It is with great sorrow I have to note the continued illness of the Rev. Mr. Saltus," he explained in his report. "During his brief, active ministry, he proved himself to be a faithful workman who needed not to be ashamed. He has the confidence and affection of this entire congregation."[40]

Thaddaeus Saltus died in June 1884. As Bishop Howe reported in 1885, "He had been only recently admitted to the Ministry, being ordained to the Diaconate February 6th, 1881, and to the Priesthood March 3rd, 1882. But short as his service was, it was quite a consecrated one and will not be found without fruit." His death was tragic on many levels. Had Saltus lived, he might have paved the way for other Black rectors to follow despite the standing committee's insistence that his case should not serve as a precedent. Reflecting on Saltus's service, Howe noted that "this ministry was earnest in Church and in private, and at the same time unobtrusive and unostentatious. I had hoped good things from it, and things which make for peace, but God let it be cut short, and God does all things well."[41]

The race issue had been festering in the Protestant Episcopal Church, and the situation was not improving as the Thaddaeus Saltus case unfolded. In April 1883, this recurring problem prompted William Mercer Green, bishop of the Mississippi Diocese and chancellor of the University of the South, to invite his fellow bishops to assemble in Sewanee, Tennessee, shortly before university commencement exercises in July to discuss the status of "the late slave population" in the Episcopal Church. Green recommended that the bishops bring at least one priest and one lay leader to address this momentous issue. As Green saw it, southern Blacks were "a race perishing in the midst of us for want of right instruction."[42]

Forty-one white men—twelve bishops, eighteen priests, and eleven laymen—representing thirteen dioceses attended the conference from July 25–July 28, 1883. They debated whether to create a separate denomination for African American church members. Ultimately, the participants decided that unity at the diocesan level was crucial, expressing the principle as "but one fold and one Chief Shepherd for all the people in any field of Ecclesiastical designation." In practical terms, this translated to one white bishop presiding over one diocese, regardless of the race of the church members. Considering their lack of faith in Blacks to assume leadership positions in any walk of life, white bishops would remain in charge of Black communicants for the foreseeable future.[43]

The so-called "Sewanee Plan" was a proposed canon that would be presented to the General Convention at the October 1883 meeting. Officially titled "Of Missionary Organizations within Constituted Episcopal Jurisdictions," the plan proposed that any diocese with a substantial Black population could create a "special Missionary Organization under the charge of the Bishop." Black church members would worship separately from white church members, while the white bishop would oversee Black parishes. To no one's surprise, Black communicants would enjoy none of the advantages of separation from whites—such as control over their own church services, buildings, and Black leadership candidates—but shoulder all the disadvantages, including subservience to whites and second-class church membership. Intelligent Black men could be educated to assume leadership positions within the church at some unspecified future time, but the proposal offered no guarantees.[44]

Black Episcopalians were noticeably absent from the Sewanee debates, but they immediately learned of the proposal. Soon after the Sewanee conference, a group of Blacks met to discuss their response to the plan. Alexander Crummell, rector of St. Luke's Church in Washington, DC, emerged as a leading figure in rejecting this plan. His views reflected the opinion of an unlikely ally, Bishop Richard Hooker Wilmer of Alabama. Wilmer attended the Sewanee conference and dissented from the adoption of what he called "class legislation."[45]

When the diocesan representatives assembled for the General Convention in Philadelphia in October 1883, the issue was the topic of much debate. The House of Bishops adopted the plan, but the proposal could not garner sufficient support within the House of Deputies. As Bishop Howe reported in 1884, the Committee on Canons refused to agree with the Sewanee recommendations, preferring to make Black conversions the work of the entire body of the church instead of carving out special missionary organizations.[46]

Porter was involved in the Sewanee conference in July, and he chose to speak on the matter during the General Convention in October. Referring to Black communicants, he admitted that they did not have much religious knowledge and "their moral standard was and is not very high." Nonetheless, white ministers were duty-bound to serve Blacks. Based on the experiences of white rectors working with Black communicants, including Porter's service at St. Mark's in Charleston, he concluded that some freed people were men and women of fine "Christian character." They were childlike, in Porter's view, and required firm direction, but African Americans could be brought into the fold. They could become good, productive Episcopalians if white bishops oversaw their efforts.[47]

Because Blacks could act as good Christians—a controversial position among some whites in the 1880s—a devoted Episcopal minister had one clear duty, namely to "preach the gospel to them." Unlike some of his contemporaries who saw the freed people as brutes who must therefore be brutalized, Porter counseled patience and kindness even as he infantilized Blacks. White church leaders must guide and instruct them on the proper course of action exactly as parents rear their children to become good citizens and well-functioning adults.[48]

For all his good intentions, Porter's proposal was only a slight modification of the Sewanee Plan. He favored the creation of a special missionary organization, but he did not specify that it would be race-based. He preferred to allow bishops and diocesan conventions to exercise discretion in deciding how such organizations would be constructed. Because this modification did not differ significantly from the Sewanee Plan, it failed to win approval.[49]

Anthony Toomer Porter in middle age. Courtesy of the Georgetown County Library Collection, Georgetown County, South Carolina.

Like Peter Fayssoux Stevens, Anthony Toomer Porter demonstrated genuine empathy for Black communicants. During the war, Porter supported the Southern Confederacy and its underlying premises, namely that the creation of a slaveholding nation was a noble cause. After the Confederate surrender, he accepted the reality of a defeated southern government even if he never rejected the values underlying a slaveholding republic. Unlike Stevens, however, Porter did not promote Black leadership within the church.

Porter believed that unity could be achieved within the diocese if Blacks accepted the terms and conditions imposed by white church leaders. As his oration at the 1883 General Convention demonstrated, his empathy was of a peculiar kind. He embraced the paternalism of the age. Everyone should be educated and accepted within the church, but Blacks should be subjected to tight controls.

Porter meant no harm. He genuinely believed that he was laboring in the best interests of all communicants, Blacks and white. As always, his labors on behalf of his communicants required funds, especially as his school grew. Even as he aged and suffered various maladies, Porter continued his fundraising trips into the late 1880s. In 1889, he traveled to England to meet with donors, staying on for a trip to Egypt. He also visited the Holy Land early in 1890 before returning to the United States in June of that year.[50]

Closer to home, Porter became nostalgic in his old age. His participation in public ceremonies honoring the men who served with him in the Confederate army indicated that although he accepted the southern surrender, he fondly recalled the good old days before Reconstruction. He revealed his sentiments on two separate ceremonies in Charleston's Washington Square. The first occasion occurred on February 23, 1891, in a ceremony laying the cornerstone for a monument in the center of the park honoring the service of the Washington Light Infantry (WLI). Forged from Carolina gray granite, the WLI monument was a 42-foot-high obelisk similar in appearance to the Washington Monument in the nation's capital and inscribed with the names of military battles as well as the names of the unit's war dead.[51]

Called to bless the dedication, Rev. Porter offered a "brief but touching prayer" that reinforced the tenets of the Lost Cause. Bowing his head, Porter asked the Lord's blessing. "We are here in Thy presence to lay the cornerstone of a Monument which we hope will last for many generations, keeping alive the memory of those who died in the conscientious discharge of duties laid upon them by their State," he said. The purpose of the monument was to "serve as a constant memorial to teach all who look upon it that it is noble to give up even life for the maintenance of what we believe to be right."[52]

The second occasion demonstrating Porter's Lost Cause sympathies occurred on June 28, 1894, in a ceremony dedicating a set of bronze panels added to the Washington Square monument. Instead of offering a prayer, this time Porter was introduced as the orator of the day. After the panels were unveiled, the former WLI chaplain stepped forward and reviewed the history of the unit. He praised the valor of men under fire, calling special attention to the brave WLI soldiers who died in the Battle of Secessionville.

Porter then turned his attention to the war's aftermath. In keeping with many white southerners' attempts to win the peace by recasting the goals of the Southern Confederacy and exaggerating the abuses of carpetbag rule during Reconstruction, he described "the decade from 1866 to 1876" as "an unwritten history." According to Porter, "I trust some graphic writer will arise to tell to future ages how the men who had fought for four years that bloody strife displayed a moral courage and a true manhood in these years of so-called peace equal to that physical courage which had been displayed on so many battlefields." Despite all that Porter had done, and continued to do, for Blacks in the South Carolina Episcopal Church as well as in his school for children of the freed people, he was still a member of the mainstream white community, as reflected in both his personal and religious views. He denounced the "so-called reconstruction period" when "negro supremacy rose up to humiliate and if possible, crush the last lingering signs of life in men who had so fought that it was an honor to receive their surrender."[53]

Monument dedications became an important ritual for many white southerners in the postbellum years, and so it was with Porter. Indeed, a dramatic episode affecting his life occurred during another monument dedication ceremony although Porter was not present. On May 30, 1895, former Confederate General Wade Hampton delivered an oration in Oakwood Cemetery in Chicago during the dedication of a monument honoring the Confederate dead. Visiting Illinois reminded Hampton of Toomer Porter's story about Lt. John A. McQueen of Company F, 15th Illinois Cavalry, the soldier who protected Toomer's family from federal troops when Columbia burned in 1865. Porter had provided McQueen with a letter addressed to General Hampton as well as any Confederate soldiers that McQueen might encounter as he departed from Columbia. The lieutenant could show the correspondence to any Confederates who might cause him problems. The letter probably saved McQueen's life.

According to Rev. John Kershaw, who was on hand for the 1895 monument ceremony, Hampton shared Porter's story about Lt. McQueen with the audience. Shortly thereafter, Hampton "observed a movement in the crowd near the platform but paid no attention to it and continued his speech until suddenly he was confronted by a large man with a big, black beard." With deep feeling, the big bearded fellow spoke. "General Hampton," he said, "I have never had the opportunity of meeting you or of presenting the letter that Dr. Porter gave me, and addressed to you, but"—drawing the letter from his pocket—"here is the letter! I cannot deliver it to you, however, for it is one of my most cherished possessions." The bearded man was the former lieutenant, John McQueen, in the flesh! Hampton had never witnessed such an exultant reaction from a crowd as he did at that moment. According to Rev. Kershaw, the men and women "cheered themselves hoarse while the tears ran down their cheeks and hand clasped hand in spontaneous outburst of comradeship." It was a memorable coda to Porter's war experiences even though he did not witness the scene.[54]

By the late 1890s, Porter was approaching his seventieth birthday. To preserve an account of his military, educational, and ecclesiastical experiences, he resolved to pen his memoirs. He had written other works about experiences, but this book was to be a comprehensive account of his life. At the suggestion of his friend Rev. Charles Frederick Hoffman, "I began, Oct. 5, 1896, to write some reminiscences of my life." After he completed the manuscript, G. P. Putnam's Sons published the memoir, *Led On! Step by Step Scenes from Clerical, Military, Educational, and Plantation Life in the South, 1828–1898*, in 1898.[55]

* * *

In his memoir, Porter confessed that before the war, he detested the institution of slavery even though he had owned slaves as a young man. He also argued that Blacks had a place within the Protestant Episcopal Church after the war. He believed that Blacks as well as whites deserved an education to allow them to become productive members of society. During his service as the rector of a predominantly African American church for a decade, he developed a measure of empathy for persons of color. He sought a unified Episcopal Church of sorts, but the unity carried a hefty price tag for Black communicants. They must understand their place within the church and act accordingly. This meant that they could have their own churches and exercise a measure of autonomy, but ultimately whites would serve as church leaders. Unlike Peter Fayssoux Stevens, who left the church when it became clear that Blacks would not be allowed to serve as leaders, Anthony Toomer Porter adopted a moderate position—it might be called benign white paternalism—choosing to work inside the PEC until shortly before his death.[56]

He died on March 30, 1902, at age seventy-four. As Bishop Ellison Capers's report in the Annual Council *Journal* noted, "On the evening of Easter Day, at his home on the Campus of the Porter Academy, the Rev. A. T. Porter, D. D., fell on sleep, dying amid the associations of his life's work, and surrounded by his devoted family." Capers marveled at the man's accomplishments. "His name and personality have been familiar to the Diocese, and to this Council, for years past," he wrote. Porter would be remembered for the "remarkable energy of his active nature; the force of his will; the School he has founded, and the great good it has done; the untiring zeal and purpose with which he supported it, up to the last; the final break-up of a strong mind, and then a brief rally, and then a pathetic ending on Easter night!"

Anthony Toomer Porter toward the end of his life. Reprinted from A. Toomer Porter, Led On! Step by Step Scenes from Clerical, Military, Educational, and Plantation Life in the South, 1828–1898 (New York and London: G. P. Putnam's Sons, the Knickerbocker Press, 1898), frontispiece. Courtesy of Reading Room 2020, Alamy Stock Photos.

Capers continued:

He was a true Evangelist. For more than half a century he was the leading spirit in Church work in upper South Carolina, and has left behind him, in the beautiful walls of Zion, and in the lasting creations of his own handiwork in Chapel and Church, memorials of his love for the worship of Zion—his zeal for the truth—his devotion to God![57]

Another commentator focused on Porter's accomplishments in education as the man's true epitaph. "During his time Dr. Porter has educated nearly 2,000 boys, fully 1,500 of whom would have had no education but for him," the author noted. "Fourteen of his students have been ordained in the Episcopal church and one in the Presbyterian church. He has sent 174 boys to college, being responsible for their expenses while in college." It was exactly the type of eulogy that Anthony Toomer Porter would have appreciated.[58]

Notes

1 After leaving General Johnston's forces, Porter traveled to Cheraw, South Carolina. When he headed for Columbia, he was traveling directly toward Union General William T. Sherman's advancing troops. Larry E. Nelson, "Sherman at Cheraw," *The South Carolina Historical Magazine* 100, no. 4 (October 1999): 332.

2 Anthony Toomer Porter, *Led On! Step by Step Scenes from Clerical, Military, Educational, and Plantation Life in the South, 1828–1898* (New York: G. P Putnam's Sons, the Knickerbocker Press, 1898), 185.

3 Porter, *Led On*, 185–8. For more on the "faithful slave" myth, see especially Carolyn E. Janney, "Written in Stone: Gender, Race, and the Heyward Shepherd Memorial," *Civil War History* 52, no. 2 (June 2006): 121–3.

4 Porter, *Led On*, 188.

5 Ibid., 189–90.

6 Ibid., 192–3.

7 Ibid., 194. The Bureau of Refugees, Freedmen, and Abandoned Lands is discussed in more detail in Chapter 5. For more on the Freedmen's Bureau, see, for example, Herman Belz, "The Freedmen's Bureau Act of 1865 and the Principle of No Discrimination According to Color," *Civil War History* 21, no. 3 (September 1975): 197–217; Robert Harrison, "New Representations of a 'Misrepresented Bureau: Reflections on Recent Scholarship on the Freedmen's Bureau," *American Nineteenth Century History* 8, no. 2 (June 2007): 205–29.

8 Porter, *Led On*, 196, 197, 198. See also Rev. A. Toomer Porter, *History of the Holy Communion Church Institute, of Charleston, South Carolina, Founded by Rev. A. Toomer Porter, A.D. MDCCCLXVII, Second Edition, Brought Down to October 1, 1875* (New York: D. Appleton and Company, 1876), 47, 64–7. For more on the episode as well as George Shrewsbury, see, for example, Winkfield Twyman, Jr., and Jennifer Richmond, *Letters in Black and White: A New Correspondence on Race in America* (Durham, NC: Pitchstone Press, 2023), 168.

9 Porter, *Led On*, 198–9. Porter's comment could be viewed in one of two ways. The charitable interpretation is that he was exercising an enlightened paternalism. Many white southerners were satisfied to leave the freed people uneducated, impoverished, and wretched. To argue that formerly enslaved persons should be educated and provided the franchise was a bold proposition for the time. A less charitable view is that Porter argued on behalf of educated, property-owning freed people knowing that they were unlikely to achieve these goals in the foreseeable future. Lacking an education or the power to vote, Blacks would remain second-class citizens in the land of their birth.

Porter could congratulate himself on his humanitarianism, secure in the knowledge that he would remain a respected member of the ruling class.

10 Porter, *Led On*, 199, 200.

11 Porter, *Led On*, 209–25. See also Anthony Toomer Porter, *The History of a Work of Faith and Love in Charleston, South Carolina* (New York: D. Appleton and Company, 1882), 6; Albert Sidney Thomas, *A Historical Account of the Protestant Episcopal Church in South Carolina, 1820–1957* (Columbia, SC: R. L. Bryan Company, 1957), 215.

12 Johnson is quoted in Porter, *Led On*, 222.

13 *Journal of the Eightieth Annual Convention of the Protestant Episcopal Church in the Diocese of South Carolina* (Charleston, SC: Walker, Evans & Cogswell, 1870), 33.

14 Porter, *Led On*, 231–5. The quote is found on page 231. See also Thomas, *A Historical Account of the Protestant Episcopal Church in South Carolina, 1820 1957*, 763.

15 Porter, *Led On*, 231–2.

16 Porter, *Led On*, 238–9. See also Rev. A.D. Mayo, "The Work of Dr. Porter in Charleston, S.C.," *Journal of Education* 15, no. 15 (April 13, 1882): 233; Thomas, *A Historical Account of the Protestant Episcopal Church in South Carolina, 1820–1957*, 763–4.

17 Porter, *Led On*, 239.

18 The report is quoted in Thomas, *A Historical Account of the Protestant Episcopal Church in South Carolina, 1820–1957*, 764.

19 *Journal of the Proceedings of the Seventy-Eighth Annual Convention of the Protestant Episcopal Church in South Carolina* (Charleston, SC: Joseph Walker, 1868), 50.

20 Porter quoted his correspondence in Porter, *Led On*, 341.

21 The quotes are found in Porter, *Led On*, 343–4. See also Mayo, "The Work of Dr. Porter in Charleston, S.C.," 233; "Rev. Dr. Anthony Toomer Porter," in *Cyclopedia of Eminent and Representative Men of the Carolinas of the Nineteenth Century, with a Brief Historical Introduction on South Carolina by General Edward McCrady, Jr., and on North Carolina by Hon. Samuel A. Ashe*, Vol. I (Madison, WS: Brant & Fuller, 1892), 494–5; Porter, *Led On*, 351–64; Thomas, *A Historical Account of the Protestant Episcopal Church in South Carolina, 1820 1957*, 766.

22 Thomas, *A Historical Account of the Protestant Episcopal Church in South Carolina, 1820–1957*, 766.

23 The resolution is quoted in Porter, *Led On*, 388.

24 Guerry is quoted in Thomas, *A Historical Account of the Protestant Episcopal Church in South Carolina, 1820–1957*, 767. See also "Bishop Guerry Dies of Bullet Wound, Was Shot by Retired Pastor, Believed Demented, Who Committed Suicide; Forgave His Assailant; Had Been Head of South Carolina Diocese of Protestant Episcopal Church Since 1908," *New York Times*, June 10, 1928, 18.

25 Karen Greene, *Porter-Gaud School: The Next Step* (Easley, SC: Southern Historical Press, 1982), 11–12; Porter, *The History of a Work of Faith and Love in Charleston, South Carolina*, 141; Porter, *Led On*, 340–64, 388–9. See also Thomas, *A Historical Account of the Protestant Episcopal Church in South Carolina, 1820 1957*, 763.

26 Porter, *Led On*, 248–9. See also *Journal of the Seventy-Ninth Annual Convention of the Protestant Episcopal Church in the Diocese of South Carolina* (Charleston, SC: Wm. G. Mazyck, 1869), 22, 27.

27 *Journal of the Eighty-Ninth Annual Convention of the Protestant Episcopal Church in the Diocese of South Carolina* (Charleston, SC: Walker, Evans & Cogswell, 1879), 40. See also "Rev. Dr. Anthony Toomer Porter," 494; Thomas, *A Historical Account of the Protestant Episcopal Church in South Carolina, 1820–1957*, 231; George Brown Tindall, *South Carolina Negroes, 1877–1900* (Columbia: University of South Carolina Press, 1952 [2003]), 195.

28 See, for example, George F. Bragg, Jr., "The Episcopal Church and the Negro Race," *Historical Magazine of the Protestant Episcopal Church* 4, no. 1 (March 1935): 50; Harold T. Lewis, *Yet with a Steady Beat: The African American Struggle for Recognition in the Episcopal Church* (Valley Forge, PA: Trinity Press International, 1996), 56–7.

29 Porter, *Led On*, 332–3. The quotes appear on page 333. See also *Journal of the Eighty-Ninth Annual Convention of the Protestant Episcopal Church in the Diocese of South Carolina*, 40; *Journal of the Ninetieth Annual Convention of the Protestant Episcopal Church in the Diocese of South Carolina* (Charleston, SC: Walker, Evans & Cogswell, 1880), 54; Lyon G. Tyler, "Drawing the Color Line in the Episcopal Diocese of South Carolina, 1876–1890: The Role of Edward McCrady, Father and Son," *The South Carolina History Magazine* 91, no. 2 (April 1990): 110, 112–13. The irony, of course, was that St. Mark's had several Black candidates who sought to become the church rector. They were ineligible owing to their race; in the meantime, the diocese experienced a shortage of white leaders in several churches.

30 *Journal of the Eighty-Ninth Annual Convention of the Protestant Episcopal Church in the Diocese of South Carolina*, 106. See also John Gary Eichelberger, Jr., "Caught in an 'Evil Infection': Postbellum Conflict in the Episcopal Diocese of South Carolina over the Role of African Americans in the Life of the Church" (master's thesis, University of the South, 2020), 91–2.

31 Porter, *Led On*, 336; *Journal of the Ninety-First Annual Convention of the Protestant Episcopal Church in the Diocese of South Carolina* (Charleston, SC: Walker, Evans & Cogswell, 1881), 72.

32 Porter, *Led On*, 308–9.

33 Thomas, *A Historical Account of the Protestant Episcopal Church in South Carolina, 1820–1957*, 449; Tindall, *South Carolina Negroes, 1877–1900*, 197.

34 *Journal of the Eighty-Ninth Annual Convention of the Protestant Episcopal Church in the Diocese of South Carolina*, 106.

35 Earlier in the report, Porter noted "I have ordained Deacon Mr. Thaddaeus Saltus, and appointed him to serve in St. Mark's Charleston." *Journal of the*

Ninety-First Annual Convention of the Protestant Episcopal Church in the Diocese of South Carolina, 41, 65, 72. See also Thomas, *A Historical Account of the Protestant Episcopal Church in South Carolina, 1820–1957*, 449.

36 *Journal of the Ninety-First Annual Convention of the Protestant Episcopal Church in the Diocese of South Carolina*, 65–6. See also Eichelberger, "Caught in an 'Evil Infection'," 94.

37 *Journal of the Ninety-Second Annual Convention of the Protestant Episcopal Church in the Diocese of South Carolina* (Charleston, SC: Walker, Evans & Cogswell, 1882), 59, 60, 63.

38 Ibid., 135.

39 *Journal of the Ninety-Third Annual Convention of the Protestant Episcopal Church in the Diocese of South Carolina* (Charleston, SC: Walker, Evans & Cogswell, 1883), 133.

40 *Journal of the Ninety-Fourth Annual Convention of the Protestant Episcopal Church in the Diocese of South Carolina* (Charleston, SC: Walker, Evans & Cogswell, 1884), 138.

41 *Journal of the Ninety-Fifth Annual Convention of the Protestant Episcopal Church in the Diocese of South Carolina* (Columbia, SC: Charles A. Calvo, 1885), 46.

42 Green is quoted in Gardiner H. Shattuck, Jr., "'One Fold and One Chief Shepherd': The Sewanee Conference of 1883 and the Beginnings of Racial Segregation in the Episcopal Church," in *Vale of Tears: New Essays on Religion and Reconstruction*, ed. Edward J. Blum and W. Scott Poole (Macon, GA: Mercer University Press, 2005), 53. See also David M. Reimers, "Negro Bishops and Diocesan Segregation in the Protestant Episcopal Church: 1870–1954," *Historical Magazine of the Protestant Episcopal Church* 31, no. 3 (September 1962): 232.

43 Shattuck, "'One Fold and One Chief Shepherd,'" 61–2; Thomas, *A Historical Account of the Protestant Episcopal Church in South Carolina, 1820 1957*, 449.

44 Gardiner H. Shattuck, Jr., *Episcopalians and Race: Civil War to Civil Rights* (Lexington: The University Press of Kentucky, 2000), 12–14; Shattuck, "'One Fold and One Chief Shepherd'," 62; Reimers, "Negro Bishops and Diocesan Segregation in the Protestant Episcopal Church," 232. See also See also Rt. Rev. W. B. W. Howe, "Paper," in *Authorized Report of the Proceedings of the Eighth Church Congress in the Protestant Episcopal Church in the United States, Held in the City of Richmond, Virginia, Tuesday, Wednesday, Thursday, and Friday, October 24th, 25th, 26th, and 27th, 1882*, ed. by the Committee on the Publication Appointed by the Executive Committee (New York: Thomas Whittaker, Publisher, Nos. 2 and 3, Bible House, 1882), 83–90.

45 Reimers, "Negro Bishops and Diocesan Segregation in the Protestant Episcopal Church," 232. See also Rhondda Robinson Thomas, "*The First Negro Priest on Southern Soil*: George Freeman Bragg, Jr. and the Struggle of Black Episcopalians in the South, 1824–1900," *Southern Quarterly* 50, no. 1 (Fall 2012): 80, 98.

46 *Journal of the Ninety-Fourth Annual Convention of the Protestant Episcopal Church in the Diocese of South Carolina*, 20–6; Shattuck, "'One Fold and One Chief Shepherd'," 65–6; Tyler, "Drawing the Color Line in the Episcopal Diocese of South Carolina, 1876–1890," 112–13.

47 A. Toomer Porter, *Speech of Rev. A. Toomer Porter, D.D., of Charleston, S.C., before the General Convention of the P.E. Church in Philadelphia, October 1883, on the Action of the Conference Held at Sewanee, Tenn., August, 1883, relative to the Work of the Church Among the Colored People of the United States* (Charleston, SC: The News and Courier Book Presses, 1883), 7.

48 Ibid., 9. See also Shattuck, "'One Fold and One Chief Shepherd'," 70.

49 Shattuck, "'One Fold and One Chief Shepherd'," 65–6; Thomas, *A Historical Account of the Protestant Episcopal Church in South Carolina, 1820 1957*, 449–50.

50 "Rev. Dr. Anthony Toomer Porter," 495.

51 *Public Ceremonies in Connection with War Memorials of the Washington Light Infantry with Orations of Gen. Wade Hampton, Hon. C. H. Simonton, Dr. A. Toomer Porter* (Charleston, SC: Edward Perry & Company, 1894), 17, 20–1.

52 Ibid., 20–1. On another occasion in 1891, Porter preached a sermon to a veterans' organization in honor of a recently deceased Confederate general, Joseph E. Johnston, during an April 26 Confederate Memorial Day celebration in Charleston. Porter lauded the former general officer as a moral exemplar, a man whose memory should provide "an incentive to our rising generation to emulate his heroic virtue." Remarking on Johnston's attempts at reconciliation following the war—the former Confederate served as a pallbearer for his rivals Ulysses S. Grant and William T. Sherman—Porter praised Johnston as a man who understood how to promote national unity while still honoring the noble values of the South. Porter is quoted in Sarah J. Purcell, *Spectacle of Grief: Public Funerals and Memory in the Civil War Era* (Chapel Hill: The University of North Carolina Press, 2022), 175.

53 *Public Ceremonies in Connection with War Memorials of the Washington Light Infantry*, 50–1.

54 Rev. Kershaw is quoted in Thomas, *A Historical Account of the Protestant Episcopal Church in South Carolina, 1820–1957*, 765–6.

55 Porter, *Led On*, 1.

56 Tyler, "Drawing the Color Line in the Episcopal Diocese of South Carolina, 1876–1890," 122.

57 *Journal of the One Hundred and Twelfth Annual Council of the Protestant Episcopal Church in the Diocese of South Carolina* (Winyah, SC: Published for the Council by the Secretary, 1902), 58–9. See also Thomas, *A Historical Account of the Protestant Episcopal Church in South Carolina, 1820 1957*, 767.

58 "Rev. Dr. Anthony Toomer Porter," 495.

9

"The Only Important Creative Theologian That the Episcopal Church in the United States Has Produced"— William Porcher DuBose

The Later Years (1865–1918)

William Porcher DuBose returned to his home near Winnsboro, South Carolina, at war's end. Like many Confederate veterans, he was demoralized by conditions in the postwar South. The Southern Confederacy was defeated on the battlefield, the town was burned, and Black Union soldiers camped near his home. No one knew what to expect. Fearful of a potential race war, white southerners nervously patrolled the streets, thankful that the "negroes were managed" by "mystery and superstition." As DuBose saw it, he and his neighbors had restored the social order. Only a few violent episodes occurred.[1]

DuBose's father had died during the war, leaving the management of his two plantations to the old man's brother-in-law, General John Bratton. Because Bratton had three of his own plantations to manage, DuBose and his wife agreed to live at Farmington, his family's main plantation home, and supervise the work necessary to restore the land and crops to profitability. It was an untenable situation despite DuBose's efforts. Lacking sufficient feed, seed, animals, and equipment, he could not make a go of the farm. Bratton eventually found a Baltimore banker to partner with him, providing much-needed capital.[2]

Relieved from his commitment to manage a plantation, DuBose accepted an assignment to oversee two congregations, St. John's Church in Winnsboro and St. Stephen's Mission in Ridgeway. The war had decimated the ranks of the Episcopal clergy, leaving far too few ministers for far too many churches. Eight months before DuBose arrived, General Sherman's troops had burned the Winnsboro Church, forcing the congregants to meet in the county courthouse. The young churchman stepped into his new role in October 1865 at almost the same time that his first child, Susie, was born. The proud parents had her baptized "at precisely the spot where I had been baptized nearly thirty years before."[3]

Many Low-Country refugees had been displaced from their homes, fleeing to safer inland communities as the Yankees looted and burned southern towns and communities. Winnsboro became a desirable destination. As a result, the church pews were usually full. Technically, DuBose was ill suited for his new role. For the first eleven months of his tenure, he was a deacon who had not been ordained a priest. That changed when Bishop Thomas F. Davis visited in September 1866. As the bishop reported, on September 9, "I preached and admitted to the Holy Order of the Priests, Rev. Wm. P. DuBose. The candidate was presented by the Rev. Mr. Obear, who, with the Rev. C. B. Walker, united in the laying on of hands." Later, Bishop Davis preached at a Black church and confirmed eight communicants.[4]

DuBose's work ethic and obvious intelligence made lasting impressions on the bishop, but the visit proved even more memorable because of the DuBose family. "Bishop Davis was at my home and one or two others of the clergy," the newly ordained priest recalled. "I happened to remember that my wife, Nannie, was with them one evening and taking part in the entertainment. The next morning, they took the train to leave us and were a little surprised to be informed of the birth the night before, May 17, of Haskell."[5]

Newly ordained, DuBose remained at his post during 1866 and 1867. He also taught Greek classes at Mt. Zion College and discovered a passion for teaching. "I had the pleasure of teaching some very bright pupils," he recalled, "and it was one of the pleasant sides of my life." They were happy years, but opportunity knocked, and he answered the call. "I would have remained there longer, but I had been invited to take the church at Abbeville."[6]

DuBose moved to Trinity Episcopal Church in Abbeville on New Year's Day 1868—the same day that his second daughter, May, was born. It was a blessed time for the young minister and his family. DuBose marveled at the beautiful church and its distinguished members. As for the town, "Abbeville had at one time been called the Athens of South Carolina." His years at Trinity were among the most enjoyable of his life. "There is much I like to remember about it," he confessed.[7]

William Porcher DuBose is pictured as a young clergyman. Courtesy of the William R. Laurie University Archives and Special Collections, the University of the South, Sewanee, Tennessee.

He especially appreciated the sense of community. Judge Wardlaw, a venerable local figure, had eight daughters, most of whom lived in the town. Some of the daughters, in turn, had children as well as other relatives who attended Trinity. Their large family "constituted a delightful community and an interesting congregation," DuBose remembered. His cousin, Octavius Porcher, had established a church school that educated many children in the area.[8]

Despite his comfortable personal situation, DuBose was deeply disturbed by political conditions in the state. Like many white southerners, he was incensed by the "carpet-bag regime" that he believed was elevating Blacks above their natural station. Violence frequently occurred at night, with mysterious fires destroying numerous barns and buildings, triggering "tremendous excitement through the whole community." He was convinced that roving bands of Black marauders were responsible for the nocturnal mayhem. Unable to depend on federal soldiers to protect the white citizenry from mob rule, "every citizen of the town was called upon to arm himself and take turns on night watch in the town," DuBose explained. "I had to buy a pistol and take my turn."[9]

He recalled two frightening episodes from that frantic time. In the first, a local judge, Samuel McGowan, was away from home when marauders burned a building on his property and broke into his house. The ruffians physically kidnapped a woman from the house. Only the screams of her old nurse "caused her to be liberated."[10]

The second episode involved DuBose himself. The young minister and his family moved into the rectory of Trinity Church after he assumed his duties. Two of DuBose's sisters-in-law came to visit and slept in a front bedroom with the infant, Susie. One night, as the family slept, someone crawled through a window and absconded with a trunk belonging to one of the ladies. As terrifying as the theft was, the situation grew worse. "Then the robber had returned, entered the room again and gone quietly around the bed, apparently searching around the pillows." Hearing the noise, "Miss Peronneau, putting out her hand, put it on the kinky head of a negro. Of course, she screamed, and the robber quickly disappeared."[11]

DuBose's tales of Black criminals running loose during Reconstruction reflected the standard white southern narrative, which reinforced the fears of many white South Carolinians that Blacks could not be trusted. In this typical narrative, rapacious Negroes were prone to rob and murder white people if left unchecked. Although the evidence of Black militants patrolling the countryside under the cover of night was greatly exaggerated, whites believed the stories. In response, white southerners argued that they must arm themselves lest they be overpowered by angry Black mobs. It was little wonder that the Ku Klux Klan arose in Abbeville and surrounding areas as early as 1868.[12]

Black violence could not be tolerated, but white violence was acceptable if employed for the right cause. In October 1868, two Republican state legislators, James Martin and Benjamin F. Randolph, died at the hands of white vigilantes near Abbeville. Martin was gunned down on October 5 as he traveled from the Abbeville Courthouse to his home. Eleven days later, Randolph was changing trains at Hodges Station in Abbeville County when three white men shot him dead in broad daylight. The assassins mounted their horses and rode away with no repercussions. Law enforcement officers did not even make a pretense of investigating the crime. Martin was an Irish immigrant who had dared to speak out in favor of Black suffrage while Randolph was a Black man who failed to know his place.[13]

"No one wanted to be violent," DuBose insisted, but self-defense was necessary to preserve white supremacy. Denied the option of self-government—"with the Yankees everywhere"—white people in South Carolina were forced to take matters into their own hands even if they had to step outside the boundaries of the law to do so. This situation led DuBose to pen the most controversial statement he ever wrote—at least controversial by later standards. "The condition of things just compelled some such organization as the Ku Klux Klan," he argued. "It was an inspiration of genius—the most discreet and successful management of the situation that could have been devised."[14]

Americans of a later age—and even some Americans at the time—were appalled by Klan excesses, but white southerners during Reconstruction believed that a vigilante group formed to police out-of-control freed people, carpetbaggers, and scalawags performed a valuable service. Rather than regarding the group as thugs and terrorists who threatened the American republic, whites such as DuBose believed that Klansmen restored a much-needed semblance of law and order. In a world where the fixed social order had been upended, an organization that promoted white supremacy was heralded as a savior of the community.[15]

As he did so often in his life when he was suffering, DuBose turned to the church for solace from the tribulations of the outside world. He threw himself into his work, and his diligence reaped numerous benefits. Virtually everyone who encountered DuBose was impressed with the man. He was a charismatic, learned figure who proved to be an inspiration to his congregation. DuBose conveyed a sense of authority and deep convictions while remaining friendly and approachable. He also attracted considerable praise after the diocesan convention met in Trinity Church from May 12–14, 1870. DuBose preached an ordination service and spent time with Bishop Davis. His reputation as a hard worker and deep thinker originated during these years.[16]

He might have followed in the footsteps of his colleagues Peter Fayssoux Stevens and Anthony Toomer Porter, spending the rest of his days preaching the Gospel in South Carolina. DuBose certainly expected to do so. Yet his life and career path changed in ways that he had not foreseen.

The change occurred because of a meeting of the trustees of the University of the South, a new institution of higher learning established in Sewanee, Tennessee. On July 12, 1871, Vice Chancellor Charles Todd Quintard, the Bishop of Tennessee, reported that the university's acting chaplain, Rev. Francis Asbury Shoup, could no longer serve. Bishop Quintard told the trustees that a replacement was needed as soon as possible. Acting with dispatch, the trustees elected the Rev. Samuel S. Harris, rector of Trinity Church in Columbus, Georgia, to serve as the university chaplain as well as a professor of moral science. After Harris declined the appointment, Quintard nominated DuBose on July 17. The trustees voted to accept the nomination, and Quintard sent a telegram to South Carolina.[17]

DuBose recalled his surprise upon receiving the news. "In the summer of 1871 there suddenly came to me a communication that was to determine the course of my whole life," he wrote. "It was a telegram from Sewanee, informing me that I had been elected *Chaplain of the University* and *Professor of Moral Science*." It was unquestionably an honor, but he had no time for reflection or deliberation. "The Board of Trustees was in session, and it was necessary to have an immediate reply. I had to make my decision without consultation with my Bishop, which was a great grief to me." Despite this unenviable circumstance, DuBose knew where his duty lay. "I returned an acceptance and prepared to make this change at the close of the year."[18]

Shortly before he was offered the post at the university, DuBose came tantalizingly close to being elected assistant bishop of the South Carolina Diocese. Owing to Bishop Davis's poor health, the assistant bishop would likely become the bishop in a short time. Balloting for the assistant bishop post began during the diocesan convention in Charleston in May 1871. The Rev. Christopher P. Gadsden, rector of St. Luke's Episcopal Church in Charleston and nephew of former Bishop Christopher E. Gadsden, initially seemed to be the likely choice. In later balloting, however, the Rev. William Bell White Howe emerged as a possible alternative. As the two candidates became deadlocked, a third possibility came to the fore. "Suddenly and absolutely unexpectedly, my name was proposed," DuBose recalled. It was not merely a ploy to break the deadlock, but "I was almost unanimously elected by the laity and came within three or four votes of election by the clergy."[19]

Had he been elected, DuBose probably would not have accepted the position in Sewanee, and the course of his professional life would have been much different. "*Fortunately*, the representatives of the two leading candidates, seeing what was likely to happen, came to an agreement and Bishop Howe was elected," DuBose later wrote. He was not dejected. In fact, in his view, "I have always regarded this as one of the most fortunate escapes of my life. It would have been one of the great misfortunes of my life if I had been elected—that I feel very forcibly."[20]

Free to move on with his new career, DuBose wrapped up his work in South Carolina within a few weeks. When he visited the University of the South for the first time, his family had not yet joined him. Lacking a permanent residence, he stayed as a guest of Josiah Gorgas and his wife. Gorgas was a former general officer and chief of ordnance in the Confederate States Army. In 1870, he came to the university as the second vice chancellor. It was a period of uncertainty as the university trustees debated the proper role of the institution. Gorgas later became president of the University of Alabama.[21]

DuBose was impressed with the general and his wife. "Both of them were factors of very great importance in determining the character of the school," he remembered. "General Gorgas was the head of the Institution and Mrs. Gorgas presided over a boarding-house with a large number of students. Between the two there was exercised a very large part of the influence which was to shape the character of Sewanee from the beginning."[22]

As DuBose recalled in an article that he published in *The Sewanee Review* in 1905,

> When I came to Sewanee in the third year of its new existence, it was only a grammar school, and it was already known, wherever the boys went through the South, by two marks: the elegant fit of their dress and the peculiar courtesy of their manner. Their tailor was fresh from Paris, and there was something in the grave, dignified and noble military courtesy of General Gorgas which left an indelible impress upon all who were long enough under him to receive it.[23]

Moving from his longtime home in South Carolina to the mountains of Tennessee to take on the tasks of sustaining a fledgling school in 1871 was risky. It was by no means certain that the new institution would survive and prosper. Nonetheless, DuBose saw promising signs. Although the institution was relatively new when he came to Tennessee, the University of the South sported an illustrious pedigree. In July 1856, Leonidas Polk, bishop of the Episcopal Diocese of Louisiana and later a Confederate general officer and founder of the Protestant Episcopal Church in the Confederate States of America, contacted the Episcopal bishops of the southern dioceses in the lower South to announce his plan for educating the children of elite southerners and training clergymen. As Polk explained it, "A cardinal purpose in the whole movement would of course be, that the institutions would be declaredly out and out Episcopal, founded by the Church for the especial benefit of her own children, for the advancement of learning generally, and for the propagation of the Gospel as she understands it."[24]

Supported by Bishop Stephen Elliott of Georgia and Bishop James Otey of Tennessee, Polk organized a university for affluent Episcopalians. In 1858, the university's board of trustees acquired the title to 9,525 acres of land approximately 30 miles northwest of Chattanooga, Tennessee. Two years later, the founders laid the cornerstone for the university's first building. The plan called for the creation of thirty-two schools within the new university with a $3 million endowment. As of 1860, the trustees had raised $500,000.[25]

As it did for many activities, the war interrupted plans for university construction. The area around Chattanooga witnessed numerous battles, and the partially constructed university structures were destroyed. Bishop Polk was killed in battle in June 1864. By the time the Southern Confederacy capitulated in 1865, the endowment was lost. With the southern states prostrate and impoverished, the creation of an Episcopal university in the hills of Tennessee seemed an unlikely prospect.[26]

With characteristic determination, Bishop Quintard threw himself into the tedious, enervating work of fundraising on behalf of the school. By 1866, he had collected enough funds to build two log cabins and a small school building. Two years later, the university opened as a college preparatory school with four professors and nine students. By 1870, enrollment stood at 125.[27]

The trustees agreed to organize the university into seven schools, with the preparatory school existing as a separate institution. Although Bishop Quintard proved to be an indefatigable fundraiser, money was always in short supply. Rev. Shoup, a professor and the university's former chaplain, joked that the school was a haven for people of "eminent respectability" who "lived together in cheerful poverty."[28]

William Porcher DuBose forged a successful academic career as a theologian at the University of the South in Sewanee, Tennessee. Courtesy of the William R. Laurie University Archives and Special Collections, the University of the South, Sewanee, Tennessee.

By the time that William Porcher DuBose agreed to become chaplain and professor of moral science three years later, the university needed new buildings to accommodate an influx of pupils. "With the consent and cooperation of my wife, Nannie, I spent the small relic of her fortune in building Palmetto Hall, which for a number of years was filled with students from South Carolina," he wrote.[29]

Increasing enrollments were encouraging indications of the institution's viability, but much work needed to be done. DuBose understood this. He had been hired to shape a nascent university into a first-rate institution of higher learning. As he recalled years later, in addition to "my duties as Chaplain and Professor of Moral Science, that would be Ethics, it was generally understood there it should be organized as soon as possible a *Theological Department* of the University." The demand for a new department grew rapidly. "The materials began very soon to present themselves among the older students, and in my second year I began preparations for such a department." For a time, DuBose was the major decision-maker for the new department. "I instigated changes for those desirous of studying for the ministry, and in the period between 1874–1876 the number of theological students reached some eight and ten students. Most of these went through their entire preparations for Holy Orders under my charge."[30]

Before DuBose arrived, the university had been modeled on a military academy. In fact, the University of the South was for all intents and purposes a military school. More than half of the faculty members were Confederate veterans, and they ran the institution on a military model. The students even wore Confederate gray uniforms until 1892. In an amazing bit of understatement, DuBose wrote that in "1871, the change was made by the organization of the University faculty and the intention on the part of the Board of Trustees of the substitution of University instead of military authority. This was a difficult process and was for some years a source of trouble." The "some years" extended for decades. Even after the university left behind its military bearing, it retained, in the words of one commentator, "its unrelenting adherence to the cultural values of 'the Lost Cause.'" University administrators proudly displayed a Confederate battle flag in the school's chapel as well as other Confederate mementos around the campus.[31]

As DuBose settled into his new position, his family joined him in Sewanee. "My brother, Robert, and my sister-in-law, Mrs. McNeely DuBose, came with me to take charge of Palmetto Hall," he wrote. "At the same time, my cousin, Mrs. Maria Porcher, built Magnolia Hall on the adjoining lot. Both were speedily filled with students, and *that* was our beginning at Sewanee."[32]

DuBose served as the university chaplain for twelve years and a professor of moral science for almost thirty-seven years. Professionally, these were happy, productive years. From the beginning of his tenure, he was a role model for his students. He started by canvassing South Carolina to recruit young men to enroll in the university. When he arrived, he brought with him a new crop of students.³³

Even as the move to Sewanee represented a professional triumph, DuBose experienced personal tragedy. He was delighted when his wife gave birth to their fourth child, a son named Samuel. As DuBose recounted the events in his memoirs, he scarcely had time to enjoy his newborn baby. "My wife's health began to fail and the ensuing winter, I left the children in charge of their aunt and took my wife, Nannie, to Charleston." She convalesced in her sister's home under the care of her brother-in-law, a doctor. She received the best care possible, but it was not enough to restore her health. "She gradually grew worse." He returned to Sewanee briefly, but "I hurried back to Charleston and in April [1872] she died." In DuBose's opinion, "I think she never did recover from certain hardships endured during the war, for she was so utterly unselfish, and thoughtful of all except herself, that she impaired her health."³⁴

His misfortunes did not end with Nannie's death. Young Samuel initially "throve and grew and was unusually well and strong" until the spring of 1874. The child suffered "a severe bronchial attack and lost his voice entirely. He lingered and lingered. I used to carry him in my arms, and he loved it. He died." DuBose was inconsolable. "I miss that little boy to this day," he wrote. "I miss him *now*. Dear little fellow! *Dear* little fellow!"³⁵

While he suffered through these heart-wrenching losses, DuBose also struggled to ensure the viability of the school. As a first step, "in order to assist in the change of discipline desired by the Trustees," the administration "determined to institute the order of government among the University students—the first introduction of the habit of the gown, I think, in this country!" DuBose never lost sight of the challenges, but he remained optimistic in the face of adversity. "It must be remembered that so soon after the war we had to deal with the results of interrupted education, and the making of the university out of such untrained and undisciplined material was a matter of much difficulty for many years among the faculty."³⁶

During the early 1870s, DuBose worked with two women from Jackson, Mississippi, Mrs. Maria Louise Yerger and Mrs. Hattie B. Kells, to move their all-girls school somewhere near Sewanee. They eventually settled on a site at Monteagle—called "Moffat" at the time—6 miles from Sewanee. "In the spring of '73, the buildings were sufficiently completed for the opening of Fairmount School, with a considerable number of pupils, all, I believe, from Mississippi and Louisiana," DuBose later wrote. "The ladies looked to me, as Chaplain of the University, to furnish them with what services were practical, which I began almost at once to do with the assistance first of Charles Gray and then of John Kershaw, theological students."³⁷

As one commentator, Moultrie Guerry, himself a chaplain at the University of the South, noted, Fairmount "furnished many a Southern woman with an education and provided many a Sewanee man with a wife." This statement

William Porcher DuBose toward the end of his life. Courtesy of the William R. Laurie University Archives and Special Collections, the University of the South, Sewanee, Tennessee.

certainly applied to DuBose. As Rev. Guerry noted, "He himself married Mrs. Yerger in 1878."[38]

In his memoirs, DuBose wrote tenderly of his second wife. She and Mrs. Kells had suffered "a very, very severe strain" organizing the school and arranging for their students to travel from Mississippi. He was concerned for Mrs. Yerger when he encountered her in Memphis as he canvassed for new students at Sewanee.

> She was in delicate health, a stranger in the city, and very much depressed by the difficulties of her task. It was in my power to give her a great many introductions and to be of great service to her, to her very manifest and

great relief. This led to an acquaintance and intimacy, which could never had occurred in my official relation with Fairmount and finally resulted in our marriage in December of the year 1878.[39]

DuBose and his new wife became fixtures at their respective schools. Generations of students revered them as exemplars. One contemporary described DuBose as

> small in stature, but this was the only way in which he could be called small. His appearance and personality were so striking that even the undiscerning were impressed. His massive forehead and deep-set eyes betokened the thinker. He was gentle but with the strength of gentleness, and although his students knew that they were in the presence of a great and good man, they did not stand in awe of him.[40]

DuBose's unusual teaching style accounted, at least in part, for his success. Unlike many learned professors who developed a course outline and imparted the same instruction using the same notes year after year, DuBose started anew with each new crop of students. As he explained in his autobiographical account, *Turning Points in My Life*,

> My method of study and of teaching has been so peculiar that I hesitate to confess it. I can never use a former note or an old manuscript. In fact, I have never accumulated or possessed any of these; I have always begun every day and every year anew, without any help from the past through any records of my own. I remember of any book only what has passed into and become part of myself.

In rejecting the "sage on the stage" model of teaching where a professor stands before students and pontificates on a learned subject, DuBose preferred to serve as a discussant, debating issues and trading ideas with his students as though he and they were on a shared journey of discovery and wonder. His willingness to learn with his students instead of acting as an all-knowing dispenser of wisdom endeared him to numerous pupils for more than thirty-five years.[41]

During these years, students recalled seeing their professor on horseback, riding into the mountains or down to the valley to preach a sermon. He spent his leisure hours talking and reading to young people both in his professional capacity and as a private man. He was both erudite and unpretentious. "His personality was impressive but never overpowering, and he encouraged his students to think for themselves," one observer recalled. "His lectures were difficult for those who were not philosophically minded, but even these never went empty away; they 'got the man' when they did not get his subtleties of thought."[42]

Numerous stories illustrated the professor's warmth and generosity. In his retrospective on DuBose's life and career, Rev. Guerry recounted one such story, possibly apocryphal. According to Guerry, the "magnetism and sincerity" of DuBose's personality were personified by his meeting with the renowned educator Helen Keller.

> It was at a reception, and the blind hostess had many hands to shake, but when she felt the hand of Dr. DuBose, she impulsively ran her fingers lightly over his small straight stature and seemed to see through them to his face, and indeed his very soul. Then she drew him quickly to her and kissed him as though she had discovered her father.[43]

DuBose's work ethic was legendary, but he was forced to back away from several commitments owing to poor health. As he recalled in his memoir, *Turning Points in My Life*,

> In 1876 a threat of failing health caused a temporary break in my courses, and theological instruction ceased until about 1880, when, with the completion of St. Luke's Hall and the organizing of a theological faculty, it was resumed upon something of an adequate scale and basis. From that time began my constructive interpretation and teaching of the New Testament.[44]

By 1877, the university's *Proceedings* noted that the theological department was a separate school. DuBose was listed as a professor of Hebrew, Exegesis, and Homiletics. The following year, the department was formally established with the Rev. Telfair Hodgson installed as the dean. Under this new dean, DuBose served as professor of New Testament Language and Interpretation, a position he held from 1878 until 1893. He also served for a time as acting professor of Old Testament Language and Interpretation.[45]

After Dean Hodgson died in 1893, DuBose became the acting dean of the school of theology. On July 31, 1894, the board of trustees elected him dean. He served in that position until he retired on June 24, 1908. For the decade following his retirement, until his death on August 18, 1918, DuBose was the dean emeritus of the school.[46]

When he became dean, the School of Theology had five departments: New Testament Language and Interpretation; Old Testament Language and Interpretation; Dogmatic Theology; Ecclesiastical History and Church Polity; and Pastoral Theology and Homiletics. DuBose taught courses in both the New and Old Testaments. Beginning in 1898, his son, William Haskell DuBose, also taught at the university.[47]

While he was at Sewanee, DuBose wrote seven books of theology and one memoir (although one book was not published until long after his death). He was in his mid-fifties before he published his first work, *The Soteriology of the New Testament*, in 1892. The summation of his decades of teaching and reflection, *Soteriology* suggested that Jesus did not die on the cross *instead* of mankind; he died *for* human beings, serving as their representative. The book explored the life of Jesus as both a human being of this world and a divine being beyond this world rather than as a remote deity divorced from the problems of mankind.[48]

His second book, *The Ecumenical Councils* (1896), served as volume three of *Ten Epochs of Church History*, a multivolume work edited by John Fulton. Unlike DuBose's other major books, *The Ecumenical Councils* did not explore the New Testament in depth. Instead, it focused on Christology—Jesus's birth, life, death, resurrection, and ascension.[49]

In *The Gospel in the Gospels* (1906), his third book, DuBose explored Jesus as he was presented in the synoptic Gospels. "How then was the so unique or exceptional personality of Jesus to be accounted for or explained?" DuBose asked at the outset. "Was He only a human individual exceptionally blessed or graced? Or, while perfect man, was He, just because perfect man, something more than man? Perfection is no mark of our common humanity and needs a very high accounting for. So, from the beginning begins a questioning which Christianity answers for itself in the Gospel of the Incarnation."[50]

His fourth book, *The Gospel According to St. Paul* (1907), focused on the Epistle to the Romans to explore the question of whether a conflict existed between Jesus and Paul. Unlike some theologians, DuBose argued that St. Paul's epistles interpreted the Gospel of Jesus Christ but did not alter it. Pauline interpretations are faithful to the idea of Jesus and the central tenets of Christianity. In DuBose's view, St. Paul fleshes out the concepts of Jesus, so to speak, without contradicting or adding to Jesus's teachings.[51]

DuBose's fifth book, *High Priesthood and Sacrifice: An Exposition of the Epistle to the Hebrews* (1908), was a compilation of lectures he delivered as an exposition of the Epistle to the Hebrews. The noted philanthropist George Atwater Jarvis provided a $10,000 endowment for a lectureship at General Theological Seminary to honor his former Pastor Benjamin Henry Paddock, the Bishop of Massachusetts from 1873–1891. Various religious figures contributed lectures to the series. *High Priesthood and Sacrifice* was DuBose's contribution.[52]

The Reason of Life (1911), his sixth book, was a Johannine interpretation of the Gospel. The term indicates a body of New Testament writings—the Gospel of John, the three Epistles of John (1 John, 2 John, and 3 John), and the Book of Revelation—attributed to John the Apostle, one of Christ's twelve disciples. Johannine texts contain unique theological perspectives, a distinct literary style, and themes not found in other New Testament writings. As DuBose noted, spiritual and natural processes of life are in continuity. "We cannot, except in the abstraction of thought, sever the continuity that runs through and unifies all life, from the lowest material up to the highest spiritual," he wrote.

> So, Christ's mission and ministry was to men's body and bodily life; the heaven He brought and preached was a heaven upon earth; the kingdom He set up was God's spirit of love, service, and sacrifice to be manifested and exercised by men among men in the world. All the work of Christ is work to be done here and now.[53]

His seventh book was a collection of eleven articles published in *The Constructive Quarterly*, from 1913 until 1920. The *Quarterly*, a publication of the Episcopal Church from 1913 through 1922, was a forum to discuss a variety of issues involving "faith, work, and thought in Christendom." In 1957, editor W. Norman Pittenger, a prolific scholar and theologian, brought together the essays in a volume titled *Unity in the Faith* to celebrate the centennial of the University of the South.[54]

DuBose's final book grew out of festivities honoring his four decades of service at Sewanee. During the week of August 2–6, 1911, the university held a series of events commemorating its most famous chaplain and professor. By this time, DuBose was a dean emeritus. He lectured several times throughout that August week. He subsequently collected his lectures and published them as *Turning Points in My Life*, an autobiographical account of how significant events in his life and times influenced his ministry as well as his theology.[55]

These works brought DuBose a measure of fame among theologians in the United States and around the globe, but he received his share of criticism as well. When he was proposed to the university board of trustees as the new dean of the theological department, Bishop Edwin Weed of Florida and Bishop Cleland Nelson of Georgia voiced objections to DuBose's candidacy. They especially questioned his orthodoxy owing to DuBose's rejection of a literal interpretation of the Bible.[56]

The objections were hardly unusual among conservative clergy. Throughout his major works, DuBose demonstrated that he was a New Testament scholar who rejected biblical literalism while maintaining the primacy of scripture. DuBose believed that the scriptures can be important without being literally true. This argument placed him in the middle of the theological debates of his day. During the nineteenth century, Fundamentalists rejected the notion that knowledge of the world and the human experience should be based primarily on reason, rationality, and empirical evidence. To literalists, the growth of a secular worldview destroyed the credibility of the Bible as the source of human knowledge and undermined the timeless values of the Gospels. In an ever-changing, fast-paced, modern world, Fundamentalists believed that a literal interpretation of the Bible provided clear answers and directives.[57]

According to DuBose, rejecting a literal interpretation of the Bible was not heresy or a repudiation of Christianity. "Truths expressed in the Scriptures in the objective or concrete form of history may be truths independently of the literal truth of the history," he wrote.

> It is not necessary to believe the story of the Garden and the Fall to be historical fact in order to find in the story the most effective primitive account of spiritual truths and realities. To say that Abraham was before Moses, the Gospel was prior to the law, is to utter a great truth quite independently of what anyone may believe about Abraham or about Moses as historical facts or factors in the actual history of the world.[58]

Although he believed that human beings should strive to make sense of the scriptures, DuBose did not accept propositional theology, or the contention that God reveals himself in propositions about divine personal nature, God's plan, or reasons that history unfolds in certain ways. For some theologians, the task is to study scripture as a series of propositions or words that must be understood as though God is sending divine messages to be decoded and interpreted. In DuBose's view, God can be understood, to the extent that He can be understood at all, primarily through acts and events.[59]

As he observed in *The Gospel According to St. Paul,*

> the fact will always remain that we receive our Christianity through the Scriptures and the Church, and that these are the tribunal of final resort for determining what Christianity is. Human reason and human experience have a great part too to play in the matter, but that is both later and different. It was not theirs to give us Christianity, but it is theirs to pass upon the question whether Christianity as given is not what it claims to be, the whole truth of ourselves, because the whole truth of God in ourselves.[60]

He approached theology and the study of scripture with a sense of humility. Man's understanding of God will always be imperfect and incomplete. This insight is reflected in St. Paul's often-quoted comment that "we see through a glass, darkly" from 1 Cor. 13:12. The ways of the Lord are inscrutable to man. Human beings look through a dim mirror as they attempt to know God. Such a realization does not mean that human beings should simply shrug their shoulders and acknowledge that they can never have a perfect understanding of God, so why strive to comprehend? Rather than surrender to nihilism and mutter a truism—"the Lord works in mysterious ways!"—human beings must engage with scripture as they seek enlightenment. The search, although imperfect and always incomplete, is a worthwhile endeavor.[61]

In a similar vein, developing a logically consistent theology does not undermine Christian faith. Indeed, theology—the study of religious experience and God's relations with the world—is the systematic study of scripture to discover whatever can be discovered about the Lord. This approach suggests that human reason is a tool by which human beings can better understand biblical writings and concepts, but it does not indicate a complete mastery of the divine. DuBose wrote in *The Gospel in the Gospels* that the

> abiding truth of Jesus Christ is within and behind and wholly independent of the ever-changing phases or stages of human knowledge. The setting has from time to time to be altered to adapt it to the changing focus or vision of advancing science, but what is really of the jewel within does not change with it; it is Jesus Christ the same yesterday, to-day, and forever.[62]

Engaging with scripture means that human beings must do more than merely read the words. They must incorporate the lessons into their lives. DuBose argued that

> we must cease to treat the phraseology, the forms, definitions, and dogmas of Christianity as sacred relics, too sacred to be handled. We must take them out of their napkins, strip them of their cerements, and turn them into current coin. We must let them do business in the life that is living now and take part in the thought and feeling and activity of the men of the world of to-day.[63]

Because we see the world through a dim mirror, "truth" can become elusive. "Truth is not an individual thing; no one of us has all of it—even all of it that is known," DuBose wrote in *Turning Points in My Life*. "Truth is a corporate possession, and the knowledge of it is a corporate process. It enters slowly and painfully into the common sense, the common experience, the common use and life of men."[64]

Human beings attempt to understand truth through lived experience—hard, bitter, devastating experience such as the loss of a spouse or a child—which means that they must be free. With that freedom, invariably they will err and hopefully learn from those errors. "The power to be free cannot be separated from the right to err," DuBose observed. The errors of human beings do not threaten the church or undermine the teachings found in scripture. DuBose argued that "the holiness of the Church is not compromised or contradicted by the weaknesses, the shortcomings, the sins of its members—any more than the efficiency of a hospital by the illness of its patients; so, the truth and life of the Church itself is not compromised by the mistakes and errors and falsities of its individual teachers and doctors."[65]

Despite its elusive nature, truth is important because both individuals and the church grow as they search for truth. The institutional church is a manmade institution, which means that it is fallible, but the church can assist individuals in advancing their knowledge of scripture. As DuBose explained in *The Ecumenical Councils*, a "complete and all-sided faith or life is not promised or given to any individual man, and no single man even with the aid of the Scriptures holds such except as the gift to him in whole or for the most part of the common thought and knowledge of the church." If a person wants to understand God, to the extent possible, he needs the church. "Only such a complex resultant of the operation of many minds and lives as we have in the Scriptures or in the church can combine the whole truth or express the sum of Christian experience."[66]

He often wrote of the need for unity in the faith. By this, DuBose meant

> that contraries do not necessarily contradict, nor need opposites always oppose. What we want is not to surrender or abolish our differences, but to unite and compose them. We need the truth of every variant opinion and the light from every opposite point of view. The least fragment is right in so far as it stands for a part of the truth. It is wrong only when, as so often, it elevates into a ground of division from the other fragments just that which in reality fits it to unite with and supplement them.[67]

The core of DuBose's theology was his contention that Jesus Christ is one person who is both fully human and fully divine. Using this Christological model, DuBose wrote that "All the great problems which have occupied Christian thought from the beginning may be reduced to a single problem, viz., the coexistence and union in one element of the two elements of the Divine and the human." Some scholars treat the Bible "as so divine as to not be at all human," but this interpretation places scripture on a higher plane where human beings cannot access it. This concern about banishing the Bible into an inaccessible level of abstraction was exactly DuBose's point when he wrote that the scriptures must not become "sacred relics, too sacred to be handled." At the same time, the other extreme is to see Christ as merely human. In this view, Jesus was a marvelous humanitarian, a gifted teacher, and a supremely wise man, but he was not divine. DuBose believed that this interpretation was as flawed as the other. Extremes must be avoided. DuBose wrote that "A Divine thing may have a human record; or in other words, Scripture may be, as to its contents, divine; as to its form, human—the treasure may be heavenly, the vessel earthen."[68]

His books made him world famous among theologians of all faiths and denominations. After he retired in 1908, DuBose was widely acknowledged as a giant within the Episcopal Church. Religious scholars who read his books and former students spread the word that he was a thinker, writer, and teacher of the first rank. He brought honor and prestige to the University of the South.[69]

DuBose remained active and engaged in church matters until shortly before his death. "His mind was keenly alive and active, and clear almost to the last moment," his son, Rev. William Haskell DuBose, remembered. Nonetheless, the old man's health declined even though his mind was active. In his eighty-second year, the retired theologian lay on his deathbed. "I am prepared and ready to go to my real home," he said. "If God should take me tonight, I would be glad. The Eternal Father, the risen Christ, the Blessed Holy Ghost have been my companions." On August 18, 1918, DuBose fell into a deep sleep from which he never awoke.[70]

Examining his life and career from cradle to grave, it is difficult to assess the legacy of this "great and good man." To innumerable students, faculty, and academics, William Porcher DuBose did much to advance the cause of Christian theology. He was a primary force behind the success and growth of the University of the South. He was a gifted teacher, writer, and thinker. He spent decades improving the life of the mind, and he developed an international reputation.

Yet, he was thoroughly a man of his time. When viewed through a prism of modern sensibilities, DuBose's antipathy toward people of color initially appears incongruous, perhaps even perverse. His intellectualism and devotion to Christian principles appear at odds with his inherent racism. A devoted follower of Jesus—a figure who represents the ideal of brotherly love and symbolizes the need to help less fortunate persons, whatever their personal characteristics—would seem to be accepting of all people, regardless of their race, creed, or color. To readers of a later age, a man of the cloth and a towering intellect would not be so provincial as to embrace unbridled white supremacy. Viewed in this manner, DuBose's affinity for a terrorist organization such as the Ku Klux Klan is off-putting and inexplicable.

This assessment ignores the history of whites in the postbellum South. For centuries, white children had been taught that the social order, with whites at the top and Blacks at the bottom, was fixed and immutable. Race, slavery, and social status were like constellations in the night sky: They might appear to be different when viewed from different perspectives, but they were nonetheless tied together in a static relationship. White southerners did not argue over the virtues or veracity of these relationships. They had existed this way since time immemorial and presumably would exist this way into the foreseeable future. "It is God's will that some races are superior to others," apologists for slavery and segregation contended, thereby mistaking manmade institutions for a divine universal plan.

That a man as conspicuously intelligent and emotionally mature as William Porcher DuBose would uncritically accept white supremacy with nary an objection says much about his experiences before, during, and after the war. He was immersed in the culture, heritage, and traditions of the Old

South. He did not know, nor care to know, about the lives and fortunes of Blacks. To him, they were servants or at least belonged in the servant class. This insight is akin to the mudsill theory, the idea that an underclass always exists to prop up the rest of society. In the Old South of DuBose's era, Black Americans comprised the underclass.[71]

Unlike Peter Fayssoux Stevens and Anthony Toomer Porter, who ministered to people of color, DuBose kept his distance. For all his brilliance as a biblical scholar with an international reputation, he was a provincial white southerner when it came to matters of race. Such a conclusion does not excuse DuBose, but perhaps it partially explains him.

Two versions of DuBose existed: The scholar who left a profound legacy of teaching and scholarship that transcended the white racist elitism of the nineteenth century and a scared husband and father who feared for himself and his family as the social order disintegrated following the war. For a hundred years after his death, these two versions coexisted. They clashed, as inevitably they would, early in the twenty-first century.

W. Norman Pittenger argued that "William Porcher DuBose was the only important creative theologian that the Episcopal Church in the United States has produced." Beginning in 1924, the University of the South honored its most famous son with a series of scholarly lectures on the anniversary of his death. For many of those years, DuBose's pro-Confederate views on race represented the traditional view of white southerners and therefore presented few problems and prompted few objections. By 2021, however, DuBose's views on race were no longer mainstream. The university recognized that "DuBose is not the name that best represents our context and what the School of Theology and our alumni have to offer the 21st-century church." As a result, the university changed the name to the "Alumni Lectures," disavowing any connection with the brilliant professor of theology and his odious views on race.[72]

By the time the university changed the name of the lecture series, DuBose was all but forgotten except among scholars of the nineteenth century Episcopal Church or historically aware alumni of the University of the South. To those who know of him, DuBose left a mixed legacy. He was noble and debased, transcendent and mundane—a man of enormous gifts and sagacity as well as a traditional white supremacist of the Old South.

Notes

1   William Porcher DuBose, "Reminiscences, 1836–1878," typescript copy transcribed by William Haskell DuBose, Southern Historical Collection, University of North Carolina at Chapel Hill, 140.

2 Ralph E. Luker, "The Crucible of Civil War and Reconstruction in the Experience of William Porcher DuBose," *The South Carolina Historical Magazine* 83, no. 1 (January 1982): 65.

3 DuBose, "Reminiscences," 141. See also Robert B. Slocum, "The Lessons of Experience and the Theology of William Porcher DuBose," *Journal of Theological Studies* 79, no. 3 (Summer 1997): 347.

4 *Journal of the Proceedings of the Seventy-Seventh Annual Convention of the Protestant Episcopal Church in South Carolina* (Charleston, SC: W. W. Deane, 1867), 43.

5 DuBose, "Reminiscences," 148.

6 Ibid., 141–2.

7 Ibid., 143–4; Luker, "The Crucible of Civil War and Reconstruction in the Experience of William Porcher DuBose," 65–6.

8 DuBose, "Reminiscences," 144.

9 Ibid., 144–5. See also Slocum, "The Lessons of Experience and the Theology of William Porcher DuBose," 347–8.

10 DuBose, "Reminiscences," 144.

11 Ibid., 145–6; Luker, "The Crucible of Civil War and Reconstruction in the Experience of William Porcher DuBose," 66.

12 Allen W. Trelease, *White Terror: The Ku Klux Klan Conspiracy and Southern Reconstruction* (Baton Rouge: Louisiana State University Press, 1999 [1971]), 72. See also Francis B. Simkins, "The Ku Klux Klan in South Carolina, 1868–1871," *The Journal of Negro History* 12, no. 4 (October 1927): 609.

13 Ibid., 72, 115–17, 349, 353.

14 DuBose, "Reminiscences," 140.

15 See, for example, Stephen Budiansky, *The Bloody Shirt: Terror After the Civil War* (New York: Penguin, 2008), 135–42; Wyn Craig Wade, *The Fiery Cross: The Ku Klux Klan in America* (New York: Touchstone, 1988), 33–59.

16 DuBose, "Reminiscences," 148. See also *Journal of the Eighty-First Annual Convention of the Protestant Episcopal Church in the Diocese of South Carolina* (Charleston, SC: Walker, Evans & Cogswell, 1871). DuBose later acknowledged that after he realized the Southern Confederacy was doomed to fail, he resolved to spend the rest of his life devoted "wholly and only to God, and to the work and life of His Kingdom." William Porcher DuBose, *Turning Points in My Life* (New York: Longmans, Green, & Company, 1912), 49–50. See also Gardiner H. Shattuck, Jr., "'This Great Day of Suffering': Redeeming Memories of the Civil War," *Anglican and Episcopal History* 81, no. 4 (December 2012): 386.

17 Donald S. Armentrout, "William Porcher DuBose: An Introduction to the Man," in *A DuBose Reader: Selections from the Writings of William Porcher DuBose*, ed. Donald S. Armentrout (Sewanne, TN: The University of the South, 1984), xviii; Arthur Benjamin Chitty, Jr., *Reconstruction at Sewanee: The Founding of the University of the South and Its First Administration*,

1857–1872 (Sewanee, TN: The University Press, 1954), 138–9; Steve Longenecker, *Pulpits of the Lost Cause: The Faith and Politics of Former Confederate Chaplains During Reconstruction* (Tuscaloosa: The University of Alabama Press, 2023), 128.

18 DuBose, "Reminiscences," 150–1. Emphases in the original. See also Ralph E. Luker, "Liberal Theology and Social Conservatism: A Southern Tradition, 1840–1920," *Church History* 50, no. 2 (June 1981): 197.

19 DuBose, "Reminiscences," 151.

20 Ibid. Emphasis in the original. See also Moultrie Guerry, "Makers of Sewanee," *The Sewanee Review* 41, no. 4 (October-December 1933): 490; John Gary Eichelberger, Jr., "Caught in an 'Evil Infection:' Postbellum Conflict in the Episcopal Diocese of South Carolina over the Role of African Americans in the Life of the Church" (master's thesis, University of the South, 2020), 43–6.

21 Chitty, *Reconstruction at Sewanee*, 140; Longenecker, *Pulpits of the Lost Cause*, 127; Sarah Woolfolk Wiggins, "Josiah Gorgas: A Victorian Father," *Civil War History* 32, no. 3 (September 1986): 231.

22 DuBose, "Reminiscences," 152–3.

23 William Porcher DuBose, "The Romance and Genius of a University," *The Sewanee Review* 13, no. 4 (October 1905): 499.

24 Polk is quoted in Glenn Robins, *The Bishop of the Old South: The Ministry and Civil War Legacy of Leonidas Polk* (Macon, GA: Mercer University Press, 2006), 120. See also Richard Tillinghast, "Sewanee and the Civil War," *Southwest Review* 99, no. 3 (June 22, 2014): 334–7.

25 Chitty, *Reconstruction at Sewanee*, 45–74, especially 60–1. See also Jon Alexander, O.P., "Introduction," in *William Porcher DuBose: Selected Writings*, ed. Jon Alexander, O.P. (New York: Paulist Press, 1988), 9; Longenecker, *Pulpits of the Lost Cause*, 126.

26 Alexander, "Introduction," 9. On Polk's death, see, for example, James Postell Jervey, "The Confederate General," *Historical Magazine of the Protestant Episcopal Church* 7, no. 4 (December 1938): 402–4; Edgar Legare Pennington, "The Confederate Episcopal Church and the Southern Soldiers," *Historical Magazine of the Protestant Episcopal Church* 17, no. 4 (December 1948): 380.

27 Ibid. See also Chitty, *Reconstruction at Sewanee*, 60, 131.

28 Rev. Shoup is quoted in Alexander, "Introduction," 9. For more on Bishop Quintard's fundraising, see especially Benjamin J. King, "Church, Cotton, and Confederates: What Charles Todd Quintard's Fundraising Trips to Great Britain Reveal About Some Nineteenth-Century Anglo-Catholics," *Anglican and Episcopal History* 90, no. 2 (June 2021): 110, 113, 118, 131, 132, 133; Longenecker, *Pulpits of the Lost Cause*, 139.

29 DuBose, "Reminiscences," 152. See also Guerry, "Makers of Sewanee," 490. In his 1981 poem "Sewanee in Ruins, Part Two," the twentieth-century poet Richard Tillinghast, himself a graduate of the University of the South, wrote of the school's recovery from the war. "Gladly they turned from the tragedy of six years gone to peaceful forests," he began. He rhapsodized about Quintard's

valiant fundraising efforts before writing, "Later came William Porcher DuBose,// a tiny silver saint who lived elsewhere,// more conversant with the tongues of angels// than of men.// Sitting on the edge of his desk in his black gown,// talking haltingly of Aristotle, he would suspend,// rapt, in some mid-air beyond our ken,// murmuring, 'The starry heavens'// We, with a glimpse of things,// would tiptoe out of the classroom."// Richard Tillinghast, "Sewanee in Ruins, Part Two," *Ploughshares* 7, no. 2 (Summer 1981): 100.

30 DuBose is quoted in Donald S. Armentrout, "William Porcher DuBose Enters the Scene," *Sewanee Theological Review* 51, no. 2 (Easter 2008): 158. Emphasis in the original.

31 DuBose, "Reminiscences," 152. See also Longenecker, *Pulpits of the Lost Cause*, 128–36; Gardiner H. Shattuck, Jr., *Episcopalians and Race: Civil War to Civil Rights* (Lexington: The University Press of Kentucky, 2000), 44.

32 DuBose, "Reminiscences," 152. Emphasis in the original. See also Chitty, *Reconstruction at Sewanee*, 139; Guerry, "Makers of Sewanee," 490.

33 DuBose, "Reminiscences," 140. See also Alexander, "Introduction," 10; Armentrout, "William Porcher DuBose," xviii; Guerry, "Makers of Sewanee," 490; Slocum, "The Lessons of Experience and the Theology of William Porcher DuBose," 342.

34 DuBose, "Reminiscences," 153–4. See also Chitty, *Reconstruction at Sewanee*, 140; Slocum, "The Lessons of Experience and the Theology of William Porcher DuBose," 348; Robert B. Slocum, "Living the Truth: An Introduction to the Theological Method and Witness of William Porcher DuBose," *St. Luke's Journal of Theology* 34, no. 1 (December 1990): 39.

35 DuBose, "Reminiscences," 154. Emphases in the original. See also Guerry, "Makers of Sewanee," 490; Slocum, "The Lessons of Experience and the Theology of William Porcher DuBose," 348; Slocum, "Living the Truth," 39.

36 DuBose, "Reminiscences," 154–5.

37 Ibid., 157.

38 Guerry, "Makers of Sewanee," 490. See also Chitty, *Reconstruction at Sewanee*, 140.

39 DuBose, "Reminiscences," 158. DuBose's second wife died in 1887. Longenecker, *Pulpits of the Lost Cause*, 128.

40 George Boggan Myers, "The Sage and the Seer of Sewanee," in William Porcher DuBose, *Unity in the Faith*, ed. W. Norman Pittenger (Greenwich, CT: The Seabury Press, 1957), 13–14.

41 DuBose, *Turning Points in My Life*, 5.

42 Myers, "The Sage and the Seer of Sewanee," 14.

43 Guerry, "Makers of Sewanee," 493.

44 DuBose, *Turning Points in My Life*, 6–7.

45 Armentrout, "William Porcher DuBose," xix-xx.

46 Ibid. xx. See also Myers, "The Sage and the Seer of Sewanee," 9; Slocum, "The Lessons of Experience and the Theology of William Porcher DuBose," 343.

47 Armentrout, "William Porcher DuBose," xviii; Slocum, "The Lessons of Experience and the Theology of William Porcher DuBose," 342–3.

48 William Porcher DuBose, *The Soteriology of the New Testament* (New York: MacMillan and Company, 1892). See also Armentrout, "William Porcher DuBose," xx–xxi; Luker, "Liberal Theology and Social Conservatism," 198; Longenecker, *Pulpits of the Lost Cause*, 143; Robert Boak Slocum, *The Theology of William Porcher DuBose: Life, Movement, and Being* (Columbia: University of South Carolina Press, 2000), 107–8; Slocum, "The Lessons of Experience and the Theology of William Porcher DuBose," 341–2.

49 DuBose wrote in the preface that "If Jesus Christ is what the church believes him to be, he is and will always be very much more in himself than our science of him. Christology will therefore never be complete; but it is quite complete enough to convince us that there is a truth in it of which while it is greater than our knowledge we may yet know more and more. No human mind can grasp the unity or organic whole of nature, yet science knows that nature is such a whole and that it can forever approximate to it. So, the church knows that Jesus Christ stands to us for a fact of God in nature and in humanity of which it may know the truth although it can forever only approximate the whole truth. There is no question to it about Christ, the only question is of our Christology, to what extent our science truly represents and expresses him." William Porcher DuBose, *The Ecumenical Councils*, 2nd ed. (Edinburgh: T & T Clark, 1897), xii. See also Slocum, *The Theology of William Porcher DuBose*, 107–8.

50 William Porcher DuBose, *The Gospel in the Gospels* (New York: Longmans, Green, & Company, 1906), 6–7. See also Harvey Hill, "The Best of Both Worlds: William Porcher DuBose Among Liberals and Conservatives," *Anglican and Episcopal History* 81, no. 1 (March 2012): 14; Henry S. Nash, "Dr. DuBose's 'Gospel in the Gospels'," *The Sewanee Review* 15, no. 1 (January 1907): 111–20.

51 Much of the book is devoted to a discussion of how Pauline interpretations support the centrality of Jesus in scripture. See, for example, DuBose's comment that "Was He not driven to the conclusion that it were better for a man to be the worst sinner and know it—than to be a so-called righteous man and unconscious of the sin that was in him? There is an absolute identity in the point of view of Jesus and of St. Paul on this point." William Porcher DuBose, *The Gospel According to St. Paul* (New York: Longmans, Green, & Company, 1907), 70. In another passage, DuBose noted, "I have elsewhere undertaken to prove that the all-inclusive principle or germ of St. Paul's most developed Gospel is distinctly stated at the beginning of every one of the canonical Gospels; is repeated at the end of one of them as being the substance of what was to be preached to the world as the Gospel of Jesus Christ; was actually after the Day of Pentecost so preached by all the Jerusalem Apostles, and preached exclusively or as practically the sole burden of their preaching; and that then finally it was taken up, identically the same, and developed by St. Paul into the complete system which he has given us, consistent everywhere with itself, in his epistles" (p. 103). In the conclusion, DuBose wrote: "Here

I leave my exposition of the Gospel of Jesus Christ as St. Paul sees it in Him and knows it in himself. According to St. Paul, as according to St. John and according to the whole mind of the New Testament, Christianity recognizes and accepts in Jesus Christ, not alone the manifestation and revelation, but the communication of God's own divine righteousness and eternal life. The Gospel is not merely a truth, it is a power and an activity. He who is in Jesus Christ is in the actual operation or working of the selfsame forces and causes which made Jesus Christ Himself humanly what He was" (p. 302). See also Slocum, *The Theology of William Porcher DuBose*, 107, 128, 157, 173–4; Dan Edwards, "Deification and the Anglican Doctrine of Human Nature: A Reassessment of the Historical Significance of William Porcher DuBose," *Anglican and Episcopal History* 58, no. 2 (June 1989): 196–212.

52 William Porcher DuBose, *High Priesthood and Sacrifice: An Exposition of the Epistle to the Hebrews* (New York: Longmans, Green, & Company, 1908). See also Slocum, *The Theology of William Porcher DuBose*, 100.

53 William Porcher DuBose, *The Reason of Life* (New York: Longmans, Green, & Company, 1911) 129. See also Armentrout, "William Porcher DuBose," xxi; Slocum, *The Theology of William Porcher DuBose*, 104.

54 William Porcher DuBose, *Unity in the Faith*, ed. W. Norman Pittenger (Greenwich, CT: The Seabury Press, 1957). See also Slocum, *The Theology of William Porcher DuBose*, 4.

55 The festivities held at Sewanee were so important to DuBose that he opened *Turning Points in My Life* with a description of the events. "During the first week of August, 1911, there was held at Sewanee, Tennessee, a reunion of those who had been my students during the thirty-six years of my active connection with the University of the South. This event had been for some time contemplated and came at a most propitious moment. Conditions could not well have conspired to make it more thoroughly successful and enjoyable." DuBose, *Turning Points in My Life*, 1. See also Slocum, "The Lessons of Experience and the Theology of William Porcher DuBose," 343–4.

56 Alexander, "Introduction," 12; Longenecker, *Pulpits of the Lost Cause*, 148. A thorough discussion of the criticism surrounding DuBose's theology is beyond the scope of this book. For more discussion on this point, see, for example, Hill, "The Best of Both Worlds," 17–20.

57 Armentrout, "William Porcher DuBose Enters the Scene," 160–1; Longenecker, *Pulpits of the Lost Cause*, 145–7.

58 DuBose, *The Gospel According to St. Paul*, 98–9.

59 In *The Soteriology of the New Testament*, DuBose wrote: "The New Testament no more gives us doctrine than nature gives us science. It gives us the facts but not the theory, the matter of all Christian doctrine, but no finished doctrine or doctrines of the whole matter of Christianity," 19–20. See also Armentrout, "William Porcher DuBose Enters the Scene," 159.

60 DuBose, *The Gospel According to St. Paul*, 14.

61 Slocum, "Living the Truth," 35.

62 DuBose, *The Gospel in the Gospels*, 78.
63 DuBose, *High Priesthood and Sacrifice*, 3.
64 DuBose, *Turning Points in My Life*, 56. See also Hill, "The Best of Both Worlds," 20–1; Slocum, "The Lessons of Experience and the Theology of William Porcher DuBose," 353, 359–60, 363; Slocum, "Living the Truth," 36–9.
65 DuBose, *Turning Points in My Life*, 139. See also Slocum, "The Lessons of Experience and the Theology of William Porcher DuBose," 361–7; Slocum, *The Theology of William Porcher DuBose*, 107–11.
66 DuBose *The Ecumenical Councils*, 28. See also Donald S. Armentrout, "DuBose's Theology: An Introduction to the Work," in *A DuBose Reader: Selections from the Writings of William Porcher DuBose,* ed. Donald S. Armentrout (Sewanee, TN: The University of the South, 1984), xxvi–xxvii.
67 DuBose, *The Gospel in the Gospels*, ix. See also Slocum, "Living the Truth," 32–3; Slocum, *The Theology of William Porcher DuBose*, 16–17, 103–6.
68 The quotes and summary of DuBose's thought are found in Armentrout, "William Porcher DuBose Enters the Scene," 159, 160. See also Edwards, "Deification and the Anglican Doctrine of Human Nature," 206–9; Hill, "The Best of Both Worlds," 17–18.
69 Another scholar recognized a philosophical theme running throughout DuBose's thought. "Those who studied with Dr. DuBose know that he was primarily an ethical philosopher and that his approach to philosophy was by the path of Aristotle's *Nicomachean Ethics*," wrote John S. Marshall in 1943. "He accepted the general moral conceptions of Aristotle and discovered a metaphysics and a theory of knowledge in the ethical positions of the Great Stagirite. He accepted a theory of reality that found its ground in the ethical life rather than in the theoretical life treated as a department of existence completely transcending the moral sphere. For DuBose the moral life is the first stage of the real and ultimate life of man, and theory is merely a contemplation or viewing of the potentiality of man reaching upward and onward to the divine." In Marshall's view, "DuBose is an Aristotelian, but he has an interpretation of the Peripatetic philosophy that brings him into the stream of thought of the Platonizing commentators of the Eastern Orthodox Church and of the Neo-Platonic interpreters that preceded them." John S. Marshall, "From Aristotle to Christ: Or the Philosophy of William Porcher DuBose," *The Sewanee Review* 51, no. 1 (January–March 1943): 148–9. In this vein, another commentator observed that "Dr. DuBose is such an impassioned student of Aristotle that in thinking of him his friends must needs recall Coleridge's generalization: 'A man is born either a Platonist or an Aristotelian.' And the generalization once in mind, it seems to follow that Dr. DuBose was born a Platonist and has made himself an Aristotelian. By nature, he is a Mystic. The intuition, rather than the induction and the syllogism, is his instinctive method. But his life has made him a Realist. He took an earnest share in one of the heroic actions of history, the Civil War. His responsibilities as a Churchman and teacher have forced his mind to substitute hands and feet for wings. Aristotle has become for him 'the master of those who think.'

Life makes some synthesis which logic puts under an anathema. Dr. Du Bose is an Aristotelian Mystic." Nash, "Dr. DuBose's 'Gospel in the Gospels'," 112. DuBose described Aristotle's influence on him this way: "I began quite early, for example, to read with an advanced class Aristotle's *Ethics*—for both the Greek and the philosophy. Unconsciously Aristotle became the basis and starting point of all my thinking. I seemed to find in him the true root and starting point of all thought or knowledge of myself: Socrates' 'Know thyself' found in him, in the third generation, its scientific response, or at least the beginning of it. I began to apply his principles and follow his lines and found that instruction built up on that foundation was not only more satisfactory to myself, but more intelligible and self-evident to the classes than upon any other system." DuBose, *Turning Points in My Life*, 6.

70 The quotes are found in Myers, "The Sage and the Seer of Sewanee," 19.

71 On the mudsill theory, see, for example, Julian S. Bach, Jr., "The Social Thought of the Old South," *American Journal of Sociology* 46, no. 2 (September 1940): 180–1. See also Edwards, "Deification and the Anglican Doctrine of Human Nature," 211–12.

72 W. Norman Pittenger, "The Significance of DuBose's Theology," in William Porcher DuBose, *Unity in the Faith*, ed. W. Norman Pittenger (Greenwich, CT: The Seabury Press, 1957), 21. See also Slocum, "Living the Truth," 28–9. On the university's decision to change the name of the lecture series, see David Paulsen, "Sewanee's School of Theology Drops Name of Slavery Apologist DuBose from Annual Lecture Series," *Episcopal News Service*, April 13, 2021, accessed November 27, 2022, https://www.episcopalnewsservice.org/2021/04/13/sewanees-school-of-theology-drops-name-of-slavery-apologist-from-annual-lecture-series/.

PART III

Conclusion

10

"We Have Passed Through a Season of Extraordinary Trial"

Divergent Views on Race in the Lives of Stevens, Porter, and DuBose

Three Episcopal clergymen, Peter Fayssoux Stevens, Anthony Toomer Porter, and William Porcher DuBose, came of age in South Carolina during the antebellum era. The values of the American South of the 1830s, 1840s, and 1850s, as well as the traditions and customs of the Protestant Episcopal Church, shaped their lives and attitudes. As with most Americans of the time, the war of 1861–5 was the most significant event in their lives. The men shared similar values and experiences from childhood until war's end. As southerners—the first Americans to lose a war—their memories were especially potent.[1]

Each man accepted notions of white supremacy over Black people, a proposition so entrenched in the majority white culture of nineteenth-century America that it needed no discussion or defense. After the war erupted, the men earnestly and eagerly supported the Confederate States of America in its quest to establish a slaveholding republic. Stevens and DuBose wore the Confederate gray and suffered wounds on the battlefield. Porter was not a soldier, but he came under fire as an army chaplain. The three men were ordained ministers in the Protestant Episcopal Church of South Carolina.

As recounted in earlier chapters of this book, many Episcopal leaders in the southern states believed they were obliged to minister to Black congregants.

Bishops instructed clergy as well as the laity to hold worship services for enslaved people living on plantations. In some cases, bishops assigned newly ordained deacons to serve as plantation missionaries. Free people of color sometimes attended white Episcopal churches in the South Carolina Low Country, although they were segregated from white parishioners.[2]

As important as these efforts were to the growth of the antebellum Episcopal Church in states like South Carolina, church leaders were not closet abolitionists dedicated to undermining the peculiar institution. Allowing whites and Blacks to attend the same churches was not a first step toward integrating the races. No southern Episcopal bishop raised a hue and cry against the immorality of human bondage. The institution was an accepted part of life in the South. Episcopalians who felt called to preach to slaves did so because of God's law. They were satisfied to leave thorny questions about the morality of man's law for others to debate. Even as they ministered to enslaved people, church leaders made it clear that Black communicants were not equal to whites. Black folks deserved to hear the word of God, but they would remain supplicants in the world of men.[3]

Since the arrival of English-speaking colonists in North America during the seventeenth century, race has played a decisive role in American history. No institution in American life was immune to its effects. For its part, the Protestant Episcopal Church in North America grappled with a conflicted view of race during the nineteenth century. Blacks were welcomed into the church, but not welcomed as full members. As early as the creation of the first Black Episcopal congregation, St. Thomas's African Church in Philadelphia in 1794, white church leaders were ambivalent about allowing Black church members to participate in church rituals. Blacks were tolerated, but not embraced. As a condition for the ordination of Absalom Jones, the first Black Episcopal minister, St. Thomas's African Church could not send delegates to the diocesan convention. Jones, a self-taught religious leader, had not mastered the required biblical languages to be ordained according to church standards. White Episcopalians who did not possess the language skills were sometimes ordained, but Jones was held to a different standard. Even if his lack of language skills disqualified Jones from ordination, it was curious that the entire congregation was disqualified from sending lay deputies to the convention in his stead. The only reasonable explanation for the disparate treatment of St. Thomas's African Church and white Episcopal churches was the presence of Black communicants in the former.[4]

As it did with so many aspects of southern life, the war disrupted the church's missionary work in South Carolina. With the Union occupation of Port Royal, Beaufort, and other small towns of the South Carolina Low Country early in the war, nearby plantation owners feared that their slaves might be liberated. To forestall what they viewed as a catastrophic development, many planters moved their households inland, complicating clergymen's efforts to preach the Gospel in slave chapels. In later years, as Sherman's army raced through the South Carolina countryside, the church experienced far worse consequences. Union soldiers and the so-called contrabands who followed Sherman's forces spread the word that emancipation was at hand. Slaves who heard the rumors were unwilling to sit by placidly listening to sermons on what God might do for them at some future date when they could immediately do something for themselves.[5]

Before the end of the war and ratification of the Thirteenth Amendment, which permanently eradicated legal slavery in the United States, enslavers had claimed dominion over the enslaved, which required them to provide necessities such as food, clothing, and shelter. Sometimes, enslavers allowed for Christian worship services to be held on the property. It was the "white Christian" thing to do, not to mention the expectation that a slave instructed in religious values such as the necessity of turning the other cheek would be more docile and easily controlled than a slave left to worship some other religion. While no one would accuse enslavers of providing creature comforts, they had cared for the enslaved if for no other reason than self-interest. In some cases, they had provided a subsistence allowance for enslaved men and women who had grown too old and feeble to work.[6]

A common southern myth portrayed the happy, contented, faithful slave. Recognizing that freedom was overrated—after all, an intellectually and morally deficient slave could not care for himself—the happy slave knew his place and settled into his role without entertaining foolish dreams of emancipation and autonomy. He was easily controlled because he was metaphorically neutered. Genteel southern manners required patrician whites to speak of the happy, contented, faithful slave as an adjunct member of the family, someone whose loyalty and obedience had earned him or her the supposedly honorific title of "aunt" or "uncle."[7]

After emancipation, former slave owners dropped all pretense of familial obligation. Freed people were expected to skedaddle off the property unless a new labor relationship could be forged. As a result, a new bond developed out of mutual dependency between landowners and freed people during the Reconstruction era. As recounted in Chapter 5, freed people enjoyed few options in the postbellum South. They engaged in agricultural or industrial labor, mostly at the lowest levels. They were itinerant wage laborers, sharecroppers, or, in rare cases, tenants with an ownership stake in the land. If it was a dirty, low-paying, back-breaking job that no one else wanted, a freed person usually did it. This new system was not quite a brother to involuntary servitude, but it was a close cousin. A freed person was tied to the land almost as though emancipation had not occurred.[8]

After southern states were "redeemed" in the 1870s—that is, after white southerners assumed positions of power in state and local governments when federal troops withdrew from the former states of the Confederacy—the Jim Crow regime arose. Jim Crow laws kept freed people politically powerless by requiring that they stay on their side of the color line in a strictly segregated political, social, and economic system. The law supported the regime, with threats of violence always lurking in the background. Black folks could not live near whites, attend the same schools, ride in the same railroad cars, eat in the same restaurants, seek medical treatment in the same hospitals, or use the same public restrooms. Discriminatory laws ensured that the races would not mingle. Segregation became the law of the land for close to a century.[9]

Many whites were content to allow segregation in society to carry over to segregation in Protestant churches. Even if freed people were allowed to join white churches, they must not become leaders. A well-known Presbyterian pastor and theologian from Virginia, Robert Lewis Dabney, who also served as Thomas J. "Stonewall" Jackson's chief of staff and biographer, spoke for many white clergymen when he observed in 1868 that Blacks should not be ordained in the church "because that race is not trustworthy for such [a] position." Dabney promised that if "you trust any portion of power over your church to Black hands, you will rue it."[10]

Two prominent laymen in the Protestant Episcopal Church of Charleston, the father-son duo of Edward McCrady, Sr., and Edward McCrady, Jr., reflected the views of many white supremacists in the Palmetto State. They saw Blacks as inherently inferior to whites, and any association with inferior peoples in religious life would degrade everyone. McCrady Sr. wrote that the "Black man with his kinky hair and the impenetrable veil which conceals his emotions" would contaminate whites, especially if miscegenation occurred. Both McCradys were lawyers and state legislators during their lengthy public careers as well as active lay leaders in the South Carolina Episcopal Church. They represented their congregations in the diocesan convention for decades. Edward McCrady Jr. was a high-ranking Confederate military officer during the war.[11]

In response to the argument that all races deserved spiritual guidance, the McCradys and many white laymen believed that Blacks did not possess the capacity for full church membership. Their intellectual development, or lack thereof, prevented them from understanding scripture or mastering church rituals. These white lay leaders were unsatisfied to leave questions of church governance to Black folks, who had shown themselves incapable of self-rule during "Black Reconstruction" in the early 1870s. As recounted in this book, the debate over race consumed the Episcopal Diocese of South Carolina for decades. Blacks could join the church, but like so much in American life, they had to be satisfied practicing their religion on the proper side of the color line. If Jim Crow could govern political, social, and economic relationships, he could govern spiritual matters as well.[12]

Even church leaders who did not share Dabney's or the McCradys' unrelentingly racist views struggled to make sense of the new era in race relations. They did so while they faced the physical devastation of the war. The loss of numerous communicants, especially Blacks, after the war provided yet more challenges. Bishop Thomas Frederick Davis of South Carolina tried to remain optimistic despite the bleak circumstances and the church's ambivalence about the loss of Blacks from the membership rolls. "We have passed through a season of extraordinary trial, necessarily drawing men's hearts to eternal considerations," he remarked. He believed that the church had helped its parishioners even in the darkest days, providing "a solace and a power in the day of their calamity." Because so many Episcopalians retained their faith in the Lord, "I am persuaded that the Church is stronger than ever in the hearts of her people."[13]

Whether the church was as strong as Bishop Davis declared was a contested proposition. What was clear was that each Episcopal minister in South Carolina, including Stevens, Porter, and DuBose, had to decide how to handle Black communicants in the new era. It was a fine line to walk—obeying the dictates of the Jim Crow regime while simultaneously encouraging Black folks not to abandon the Protestant Episcopal Church.

* * *

As the author of a family history later concluded, "In the years following the war, Peter Fayssoux Stevens felt a great urgency to help the colored people, particularly the children, get a basic education in secular matters as well as in the Christian Gospel." Stevens believed that Blacks would be inclined to stay within the Protestant Episcopal Church—or return to the fold, if they had already left—if they could "become ministers of the Gospel to their own people." Moreover, Stevens "encouraged the colored people to organize their own congregations, to be ready to receive their own ministers."[14]

He struggled with this task for a decade. When the Protestant Episcopal Church of South Carolina refused to ordain Black ministers or allow Black congregations to take part in church conventions or governing decisions, Stevens left the church of his youth for the Reformed Episcopal Church. He did not take such a drastic step lightly. After his candidate for ordination was not considered despite repeated entreaties, Stevens reacted decisively. "The evidence was too clear to my mind," he wrote in an 1875 letter to William B.W. Howe, who had become bishop following Thomas Davis's death in 1871. "That these men were rejected because of their race was . . . apparent." The obvious racism in the church leaders' reactions to Black Episcopalians left Stevens in an untenable position. In his opinion,

> my success, and that of others, in winning these people to the Church, despite . . . the Church's position towards them, had convinced me of the impossibility of the two races working harmoniously and effectively in the same diocesan organization. The colored element if fairly dealt with would be in the majority or at least constitute so large a proportion as to excite jealousy and strife.[15]

Stevens was convinced that the Episcopal Church of South Carolina—before, during, and after the war—had made promises to the freed people and those promises had not been kept. "At the Convention in 1866 (I think) by a unanimous vote of that Convention the Church extended the right hand to the colored people inviting them to form congregations and present suitable persons for the ministry," he explained to Bishop Howe. "Thus encouraged by the Church and sustained by the Bishop I returned to my work and for the first time proposed organization to these people. The result, as you know, was in time the formation of respectable congregations and two postulants pursuing their studies for the ministry."[16]

The Protestant Episcopal Church betrayed the few remaining Black communicants who had not left the fold in 1865. Stevens could not stand by and do nothing. He felt compelled to join the Reformed Episcopal Church, which allowed freed people to become leaders and form their own churches. In Stevens' view, turning his back on the Protestant Episcopal Church of South Carolina, which had been his home since the 1850s, and abandoning the people and institutions that had nurtured him was agonizing. To join a new church originally formed in New York City, far away in time and disposition from South Carolina, was another bold move. Stevens acted owing to his firm conviction that Blacks, regardless of their status in the postwar South, should be welcomed into the church. "Some day our people will find that the colored man does not wait for his 'white friend' to do all his thinking," he wrote in correspondence from 1875.[17]

"Born and reared in the Episcopal Church, I have ever loved it and will love it to the day of my death," he confessed toward the end of his letter to Bishop Howe. Yet he must act as a matter of conscience. "Believe me, Reverend Sir, that it costs me no little pain to sever the ties of a lifetime. If I have erred, I need your prayers and ask the forgiveness of you and my brethren for brethren they still are tho[ugh] they may not acknowledge it."[18]

This unwavering faith in the necessity of the church welcoming Black folks into the pews transformed Peter Fayssoux Stevens into an extraordinary public figure for his time. His behavior is puzzling when considered in the context of his life before and during the war. His casual acceptance of the values and traditions of the white antebellum South and his support for the Southern Confederacy were consistent with his life as a young man growing up in South Carolina. He studied at The Citadel, an institution specifically designed to defend whites in South Carolina from marauding Blacks. It was only natural that Stevens, as the eventual leader of The Citadel, would take up arms to defend the Southland and her way of life from what he viewed as a northern invasion.

Geography was important to Stevens's postwar life. He spent most of his career ministering in the South Carolina Low Country, in and around Charleston. Compared with many other areas of the state, the Low Country witnessed relatively little racial violence during the Reconstruction era.

Blacks and whites frequently lived in proximity to each other. Because the Low Country had a large Black population and because Bishop Thomas Davis had decreed before the war that ministers should evangelize Blacks, Stevens became comfortable working among people of color.[19]

Stevens's postwar actions were entirely consistent with his faith and his character. The war and his ministry among Blacks changed him. Unlike many whites who kept Black people at arm's length, avoiding all contact save interactions with domestic servants and agricultural laborers, Rev. Stevens knew the freed people and shared their concerns. He saw how they lived, worked, loved, and died. He recognized them as individuals deserving of at least a modicum of approbation. Although he was not an integrationist or a champion of equality of the races, he believed that promises made must be promises kept. The church must welcome all of God's creatures into the fold. Stevens was a man of faith who was not satisfied to preach from a pulpit far removed from the congregation. He practiced what he preached. His life was a testament to his faith.[20]

Anthony Toomer Porter never joined the Reformed Episcopal Church, but he shared many of Rev. Stevens's values. Before the war, Porter had welcomed Black people into his church. He retained his belief in white superiority over Blacks, but he also believed that the Protestant Episcopal Church should welcome Black congregants into the church and help improve their lives. Moreover, he thought that education was crucial for everyone's success—Blacks and whites alike—within and without the church.[21]

Building schools would be Toomer Porter's gift to his church and community. In April 1866, he traveled to the northern states and raised enough money to open a school for hundreds of children of the freed people. On the heels of establishing his school for Blacks, Porter founded the Holy Communion Church Institute to educate white children. In October 1867, still grieving the death of his son almost exactly three years earlier, Porter was called to "Take up your work and do it." Initially puzzled as to what his work should be, he experienced an epiphany. "Gradually, the light seemed to break upon me, showing me, although then dimly, the way. I remembered that I had at my command a large building, which I had erected before the war as a Sunday school and an industrial school-house," he recalled. "This I could use for a schoolroom."[22]

The Holy Communion Church Institute changed its name to the Porter Academy in 1886 before becoming the Porter Military Academy. As discussed in Chapter 8, Porter sought to acquire the US Arsenal on Ashley Avenue in Charleston as the new site for his school. He convinced South Carolina's two US senators, former Confederate generals Matthew Butler and Wade Hampton, to sponsor legislation effecting the transfer. Two former opposing general officers, Joseph E. Johnston of the Confederacy and William T. Sherman of the Union, voiced support for the transfer. The bill passed both houses of Congress and President Rutherford B. Hayes signed it into law.

The US government conveyed the land to Porter for use as his school and, on January 8, 1880, he took possession of the former arsenal.[23]

In the meantime, in May 1878, Bishop William B. W. Howe directed Porter to serve as the rector of St. Mark's Church, a congregation of mostly Blacks in Charleston. For years, Porter divided his time and attention between St. Mark's and the Church of the Holy Communion. St. Mark's had lost its minister and was suffering from chronically poor finances.[24]

Porter initially demurred, pleading overwork, but Howe would not take "no" for an answer. The bishop explained that the church needed someone with an understanding of financial matters. Recognizing that he was the right man for the job, Porter eventually agreed to serve. He spent almost a decade at the helm.[25]

Porter found himself in the middle of the debate about race in the postwar Protestant Episcopal Church in South Carolina. Always seeking a compromise, he crafted a moderate position. Black people could join the church, but their activities would be scrutinized and directed by white bishops and lay leaders. It was a stance almost certain to infuriate everyone. For conservatives, Porter was too accommodating to people of color. For Black communicants, his position was paternalistic and demeaning.[26]

His most direct statement on Blacks in the postwar Episcopal Church came in a speech he delivered at the annual convention of the Episcopal Church in October 1883. Porter was reacting to the continuing problem of the ecclesiastical status of Blacks. Episcopal leaders wanted to keep Blacks in the church and accountable to white clergy—a position that Porter supported—but the method for overseeing and administering Black churches was contentious. In July 1883, Episcopal bishops, priests, and lay people assembled at the University of the South in Sewanee, Tennessee, to hash out this question.

Conference attendees were familiar with the example of the Methodist Episcopal Church of the South, which had created the Colored Methodist Episcopal Church with their own ordained pastors and bishops. Although Black Methodists were not equal to whites, they enjoyed a level of autonomy over their own affairs. The Episcopal leadership rejected the Methodist model as well as a plan, proposed by Texas Bishop Alexander Gregg, to create a new position, a suffragan, or assistant bishop, to evangelize Blacks. After several days of debate, the conferees approved a plan to create a "special Missionary organization" for each diocese that contained large numbers of Blacks. Blacks would still worship separately from whites, but they would fall under the authority of the white diocesan bishop.[27]

Black Episcopalians did not find much to recommend the Sewanee Plan, and they vehemently argued against it. When the diocesan representatives assembled for the general convention in Philadelphia in October 1883, the plan was the topic of much debate. The House of Bishops adopted the plan, but the proposal could not garner sufficient support within the House of Deputies. Against this backdrop, Toomer Porter delivered his speech.[28]

He admitted that Blacks were not equal to whites, a fundamental position of the Jim Crow South. Referring to his experience ministering to Blacks before and during the war, Porter observed, "We will grant on average that their religious knowledge was not very much; that their moral standard was and is not very high." Nonetheless, this acknowledgment did not relieve ministers from their duty. Based on the experiences of white rectors working with Black communicants, "some of us know there are to be found among these people in our midst as fine specimens of Christian character—men and women—possessed of the finest traits which adorn the human family."[29]

Because Blacks could act as good Christians—a controversial position among some whites in the 1880s—a good Episcopal minister had one clear duty: "Just exactly what we would do to any other men anywhere in the world—preach the gospel to them—the old, old story unimproved by modern criticisms. Tell them of the Jesus who loved them and died for them: who loves them and now intercedes for them." Porter's speech was hailed as a "spirited presentation." It demonstrated his commitment to help Blacks progress in the church, but only within prescribed limits.[30]

The Sewanee Plan failed, at least in part, owing to objections from Blacks, yet it was a pyrrhic victory. By the end of the 1880s, the South Carolina diocese had segregated into Black and white churches, with the latter firmly controlling the former. Some white ministers questioned whether the Episcopal Church was now a "race church," but the new arrangement suited ardent white supremacists. They could claim that the church ministered to Blacks while church members were not forced to associate with the undesirables. At the same time, Black communicants were not left to their own devices. They were forced to submit to the decisions of white church leaders. For Black Episcopalians, it was the worst of all possible worlds. They could not worship with whites, but they were not free to set their own rules. The arrangement became a de facto acceptance of the Sewanee Plan.[31]

Porter empathized with Black communicants, although his empathy had its limits. He spent much of his life and career surrounded by Blacks and interacting with them. As a plantation owner during the antebellum era, he had treated his slaves as fairly as the institution would allow. Although he did not emancipate his slaves when he severed his plantation ties to enter the ministry, he sold them to a purchaser who promised not to break up enslaved families. As a newly ordained minister, he welcomed Blacks into his prewar church.

During the war, Porter supported the Southern Confederacy as a chaplain. He believed in the southern cause and expressed few reservations about secession other than practical concerns regarding the difficulty in fighting northern soldiers who enjoyed superior resources. He believed the southern myths about the avariciousness and moral failings of Union troops.

After Appomattox, he accepted the reality of a defeated southern government. Unlike some unreconstructed rebels who aimed their vitriol at the freed people, Porter adapted well to the postwar world. He never renounced the values of the Old South, but he learned to navigate through changing times. He had never approved of the peculiar institution, and he did not lament the loss of slavery. Although South Carolina had been decimated by the fighting, Porter was not discouraged. He threw himself into the task of rebuilding, soliciting funds from northern sources, and constructing separate schools for Black and white children.

Porter believed in the mission of the Protestant Episcopal Church and suggested that harmony could be achieved if Black clergymen made decisions for their congregations under the tutelage of a white bishop. He never saw Blacks as equal to whites in all respects, but he thought that everyone, regardless of race, should receive a high-quality education and enjoy the freedom to worship in the church of his choosing. Jim Crow was a powerful force in every aspect of American life, however, including the church. Although he did not support the harshest strictures of the Jim Crow regime, Porter accepted the reality of a deeply segregated and divided church. He saw no other options. For him, unlike his colleague Peter Fayssoux Stevens, leaving the Protestant Episcopal Church was not an option.[32]

The war changed Stevens and Porter. They accepted the reality of the lost Confederacy and struggled to find a place for freed people in the postbellum church, although Stevens eventually left the church to join the reform movement. By contrast, William Porcher DuBose possessed different sensibilities. He held a traditional white southern perspective on the race question. Before the war, the DuBoses owned plantations and slaves. Young DuBose never disavowed the institution. Every encounter he had with Blacks before, during, and after the war reinforced his belief in their inferiority. He accepted the values of white supremacy and never deviated from those beliefs.

DuBose suffered mightily for his beliefs. He donned a Confederate uniform during the war and fought to create a slaveholding government. An undeniably brave, enthusiastic soldier, he was wounded multiple times, taken prisoner, exchanged, and returned to the ranks. He was left embittered by his experiences, distrustful of Union soldiers, demoralized by the carpetbagger regime in the early years of Reconstruction, and desperate to ensure that law and order prevailed throughout the postwar South.[33]

"When at the close of the war I returned home and as soon as possible entered upon my permanent ministry, conditions with us were for some years no better than in war," he wrote in his memoir, *Turning Points in My Life*. "My family had been a wealthy one before the war, but that was now utterly impoverished." Aside from his diminished personal circumstances, "the country was stript of the barest means of subsistence; our social and political condition was unendurable and hopeless."[34]

When he surveyed his family's homestead in April 1865, DuBose was dispirited. "At last we arrived at Winnsboro. The town had been pretty well burnt. There were not only Yankee troops, but *negro* troops, encamped near our home. These men seemed to be under very little discipline because they ranged and roamed through the country, more and more demoralizing the native negroes."[35]

The comment about "native negroes" reflected white attitudes about the character of Black "types." Some Black folks—the "native negroes"—had lived for generations in the South under white control. They knew their place in the social hierarchy, and they strayed from the prescribed boundaries at their peril. Black Union troops, by contrast, were free men armed with guns and acting under the imprimatur of the US government. They were supposed to be subject to military discipline, but because of their race and their exposure to dangerous northern ideals, "they ranged and roamed through the country, more and more demoralizing the native negroes." The "good" Blacks were as alarmed by the behavior of foreign Blacks under the Reconstruction regime as whites were.

Worse than the demoralization of the "native negroes" was the possibility that the attitudes of the Black troops might influence southern Blacks. "Uppity" ideas undermined social relations between the races. "The negroes, who up to that time had been with ourselves, were gradually alienated, and even those who were profoundly faithful, for safety to themselves were forced to be silent and secretive with us, so that we never knew what was going on," DuBose wrote. It was an untenable situation. "There were nights when at the negro quarters, a quarter of a mile from the house, we could hear the noisy carryings on of negro soldiers from Winnsboro. It might have been very dangerous."[36]

In his memoirs, DuBose explained that his attitude toward Reconstruction was shaped by the lawlessness that he witnessed beginning in 1865. "The carpet-bag regime was at its height and its worst," he recalled. "The negroes were influenced and became for a time very dangerous." Like many southerners, he longed for the day when Union troops departed and southern leaders could restore law and order, replacing "roaming" Blacks with white southerners who would not tolerate the permissiveness of the carpetbagger, the scalawag, and the freed people.[37]

Aside from his sensibilities, DuBose's postwar experiences in the church were markedly different from Stevens's and Porter's biracial ministries. While those two clergymen remained in the South Carolina Low Country and ministered to whites as well as freed people, DuBose served in all-white churches in the middle of the state, closer to the capital in Columbia. Later, when he moved to Abbeville, he lived in the Up Country, where racial violence was frequent. Segregated from the day-to-day lives of Blacks, DuBose saw freed people as the "other," an alien, inferior race with whom he enjoyed little day-to-day interaction. When he did encounter Blacks, he expected them to be subservient to his needs and desires. When they were not, he viewed them as "very dangerous."[38]

Despite the uncertainty of the times, DuBose knew that his place was in the Protestant Episcopal Church. Following his ordination as priest on September 9, 1866, he served in St. John's Parish in Fairfield, which included St. Stephen's Episcopal Church, as well as St. John's Church in Winnsboro. Because Union troops under General Sherman had burned the Winnsboro Church, DuBose and his congregation worshipped at the courthouse.[39]

In 1868, DuBose moved on to Trinity Episcopal Church in Abbeville, South Carolina. There, he observed numerous episodes of crime and destruction, which he attributed to Black soldiers and freed people running amok. Three years later, he was elected chaplain and professor of moral science at the University of the South in Sewanee, Tennessee. He left South Carolina permanently, living out the remainder of his life in Tennessee. DuBose eventually helped to establish the school of theology at Sewanee. He was associated with the university until he retired in 1908.[40]

As illustrated throughout this book, DuBose's prewar experiences were almost identical to Stevens's and Porter's experiences. The divergence came during Reconstruction. Unlike Stevens and Porter, DuBose encountered Blacks only under adverse circumstances. He did not minister to Blacks or visit their homes. He did not invite them into his church. He saw them as undisciplined brutes, subhuman. When he referenced them in his written work, invariably he used pejorative language, such as a passage describing the "kinky head of a negro." He feared that marauding bands of Blacks would harm him or his family, and he admired the Ku Klux Klan—"an inspiration of genius"—because the Klan pledged to control the heretofore uncontrollable "other."[41]

DuBose saw his duty through the eyes of a white southerner. He grieved the death of the Confederate States of America, as did many of his congregants. He and they felt the pain of Confederates brought low by Union soldiers, carpetbaggers, scalawags, and dangerous Negroes. During their hour of need in an uncertain, dangerous world, the white communicants in his church sought solace. Rev. DuBose intended to provide that solace.

Stevens and Porter believed that the spiritual needs of communicants, white and Black, required unity in the church. Even if Blacks were not socially equal to whites, they deserved consideration in the church because they enjoyed the consideration of God. This attitude was fostered by serving in proximity with Blacks. DuBose, by contrast, had little to do with Blacks. His focus was on his white congregants and their desire to avoid associating with Blacks unless they required the services of day laborers or domestic servants.

The duty of a Christian minister, at least in part, is to help communicants deal with the challenges of life and understand the word of God regarding the afterlife. Stevens and Porter believed that they fulfilled that duty by ministering to all people, whatever their race. DuBose disagreed. His constituency consisted of resentful whites who could not or would not accept freed people in the church.

The disparate attitudes of Stevens and Porter compared to DuBose owed as much to their conceptions of social mores as to their views on ecclesiastical doctrine. In the words of one commentator, DuBose accepted that "the peculiar function of priests in their human qualities" was "to bear the burdens of a defeated people—a disenfranchised and impoverished elite, beset by carpetbagging enemies, traitorous scalawags, ungrateful and dangerous Negroes in their midst."[42]

DuBose reflected the social views of most white South Carolinians of his time. He was the least tolerant of the three clergymen when it came to race. Despite his many accomplishments, he did not regard Blacks sympathetically. He joined the faculty at the University of the South, an institution devoted to the Lost Cause, a mythology that extolled the virtues of the whites-only culture of the antebellum era. Sewanee was, in the words of a report from the university's Roberson Project on Slavery, Race, and Reconciliation, the "only institution of higher education designed from the start to represent, protect, and promote the South's civilization of bondage; and launched expressly for the slaveholding society of the South." Moreover, in

> Sewanee's first several decades after the Civil War, its identity as 'a child of the Confederacy' emerged in many ways: Those who held key leadership roles typically had been slave owners, defenders of slavery and secession, and Confederate military leaders; and some of the most consequential donors had been the owners or beneficiaries of some of the largest slavery-based plantations in the antebellum South.

DuBose was a part of this tradition, and he never seriously questioned it.[43]

The Protestant Episcopal Church encouraged ministers to proselytize Blacks, but it did not allow Black communicants to enjoy the same privileges or opportunities for advancement as church leaders that whites enjoyed, which explains Stevens's decision to embrace the Reformed Episcopal Church during the 1870s. Stevens's opinions on race were shaped by his experiences ministering to Blacks, not solely by church doctrine. Similarly, Anthony Toomer Porter had been around Black folks for much of his life, first as an enslaver and later acting under Rev. Alexander Glennie's guidance as a minister on antebellum slave plantations. He exhibited empathy for the enslaved and later the freed people. William Porcher DuBose did not share Stevens's and Porter's experiences or sensibilities.

The three men came to the church at different times, and timing was important. Porter was ordained during the antebellum era in 1854, and Stevens on the eve of the war in 1861. Although he became a deacon in 1863, DuBose was not ordained a priest until 1866, during Reconstruction.

When Porter and Stevens assumed their ministerial duties, they viewed proselytizing Blacks as a crucial duty of Episcopal ministers. Thomas Frederick Davis, the Episcopal Bishop of South Carolina from 1853 until 1871, encouraged Blacks to join the church. It was natural that Porter and Stevens accepted Davis's direction on this point. When they were ordained, the peculiar institution still existed and provided a measure of social control between the races.

Younger than Stevens and Porter, DuBose did not become a priest until after the war. Still reeling from battlefield losses and the social upheaval precipitated by the end of slavery in 1865, many white southerners viewed the freed people with suspicion and resentment, fearing an imminent race war. DuBose was one of those whites who looked on the racial violence with growing alarm. Moreover, when DuBose and his young family moved to Abbeville, South Carolina, in 1868, violence between the Ku Klux Klan and Blacks was at a fever pitch. He became the rector of Trinity Episcopal Church in Abbeville at precisely the time when the Klan spread to the South Carolina Up Country.[44]

In his study of Ku Klux Klan violence during Reconstruction, Allen W. Trelease noted that Klan-related violence was especially prevalent in South Carolina beginning in 1868, "but it was restricted almost entirely to twelve northwestern counties in which the balance between races and parties was more equal than elsewhere in the state." Klan leaders harassed white Republicans and assailed them at every opportunity. According to Trelease, "In Abbeville, still the worst county in this respect, harassment extended to the political assassination of two legislators."[45]

In addition to the racial violence of 1868, Trinity Episcopal Church was the home of Abbeville's gentry before the war. DuBose later wrote that the "church at Abbeville was one of the most beautiful in the state and its congregation and community one of the most distinguished." He remembered that "Many of the most distinguished men of the state had been born there, and many more had been educated there at the famous old school at Willington, by the famous old teacher, Dr. Waddell." After the war, as DuBose became the rector at Trinity, many former Confederate leaders were congregants. "In my congregation there were a number of leading lawyers, judges, etc.," he wrote. DuBose was surrounded by the Old South elite. He and they were fearful of the freedmen and the loss of control over Black folks. After three years in this environment, DuBose departed for the University of the South, an institution founded by former Confederate leaders. No wonder he looked on freed people as undesirables.[46]

Living in the South Carolina Low Country in 1868, Peter Fayssoux Stevens and Anthony Toomer Porter did not experience the hysteria of freed people supposedly marauding through the countryside and Klan violence against anyone suspected of sympathizing with them. Charleston was the epicenter of the movement to attract Black folks back to the Episcopal

Church following the mass exodus at war's end. So devoted was Rev. Stevens to the cause that he left the Protestant Episcopal Church rather than bear witness to inequities based on racial discrimination within the church hierarchy. Porter chose to work within the church, but DuBose was not concerned with attracting Blacks to the church.[47]

Although clergymen insisted that politics should not affect the decisions of the church, no one was immune to the political events of the 1860s and 1870s. Stevens, Porter, and DuBose struggled with questions about Black communicants and their role in the church at precisely the time when South Carolinians were confronting the role of Republicans and the freed people in state government. The year 1868 proved to be critical. That was the year that William Porcher DuBose moved to Trinity Episcopal Church in the Up Country. Around that same time, the Ku Klux Klan arose in South Carolina. It was also the year that the Republicans drafted a new state constitution. Whites reviled this short-lived iteration of state government because it provided significant legal rights and civil liberties to the freed people. Within less than a decade, however, the popular Democrat and staunch white supremacist Wade Hampton became governor and redeemed the state. The freed people's gains were reversed with the demise of the state's Republican Party. It was no accident that Stevens's decision to leave the Episcopal Church of South Carolina in 1875 occurred as the Reconstruction regime disintegrated. The growing hostility of the South Carolina Episcopal Church toward people of color consciously or unconsciously reflected the declining political fortunes of the Republican Reconstruction government.[48]

A minister of any denomination had three choices regarding Black communicants. If the minister disagreed with the church's decision to allow Blacks in the church while denying them full membership, the minister could petition for a change. He could abandon the church if the change did not occur, as Rev. Stevens did. Alternatively, the minister could petition for change but work within the church even if the change did not occur, as Rev. Porter chose to do. Finally, a minister could accept the church's decision to discriminate against Black communicants and defend that decision as necessary to the social order, as Rev. DuBose did.

Three nineteenth-century white southern gentlemen with similar backgrounds were called to serve God through the Episcopal Church. Each man answered the call. Yet each man answered in his own way, forging a distinct path. Comparing and contrasting the lives and careers of these three Episcopal ministers of the nineteenth century—Peter Fayssoux Stevens, Anthony Toomer Porter, and William Porcher DuBose—reveals the varying attitudes on race among similarly situated men of God. A minister devoted to spreading the Gospel can understand his duty far differently than his brethren, and the repercussions can be far-reaching. God is perfect, but human beings never are.

Notes

1 The literature on American memory and the Civil War is voluminous. See especially David W. Blight, *Race and Reunion: The Civil War in American Memory* (Cambridge, MA: The Belknap Press of Harvard University Press, 2001). See also, for example, Grace Elizabeth Hale, "The Lost Cause and the Meaning of History," *OAH Magazine of History* 27, no. 1 (January 2013): 13–17; Malinda Maynor Lowery, "The Original Southerners: American Indians, the Civil War, and Confederate Memory," *Southern Cultures* 25, no. 4 (Winter 2019): 16–35; Jack P. Maddex, Jr., "Pollard's *The Lost Cause Regained*: A Mask for Southern Accommodation," *The Journal of Southern History* 40, no. 4 (November 1974): 595–612; Stuart McConnell, "The Civil War and Historical Memory: A Historiographical Survey," *OAH Magazine of History* 8, no. 1 (Fall 1993): 3–6; John A. Simpson, "The Cult of the 'Lost Cause,'" *Tennessee Historical Quarterly* 34, no. 4 (Winter 1975): 350–61; Charles Reagan Wilson, "The Religion of the Lost Cause: Ritual and Organization of the Southern Civil Religion, 1865–1920," *The Journal of Southern History* 46, no. 2 (May 1980): 219–38.

2 T. Felder Dorn, *Challenges on the Emmaus Road: Episcopal Bishops Confront Slavery, Civil War, and Emancipation* (Columbia, SC: University of South Carolina Press, 2013), 71. See also N. Brooks Graebner, "The Preparation and Admission of Black Clergy in the Episcopal Diocese of North Carolina: The Training School at St. Augustine's in Raleigh, 1867–1894," *North Carolina Historical Review* 102, no. 1 (January 2025): 36–7.

3 J. Carleton Hayden, "After the War: The Mission and Growth of the Episcopal Church Among Blacks in the South, 1865–1877," *Historical Magazine of the Protestant Episcopal Church* 42, no. 4 (December 1973): 403–9; Gardiner H. Shattuck, Jr., *Episcopalians and Race: Civil War to Civil Rights* (Lexington: The University Press of Kentucky, 2000), 8.

4 Jennifer Snow, "The Altar and the Rail: 'Catholicity' and African American Inclusion in the 19th Century Episcopal Church," *Religions* 12, no. 224 (March 2021): 3–5. See also Harold T. Lewis, *Yet with a Steady Beat: The African American Struggle for Recognition in the Episcopal Church* (Valley Forge, PA: Trinity Press International, 1996), 14, 27–31. For more on Absalom Jones, see, for example, Ann C. Lammers, "The Rev. Absalom Jones and the Episcopal Church: Christian Theology and Black Consciousness in a New Alliance: Essays in the Social Gospel in England and America and Honoring the Diocese of Nebraska and the Diocese of Pennsylvania," *Historical Magazine of the Protestant Episcopal Church* 51, no. 2 (June 1982): 178–83. For more on St. Thomas's African Church, see Darrell Tiller, "The African Episcopal Church of St. Thomas, West Philadelphia," *Anglican and Episcopal History* 91, no. 2 (June 2022): 210–13.

5 Dorn, *Challenges on the Emmaus Road*, 198–201. See also David B. Cheesebrough, "'There Goes Your Damned Gospel Shop!' The Churches and Clergy as Victims of Sherman's March Through South Carolina," *The South Carolina Historical Magazine* 92, no. 1 (January 1991): 15–33.

6   Shattuck, *Episcopalians and Race*, 7–9. See also Richard W. Murphy. *The Nation Reunited: War's Aftermath* (Alexandria, VA: Time-Life Books), 42–4.

7   This view of slaves as racially inferior people who were both uncivilized and naturally happy, like some form of human chattels, was a popular interpretation of slavery among white historians for generations. See especially Ulrich Bonnell Phillips, *American Negro Slavery: A Survey of the Supply, Employment and Control of Negro Labor as Determined by the Plantation Régime* (New York: D. Appleton and Company, 1918). For a subsequent criticism of this interpretation, see, for example, Eugene D. Genovese, *Roll, Jordan, Roll: The World the Slaves Made* (New York: Pantheon, 1974), 144–7; James Oliver Horton and Lois E. Horton, *Slavery and the Making of America* (New York: Oxford University Press, 2005), 8–9.

8   See, for example, Lee J. Alston and Kyle D. Kauffman, "Up, Down, and Off the Agricultural Ladder: New Evidence and Implications of Agricultural Mobility for Blacks in the Postbellum South," *Agricultural History* 72, no. 2 (Spring 1998): 263–79; Eric Foner, *Reconstruction: America's Unfinished Revolution: 1863 1877* (New York: Francis Parkman Prize Edition, History Book Club, 2005 [1988]), 404–11; Murphy. *The Nation Reunited*, 42–4; Roger L. Ransom and Richard L. Sutch, *One Kind of Freedom: The Economic Consequences of Emancipation*, 2nd ed. (Cambridge: Cambridge University Press, 2001), 95.

9   The literature on this point is voluminous. See, for example, Edward L. Ayers, *The Promise of the New South: Life After Reconstruction*, Fifteenth Anniversary ed. (New York: Oxford University Press, 2007), 434; Leon F. Litwack, *Trouble in Mind: Black Southerners in the Age of Jim Crow* (New York: Knopf, 1998), 233; C. Vann Woodward, *Origins of the New South, 1877–1913* (Baton Rouge: Louisiana State University Press, 1951), 104–6; C. Vann Woodward, *The Strange Career of Jim*, 2nd ed. (Oxford: Oxford University Press, 1966), 54–8.

10 Dabney is quoted in Allen C. Guelzo, *For the Union of Evangelical Christendom: The Irony of the Reformed Episcopalians* (University Park: The Pennsylvania State University Press, 1994), 220. As a fierce apologist for slavery as well as the values of the Old South, Dabney looked forward to the day when "a retributive Providence" would smite the Union and lead the way toward a restored Southern Confederacy. See also William A. Clebsch, "Christian Interpretations of the Civil War," *Church History* 30, no. 2 (June 1961): 214–15.

11 McCrady is quoted in Lyon G. Tyler, "Drawing the Color Line in the Episcopal Diocese of South Carolina, 1876–1890: The Role of Edward McCrady, Father and Son," *The South Carolina Historical Magazine* 91, no. 2 (April 1990): 108.

12 For more on Edward McCrady, Jr., see Charles J. Holden, "'The Public Business Is Ours': Edward McCrady, Jr., and Conservative Thought in Post-Civil War South Carolina, 1865–1900," *The South Carolina Historical Magazine* 100, no. 2 (April 1999): 124–42.

13 Bishop Davis is quoted in Dorn, *Challenges on the Emmaus Road*, 400.

14 Marion Stevens Eberly, "Our Stevens Family," unpublished manuscript, December 1979, typescript copy, Citadel Archives, 10–11.
15 Stevens is quoted in Ibid., 13. Bishop Howe and many Episcopal clergy in South Carolina supported allowing Black laymen and clergy to join the church and participate, for example, in the diocesan convention. Howe set forth his position in Rt. Rev. W. B. W. Howe, "Paper," in *Authorized Report of the Proceedings of the Eighth Church Congress in the Protestant Episcopal Church in the United States, Held in the City of Richmond, Virginia, Tuesday, Wednesday, Thursday, and Friday, October 24th, 25th, 26th, and 27th, 1882*, ed. by the Committee on the Publication Appointed by the Executive Committee (New York: Thomas Whittaker, Publisher, Nos. 2 and 3, Bible House, 1882), 83–90. Most of the laity did not agree with this position. Tyler, "Drawing the Color Line in the Episcopal Diocese of South Carolina, 1876–1890," 107.
16 Stevens is quoted in Eberly, "Our Stevens Family," 12.
17 Peter Fayssoux Stevens to editors of *The Record*, August 23, 1875, Correspondence 1875 file, DuPre-Moseley Family Collection, the Kennedy Room of Local History and Genealogy, Spartanburg County Public Libraries, Spartanburg, South Carolina.
18 Stevens is quoted in Eberly, "Our Stevens Family," 14, 16.
19 Ralph E. Luker, "The Crucible of Civil War and Reconstruction in the Experience of William Porcher Dubose," *The South Carolina Historical Magazine* 83, no. 1 (January 1982): 66–8; Herbert Geer McCarriar, Jr., "A History of the Missionary Jurisdiction of the South of the Reformed Episcopal Church 1874–1970," *Historical Magazine of the Protestant Episcopal Church* 41, no. 2 (June 1972): 199–203; Allen W. Trelease, *White Terror: The Ku Klux Klan Conspiracy and Southern Reconstruction* (Baton Rouge: Louisiana State University Press, 1999 [1971]), 72, 115–17, 349, 353; Richard Zuczek, *State of Rebellion: Reconstruction in South Carolina* (Columbia: University of South Carolina Press, 1996), 55–9.
20 "Colored Ministers Will Act at Rev. P. F. Stevens Burial; Body of Leader in Reformed Episcopal Church, Who Died Sunday, Will Sleep in Magnolia," *The State* [Columbia, South Carolina], January 11, 1910, n.p.
21 A. Toomer Porter, *Led On! Step by Step Scenes from Clerical, Military, Educational, and Plantation Life in the South, 1828–1898* (New York: G. P Putnam's Sons, the Knickerbocker Press, 1898), 97–8.
22 A. Toomer Porter, *The History of a Work of Faith and Love in Charleston, South Carolina* (New York: D. Appleton and Company, 1882), 6–8. The quote comes from page 8.
23 Porter, *The History of a Work of Faith and Love in Charleston, South Carolina*, 141; Porter, *Led On*, 340–64. See also Albert Sidney Thomas, *A Historical Account of the Protestant Episcopal Church in South Carolina, 1820–1957* (Columbia, SC: R. L. Bryan Company, 1957), 763.
24 Thomas, *A Historical Account of the Protestant Episcopal Church in South Carolina, 1820–1957*, 231.

25 Porter, *Led On*, 332–3. See also Tyler, "Drawing the Color Line in the Episcopal Diocese of South Carolina, 1876–1890," 110, 112–13.
26 Porter, *Led On*, 308–9.
27 Howe, "Paper," 83–90. See also Gardiner H. Shattuck, Jr., "'One Fold and One Chief Shepherd': The Sewanee Conference of 1883 and the Beginnings of Racial Segregation in the Episcopal Church," in *Vale of Tears: New Essays on Religion and Reconstruction*, ed. Edward J. Blum and W. Scott Poole (Macon, GA: Mercer University Press, 2005), 53–72; Shattuck, *Episcopalians and Race*, 12–14; David M. Reimers, "Negro Bishops and Diocesan Segregation in the Protestant Episcopal Church: 1870–1954," *Historical Magazine of the Protestant Episcopal Church* 31, no. 3 (September 1962): 232; Thomas, *A Historical Account of the Protestant Episcopal Church in South Carolina, 1820–1957*, 449–50.
28 Tyler, "Drawing the Color Line in the Episcopal Diocese of South Carolina, 1876–1890," 112–13. See also Reimers, "Negro Bishops and Diocesan Segregation in the Protestant Episcopal Church," 232.
29 A. Toomer Porter, *Speech of Rev. A. Toomer Porter, D.D., of Charleston, S.C., before the General Convention of the P.E. Church in Philadelphia, October 1883, on the Action of the Conference Held at Sewanee, Tenn., August, 1883, Relative to the Work of the Church Among the Colored People of the United States* (Charleston, SC: The News and Courier Book Presses, 1883), 7.
30 Ibid., 9.
31 Shattuck, *Episcopalians and Race*, 14–16; Tyler, "Drawing the Color Line in the Episcopal Diocese of South Carolina, 1876–1890," 113.
32 Tyler, "Drawing the Color Line in the Episcopal Diocese of South Carolina, 1876–1890," 122.
33 W. Eric Emerson and Karen Stokes, "Introduction," in William Porcher DuBose, *Faith, Valor, and Devotion: The Civil War Letters of William Porcher DuBose*, ed. W. Eric Emerson and Karen Stokes (Columbia, SC: The University of South Carolina Press, 2010), xvii–xxv; Luker, "The Crucible of Civil War and Reconstruction in the Experience of William Porcher Dubose," 53–64.
34 William Porcher DuBose, *Turning Points in My Life* (New York: Longmans, Green, & Company, 1912), 51.
35 William Porcher DuBose, "Reminiscences, 1836–1878," typescript copy transcribed by William Haskell DuBose, Southern Historical Collection, University of North Carolina at Chapel Hill, 139–40. Emphasis in the original.
36 Ibid., 140.
37 Ibid., 144. See also Zuczek, *State of Rebellion*, 59.
38 DuBose, "Reminiscences," 140.
39 W. Eric Emerson and Karen Stokes, "Epilogue," in William Porcher DuBose, *Faith, Valor, and Devotion: The Civil War Letters of William Porcher DuBose*, ed. W. Eric Emerson and Karen Stokes (Columbia: The University of South Carolina Press, 2010), 334. See also Cheesebrough, "'There Goes Your Damned Gospel Shop!'," 26–8.

40 DuBose, "Reminiscences," 139–51; Emerson and Stokes, "Epilogue," 334.

41 DuBose, "Reminiscences," 139–46. Yet one must acknowledge that history is not always linear, and people are not always ideologically consistent. At the end of the century, DuBose claimed that he voted for Republican William McKinley for president. In 1912, he supported Theodore Roosevelt's Bull Moose Progressive Party. Steve Longenecker, *Pulpits of the Lost Cause: The Faith and Politics of Former Confederate Chaplains During Reconstruction* (Tuscaloosa: The University of Alabama Press, 2023), 131, 201.

42 Luker, "The Crucible of Civil War and Reconstruction in the Experience of William Porcher Dubose," 69.

43 The University of the South, "A Research Summary on Slavery and Race at the University of the South and in the Community of Sewanee," the Roberson Project on Slavery, Race, and Reconciliation, accessed July 15, 2021, https://new.sewanee.edu/roberson-project/learn-more/research-summary/.

44 DuBose, "Reminiscences," 143–4. For the rise of the Ku Klux Klan in Abbeville, see especially Herbert Shapiro, "The Ku Klux Klan During Reconstruction: The South Carolina Episode," *The Journal of Negro History* 49, no. 1 (January 1964): 35–6, 37. See also Jerry L. West, *The Reconstruction Ku Klux Klan in York County, South Carolina, 1865–1877* (Jefferson, NC and London: McFarland & Company, Inc., 2002), 32, 33, 40; Lou Falkner Williams, *The Great South Carolina Ku Klux Klan Trials, 1871–1872* (Athens: University of Georgia Press, 1996), 20–2.

45 The quotes are found in Trelease, *White Terror*, 115, 116. See also pages 72, 349, 353. See also Walter Edgar, *South Carolina: A History* (Columbia: University of South Carolina Press, 1998), 398, 399–401; Luker, "The Crucible of Civil War and Reconstruction in the Experience of William Porcher Dubose," 66–8; Francis B. Simkins, "The Ku Klux Klan in South Carolina, 1868–1871," *The Journal of Negro History* 12, no. 4 (October 1927): 608; Richard Zuczek, "The Federal Government's Attack on the Ku Klux Klan: A Reassessment," *The South Carolina Historical Magazine* 97, no. 1 (January 1996): 48–9, 55, 59, 60.

46 DuBose is quoted in DuBose, "Reminiscences," 143–4. See also Jon Alexander, O. P., "Introduction," in William Porcher DuBose, *Selected Writings*, ed. Jon Alexander, O. P. (New York and Mahwah: Paulist Press, 1988), 8; Larry S. Bell and Marvin L. Cann, "Silver Spoons and Spyglasses: The Lifestyle of the Abbeville Gentry, 1820–1860," *The South Carolina Historical Magazine* 115, no. 4 (October 2014): 317–18; Luker, "The Crucible of Civil War and Reconstruction in the Experience of William Porcher Dubose," 66–8.

47 Eberly, "Our Stevens Family," 11–12; McCarriar, "A History of the Missionary Jurisdiction of the South of the Reformed Episcopal Church 1874–1970," 203; Porter, *Led On*, 223–5.

48 Eberly, "Our Stevens Family," 14, 16. See also Edgar, *South Carolina*, 401–6; Zuczek, *State of Rebellion*, 167–80, 188–92.

REFERENCES

Adams, Henry. *The Education of Henry Adams.* Washington, DC: Self, 1907.
Ahlstrom, Sydney E. *A Religious History of the American People.* 2nd ed. New Haven, CT: Yale University Press, 2004.
Albright, Raymond W. *A History of the Protestant Episcopal Church.* New York: Macmillan, 1964.
Alexander, Jon, O.P., Editor. *William Porcher DuBose: Selected Writings.* New York: Paulist Press, 1988.
Alston, Lee J., and Kyle D. Kauffman. "Up, Down, and Off the Agricultural Ladder: New Evidence and Implications of Agricultural Mobility for Blacks in the Postbellum South." *Agricultural History* 72, no. 2 (Spring 1998): 263-79.
Andrew, Rod Jr. *Wade Hampton: Confederate Warrior to Southern Redeemer.* Chapel Hill: The University of North Carolina Press, 2008.
Armentrout, Donald S., Editor. *A DuBose Reader: Selections from the Writings of William Porcher DuBose.* Sewanee, TN: The University of the South, 1984.
Armentrout, Donald S. "William Porcher DuBose Enters the Scene." *Sewanee Theological Review* 51, no. 2 (Easter 2008): 157-68.
Authorized Report of the Proceedings of the Eighth Church Congress in the Protestant Episcopal Church in the United States, Held in the City of Richmond, Virginia, Tuesday, Wednesday, Thursday, and Friday, October 24th, 25th, 26th, and 27th, 1882. Edited by the Committee on the Publication Appointed by the Executive Committee. New York: Thomas Whittaker, Publisher, Nos. 2 and 3, Bible House, 1882.
Aycrigg, Benjamin. *Memoirs of the Reformed Episcopal Church and the Protestant Episcopal Church in the Contemporary Reports Respecting these and The Church of England, Extracted from the Public Press, Analysed and Compared with Proven History.* New York: Edward O. Jenkins, 1880.
Ayers, Edward L. *The Promise of the New South: Life After Reconstruction.* Fifteenth Anniversary ed. New York: Oxford University Press, 2007.
Bach, Julian S. Jr. "The Social Thought of the Old South." *American Journal of Sociology* 46, no. 2 (September 1940): 179-88.
Badders, Hurley E. *Remembering South Carolina's Old Pendleton District.* Charleston, SC: History Press, 2006.
Bailey, Kenneth K. "The Post Civil War Racial Separations in Southern Protestantism: Another Look." *Church History* 46, no. 4 (December 1977): 453-73.
Baker, Gary L. *Cadets in Gray: The Story of the Cadets of the South Carolina Military Academy and the Cadet Rangers in the Civil War.* Columbia, SC: Palmetto Bookworks, 1989.

Bartley, Abel A. "The Fourteenth Amendment: The Great Equalizer of the American People." *Akron Law Review* 36, no. 3 (2003): 475-90.

Beale, Howard K. *The Critical Year: A Study of Andrew Johnson and Reconstruction.* New York: Frederick Ungar, 1958 [1930].

Bearden Robert E. L. Jr. "The Episcopal Church in the Confederate States." *The Arkansas Historical Quarterly* 4, no. 4 (Winter 1945): 269-75.

Beckert, Sven. *Empire of Cotton: A Global History.* New York: Vintage Books, 2015.

Bell, John L. Jr. "Andrew Johnson, National Politics, and Presidential Reconstruction in South Carolina." *The South Carolina Historical Magazine* 82, no. 4 (October 1981): 354-66.

Bell, Larry S., and Marvin L. Cann. "Silver Spoons and Spyglasses: The Lifestyle of the Abbeville Gentry, 1820-1860." *The South Carolina Historical Magazine* 115, no. 4 (October 2014): 304-24.

Belz, Herman. *Reconstructing the Union: Theory and Policy During the Civil War.* Ithaca, NY: Cornell University Press, 1969.

Belz, Herman. "The Freedmen's Bureau Act of 1865 and the Principle of No Discrimination According to Color." *Civil War History* 21, no. 3 (September 1975): 197-217.

Bennett, Robert A. "Black Episcopalians: A History from the Colonial Period to the Present." *Historical Magazine of the Protestant Episcopal Church* 43, no. 3 (September 1974): 231-45.

Birnie, C. W. "Education of the Negro in Charleston, South Carolina, Prior to the Civil War." *The Journal of Negro History* 12, no. 1 (January 1927): 13-21.

Birnie, Cassandra Maxwell. "Race and Politics in Georgia and South Carolina." *Phylon (1940-1956)* 13, no. 3 (Third Quarter 1952): 235-44.

"Bishop Guerry Dies of Bullet Wound, Was Shot by Retired Pastor, Believed Demented, Who Committed Suicide; Forgave His Assailant; Had Been Head of South Carolina Diocese of Protestant Episcopal Church Since 1908." *New York Times*, June 10, 1928, 18.

Blair, William A. "Finding the Ending of America's Civil War." *The American Historical Review* 120, no. 5 (December 2015): 1753-66.

Blight, David W. *Race and Reunion: The Civil War in American Memory.* Cambridge, MA: The Belknap Press of Harvard University Press, 2001.

Blum, Edward J. *Reforging the White Republic: Race, Religion, and American Nationalism, 1865-1898.* Baton Rouge: Louisiana State University Press, 2005.

Bogue, Allan G. "Historians and Radical Republicans: A Meaning for Today." *The Journal of American History* 70, no. 1 (June 1983): 7-34.

Bolton, S. Charles. *Southern Anglicanism: The Church of England in Colonial South Carolina.* Westport, CT: Greenwood Press, 1982.

Bond, Colonel O. J. *The Story of the Citadel.* Richmond, VA: Garrett and Massie, 1936.

Booth, Ted. "Trapped by His Hermeneutic: An Apocalyptic Defense of Slavery." *Anglican and Episcopal History* 87, no. 2 (June 2018): 159-79.

Bragg, George Freeman. *The Episcopal Church and the Black Man.* Baltimore, MD: Self Published, 1918.

Bragg, George Freeman, D.D. *History of the Afro-American Group of the Episcopal Church.* Baltimore, MD: Church Advocate Press, 1922.

Bragg, George Freeman, Jr. "The Episcopal Church and the Negro Race." *Historical Magazine of the Protestant Episcopal Church* 4, no. 1 (March 1935): 47–52.

Brewer, H. Peers. "The Protestant Episcopal Freedman's Commission, 1865-1878." *Historical Magazine of the Protestant Episcopal Church* 26, no. 4 (December 1957): 361–81.

Brown, Lawrence L. "The Americanization of the Episcopal Church." *Historical Magazine of the Protestant Episcopal Church* 44, no. 5 (December 1975): 33–51.

Bryant, Douglas H. "Unorthodox and Paradox: Revisiting the Ratification of the Fourteenth Amendment." *Alabama Law Review* 53, no. 2 (Winter 2003): 555–81.

Budiansky, Stephen. *The Bloody Shirt: Terror After the Civil War.* New York: Penguin, 2008.

Burnett, Gene M. *Florida's Past: People and Events That Shaped the State.* Sarasota, FL: Pineapple Press, 1986.

Burton, Georganne B., and Orville Vernon Burton. "Lucy Holcombe Pickens, Southern Writer." *The South Carolina Historical Magazine* 103, no. 4 (October 2002): 296–324.

Burton, Orville Vernon. "Race and Reconstruction: Edgefield County, South Carolina." *Journal of Social History* 12, no. 1 (October 1978): 31–56.

Calabresi, Steven G., and Christopher S. Yoo. "The Unitary Executive During the Second Half-Century." *Harvard Journal of Law & Public Policy* 26, no. 3 (Summer 2003): 667–801.

Caldwell, Ronald James. *A History of the Episcopal Church Schism in South Carolina.* Eugene, OR: Wipf & Stock, 2017.

Campbell, Jacqueline G. "'Terrible Has Been the Storm': William T. Sherman's Own Soldiers Were Shocked by the Destruction They Left Behind in South Carolina." *Civil War Times* 51, no. 1 (February 2012): 36–43.

Capers, Ellison. *A Sermon Preached in Commemoration of the Episcopate of Rt. Rev. William Bell White Howe, D.D., the Sixth Bishop of the Diocese of South Carolina.* Greenville, SC: Shannon & Co., Printers and Binders, 1895.

Carney, Judith A. "From Hands to Tutors: African Expertise in the South Carolina Rice Economy." *Agricultural History* 67, no. 3 (Summer 1993): 1–30.

Carr, Matthew. *Sherman's Ghosts: Soldiers, Civilians, and the American Way of War.* New York: The Free Press, 2015.

Carter, Paul A. "The Reformed Episcopal Schism of 1873: An Ecumenical Perspective." *Historical Magazine of the Protestant Episcopal* Church 33, no. 3 (September 1964): 225–38.

Carwardine, Richard. *Lincoln: A Life of Purpose and Power.* New York: Knopf, 2003.

Castel, Albert. *The Presidency of Andrew Johnson.* Lawrence: The University Press of Kansas, 1979.

Cheesebrough, David B. "'There Goes Your Damned Gospel Shop!' The Churches and Clergy as Victims of Sherman's March Through South Carolina." *The South Carolina Historical Magazine* 92, no. 1 (January 1991): 15–33.

Cheshire, Joseph Blount, D.D. *The Church in the Confederate States: A History of the Protestant Episcopal Church in the Confederate States.* New York: Longmans, Green, & Company, 1912.

Chitty, Arthur Benjamin Jr. *Reconstruction at Sewanee: The Founding of the University of the South and Its First Administration, 1857-1872*. Sewanee, TN: The University Press, 1954.

Civil Rights Act of 1866 14 Stat. 27-30 (1866).

Clebsch, William A. "Christian Interpretations of the Civil War." *Church History* 30, no. 2 (June 1961): 212-22.

Clifton, Denzil T. "Anglicanism and Negro Slavery in Colonial America." *Historical Magazine of the Protestant Episcopal Church* 39, no. 1 (March 1970): 29-70.

"Colored Ministers Will Act at Rev. P. F. Stevens Burial; Body of Leader in Reformed Episcopal Church, Who Died Sunday, Will Sleep in Magnolia." *The State* [Columbia, South Carolina], January 11, 1910, n.p.

Comminey, Shawn. "The Society for the Propagation of the Gospel in Foreign Parts and Black Education in South Carolina, 1702-1764." *The Journal of Negro History* 84, no. 4 (Autumn 1999): 360-9.

Conrad, James Lee. *The Young Lions: Confederate Cadets at War*. Mechanicsburg, PA: Stackpole Books, 1997.

Cornelius, Janet Duitsman. *Slave Missions and the Black Church in the Antebellum South*. Columbia: University of South Carolina Press, 1999.

Cornish, Dudley Taylor. *The Sable Arm: Negro Troops in the Union Army, 1861-1865*. New York: Longmans, Green and Company, 1956.

Cox, LaWanda Fenlason. "The Promise of Land for the Freedmen." *Mississippi Valley Historical Review* 45, no. 3 (December 1958): 413-40.

Cox, LaWanda Fenlason. *Lincoln and Black Freedom: A Study in Presidential Leadership*. Columbia: University of South Carolina Press, 1994 [1981].

Cummins, A. M. *Memoir of George David Cummins, DD., First Bishop of the Reformed Episcopal Church, By His Wife*. New York: Dodd, Mead & Company, 1878.

Cummins, George D. *Following the Light: A Statement of the Author's Experiences Resulting in a Change of Views Respecting the Prayer-Book of the Protestant Episcopal Church, and of the Reasons for Changing the Direction of Ministerial Labors in the Gospel of Christ*. Philadelphia, PA: James A. Moore, 1876.

Currie, David P. "The Reconstruction Congress." *University of Chicago Law Review* 75, no. 1 (2008): 383-495.

Daly, John Patrick. *When Slavery Was Called Freedom: Evangelism, Proslavery, and the Causes of the Civil War*. Lexington: University Press of Kentucky, 2002.

Dawes, Anna Laurens. *Charles Sumner*. New York: Dodd, Mead and Company, 1892.

Detzer, David. *Allegiance: Fort Sumter, Charleston, and the Beginning of the Civil War*. New York: Harcourt, 2001.

DeWitt, David Miller. *The Impeachment and Trial of Andrew Johnson, Seventeenth President of the United States: A History*. New York: The MacMillan Company, 1903.

Donald, David Herbert. *The Politics of Reconstruction, 1863-1867*. Baton Rouge: Louisiana State University Press, 1965.

Donald, David Herbert. *Lincoln*. New York: Simon & Schuster, 1995.

Dorn, T. Felder. *Challenges on the Emmaus Road: Episcopal Bishops Confront Slavery, Civil War, and Emancipation*. Columbia: University of South Carolina Press, 2013.

Du Bois, W. E. B. *The Souls of Black Folk: Essays and Sketches*. 8th ed. Chicago: A. C. McClurg & Company, 1909.

DuBose, William Porcher. *The Soteriology of the New Testament*. New York: MacMillan and Company, 1892.

DuBose, William Porcher. *The Ecumenical Councils*. Second Edition. Edinburgh: T & T Clark, 1897.

DuBose, William Porcher. "The Romance and Genius of a University." *The Sewanee Review* 13, no. 4 (October 1905): 496–502.

DuBose, William Porcher. *The Gospel in the Gospels*. New York: Longmans, Green & Company, 1906.

DuBose, William Porcher. *The Gospel According to St. Paul*. New York: Longmans, Green & Company, 1907.

DuBose, William Porcher. "Ellison Capers." *The Sewanee Review* 16, no. 3 (July 1908): 368–73.

DuBose, William Porcher. *High Priesthood and Sacrifice: An Exposition of the Epistle to the Hebrews*. New York: Longmans, Green, & Company, 1908.

DuBose, William Porcher. *The Reason of Life*. New York: Longmans, Green, & Company, 1911.

DuBose, William Porcher. *Turning Points in My Life*. New York: Longmans, Green & Company, 1912.

DuBose, William Porcher. *Unity in the Faith*. Greenwich, CT: The Seabury Press, 1957.

DuBose, William Porcher. *Selected Writings*. Edited by Jon Alexander. O.P. New York: Paulist Press, 1988.

DuBose, William Porcher. *Faith, Valor, and Devotion: The Civil War Letters of William Porcher DuBose*. Edited by W. Eric Emerson and Karen Stokes. Columbia: University of South Carolina Press, 2010.

DuBose, William Porcher. Letter from W. P. DuBose to Mrs. Joseph Huger, March 5, 1898. Habersham Elliott Papers, Southern Historical Collection, University of North Carolina at Chapel Hill.

DuBose, William Porcher. "Reminiscences, 1836-1878." Typescript copy transcribed by William Haskell DuBose, Southern Historical Collection University of North Carolina at Chapel Hill.

DuBose, William Porcher, and B. J. Ramage. "Wade Hampton." *The Sewanee Review* 10, no. 3 (July 1902): 364–73.

Duffy, John. "Yellow Fever in Colonial Charleston." *The South Carolina Historical and Genealogical Magazine* 52, no. 4 (October 1951): 189–97.

Dunkerly, Robert M., Donald C. Pfanz, and David R. Ruth. *No Turning Back: A Guide to the 1864 Overland Campaign, from the Wilderness to Cold Harbor, May 4–June 13, 1864*. Emerging Civil War Series. El Dorado Hills, CA: Savas Beatie, 2014.

Dunning, William Archibald. *Reconstruction, Political and Economic, 1865-1877*. The American Nation: A History. Vol. II. New York: Harper & Row, 1962 [1907].

DuPre-Moseley Family Collection, the Kennedy Room of Local History and Genealogy, Spartanburg County Public Libraries, Spartanburg, South Carolina.

Durden, Robert F. "The Prostrate State Revisited: James S. Pike and South Carolina Reconstruction." *The Journal of Negro History* 39, no. 2 (April 1954): 87–110.

Durden, Robert F. "The Establishment of Calvary Protestant Episcopal Church for Negroes in Charleston." *South Carolina Historical Magazine* 65, no. 2 (April 1964): 63-84.

Dyer, Brainerd. "The Treatment of Colored Union Troops by the Confederates, 1861-1865." *The Journal of Negro History* 20, no. 3 (July 1935): 273-86.

Eberly, Marion Stevens. "Our Stevens Family." Unpublished manuscript, December 1979. Typescript copy, Citadel Archives.

Edgar, Walter. *South Carolina: A History*. Columbia: University of South Carolina Press, 1998.

Editors of Time-Life Books. *Voices of the Civil War: Charleston*. New York: Time-Life Books, 1997.

Edwards, Dan. "Deification and the Anglican Doctrine of Human Nature: A Reassessment of the Historical Significance of William Porcher DuBose." *Anglican and Episcopal History* 58, no. 2 (June 1989): 196-212.

Egerton, Douglas R. *Year of Meteors: Stephen Douglas, Abraham Lincoln, and the Election That Brought on the Civil War*. London: Bloomsbury Press, 2010.

Eichelberger, John Gary Jr. "Caught in an 'Evil Infection': Postbellum Conflict in the Episcopal Diocese of South Carolina over the Role of African Americans in the Life of the Church." Master's Thesis, University of the South, 2020.

The Equal Justice Initiative (EJI). *Reconstruction in America: Racial Violence after the Civil War, 1865-1876*. Montgomery, AL: EJI, 2020.

Everitt, David. "War on Terror." *American History* 38, no. 2 (June 2003): 26-33.

Ex Parte Milligan, 71 U.S. 2 (1866).

Faust, Drew Gilpin. "A Southern Stewardship: The Intellectual and the Proslavery Argument." *American Quarterly* 31, no. 1 (Spring 1979): 63-80.

Ferleger, Louis. "Sharecropping Contracts in the Late-Nineteenth-Century South." *Agricultural History* 67, no. 3 (Summer 1993): 31-46.

Fickling, Susan Markey. "Slave-Conversion in South Carolina, 1830-1860." Master's Thesis, University of South Carolina, 1924.

Field, Ron. "Clothing the Confederate Soldiers of South Carolina, 1861-1865." *Military Collector & Historian* 70, no. 1 (Spring 2018): 88-93.

Flood, Charles Bracelen. *1864: Lincoln at the Gates of History*. New York: Simon & Schuster, 2009.

Folsom, Burton Jr. "Andrew Johnson and the Constitution." *Ideas on Liberty* 53, no. 8 (September 2003): 32-3.

Foner, Eric. *Reconstruction: America's Unfinished Revolution: 1863-1877*. New York: Francis Parkman Prize Edition, History Book Club, 2005 [1988].

Foner, Eric. *Forever Free: The Story of Emancipation and Reconstruction*. Illustrations Edited with a Commentary by Joshua Brown. New York: Knopf, 2005.

Ford, Lacy K. "Rednecks and Merchants: Economic Development and Social Tensions in the South Carolina Upcountry, 1865-1900." *The Journal of American History* 71, no. 2 (September 1984): 294-318.

Ford, Lacy K. *Origins of Southern Radicalism: The South Carolina Upcountry, 1800-1860*. Oxford: Oxford University Press, 1988.

Ford, Lacy K. "Reconsidering James Petigru: Unionist and Civic Reformer in a Radical Age." *The South Carolina Historical Magazine* 122, no. 3 (July 2021): 124-47.

Ford, Lacy K. "Christian Paternalism and the Contested Ideology of Slaveholding in Charleston and the South Carolina Low Country, 1845-1865." *The Journal of Southern History* 90, no. 1 (February 2024): 45-78.

Foster, Gaines M. "Bishop Cheshire and Black Participation in the Episcopal Church: The Limitations of Religious Paternalism." *The North Carolina Historical Review* 54, no. 1 (January 1977): 49-65.

Franklin, John Hope. *Reconstruction: After the Civil War*. Chicago, IL: The University of Chicago Press, 1961.

Freeman, Douglas Southall. *Lee's Lieutenants: A Study in Command*. New York: Scribner, 1998 [1940].

Genovese, Eugene D. *Roll, Jordan, Roll: The World the Slaves Made*. New York: Pantheon, 1974.

Genovese, Michael A. *The Power of the American Presidency, 1789-2000*. New York: Oxford University Press, 2001.

Goen, C. C. "Broken Churches, Broken Nation: Regional Religion and North-South Alienation in Antebellum America." *Church History* 52, no. 1 (March 1983): 21-35.

Goodwin, Doris Kearns. *Team of Rivals: The Political Genius of Abraham Lincoln*. New York: Simon & Schuster, 2005.

Gore, Blinzy L. *On a Hilltop High: The Origin and History of Claflin College to 1984*. Spartanburg, SC: The Reprint Company, 1994.

Gould, Lewis. *Grand Old Party: A History of the Republicans*. New York: Random House, 2003.

Graebner, N. Brooks. "The Preparation and Admission of Black Clergy in the Episcopal Diocese of North Carolina: The Training School at St. Augustine's in Raleigh, 1867-1894." *North Carolina Historical Review* 102, no. 1 (January 2025): 36-76.

Greene, Karen. *Porter-Gaud School: The Next Step*. Easley, SC: Southern Historical Press, 1982.

Guelzo, Allen C. *For the Union of Evangelical Christendom: The Irony of the Reformed Episcopalians*. University Park: The Pennsylvania State University Press, 1994.

Guelzo, Allen C. "A Sufficiently Republican Church: George David Cummins and the Reformed Episcopalians in 1873." *The Filson Club History Quarterly* 69, no. 2 (April 1995): 115-39.

Guelzo, Allen C. *Lincoln's Emancipation Proclamation: The End of Slavery in America*. New York: Simon & Schuster, 2006.

Guerry, Moultrie. "Makers of Sewanee." *The Sewanee Review* 41, no. 4 (October-December 1933): 483-94.

Habersham Elliott Papers, Southern Historical Collection, University of North Carolina at Chapel Hill.

Hahn, Steven. *A Nation Under Our Feet: Black Political Struggles in the Rural South from Slavery to the Great Migration*. Cambridge, MA: The Belknap Press of Harvard University Press, 2005.

Hale, Grace Elizabeth. "The Lost Cause and the Meaning of History." *OAH Magazine of History* 27, no. 1 (January 2013): 13-17.

Hall, Kermit L. "Political Power and Constitutional Legitimacy: The South Carolina Ku Klux Klan Trials, 1871-1872." *Emory Law Journal* 33, no. 4 (Fall 1984): 921-51.

Harrill, J. Albert. "The Use of the New Testament in the American Slave Controversy: A Case History in the Hermeneutical Tension between Biblical Criticism and Christian Moral Debate." *Religion and American Culture: A Journal of Interpretation* 10, no. 2 (Summer 2000): 149-86.

Harris, William C. *With Charity for All: Lincoln and the Restoration of the Union.* Lexington: University Press of Kentucky, 1999.

Harrison, Robert. "New Representations of a 'Misrepresented Bureau': Reflections on Recent Scholarship on the Freedmen's Bureau." *American Nineteenth Century History* 8, no. 2 (June 2007): 205-29.

Hatcher, Richard W. III. *Thunder in the Harbor: Fort Sumter and the Civil War.* El Dorado Hills, CA: Savas Beatie, 2024.

Hayden, J. Carleton. "Conversion and Control: Dilemma of Episcopalians in Providing for the Religious Instructions of Slaves, Charleston, South Carolina, 1845-1860." *Historical Magazine of the Protestant Episcopal Church* 40, no. 2 (June 1971): 143-71.

Hayden, J. Carleton. "After the War: The Mission and Growth of the Episcopal Church Among Blacks in the South, 1865-1877." *Historical Magazine of the Protestant Episcopal Church* 42, no. 4 (December 1973): 403-27.

Hennessey, Melinda Meek. "Racial Violence during Reconstruction: The 1876 Riots in Charleston and Cainhoy." *The South Carolina Historical Magazine* 86, no. 2 (April 1985): 100-12.

Henry, Robert Selph. *The Story of Reconstruction.* New York: Konecky & Konecky, 1999.

Hesseltine, William Best. *Civil War Prisons: A Study in War Psychology.* Columbus: Ohio State University Press, 1930.

Hesseltine, William Best. *Lincoln's Plan of Reconstruction.* Chicago: Quadrangle Books, 1967.

Hill, Harvey. "The Best of Both Worlds: William Porcher DuBose Among Liberals and Conservatives." *Anglican and Episcopal History* 81, no. 1 (March 2012): 1-21.

Holden, Charles J. "'The Public Business Is Ours': Edward McCrady, Jr. and Conservative Thought in Post-Civil War South Carolina, 1865-1900." *The South Carolina Historical Magazine* 100, no. 2 (April 1999): 124-42.

Holmes, David L. "The Episcopal Church and the American Revolution." *Historical Magazine of the Protestant Episcopal Church* 47, no. 3 (September 1978): 261-91.

Holzer, Harold. "A Promise Fulfilled." *Civil War Times* 48, no. 6 (December 2009): 28-35.

Holzer, Harold. *Lincoln: How Abraham Lincoln Ended Slavery in America.* New York: Newmarket Press, an Imprint of HarperCollins, 2012.

Hood, R. E. "From a Headstart to a Deadstart: The Historical Basis for Black Indifference Toward the Episcopal Church 1800-1860." *Historical Magazine of the Protestant Episcopal Church* 51, no. 3 (September 1982): 269-96.

Horton, James Oliver, and Lois E. Horton. *Slavery and the Making of America.* New York: Oxford University Press, 2005.

Howe, Daniel Walker. *What Hath God Wrought: The Transformation of America, 1815-1848*. New York: Oxford University Press, 2007.

Howe, Rev. W. B. W. *Cast Down, But Not Forsaken! A Sermon Delivered in St. Philip's Church, Charleston, December 15, 1861, Being the Sunday After the Great Fire*. Charleston, SC: Steam-Power Presses of Evans & Cogswell, 1861.

Howe, Rt. Rev. W. B. W. "Paper." In *Authorized Report of the Proceedings of the Eighth Church Congress in the Protestant Episcopal Church in the United States, Held in the City of Richmond, Virginia, Tuesday, Wednesday, Thursday, and Friday, October 24th, 25th, 26th, and 27th, 1882*. Edited by the Committee on the Publication Appointed by the Executive Committee, 83–90. New York: Thomas Whittaker, Publisher, Nos. 2 and 3, Bible House, 1882.

Huger, Daniel E. Chairman of the Standing Committee. *Proceedings of the Meeting in Charleston, S.C., May 13-15, 1845, on the Religious Instruction of the Negroes, together with the Report of the Committee, and the Address to the Public. Pub. by Order of the Meeting*. Charleston, SC: B. Jenkins, 1845.

Hughes, Robert M. "Joseph Eggleston Johnston: Soldier and Man." *The William and Mary College Quarterly Historical Magazine Second Series* 13, no. 2 (April 1933): 63–84.

Hyman, Harold M. *The Radical Republicans and Reconstruction, 1861-1870*. Indianapolis, IN: Bobbs-Merrill, 1967.

Jackson, James Conroy. "The Religious Education of the Negro in South Carolina Prior to 1850." *Historical Magazine of the Protestant Episcopal Church* 36, no. 1 (March 1967): 35–61.

Jackson, Luther P. "Religious Instruction of Negroes, 1830-1860, with Special Reference to South Carolina." *The Journal of Negro History* 15, no. 1 (January 1930): 72–114.

Janney, Carolyn E. "Written in Stone: Gender, Race, and the Heyward Shepherd Memorial." *Civil War History* 52, no. 2 (June 2006): 117–41.

Jervey, James Postell. "The Confederate General." *Historical Magazine of the Protestant Episcopal Church* 7, no. 4 (December 1938): 389–404.

Johnson, Jessica. "Washington Light Infantry Turns 200; Group Named for 1st President Organized in 1807 as Militia." *The Post and Courier* [Charleston, SC], February 21, 2007, B1.

Johnson, Michael P. "Denmark Vesey and His Co-Conspirators." *The William and Mary Quarterly* Third Series, 58, no. 4 (October 2001): 915–76.

Jones, Newton B. "The Washington Light Infantry at the Bunker Hill Centennial." *The South Carolina Historical Magazine* 65, no. 4 (October 1964): 195–204.

Journal of the Proceedings of the Sixty-Fifth Annual Convention of the Protestant Episcopal Church in South Carolina. Charleston, SC: A. E. Miller, 1854.

Journal of the Proceedings of the Sixty-Eighth Annual Convention of the Protestant Episcopal Church in South Carolina (Charleston, SC: A. E. Miller, 1857.

Journal of the Proceedings of the Seventieth Annual Convention of the Protestant Episcopal Church in South Carolina. Charleston, SC: A. E. Miller, 1859.

Journal of the Proceedings of the Seventy-Sixth Annual Convention of the Protestant Episcopal Church in South Carolina. Charleston, SC: Joseph Walker, 1866.

Journal of the Proceedings of the Seventy-Seventh Annual Convention of the Protestant Episcopal Church in South Carolina. Charleston, SC: W. W. Deane, 1867.

Journal of the Proceedings of the Seventy-Eighth Annual Convention of the Protestant Episcopal Church in South Carolina. Charleston, SC: Joseph Walker, 1868.

Journal of the Seventy-Ninth Annual Convention of the Protestant Episcopal Church in the Diocese of South Carolina. Charleston, SC: Wm. G. Mazyck, 1869.

Journal of the Eightieth Annual Convention of the Protestant Episcopal Church in the Diocese of South Carolina. Charleston, SC: Walker, Evans & Cogswell, 1870.

Journal of the Eighty-First Annual Convention of the Protestant Episcopal Church in the Diocese of South Carolina. Charleston, SC: Walker, Evans & Cogswell, 1871.

Journal of the Eighty-Third Annual Convention of the Protestant Episcopal Church in the Diocese of South Carolina. Charleston, SC: Walker, Evans & Cogswell, 1873.

Journal of the Eighty-Fourth Annual Convention of the Protestant Episcopal Church in the Diocese of South Carolina. Charleston, SC: Walker, Evans & Cogswell, 1874.

Journal of the Eighty-Fifth Annual Convention of the Protestant Episcopal Church in the Diocese of South Carolina. Charleston, SC: Walker, Evans & Cogswell, 1875.

Journal of the Eighty-Sixth Annual Convention of the Protestant Episcopal Church in the Diocese of South Carolina. Charleston, SC: Walker, Evans & Cogswell, 1876.

Journal of the Proceedings of the Fourth General Council of the Reformed Episcopal Church, Held in Emmanuel Church, Ottawa, Ontario, Canada, Commencing Wednesday, July 12, and Ending Monday, July 17, 1876, Published by Order of the General Council. Philadelphia, PA: James A. Moore, 1876.

Journal of the Proceedings of the Fifth General Council of the Reformed Episcopal Church, Held in the Chapel of the Second Reformed Episcopal Church, Philadelphia, PA, Commencing Wednesday, May 9, and Ending Tuesday, May 15, 1877, Published by Order of the General Council. Philadelphia, PA: James A. Moore, 1876.

Journal of the Eighty-Seventh Annual Convention of the Protestant Episcopal Church in the Diocese of South Carolina. Charleston, SC: Walker, Evans & Cogswell, 1877.

Journal of the Proceedings of the Sixth General Council of the Reformed Episcopal Church, Held in Emmanuel Church, Newark, New Jersey, Commencing Wednesday, May 8, and Ending Monday, May 13, 1878, Published by Order of the General Council. Philadelphia, PA: James A. Moore, 1878.

Journal of the Eighty-Ninth Annual Convention of the Protestant Episcopal Church in the Diocese of South Carolina. Charleston, SC: Walker, Evans & Cogswell, 1879.

Journal of the Proceedings of the Seventh General Council of the Reformed Episcopal Church, Held in Christ Church, Chicago, Illinois, Commencing Wednesday, May 28th, and Ending Wednesday, June 4th, 1879, Published by Order of the General Council. Philadelphia, PA: James A. Moore, 1879.

Journal of the Ninetieth Annual Convention of the Protestant Episcopal Church in the Diocese of South Carolina. Charleston, SC: Walker, Evans & Cogswell, 1880.

Journal of the Ninety-First Annual Convention of the Protestant Episcopal Church in the Diocese of South Carolina. Charleston, SC: Walker, Evans & Cogswell, 1881.

Journal of the Proceedings of the Eighth General Council of the Reformed Episcopal Church, Held in the First Reformed Episcopal Church in New York City, Commencing Wednesday, May 25th, and Ending Monday, May 30th, 1881, Published by Order of the General Council. Philadelphia, PA: James A. Moore, 1881.

Journal of the Ninety-Second Annual Convention of the Protestant Episcopal Church in the Diocese of South Carolina. Charleston, SC: Walker, Evans & Cogswell, 1882.

Journal of the Ninety-Third Annual Convention of the Protestant Episcopal Church in the Diocese of South Carolina. Charleston, SC: Walker, Evans & Cogswell, 1883.

Journal of the Proceedings of the Bishops, Clergy, and Laity of the Protestant Episcopal Church in the United States of America. Philadelphia, PA: The Protestant Episcopal Church, 1883.

Journal of the Proceedings of the Ninth General Council of the Reformed Episcopal Church, Held in Bishop Cummins' Memorial Church, Baltimore, Maryland, Commencing Wednesday, May 23rd, and Ending Monday, May 28, 1883, Published by Order of the General Council. Philadelphia, PA: William Syckelmoore, 1883.

Journal of the Ninety-Fourth Annual Convention of the Protestant Episcopal Church in the Diocese of South Carolina. Charleston, SC: Walker, Evans & Cogswell, 1884.

Journal of the Ninety-Fifth Annual Convention of the Protestant Episcopal Church in the Diocese of South Carolina. Columbia, SC: Charles A. Calvo, 1885.

Journal of the Proceedings of the Eleventh General Council of the Reformed Episcopal Church, Held in the Second Reformed Episcopal Church, Philadelphia, Commencing Wednesday, May 25th, and Ending Monday, May 30, 1887, Published by Order of the General Council. Philadelphia, PA: Reformed Episcopal Publication Society, Limited, 1887.

Journal of the Proceedings of the Twelfth General Council of the Reformed Episcopal Church, Held in the First Reformed Episcopal Church, Boston, Commencing Wednesday, May 22nd, and Ending Monday, May 27, 1889, Published by Order of the General Council. Philadelphia, PA: James A. Moore, 1889.

Journal of the Proceedings of the Fourteenth General Council of the Reformed Episcopal Church, Held in Christ Church, Chicago, Illinois, Commencing Wednesday, June 6th, and Ending Monday, June 11th, 1894, Published by Order of the General Council. Philadelphia, PA: James A. Moore, 1894.

Journal of the One Hundred and Fifth Annual Council of the Protestant Episcopal Church in the Diocese of South Carolina a Held in Grace Church, Camden, on the 8th, 9th, and 10th of May 1895. Greenville, SC: Shannon & Co., Printers and Binders, 1895.

Journal of the Proceedings of the Fifteenth General Council of the Reformed Episcopal Church, Held in First Church, New York City, Commencing Wednesday, June 9th, and Ending Monday, June 14th, 1897, Published by Order of the General Council. Philadelphia, PA: Reformed Episcopal Publication Society, 1897.

Journal of the One Hundred Twelfth Annual Convention of the Protestant Episcopal Church in the Diocese of South Carolina. Winyah, SC: Published for the Council by the Secretary, 1902.

Journal of the Proceedings of the Seventeenth General Council of the Reformed Episcopal Church, Held in St. Paul's Church, Chicago, Illinois, Commencing Wednesday, May 20th, and Ending Monday, May 25, 1903, Published by Order of the General Council. Philadelphia, PA: James M. Armstrong, 1903.

Journal of the Proceedings of the Nineteenth General Council of the Reformed Episcopal Church, Held in St. Paul's Church, Philadelphia, Penna., Commencing Wednesday, May 19th, and Ending Saturday, May 22nd, 1909, Published by Order of the General Council. Philadelphia, PA: James A. Armstrong, 1909.

Journal of the Proceedings of the Twentieth General Council of the Reformed Episcopal Church, Held in Christ Memorial Church, Philadelphia, Pennsylvania, Commencing Wednesday, May 15th, and Ending Saturday, May 18, 1912, Published by Order of the General Council. Philadelphia, PA: James M. Armstrong, 1912.

Kaczorowski, Robert J. "Congress' Power to Enforce Fourteenth Amendment Rights: Lessons from Federal Remedies the Framers Enacted." *Harvard Journal on Legislation* 42, no. 1 (Winter 2005): 187-283.

Kantrowitz, Stephen. *Ben Tillman & the Reconstruction of White Supremacy*. Chapel Hill: The University of North Carolina Press, 2000.

Keegan, John. *The American Civil War: A Military History*. New York: Knopf, 2009.

Kendi, Ibram X. *Stamped from the Beginning: The Definitive History of Racist Ideas in America*. New York: Nation Books, 2016.

Kendrick, Benjamin B. *The Journal of the Joint Committee of Fifteen on Reconstruction, 39th Congress, 1865-1867*. Clark, NJ: The Law Book Exchange, Ltd., 2005 [1914].

King, Benjamin J. "Church, Cotton, and Confederates: What Charles Todd Quintard's Fundraising Trips to Great Britain Reveal About Some Nineteenth-Century Anglo-Catholics." *Anglican and Episcopal History* 90, no. 2 (June 2021): 109-33.

King, Ronald F. "Counting the Votes: South Carolina's Stolen Election of 1876." *Journal of Interdisciplinary History* 32, no. 2 (Autumn 2001): 169-91.

Klarman, Michael J. *From Jim Crow to Civil Rights: The Supreme Court and the Struggle for Equality*. New York: Oxford University Press, 2004.

Kraditor, Aileen S. *Means and Ends in American Abolitionism: Garrison and His Critics on Strategy and Tactics, 1834-1850*. New York: Vintage Books, 1969.

Krannawitter, Thomas L. *Vindicating Lincoln: Defending the Politics of Our Greatest President*. Lanham, MD: Rowman & Littlefield, 2008.

Lammers, Ann C. "The Rev. Absalom Jones and the Episcopal Church: Christian Theology and Black Consciousness in a New Alliance: Essays in the Social Gospel in England and America and Honoring the Diocese of Nebraska and the Diocese of Pennsylvania." *Historical Magazine of the Protestant Episcopal Church* 51, no. 2 (June 1982): 159-84.

Langguth, A. J. *After Lincoln: How the North Won the Civil War and Lost the Peace*. New York: Simon & Schuster, 2014.

Larson, Erik. *The Demon of Unrest: A Saga of Hubris, Heartbreak, and Heroism at the Dawn of the Civil War*. New York: Crown, 2024.

Latzko, David A. "Mapping the Short-run Impact of the Civil War and Emancipation on the South Carolina Economy." *The South Carolina Historical Magazine* 116, no. 4 (October 2015): 258-79.

Lemann, Nicholas. *Redemption: The Last Battle of the Civil War*. New York: Farrar, Straus & Giroux, 2006.

Lesser, Charles H. *Relic of the Lost Cause: The Story of South Carolina's Ordinance of Secession*. 2nd. ed. Columbia: University of South Carolina Press, 2012.

Lewis, Harold T. *Yet with a Steady Beat: The African American Struggle for Recognition in the Episcopal Church*. Valley Forge, PA: Trinity Press International, 1996.

Lippy, Charles H. "Chastized by Scorpions: Christianity and Culture in Colonial South Carolina, 1669-1740." *Church History* 79, no. 2 (June 2010): 253-70.

Little, Thomas J. "The Origins of Southern Evangelicalism: Revivalism in South Carolina, 1700-1740." *Church History* 75, no. 4 (December 2006): 768-808.

Litwack, Leon F. *Been in the Storm So Long: The Aftermath of Slavery*. New York: Vintage Books, 1979.

Litwack, Leon F. *Trouble in Mind: Black Southerners in the Age of Jim Crow*. New York: Knopf, 1998.

Livingstone, David. "The Emancipation Proclamation, the Declaration of Independence, and the Presidency: Lincoln's Model of Statesmanship." *Perspectives on Political Science* 28, no. 4 (Fall 1999): 203-10.

London, Lawrence F. "The Literature of the Church in the Confederate States." *Historical Magazine of the Protestant Episcopal Church* 17, no. 4 (December 1948): 345-55.

Longenecker, Steve. *Pulpits of the Lost Cause: The Faith and Politics of Former Confederate Chaplains During Reconstruction*. Tuscaloosa: The University of Alabama Press, 2023.

Lowery, Malinda Maynor. "The Original Southerners: American Indians, the Civil War, and Confederate Memory." *Southern Cultures* 25, no. 4 (Winter 2019): 16-35.

Luker, Ralph E. "Liberal Theology and Social Conservatism: A Southern Tradition, 1840-1920." *Church History* 50, no. 2 (June 1981): 193-204.

Luker, Ralph E. "The Crucible of Civil War and Reconstruction in the Experience of William Porcher DuBose." *The South Carolina Historical Magazine* 83, no. 1 (January 1982): 50-71.

Luker, Ralph E. *A Southern Tradition in Theology and Social Criticism 1830-1930: The Religious Liberalism and Social Conservatism of James Warley Miles, William Porcher DuBose and Edgar Gardner Murphy*. Studies in American Religion 11. New York: The Edwin Mellen Press, 1984.

Maddex, Jack P. Jr. "Pollard's *The Lost Cause Regained*: A Mask for Southern Accommodation." *The Journal of Southern History* 40, no. 4 (November 1974): 595–612.

Manning, Chandra. *What This Cruel War Was Over: Soldiers, Slavery, and the Civil War*. New York: Knopf, 2007.

Manross, William Wilson. "The Episcopal Church and Reform." *Historical Magazine of the Protestant Episcopal Church* 12, no. 4 (December 1943): 339–66.

Mantell, Martin E. *Johnson, Grant, and the Politics of Reconstruction*. New York: Columbia University Press, 1973.

Marshall, John S. "From Aristotle to Christ: Or the Philosophy of William Porcher DuBose." *The Sewanee Review* 51, no. 1 (January–March 1943): 148–59.

Martinez, J. Michael. *Life and Death in Civil War Prisons*. Nashville, TN: Rutledge Hill Press, 2004.

Martinez, J. Michael. *Carpetbaggers, Cavalry, and the Ku Klux Klan: Exposing the Invisible Empire During Reconstruction*. Lanham, MD: Rowman & Littlefield, 2007.

Martinez, J. Michael. *Coming For to Carry Me Home: Race in America from Abolitionism to Jim Crow*. Lanham, MD: Rowman & Littlefield, 2012.

Martinez, J. Michael. *A Long Dark Night: Race in America from Jim Crow to World War II*. Lanham, MD: Rowman & Littlefield, 2016.

Mason, Lockert B. "Separation and Reunion of the Episcopal Church 1861-1865: The Role of Bishop Thomas Atkinson." *Anglican and Episcopal History* 59, no. 3 (September 1990): 345–65.

Mason, Matthew. *Slavery and Politics in the Early American Republic*. Chapel Hill: University of North Carolina Press, 2006.

Mathews, Donald G. *Religion in the Old South*. Chicago, IL: The University of Chicago Press, 1977.

Mayo, Rev. A. D. "The Work of Dr. Porter in Charleston, S.C." *Journal of Education* 15, no. 15 (April 13, 1882): 233–4.

McCarriar, Herbert Geer Jr. "A History of the Missionary Jurisdiction of the South of the Reformed Episcopal Church 1874-1970." *Historical Magazine of the Protestant Episcopal Church* 41, no. 2 (June 1972): 197–220.

McCarriar, Herbert Geer Jr. "History of the Missionary Jurisdiction of the South of the Reformed Episcopal Church 1874-1970: Part II." *Historical Magazine of the Protestant Episcopal Church* 41, no. 3 (September 1972): 287–315.

McConnell, Samuel David, D. D. *History of the American Episcopal Church from the Planting of the Colonies to the End of the Civil War*. New York: Thomas Whittaker, 1890.

McConnell, Stuart. "The Civil War and Historical Memory: A Historiographical Survey." *OAH Magazine of History* 8, no. 1 (Fall 1993): 3–6.

McCurry, Stephanie. *Masters of Small Worlds: Yeoman Households, Gender Relations, & Political Culture of the Antebellum South Carolina Low Country*. New York: Oxford University Press, 1995.

McFeely, William S. *Grant: A Biography*. New York: W. W. Norton, 1981.
McKitrick, Eric L. *Andrew Johnson and Reconstruction*. New York: Oxford University Press, 1988 [1960].
McPherson, James M. *Battle Cry of Freedom: The Civil War Era*. New York: Ballantine Books, 1988.
McPherson, James M. *What They Fought For, 1861-1865*. Baton Rouge: Louisiana State University Press, 1994.
Mead, Loren B. *Financial Meltdown in the Mainline?* Lanham, MD: Rowman & Littlefield, 1998.
Mead, Loren B. *Five Challenges for the Once and Future Church*. Lanham, MD: Rowman & Littlefield, 1996.
Mead, Loren B. *New Hope for Congregations*. New York: Seabury Press, 1972.
Mead, Loren B. *The Once and Future Church: Reinventing the Congregation for a New Mission Frontier*. Lanham, MD: Rowman & Littlefield, 1991.
Mead, Loren B. *The Parish is the Issue: What I Learned and How I Learned It*. New York: Morehouse Publishing, 2015.
Mead, Loren B. *Transforming Congregations for the Future*. Lanham, MD: Rowman & Littlefield, 1994.
Mead, Loren B., and J. Michael Martinez. "A Southern White Clergyman, the Freed People, and the Nineteenth-Century Episcopal Church." *Journal of Anglican Studies* 22, no. 1 (May 2024): 290-309.
Mead, Loren B., and J. Michael Martinez. "Three Ministers, Black Communicants, and the Civil War Era." *Anglican and Episcopal History* 92, no. 3 (September 2023): 398-426.
Means, Howard. *The Avenger Takes His Place: Andrew Johnson and the 45 Days That Changed the Nation*. New York: Harcourt, Inc., 2006.
Mercantini, Jonathan. "The Great Carolina Hurricane of 1752." *The South Carolina Historical Magazine* 103, no. 4 (October 2002): 351-65.
Milton, George Fort. *The Age of Hate: Andrew Johnson and the Radicals*. New York: Coward-McCann, Inc., 1930.
Mohler, Mark. "The Episcopal Church and National Reconciliation, 1865." *Political Science Quarterly* 41, no. 4 (December 1926): 567-95.
Morgan, James A. *Six Miles from Charleston, Five Minutes to Hell: The Battle of Secessionville, June 16, 1862*. El Dorado Hills, CA: Savas Beatie, 2022.
Mullin, Robert Bruce. "Biblical Critics and the Battle Over Slavery." *Journal of Presbyterian History* 61, no. 2 (Summer 1983): 210-26.
Murphy Richard W. *The Nation Reunited: War's Aftermath*. Alexandria, VA: Time-Life Books, 1987.
Myers, George Boggan. "The Sage and Seer of Sewanee." In *Unity in the Faith*. Edited by W. Norman Pittenger, 1-20. Greenwich, CT: The Seabury Press, 1957.
Nash, Henry S. "Dr. DuBose's 'Gospel in the Gospels.'" *The Sewanee Review* 15, no. 1 (January 1907): 111-20.
"Necrology: Ellison Capers." *The South Carolina Historical and Genealogical Magazine* 9, no. 3 (July 1908): 166-9.
Nelson, Larry E. "Sherman at Cheraw." *The South Carolina Historical Magazine* 100, no. 4 (October 1999): 328-54.
Newell, Clayton R., and Charles R. Shrader. "The U.S. Army's Transition to Peace, 1865-66." *The Journal of Military History* 77, no. 3 (July 2013): 867-94.

Noll, Mark A. *The Civil War as a Theological Crisis*. Chapel Hill: The University of North Carolina Press, 2006.

Oakes, James. *Freedom National: The Destruction of Slavery in the United States, 1861-1865*. New York: W. W. Norton, 2013.

Official Register of the Officers and Cadets at the South Carolina Military Academies. The Citadel Archives & Museum, 1849. https://citadeldigitalarchives.omeka.net/items/show/3.

Olwell, Robert. *Masters, Slaves & Subjects: The Culture of Power in the South Carolina Low Country, 1740-1790*. Ithaca, NY: Cornell University Press, 1998.

O'Malley, Gregory E. "Slavery's Converging Ground: Charleston's Slave Trade as the Black Heart of the Lowcountry." *The William and Mary Quarterly* 74, no. 2 (April 2017): 271-302.

Orr, Peter. "'Slaves, Submit to Your Masters': Understanding and Applying the Slavery Passages in the Bible." *JSTOR*. Accessed June 7, 2025. https://jstor.org/stable/community.32028934.

Oshatz, Molly. "No Ordinary Sin: Antislavery Protestants and the Discovery of the Social Nature of Morality." *Church History* 79, no. 2 (June 2010): 334-58.

Pennington, Edgar Legare. "The Confederate Episcopal Church and the Southern Soldiers." *Historical Magazine of the Protestant Episcopal Church* 17, no. 4 (December 1948): 356-83.

Pennington, Edgar Legare. "The Organization of the Protestant Episcopal Church in the Confederate States of America." *Historical Magazine of the Protestant Episcopal Church* 17, no. 4 (December 1948): 308-38.

Perman, Michael. *The Road to Redemption: Southern Politics, 1869-1879*. Chapel Hill: The University of North Carolina Press, 1984.

Perry, William Stevens. *The History of the American Episcopal Church, 1587-1883*. Vol. II. Boston: J.R. Osgood, 1885.

Perry, William Stevens. *The Bishops of the American Church, Past and Present. Sketches, Biographical and Bibliographical, of the Bishops of the American Church with a Preliminary Essay on the Historic Episcopate and Documentary Annals of the Introduction of the Anglican Line of Succession into America*. New York: The Christian Literature Company, 1897.

Phillips, Ulrich Bonnell. *American Negro Slavery: A Survey of the Supply, Employment and Control of Negro Labor as Determined by the Plantation Régime*. New York: D. Appleton and Company, 1918.

Pittenger, W. Norman. "The Significance of DuBose's Theology." In *Unity in the Faith*. Edited by W. Norman Pittenger, 21-31. Greenwich, CT: The Seabury Press, 1957.

Platt, Warren C. "The Reformed Episcopal Church: The Origins and Early Development of Its Ideological Expression." *Historical Magazine of the Protestant Episcopal Church* 52, no. 3 (September 1983): 245-73.

Poole, W. Scott. "Religion, Gender, and the Lost Cause in South Carolina's 1876 Governor's Race: 'Hampton or Hell!'." *The Journal of Southern History* 68, no. 3 (August 2002): 573-98.

Porter, Anthony Toomer. *The History of a Work of Faith and Love in Charleston, South Carolina*. New York: D. Appleton and Company, 1882.

Porter, Anthony Toomer. *Speech of Rev. A. Toomer Porter, D.D., of Charleston, S.C., before the General Convention of the P.E. Church in Philadelphia,*

October 1883, on the Action of the Conference Held at Sewanee, Tenn., August, 1883, relative to the Work of the Church Among the Colored People of the United States. Charleston, SC: The News and Courier Book Presses, 1883.

Porter, Anthony Toomer. *Led On! Step by Step Scenes from Clerical, Military, Educational, and Plantation Life in the South, 1828-1898*. New York: G. P Putnam's Sons, the Knickerbocker Press, 1898.

Porter, Rev. A. Toomer. *History of the Holy Communion Church Institute, of Charleston, South Carolina, Founded by Rev. A. Toomer Porter, A.D. MDCCCLXVII, Second Edition, Brought Down to October 1, 1875*. New York: D. Appleton and Company, 1876.

Posey, Walter B. "The Protestant Episcopal Church: An American Adaptation." *The Journal of Southern History* 25, no. 1 (February 1959): 3-30.

Power, J. Tracy. "'An Affair of Outposts': The Battle of Secessionville, June 16, 1862." *Civil War History* 38, no. 2 (June 1992): 156-72.

Powers, Bernard E. Jr. "Community Evolution and Race Relations in Reconstruction Charleston, South Carolina." *The South Carolina Historical Magazine* 101, no. 3 (July 2000): 214-33.

Price, Mrs. Annie Darling. *A History of the Formation and Growth of the Reformed Episcopal Church, 1873-1902*. Philadelphia, PA: James M. Armstrong, 1902.

Public Ceremonies in Connection with War Memorials of the Washington Light Infantry with Orations of Gen. Wade Hampton, Hon. C. H. Simonton, Dr. A. Toomer Porter. Charleston, SC: Edward Perry & Company, 1894.

Purcell, Sarah J. *Spectacle of Grief: Public Funerals and Memory in the Civil War Era*. Chapel Hill: The University of North Carolina Press, 2022.

Pyszka, Kimberly. "'Built for the Publick Worship of God, according to the Church of England': Anglican Landscapes and Colonialism in South Carolina." *Historical Archaeology* 47, no. 4 (December 2013): 1-22.

Quarles, Benjamin. *The Negro in the Civil War*. Cambridge, Mass.: Da Capo, 1988 [1953].

Rable, George C. *But There Was No Peace: The Role of Violence in the Politics of Reconstruction*. Athens: University of Georgia Press, 1984.

Ramsey, William L. "'Something Cloudy in Their Looks': The Origins of the Yamasee War Reconsidered." *The Journal of American History* 90, no. 1 (June 2003): 44-75.

Rankin, David C. "The Impact of the Civil War on the Free Colored Community of New Orleans." *Perspectives in American History* 11, no. 1 (1977-1978): 377-416.

Ransom, Roger L., and Richard L. Sutch. *One Kind of Freedom: The Economic Consequences of Emancipation*. 2nd ed. Cambridge: Cambridge University Press, 2001.

Reidenbaugh, Lowell. "Kershaw, Joseph B." In *MacMillan Information Now Encyclopedia: The Confederacy*. Edited by Richard N. Current, 313. New York: MacMillan Reference USA, 1993.

Reimers, David M. "Negro Bishops and Diocesan Segregation in the Protestant Episcopal Church: 1870-1954." *Historical Magazine of the Protestant Episcopal Church* 31, no. 3 (September 1962): 231-42.

"Rev. Dr. Anthony Toomer Porter." In *Cyclopedia of Eminent and Representative Men of the Carolinas of the Nineteenth Century, with a Brief Historical Introduction on South Carolina by General Edward McCrady, Jr., and on North Carolina by Hon. Samuel A. Ashe.* Vol. I, 493-5. Madison, WI: Brant & Fuller, 1892.

Ricards, Sherman L., and George M. Blackburn. "A Demographic History of Slavery: Georgetown County, South Carolina, 1850." *The South Carolina Historical Magazine* 76, no. 4 (October 1975): 215-24.

Robertson, David. *Denmark Vesey: The Buried Story of America's Largest Slave Rebellion and the Man Who Led It.* New York: Vintage Books, 2000.

Robins, Glenn. *The Bishop of the Old South: The Ministry and Civil War Legacy of Leonidas Polk.* Macon, GA: Mercer University Press, 2006.

Salomon, Richard G. "Mother Church—Daughter Church—Sister Church: The Relations of the Protestant Episcopal Church and the Church of England in the 19th Century." *Historical Magazine of the Protestant Episcopal Church* 21, no. 4 (December 1952): 417-46.

Savage, John. *The Life and Public Speeches of Andrew Johnson, Seventeenth President of the United States, Including His State Papers, Speeches, and Addresses.* New York: Derby & Miller, 1866.

Saville, Julie. *The Work of Reconstruction: From Slave to Wage Laborer in South Carolina, 1860-1870.* Cambridge: Cambridge University Press, 1994.

Scarborough, William Kaufman. *Masters of the Big House: Elite Slaveholders in the Mid-Nineteenth Century South.* Baton Rouge: Louisiana State University Press, 2006.

Scarborough, William Kaufman. "Propagandists for Secession: Edmund Ruffin of Virginia and Robert Barnwell Rhett of South Carolina." *The South Carolina Historical Magazine* 112, no. 3/4 (July-October 2011): 126-38.

Scruggs, C. Eugene. *Tramping with the Legion: A Carolina Rebel's Story.* Victoria, BC: Trafford Publishing, 2006.

Shanks, Caroline L. "The Biblical Anti-Slavery Argument of the Decade 1830-1840." *The Journal of Negro History* 16, no. 2 (April 1931): 132-57.

Shanks, Harry T. "The Reunion of the Episcopal Church, 1865." *Church History* 9, no. 2 (June 1940): 120-40.

Shapiro, Herbert. "The Ku Klux Klan During Reconstruction: The South Carolina Episode." *The Journal of Negro History* 49, no. 1 (January 1964): 34-55.

Shattuck, Gardiner H. Jr. *Episcopalians and Race: Civil War to Civil Rights.* Lexington: The University Press of Kentucky, 2000.

Shattuck, Gardiner H. Jr. "'One Fold and One Chief Shepherd': The Sewanee Conference of 1883 and the Beginnings of Racial Segregation in the Episcopal Church." In *Vale of Tears: New Essays on Religion and Reconstruction.* Edited by Edward J. Blum and W. Scott Poole, 53-72. Macon, GA: Mercer University Press, 2005.

Shattuck, Gardiner H. Jr. "'This Great Day of Suffering': Redeeming Memories of the Civil War." *Anglican and Episcopal History* 81, no. 4 (December 2012): 377-89.

Sheehan-Dean, Aaron. "The Long Civil War: A Historiography of the Consequences of the Civil War." *The Virginia Magazine of History and Biography* 119, no. 2 (2011): 106-53.

Simkins, Francis Butler. "The Ku Klux Klan in South Carolina, 1868-1871." *The Journal of Negro History* 12, no. 4 (October 1927): 606-47.

Simkins, Francis Butler. "Ben Tillman's View of the Negro." *The Journal of Southern History* 3, no. 2 (May 1937): 161-74.

Simkins, Francis Butler, and Charles Pierce Roland. *A History of the South*. 4th ed. New York: Knopf, 1972.

Simpson, Brooks D. *Let Us Have Peace: Ulysses S. Grant and the Politics of War and Reconstruction, 1861-1868*. Chapel Hill: The University of North Carolina Press, 1991.

Simpson, Brooks D. *The Reconstruction Presidents*. Lawrence: The University Press of Kansas, 1998.

Simpson, Brooks D. "Mission Impossible: Reconstruction Policy Reconsidered." *Journal of the Civil War Era* 6, no. 1 (March 2016): 85-102.

Simpson, John A. "The Cult of the 'Lost Cause'." *Tennessee Historical Quarterly* 34, no. 4 (Winter 1975): 350-61.

Slap, Andrew L. "The Spirit of '76: The Reconstruction of History in the Redemption of South Carolina." *The Historian* 63, no. 4 (Summer 2001): 769-85.

Slap, Andrew L. *The Doom of Reconstruction: The Liberal Republicans in the Civil War Era*. New York: Fordham University Press, 2010.

Slocum, Robert B. "Living the Truth: An Introduction to the Theological Method and Witness of William Porcher DuBose." *St. Luke's Journal of Theology* 34, no. 1 (December 1990): 28-40.

Slocum, Robert B. "The Lessons of Experience and the Theology of William Porcher DuBose." *Journal of Theological Studies* 79, no. 3 (Summer 1997): 341-68.

Slocum, Robert B. *The Theology of William Porcher DuBose: Life, Movement, and Being*. Columbia: University of South Carolina Press, 2000.

Slocum, Robert B. "A Soldier's Faith: The Civil War Experiences and Reflections of William Porcher DuBose." *Journal of Anglican Studies* 16, no. 2 (November 2018): 170-87.

Smith, Henry A. M. "The Baronies of South Carolina." *The South Carolina Historical and Genealogical Magazine* 13, no. 1 (January 1912): 3-20.

Smith, John David, and J. Vincent Lowery, Editors. *The Dunning School: Historians, Race, and the Meaning of Reconstruction*. Lexington: University Press of Kentucky, 2013.

Smith, W. Thomas Jr. "Big Red & *The Star of the West*." *Sandlapper: The Magazine of South Carolina* 22, no. 1 (Spring 2011): 28-30.

Snow, Jennifer. "The Altar and the Rail: 'Catholicity' and African American Inclusion in the 19th Century Episcopal Church." *Religions* 12, no. 224 (March 2021): 1-19.

Speer, Lonnie R. *Portals to Hell: Military Prisons of the Civil War*. Mechanicsburg, PA: Stackpole Books, 1997.

Stagg, J. C. A. "The Problem of Klan Violence: The South Carolina Up-Country, 1868-1871." *Journal of American Studies* 8, no. 3 (December 1974): 303-18.

Stampp, Kenneth M. *The Era of Reconstruction, 1865-1877*. New York: Alfred A. Knopf, 1965.

Stevens, Peter Fayssoux. "Autobiography." Unpublished, manuscript, n.d. Handwritten copy, DuPre-Moseley Family Collection, the Kennedy Room of Local History and Genealogy, Spartanburg County Public Libraries, Spartanburg, South Carolina.

Stewart, David O. *Impeached: The Trial of President Andrew Johnson and the Fight for Lincoln's Legacy.* New York: Simon & Schuster, 2009.

Strange, Thomas. "Alexander Crummell and the Anti-Slavery Dilemma of the Episcopal Church." *Journal of Ecclesiastical History* 70, no. 4 (October 2019): 767-84.

Thomas, Albert Sidney. "A Sketch of the History of the Church in South Carolina." *Historical Magazine of the Protestant Episcopal Church* 4, no. 1 (March 1935): 1-12.

Thomas, Albert Sidney. "The Protestant Episcopal Society for the Advancement of Christianity in South Carolina." *Historical Magazine of the Protestant Episcopal Church* 21, no. 4 (December 1952): 447-60.

Thomas, Albert Sidney. *A Historical Account of the Protestant Episcopal Church in South Carolina, 1820-1957.* Columbia, SC: R. L. Bryan Company, 1957.

Thomas, Brook. "The Unfinished Task of Grounding Reconstruction's Promise." *Journal of the Civil War Era* 7, no. 1 (March 2017): 16-38.

Thomas, John Peyre. *The History of the South Carolina Military Academy, with Appendices.* Charleston, SC: Walker, Evans & Cogswell Co., 1893.

Thomas, Rhondda Robinson. "*The First Negro Priest on Southern Soil*: George Freeman Bragg, Jr. and the Struggle of Black Episcopalians in the South, 1824-1900." *Southern Quarterly* 50, no. 1 (Fall 2012): 79-101.

Tiller, Darrell. "The African Episcopal Church of St. Thomas, West Philadelphia." *Anglican and Episcopal History* 91, no. 2 (June 2022): 210-13.

Tillinghast, Richard. "Sewanee in Ruins, Part Two." *Ploughshares* 7, no. 2 (Summer 1981): 99-104.

Tillinghast, Richard. "Sewanee and the Civil War." *Southwest Review* 99, no. 3 (June 22, 2014): 327-44.

Tindall, George Brown. "The Campaign for the Disfranchisement of Negroes in South Carolina." *The Journal of Southern History* 15, no. 2 (May 1949): 212-34.

Tindall, George Brown. *South Carolina Negroes, 1877-1900.* Columbia, SC: University of South Carolina Press, 2003 [1952].

Todd, Richard C. "C.G. Memminger and the Confederate Treasury Department." *The Georgia Review* 12, no. 4 (Winter 1958): 396-410.

Trefousse, Hans L. *The Radical Republicans: Lincoln's Vanguard for Racial Justice.* New York: Knopf, 1969.

Trefousse, Hans L. *Impeachment of a President: Andrew Johnson, the Blacks, and Reconstruction.* Bronx, NY: Fordham University Press, 1999 [1975].

Trelease, Allen W. *White Terror: The Ku Klux Klan Conspiracy and Southern Reconstruction.* Baton Rouge: Louisiana State University Press, 1999 [1971].

Twyman, Winkfield Jr., and Jennifer Richmond. *Letters in Black and White: A New Correspondence on Race in America.* Durham, NC: Pitchstone Press, 2023.

Tyler, Lyon G. "James Louis Petigru: Freedom's Champion in a Slave Society." *The South Carolina Historical Magazine* 83, no. 4 (October 1982): 272-86.

Tyler, Lyon G. "God and Mr. Petigru: Episcopal Attitudes Toward Faith and Doctrine in Antebellum South Carolina." *Historical Magazine of the Protestant Episcopal Church* 52, no. 3 (September 1983): 229-43.

Tyler, Lyon G. "Drawing the Color Line in the Episcopal Diocese of South Carolina, 1876-1890: The Role of Edward McCrady, Father and Son." *The South Carolina Historical Magazine* 91, no. 2 (April 1990): 107-24.

United States Senate. *Trial of Andrew Johnson, President of the United States, Before the Senate of the United States, on Impeachment by the House of Representatives from High Crimes and Misdemeanors.* Vol. I. Washington, DC: U.S. Government Printing Office, 1868.

The University of the South. "A Research Summary on Slavery and Race at the University of the South and in the Community of Sewanee." The Roberson Project on Slavery, Race, and Reconciliation. Accessed July 15, 2021. https://new.sewanee.edu/roberson-project/learn-more/research-summary/.

Vorenberg, Michael. *Final Freedom: The Civil War, the Abolition of Slavery, and the Thirteenth Amendment.* Cambridge: Cambridge University Press, 2001.

Vorenberg, Michael. *Lincoln's Peace: The Struggle to End the American Civil War.* New York: Knopf, 2025.

Wade, Rev. Dr. Francis H. "Confederate Colonel and Priest Promotes Racial Reconciliation." *The Historiographer* 61, no. 3 (Summer 2021): 1, 8-10.

Wade, Wyn Craig. *The Fiery Cross: the Ku Klux Klan in America.* New York: Touchstone, 1988.

Waldstreicher, David. *Slavery's Constitution: From Revolution to Ratification.* New York: Hill and Wang, 2009.

Wallace, D. D. "The Question of the Withdrawal of the Democratic Presidential Electors in South Carolina in 1876." *The Journal of Southern History* 8, no. 3 (August 1942): 374-85.

Wallace, Jessica L. "Endangering the 'Peace and Safety of the Community': Anglican Religious Authority and South Carolina's Great Awakening." *The South Carolina Historical Magazine* 118, no. 2 (April 2017): 100-31.

Walther, Eric H. *The Fire-Eaters.* Baton Rouge: Louisiana State University Press, 1992.

Walther, Eric H. *The Shattering of the Union: America in the 1850s.* Wilmington, DE: SR Books, 2004.

Weigley, Russell F. *A Great Civil War: A Military and Political History, 1861-1865.* Bloomington: Indiana University Press, 2000.

West, Jerry L. *The Reconstruction Ku Klux Klan in York County, South Carolina, 1865-1877.* Jefferson, NC: McFarland & Company, Inc., 2002.

White Ronald C. Jr. *The Eloquent President: A Portrait of Lincoln Through His Words.* New York: Random House, 2005.

White, Ronald C. Jr. *A. Lincoln: A Biography.* New York: Random House, 2009.

Wiggins, Sarah Woolfolk. "Josiah Gorgas: A Victorian Father." *Civil War History* 32, no. 3 (September 1986): 229-46.

Williams, George W. *A History of the Negro Troops in the War of the Rebellion, 1861-1865.* New York: Harper & Brothers, 1888.

Williams, Lou Falkner. *The Great South Carolina Ku Klux Klan Trials, 1871-1872.* Athens: University of Georgia Press, 1996.

Williams, Patrick G. *Beyond Redemption: Texas Democrats After Reconstruction.* College Station: Texas A&M University Press, 2007.

Williams, T. Harry. *Lincoln and the Radicals.* Madison : The University of Wisconsin Press, 1965.

Williamson, Joel. *After Slavery: The Negro in South Carolina During Reconstruction, 1861-1877.* Chapel Hill: University of North Carolina Press, 1965.

Wilson, Charles Reagan. "The Religion of the Lost Cause: Ritual and Organization of the Southern Civil Religion, 1865-1920." *The Journal of Southern History* 46, no. 2 (May 1980): 219-38.

Winik, Jay. *April 1865: The Month That Saved America.* New York: HarperCollins, 2001.

Witcover, Jules. *Party of the People: A History of the Democrats.* New York: Random House, 2003.

Wood, A. E., and W. T. Sherman. "The Burning of Columbia." *The North American Review* 146, no. 377 (April 1888): 400-4.

Wood, Bradford J. "'A Constant Attendance on God's Alter': Death, Disease, and the Anglican Church in Colonial South Carolina, 1706-1750." *The South Carolina Historical Magazine* 100, no. 3 (July 1999): 204-20.

Woodward, C. Vann. *Origins of the New South, 1877-1913.* Baton Rouge: Louisiana State University Press, 1951.

Woodward, C. Vann. *The Strange Career of Jim Crow.* 2nd ed. Oxford: Oxford University Press, 1966.

Yoo, John. *Crisis and Command.* New York: Kaplan Publishing, 2009.

Zuck, Lowell H. "The American Anti-Slavery Movement in the Churches Before the Civil War." *Zeitschrift für Religions-und Geistesgeschichte* 17, no. 4 (January 1965): 353-64.

Zuczek, Richard. "The Federal Government's Attack on the Ku Klux Klan: A Reassessment." *The South Carolina Historical Magazine* 97, no. 1 (January 1996): 47-64.

Zuczek, Richard. "The Last Campaign of the Civil War: South Carolina and the Revolution of 1876." *Civil War History* 42, no. 1 (March 1996): 18-31.

Zuczek, Richard. *State of Rebellion: Reconstruction in South Carolina.* Columbia: University of South Carolina Press, 1996.

INDEX

Note: Page numbers followed by 'n' indicate note numbers.

Abbeville (South Carolina)   17, 124, 218, 220, 257–60
  County (South Carolina)   220
  Courthouse   220
abolitionism   xiii, 12, 45, 116
abolitionists   5, 44, 248
Abraham   232
Acts 17:26   8
Acts of the Holy Apostles   64
Adams, Henry   111
Africa   44
African Methodist Episcopal Church   18, 143, 181
Ahlstrom, Sydney E.   5
Aiken County (South Carolina)   126
Aiken, William Jr.   115
Aiken's Landing   93
Alabama   119, 140, 206
Alban Institute   x, xi, xvi
Albemarle Road (Charleston, South Carolina)   201
Alexander II   59 n.61
All Saints Church (Waccamaw, South Carolina)   68, 145
American Colonization Society   44
American Revolution   6, 7, 10, 26 n.12, 44, 116
Anderson (South Carolina)   76, 96, 101, 172, 193
Anderson, Robert   45–6, 48, 50, 58 n.34, 73, 74, 89
Anglican Church   6, 28 n.24, 87, 131 n.17, 152
Anglican and Episcopal History (journal)   xix, xx

Anglo-Catholicism   153
antebellum era (generally)   127
Antietam, Battle of (Sharpsburg)   xi, 13, 53
Apostles' Creed   154
Appomattox Court House (Virginia)   xiv, 101
Archives of the Episcopal Church   xx
Aristotle   239 n.30, 242–3 n.69
Aristotelianism; *see* Aristotle
Arkansas   119
Armstrong, Nathaniel W.   47
Army of Northern Virginia   53, 98
Army of the United States   73, 121, 149, 200, 253, 258
Army of the United States, Department of South Carolina   117
Arsenal Academy; *see* The Citadel (South Carolina Military Academy)
Ashley Avenue (Charleston, South Carolina)   200, 253
Ashley, James   118
Ashley River (South Carolina)   52, 90
Atkinson (Mrs.)   86
Atkinson, Susan Magdalene; *see* Porter, Susan Magdalen Atkinson
Atlanta Campaign   60 n.72
Atlanta University   114
Austin (Texas)   xx
Averasboro (North Carolina)   100
Aycrigg, Benjamin   189 n.35

Bagatelle (horse)   86
Baltimore (Maryland)   92, 93, 149, 153, 200, 217

Baptist Church   7, 40, 143
battery Gregg   74
Bayou Teche (Louisiana)   60 n.72
Beaufort (South Carolina)   48, 113, 248
Beauregard, P. G. T.   50
Bee, Anne Fayssoux   38, 55 n.5
Bee, Barnard Elliot (P.F. Stevens's brother)   37
Bee, Barnard Elliot Jr.   55 n.5
Bee, Barnard Elliot Sr.   38, 55 n.5
Benevolent Society   71
Bennett, Granville   x
Bennett Place   15
Bennett, S. L.   146, 198
Bentonville (North Carolina)   59 n.47, 100
Berkeley County (South Carolina)   x
Berney, W. H.   158–9
Bethlehem Church   173
Bible, Christian   64, 65, 153
Bishop Cummins Training School   20, 177, 180
Black Codes   116–17
Black Oak Parish   51, 54, 171; see also Trinity Episcopal Church
"Black Reconstruction"; see Black Republican Rule
Black Republican Rule   121, 132 n.38, 250
Black soldiers   92, 104 n.44, 217
Blacklock, John Freer   65
Bloomsbury (publisher)   xix
Blue Ridge Mountains   122
Blum, Edward J.   127
Board of Missions of the South Carolina Episcopal Church   143–5, 151
Book of Common Prayer   6, 54, 155, 173
Book of Revelation   230
Boonsboro Gap, Battle of (South Mountain)   13, 53, 84–5, 91, 93
Boston Harbor   111
"Bourbons"   134 n.47
Bowen, Nathaniel   8, 9, 11
Boyce, William Waters   115

Brashear City (Louisiana)   60 n.72
Bratton, Betsy DuBose   90
Bratton, John Simpson   90, 217
British North Carolina   10
Broad Street (Charleston)   72
Brown, Richard   xix
Buchanan, James   45
Bull Run, First Battle of (First Manassas)   55 n.5, 74, 90
Bull Run, Second Battle of (Second Manassas)   13, 16, 53, 83–4, 91
Bureau of Refugees, Freedmen, and Abandoned Lands; see Freedmen's Bureau
Butler, Matthew   200, 201, 253

Caesar, Julius   xv
Cainhoy (South Carolina)   125
Calhoun, John C.   41, 44
Calvary Episcopal Church   18, 142, 144, 169, 173, 174
Camden (South Carolina)   11, 16, 70, 77, 88, 89, 97, 100, 137, 147
Canaan   5
Canada   180
Capers, Ellison   50, 57 n.15, 134 n.46, 148, 160, 167 n.78, 210–11
Capers, Mary Singletary; see Stevens, Mary Singletary Capers
Capers, William   40
Cardozo, Francis L.   120
Carlisle (Pennsylvania)   152
carpetbaggers   19, 119, 125, 178, 209, 219, 221, 256–9
Castle Pinckney   73
Catholicism   7, 156
Cedar Creek, Battle of   99
census of 1850   30 n.33
Central Methodist Church   178
Chamberlain, Daniel H.   125–7
Chapel Hill (North Carolina)   x
Chapofo (plantation)   23 n.1, 24 n.1, 37–8, 56 n.7
Charles II (King of England)   6
Charleston (South Carolina)   xv, xx, 185, 201, 226

and the antebellum era 11, 14, 23
  n.1, 30 n.31, 37, 39, 40, 44, 56
  n.7, 68, 70, 195
and the Civil War 13, 14, 16,
  45–52, 71–6, 89, 90, 94, 97,
  100, 149, 193
and the Episcopal Church of South
  Carolina 8, 15, 18, 28 n.24, 54,
  87, 137, 142, 144–8, 156–60,
  169, 173, 197–9, 202, 206, 222,
  250, 252–4
and Reconstruction 20, 21, 119,
  122, 123, 125, 194, 200, 260–1
and Redemption 208
and the Reformed Episcopal
  Church of South Carolina 177,
  180–2
Charleston Agricultural
  Society 29 n.29
Charleston Arsenal 70
Charleston County Schools 182
Charleston
  cyclone of 1885 202
  earthquake of 1886 181, 202
  Harbor (South Carolina) 13, 48,
    73, 89
  hurricane of 1893 181
Charlottesville (Virginia) 87
Chattanooga (Tennessee) 96, 223
Cheraw (South Carolina) 100, 193
Chester (Rev.) 63
Chestnut, James, Jr. 45, 73
Chicago (Illinois) 153, 209
Christ Church (Baltimore,
  Maryland) 153
Christ Church (Norfolk, Virginia) 153
Christ, Jesus xv, xvi, 7, 9, 25 n.8, 64,
  70, 73, 140, 184, 230, 231, 233–5,
  240 n.49, 240–1 n.51, 255
Christianity 230, 232–4, 241 n.59
Christology 230, 234, 240 n.49
Church of Christ 151
Church of England; *see* Anglican
  Church
Church of the Holy Communion xx,
  15, 41, 70, 74, 163 n.29, 196,
  200, 202, 254

Church of the Holy Family x
The Church Intelligencer
  (publication) 141
The Citadel (South Carolina Military
  Academy) xi, xx, 4, 13, 16, 41,
  42, 51–4, 58–9 n.47, 86–8, 90,
  94, 98, 185, 252
  origins of 39–40
  reopening after the Civil War 182
Citadel Cadets and *Star of the
  West* 47–50, 59 n.50, 89
Civil Rights Bill of 1866 117
Civil rights movement x
Civil War x, xiii, xiv, 3, 45, 49, 59
  n.47, 71, 113, 136 n.58
  and Anthony Toomer xiv, 4,
    15, 21, 68, 74–7, 160, 193,
    199, 247
  and the Episcopal Church of North
    America 7, 153, 223
  and the Episcopal Church of South
    Carolina 137, 140, 148,
    160, 172
  and Peter Fayssoux Stevens xi,
    xiv, 4, 13–14, 45–55, 160,
    185, 247
  and William Porcher DuBose xiv,
    4, 15–17, 83–5, 160, 236, 242
    n.69, 247
The Civil War as a Theological Crisis
  (book) 25 n.8
Claflin College 182
Claremont (New Hampshire) 147
Clay, Henry 44
Colcock, C. J. 201
Cold Harbor, Battle of 98, 100
Cole, Abby xx
Colored Methodist Episcopal
  Church 254
Columbia (South Carolina) xx, 8,
  15, 17, 39, 40, 51, 65, 71, 72,
  76, 85, 100, 115, 116, 140, 142,
  174, 193, 257
  burning of 63, 76–7, 81 n.62, 209
Columbia University 132 n.38
Columbus, Georgia 221
Confederate battle flag 225

"Confederate Colonel and Priest Promotes Racial Reconciliation" (article)   xvi–xvii
Confederate flag   x, xvii
Confederate Memorial Day   216 n.52
Confederate States of America (CSA)   xv, xvi, 17–19, 27 n.17, 113, 114, 118, 130 n.14, 172, 249, 263 n.10
 and Anthony Toomer Porter   72, 76, 77, 193, 194, 197, 200, 208, 209, 247, 253, 255, 256
 and the Episcopal Church of South Carolina   140, 141, 143, 148, 149, 156
 and Peter Fayssoux Stevens   51, 55, 60 n.72, 185, 247, 252, 256
 surrender of   111–12, 141, 142, 223
 and William Porcher DuBose   21, 96, 97, 99, 217, 237 n.16, 247, 258
Confederate States Army   xi, 51, 123, 125, 134 n.46, 178, 208, 222
Confederate States Congress   115
Congaree River (South Carolina)   76
Congress of the United States   41, 115, 118, 119, 197, 201
Connecticut   62
Conner, James   74
Constitution of the United States   5, 22, 23, 72
Constitutional Convention   xvi
The Constructive Quarterly (publication)   231
Convention of the Diocese of South Carolina   11
Convention of the People of South Carolina; *see* South Carolina Constitutional Convention of 1865
Cooper, Peter   63
Cooper River (South Carolina)   85
Cornerstone Speech   xvi
cotton gin   5
Crowson, Charles Mason   52
Crummell, Alexander   206

CSS J.A. Cotton (ship)   60 n.72
Cummings Point (South Carolina)   50
Cummins, George David   151-6, 160, 174, 175, 177–8, 189 n.35
 photograph of   155

Dabney, Robert Lewis   250, 263 n.10
Davis, Thomas Frederick: and Anthony Toomer Porter   200
 as bishop of South Carolina   10–12, 17, 18, 137–9, 142–7, 164 n.39, 222, 251, 260
 and Peter Fayssoux Stevens   144, 145, 170–1, 253
 photograph of   138
 and William Porcher DuBose   16, 87–90, 97, 218, 221
Dawson, Lawrence (Laurens)   170, 172–3, 176, 177, 186–7 n.5, 203
Day of Pentecost   240 n.51
Dehon, Theodore   8
Delaware   153
Delaware River   92
Democratic Party   125, 127, 201
Denison (Rev.)   41
Depass, Sam   94
Dew, Thomas R.   12
Dickinson College   152
Diocese of the South Carolina Episcopal Church; *see* Episcopal Church of South Carolina
Dismal Swamp Canal   62
Dix, John A.   91
Dix-Hill Cartel   91
DuBose, Anne Barnwell "Nannie" Peronneau   89, 90, 94–7, 99, 101, 218, 225, 226
DuBose, Jane Porcher   85, 90–1
DuBose, Maria Louise Yerger   226–8
DuBose, May   218
DuBose, McNeely (Mrs.)   225
DuBose, Robert   100, 225
DuBose, Samuel   226
DuBose, Susie   218, 220
DuBose, Theodore Samuel Marion   85, 86, 90, 217

INDEX

DuBose, William Haskell 218, 229, 235
DuBose, William Porcher: and Anthony Toomer Porter 221
  background of xi, xv, xvii, xviii, xix, xx, 4, 12–13, 15–17, 85–9, 247
  and the Civil War 15–17, 52, 83–5, 89–101, 236, 242 n.69, 247
  death and legacy of 235–6
  and the Episcopal Church of South Carolina 19, 57 n.15, 147, 160, 218–22, 258, 261
  and the freed people 124, 141, 160, 220–1, 236, 251, 256, 261
  and Peter Fayssoux Stevens 16, 83, 90, 94, 95, 174–5, 188 n.22
  photographs of 88, 219, 224, 227
  postwar career of 21–3, 111, 127, 135 n.50, 217–36, 259
  theology of 229–34
Dudleys (DuBose family friends) 93
due process of law 116
Dunning, William Archibald 132 n.38
Durham (North Carolina) 15
Dwight, Richard 86
Dwight, R. Y. 91

Early, Jubal 16, 99
East Coast Railway 95
Eastern Orthodox Church 242 n.69
Eberly, Marion Stevens xx, 169–70
The Ecumenical Councils (book) 230, 234
Edgefield County (South Carolina) 126, 134 n.47
The Education of Henry Adams (book) 111
Edwards, Catharine Gadsden 148
Egypt 208
Elgin (Ohio) 77
Elizabeth (New Jersey) 61
Ellenton (South Carolina) 125
Elliott, John H. 96
Elliott, Stephen 223

emancipation 4, 9, 22, 67, 113, 114, 123, 149, 249, 255
Emancipation Proclamation 112
Emerson, Ralph Waldo 38
Emmanuel Chapel 170
England 200, 208
Episcopal Church of the Confederate States of America 17–18, 223
Episcopal Church of Louisiana 223
Episcopal Church of Mississippi 205
Episcopal Church of North America xiii, xvi, 5–8, 28, 127, 141, 143, 146, 153–5, 160, 206–7, 236, 248, 259
  organization of 33 n.63
  and the Second Great Awakening 12
Episcopal Church of the South 18
Episcopal Church of South Carolina xiii, xiv, xv, xviii, 6–13, 17, 18, 26 n.12, 30 n.31, 137, 140, 142–9, 151, 156–60, 166 n.74, 169, 250, 251, 264 n.15
  and Anthony Toomer Porter xv 3, 4, 13, 15, 16, 19, 21, 23, 33 n.64, 68, 71, 146, 160, 163 n.29, 196, 201–12, 247, 253–6
  and High Churchmen 7–8, 12
  and Low Churchmen 7–8, 156, 173
  and Peter Fayssoux Stevens xi, xv, 3, 4, 13, 19, 20, 23, 33 n.64, 44–5, 51, 140, 144, 169–77, 186, 247, 251–3, 261
  and William Porcher DuBose xv, 3, 4, 13, 19, 23, 87, 88, 97, 101, 234, 247, 258
Episcopal Diocesan Convention 61
Episcopal Prayer Book; *see Book of Common Prayer*
Epistles of John 230
Epistle to the Romans 230
Epistles 64
Ethics (book by Aristotle) 243 n.69
Europe 111

294 INDEX

Evangelical Educational Society 186 n.5
Evans, Nathan George "Shanks" 52–3
Evans's Brigade 52–3
Exchange Hotel (Richmond) 93
Exod. 21:16 5, 25 n.8

Fairfield District (South Carolina) 86, 258
Fairmount School 226, 228
Fall from Grace 232
Fallows, Samuel 179, 180, 182–3
Falls Church (Virginia) xi
Farmington (plantation) 15, 85, 217
Farrow, Joseph 152
Fayssoux, Peter 37
Fayssoux, Sarah Johnston; see Stevens, Sarah
Ferguson, Frank C. 170, 172–3, 176–8, 182, 186 n.5, 203
Ferguson, Thomas 59 n.50
15th Illinois Cavalry, Company F 77, 209
Finney, Charles 5
Fire-Eaters 72
First Baptist Church of Columbia (South Carolina) 115
Fisk University 114
Flagg, Allard H. 68
Florence (South Carolina) xviii
Florida 23 n.1, 38, 56 n.7, 112, 140, 184, 231
Foley, Ehren xx
Following the Light (pamphlet) 153
Forrest, Edward A. 17pino
Fort Delaware 16, 92–3
Fort Moultrie 45–6, 50, 58 n.34, 73, 74
Fort Sumter (South Carolina) 54: and *Star of the West* episode 13, 45–50
 and the start of the Civil War 17, 51, 58 n.34, 73, 74, 89
Fortieth Congress 119
"40 acres and a mule"; see Special Field Orders Number 15

Founders (American) 5
Fourteenth Amendment 117–18
Fourth Cavalry 81 n.62
Franklin Street School 145, 146, 198
freed people xiii, 113, 117, 123, 128 n.4, 249, 259, 261
 and Anthony Toomer Porter 194, 197, 199, 209, 210, 212–13 n.9, 236, 256, 260
 and the Episcopal Church of North America 3, 18, 127, 143, 206–7
 and the Episcopal Church of South Carolina xv, 19, 143, 145, 149–51, 159, 164 n.39, 172, 173
 and Peter Fayssoux Stevens 19–20, 124, 160, 169–70, 173–5, 178, 185–6, 236, 251–3, 256, 260
 and William Porcher DuBose 220–1, 236, 256–8, 260
Freedmen's Aid Commission 143, 144
Freedmen's Bureau 112–14, 194–5, 197
French Huguenots 85, 87
Front Royal (Virginia) 99
Fuel Society 71
Fulton, John 230
"Fundamental Constitutions" 6
Fundamentalists 231–2
"fusion" party 133 n.41

Gadsden, Christopher E. 8, 11, 137, 147, 148, 222
Gadsden, Christopher P. 147, 163 n.35, 222
Gadsden, James 23 n.1, 56 n.7
Gaillard, Franklin 97, 98
Gaillard, Henry 86
Gaillard, Willie 86
Garden, Alexander 28–9 n.24
Garden of Eden 232
Garment Society 71
Gary, Martin Witherspoon 126
Gary Plan 126
Gaud School; see Porter Gaud School
Geary, John W. 100
Gen. 9:25–27 5

General Clinch (ship)   48
General Convention of the Church in the United States; *see* General Convention of the Protestant Episcopal Church
General Convention of the Protestant Episcopal Church   33 n.63, 146
General Theological Seminary   230
Georgetown (South Carolina)   14, 41, 61, 62, 64, 68–70, 76
Georgetown County (South Carolina) Digital Library   xx
Georgia   65, 73, 100, 112, 114, 119, 140, 179, 184, 223, 231
German Riflemen   49
gerrymandering   121–2
Gettysburg (Pennsylvania)   96
Gibraltar   111
Gilded Age   174
Glennie, Alexander   68, 145, 259
Gordonsville (Virginia)   53
Gorgas, Amelia Gayle   222
Gorgas, Josiah   222, 223
The Gospel According to St. Paul (book)   230, 232
The Gospel in the Gospels (book)   230, 233
The Gospel of John   230
Gospels   8, 13, 19, 40, 53, 64, 231, 240–1 n.51
G. P. Putnam's Sons   210
Grace Baptist Church   137
Grant, Ulysses S.   96–9, 124–6, 194, 216 n.52
Grant administration   125
Gray, Charles   226
Great Britain   91
Great Stagirite   242 n.69
Green, William Mercer   205
Greeneville (Tennessee)   97
Gregg, Alexander   254
gubernatorial election of 1876   125–7
Guerry, Moultrie   226, 227, 229
Guerry, William Alexander   201

Habeas corpus   124
Hagerstown (Maryland)   84
Haiti   44
Halleck, Henry   92
Ham   5
Hamburg (South Carolina) riot   125, 134 n.47
Hampton III, Wade   22, 77, 123–7, 133–4 n.46, 134 n.47, 135 n.50, 200, 201, 209–10, 253, 261
Hampton Institute   114
Hampton Legion   74
Hardee, William   76
Harris, Samuel S.   221
Hat and Shoe Society   71
Hatch, Lemuel M.   71
Hatteras, Cape   63
Hayes, Rutherford B.   126–7, 135 n.57, 200, 201, 253
Haynesworth, George Edward "Tuck"   49, 58–9 n.47
Hellhole Swamp (South Carolina)   x
High Churchmen; *see* Episcopal Church of South Carolina
High Priesthood and Sacrifice: An Exposition of the Epistle to the Hebrews (book)   230
Hill, D. H.   91
Historically black colleges and universities (HBCUs)   114
The Historiographer (publication)   xvi
Hodges Station   220
Hodgson, Telfair   229
Hoffman, Charles Frederick   210
Holcombe Legion   13, 16, 51–3, 83–4, 90, 91, 95, 97, 174; *see also* DuBose, William Porcher Stevens, Peter Fayssoux
Holcombe's Legion; *see* Holcombe Legion
Holy Communion Church; *see* Church of the Holy Communion
Holy Communion Church Institute   21, 199, 200, 253
Holy Ghost   235
Holy Land   208
Holy Scriptures   154, 234
Home Mission for colored persons and freedmen   146

Hopkins, John Henry 18
House of Representatives of the United States 117, 118
Howard, Oliver O. 113, 114, 197
Howard, Robert T. 69
Howe, James Blake 147
Howe, William Bell White 147–52, 157–60, 164 n.39, 171–2, 175–7, 188 n.26, 202, 205, 206, 222, 251–2, 254, 264 n.15
  photograph of 150
Huger, Joseph (Mrs.) 21
Huguenin, Thomas A. 54–5
Huguenots; *see* French Huguenots

impeachment 115; *see also* Johnson, Andrew
industrial school for girls (South Carolina) 70–1
interracial marriage 117

Jackson (Mississippi) 96, 97
Jackson, Thomas J. "Stonewall" 55 n.5, 194, 250
Jamaica 37
James Island 75
James Island, First Battle of 75
James River (Virginia) 93
Jarvis, George Atwater 230
Jellico, Jerry xx
Jenkins, Micah 98
Jerusalem Apostles 240 n.51
Jessie Ball duPont Library xx
Jesus; *see* Christ, Jesus
Jim Crow x, xiii, xv, 127, 172, 179, 249–50
  and Christian churches xvii, 173, 235, 256
  and the Episcopal Church xvii, 19, 22, 158, 171–2, 203, 251, 255
Job (biblical figure) 148
Johannine interpretation of the Gospel 230
John the Apostle 230
Johnson administration 113, 118, 119

Johnson, Andrew: and the freed people 112, 197
  and the Radical Republicans 114–15, 117–19
  and Reconstruction generally 114–15, 130 n.14
  and South Carolina 115–17
Johnson, Benjamin 174, 175, 178
Johnson, Malcolm 38
Johnson, Mandi D. xx
Johnston, Joseph E. 15, 17, 77, 96, 97, 100, 101, 193, 200, 216 n.52, 253
Joint Committee on Reconstruction 117, 118
Joint Committee on the Conduct of the War 117
Jones, Absalom 248
Journal of Anglican Studies xix
Journal of the First General Council of the Reformed Episcopal Church 154

Keitt, Laurence M. 100
Keitt's Regiment 100–1
Keller, Helen 229
Kells, Hattie B. 226, 227
Kennedy Room of Local History and Genealogy xx
Kennesaw (Georgia) xvi
Kennesaw State University xvii
Kentucky 151, 153
Kentucky Diocese of the Episcopal Church 152, 153
Kershaw, John 209–10, 226
Kershaw, Joseph B. 16, 97
Kershaw's brigade 16, 17, 97–101, 105 n.76
King, Martin Luther x
Kinston (North Carolina) 95–6
Ku Klux Klan xvii
  in South Carolina 122–4, 133 n.46, 179
  and William Porcher DuBose 23, 220, 221, 235, 258, 260, 261
Kujawa-Holbrook, Sheryl xx

Lankes, Andrew   xx
The Last Days of Pompeii (book)   63
Latane, James Allen   185
Laurens County (South Carolina)   126
Led On! Step by Step Scenes from Clerical, Military, Educational, and Plantation Life in the South   1828–98 (book)   210
Lee, Alfred   153
Lee, Robert E.   13–14, 53, 84, 98–101, 194
Liberia (Africa)   44
Lincoln, Abraham   5, 45, 66, 71, 89, 112, 114, 115
Lincoln administration   92
Lincoln assassination   115
Lincoln-Douglas debates   66
Locke, John   6
Lockhart, Matthew A.   xx
Longstreet's Corps   83
Lords Proprietors   6
Lord's Supper   154
Lost Cause   22, 134 n.46, 208, 225, 259
Louisiana   17, 140, 226
Low Churchmen; *see* Episcopal Church of South Carolina

McCrady, Edward M., Jr.   157, 159, 172, 250
McCrady, Edward M., Sr.   157, 159, 166 n.74, 172, 250
McCray, George W.   200
McGowan, John   48–50
McGowan, Samuel   220
McQueen, John A.   77, 200, 209–10
Magnolia Cemetery   21, 76, 185, 199
Magnolia Hall   225
Main Street (Columbia, South Carolina)
Malvern Hill, Battle of   53, 91
Manassas, First Battle of; *see* Bull Run, First Battle of
Manassas, Second Battle of; *see* Bull Run, Second Battle of
Manly, Basil Sr.   40

Marine Hospital (Charleston, South Carolina)   146, 197, 198
Marion Square (Charleston, SC)   39
Marshall, John S.   242 n.69
Martin, James   220
Martinez, Mike   xi–xii
Maryland   13, 54, 84
Mason-Dixon Line   5, 179, 180
Massachusetts   111, 230
Mead, Chris   xix
Mead, Loren B.   x–xii, xiv–xix, xx–xxi
Mead, Phil   xix
Mead, Polly   xi, xvii
Mead, Walter Russell   x–xii, xix, xx
Means, Colonel   98
Memminger, Christopher   72
Memphis (Tennessee)   227
Methodist Church   7, 40, 44, 143, 152–3
Methodist Episcopal Church   152, 254
Mexico   47
Mid-Atlantic states   7
Middle St. John's Parish   144, 171
Miller, Ellie   xx
miscegenation   121, 157, 250
Mississippi   96, 97, 119, 126, 140, 226, 227
Mobley, J. S.   181
Moffat; *see* Monteagle
Monroe, James   44
Monroe (Georgia)   xxi
Monrovia (Liberia)   44
Monteagle   226
Montgomery (Alabama)   17, 140
Morris Island (South Carolina)   74, 75
and *Star of the West* episode   13, 47–50
Morristown (New Jersey)   63
Moultrie House (Sullivan's Island)   74
Mt. Pisgah Reformed Episcopal Church   181
Mount Zion College   14, 65, 86, 218
Mount Zion Schools   86
Myrtle Beach (South Carolina)   48

Nassau Street (Charleston, South Carolina) 182
National Episcopal Historians and Archivists xvi
Navy of the United States 75
Nazareth Chapel 20, 170, 173
Nelson, Cleland 231
Neo-Platonism 242 n.69
New Haven (Connecticut) 61, 62
New England 4, 7
New Hampshire 147
New Jersey 64, 118
New Testament 12, 35 n.80, 154, 229–31, 241 n.51, 241 n.59
New York 48, 63
New York City 19, 137, 152, 154, 173, 200, 252
Newark, New Jersey x 200
Newbury (South Carolina) 177
Newberry and Laurens Railroad 40
Newport (Rhode Island) 62
Nicholson, W. R. 180
Nicomachean Ethics (book) 242 n.69
nihilism 232
Noah 5
Noll, Mark 25 n.8
Norfolk (Virginia) 153
North Carolina 10, 17, 77, 100, 101, 112, 119
North Carolina mountains 88
North Island (South Carolina) 63, 68
nullification 42

Oakley (South Carolina) 173
Oakwood Cemetery (Chicago, Illinois) 209
Obear, Mr. 218
"Of Missionary Organizations within Constituted Episcopal Jurisdictions"; *see* Sewanee Plan
Ohio 114, 118, 120
Old South 235–6
Old Testament 12, 64, 154
1 Cor. 13:13 232
Orangeburg (South Carolina) 100, 142
Orphan Home 200

Orr, James Lawrence 115, 116
Otey, James 223
Overland Campaign 98
Oxford Movement 152, 153

Paddock, Benjamin Henry 230
Palmer, Harriett Rebecca; *see* Stevens, Harriett Rebecca Palmer
Palmetto Guards 50
Palmetto Hall 225
Paris (France) 223
Parishes (political) 131 n.17
Partridge's Academy 85
Paul 16, 25 n.8
Pea Patch Island 92
Pearl River (Mississippi) 96
Peachtree Creek, Battle of 60 n.72
peculiar institution; *see* slavery
Pendleton (South Carolina) 38, 39, 56 n.7
Pengelly, Arthur L. 185
Pennsylvania 118
Peronneau, Anne Barnwell "Nannie"; *see* DuBose, Anne Barnwell "Nannie" Peronneau
Peronneau, Miss (William Porcher DuBose's sister-in-law) 220
Perry, Benjamin Franklin 115–17
Petersburg (Virginia) 98–100
Petigru, James L. 45, 72
Philadelphia (Pennsylvania) xvi, 18, 68, 180, 200, 206
Pickens, Francis W. 46–7, 51, 89
Pickens, Lucy Holcombe 51, 59 n.61
Pickens, Samuel 59 n.50
Pinckney, Charles Cotesworth (1746–1825) 30 n.29
Pinckney, Charles Cotesworth (1789–1865) 29–30 n.29
Pineville (South Carolina) 173
Pinopolis (South Carolina) x, xviii 51, 170, 171, 173, 174, 177
Pittenger, W. Norman 231, 236
Platonism 242 n.69
Polk, Leonidas 17, 223
Pope, John 53

Porcher, Maria 225
Porcher, Octavius 219
Porcher, Sam 87
Port Royal (South Carolina) 51, 53, 248
Porter Academy; *see* Porter Gaud School
Porter, Anthony Toomer: background of xi, xiv–xv, xvii, xviii, xix, 4, 12–17, 61–74, 145, 247
 and the Civil War 15, 68, 74–7, 160, 193, 199, 208, 247
 death and legacy of 210–12
 and the Episcopal Church of South Carolina 19, 33 n.64, 146, 160, 163 n.29, 196, 201–8, 210–12, 254, 261
 and the freed people 124, 160, 197, 199, 202–10, 212–13 n.9, 236, 251, 260, 261
 and Peter Fayssoux Stevens 41
 photographs of 69, 198, 207, 211
 postwar career of 20–1, 111, 127, 193–212, 216 n.52, 253–6, 258–9
 and William Porcher DuBose 221
Porter, Charlotte 63, 64
Porter, Esther Ann Toomer 61, 63
Porter Gaud Academy; *see* Porter Gaud School
Porter Gaud School xv, 20–1, 201, 210, 253–4
Porter, John (Anthony Toomer Porter's brother) 63, 64
Porter, John, Jr. 61, 62, 64
Porter, John, Sr. 62
Porter, John Toomer (Anthony Toomer Porter's son) 70, 75–6
Porter Military Academy; *see* Porter Gaud School
Porter, Susan Magdalen Atkinson 68, 69
Porter, Theodore 70
Potomac River (Virginia) 93
Presbyterian Church 7, 71, 212
Preston, Sam 93
Primus Plot of 1720 10

Prince George Winyah Episcopal Church 69
Proclamation 153 118
Proclamation of Amnesty and Reconstruction 114–15
Protestant Episcopal Church; *see* Episcopal Church of North America
Protestant Episcopal Society for the Advancement of Christianity 8
Pyne, Thomas 12, 31 n.39

Quintard, Charles Todd 221, 223–4, 238 n.28, 238–9 n.29

Radical Republicans 114–19, 125
Raleigh (North Carolina) 77, 96, 186 n.5, 193
Ramage, Burr James 22, 35 n.80, 135 n.50
Randolph, Benjamin F. 220
Rappahannock River 53, 83
Rappahannock Station, First Battle of 13, 53
The Reason of Life (book) 230
rebel yell 72
Reconstruction xiii, xiv, xv, xvii, 115, 117, 118, 120–2, 124, 125, 127, 132 n.33, 132 n.38, 136 n.58, 249, 261
 and Anthony Toomer Porter 4, 20–1, 64, 127, 197, 200, 208, 258
 and Christian churches xvi, 19, 172
 and the Episcopal Church xvii, 137, 143–4, 156
 and Peter Fayssoux Stevens 4, 19–20, 127, 252–3, 258
 and William Porcher DuBose 4, 21–3, 127, 220–1, 256–9
Reconstruction Act of 1867 (first) 118, 119
Reconstruction Act of 1867 (second) 119
Reconstruction Act of 1867 (third) 119

Reconstruction Act of 1867 (fourth) 132 n.33
Reconstruction proclamation 134; *see* Proclamation of Amnesty and Reconstruction
Red Shirts 125, 126, 133 n.46
Redeemer Church 173
Redemption 124, 127, 134 n.46, 172, 249
Reforging the White Republic (book) 127
Reformed Episcopal Church: formation of xi, 13, 152–6, 173, 189 n.35, 253
 and the freed people 18, 156, 173–4
 and Peter Fayssoux Stevens 19–20, 175–86, 203, 251, 252, 259
Reformed Episcopal Parochial School 182
"Religious Instruction of Our Negroes" 8–10
Republican Party 45, 121, 125, 127, 201, 220, 261
Revolutionary War; *see* American Revolution
Reynolds, Dr. 76, 77
Rice cultivation (South Carolina) 62, 78 n.4
Richmond (Virginia) 52, 90, 91, 93, 98, 153
Ridgeway (South Carolina) 218
Roberson Project on Slavery, Race, and Reconciliation 259
Robertson & Blacklock 14, 65
Rom. Ch. 5, vv. 1 and 2 54
Rome (Italy) 154
Roseland (plantation) 86
Rowman & Littlefield (publisher) xix
Rudolph, Robert Livingston 184, 185
Russia 59 n.61
Rutledge Street (Charleston) 70

St. Andrew's Church (Wilmington, Delaware) 153
St. Andrew's Hall (Charleston) 72
St. Augustine's College 170
St. Augustine's Training School 186 n.5
St. James's Church (Richmond, Virginia) 153
St. John's/Berkeley (South Carolina) 14, 54, 147, 174, 258
St. John's Church (Winnsboro, South Carolina) 218, 258
St. Luke's Church (Washington, DC) 206
St. Luke's Episcopal Church (Charleston, South Carolina) 147, 177, 222
St. Luke's Hall 229
St. Luke's Seminary xvii
St. Mark's Episcopal Church 18, 21, 142, 144, 156–60, 166 n.74, 169, 172, 174, 202–6, 254
St. Michael's Church 87, 137
St. Paul 230, 232, 240–1 n.51
St. Paul's Episcopal Church (Baltimore, Maryland) 149
St. Paul's Episcopal Church (Pendleton, South Carolina) 39, 149
St. Peter's Episcopal Church 41
St. Philip's Church (Charleston, South Carolina) 28 n.24, 145, 147–9
St. Stephen's Church 100
St. Stephen's Church (Ridgeway, South Carolina) 218, 258
St. Stephen's Church (Summerville, South Carolina) 144, 171, 174
Saltus, Thaddaeus 203–5
Sampit River (South Carolina) 62
Santee River (South Carolina) 85
Savannah (Georgia) 16, 89, 97
Saxton, Rufus B. 113
scalawags 19, 119, 221, 257–9
Scott, Robert K. 120, 123
Scott, Winfield 48
Scriptures; *see* Holy Scriptures
Sea Islands (South Carolina) 112
Seabrook, J. B. 202
secession 3, 15, 22, 41–2, 45, 46, 71–3, 89, 116, 259
secession ordinance 45, 89, 115

Secessionville, Battle of 15, 75, 209
Second Great Awakening 12
Second Reformed Episcopal
  Church 180
Segregation; *see* Jim Crow
Senate of the United States 117, 118
Seven Days Battles 53
Seven Pines, Battle of 90
Sewanee Plan 160, 205–7, 254–5
The Sewanee Review
  (publication) 222–3
"Sewanee in Ruins" (poem) 238–9 n.29
Sewanee, Tennessee xv, xvii, 15,
  124, 160, 163 n.35, 174, 205,
  221, 222, 224–7, 229, 231, 241
  n.55, 254, 258, 259; *see also*
  University of the South
Seward, William 118
Shand, Peter J. 142
Shanklin (Rev.) 40–1
sharecropping 122, 127, 249
Sharpsburg; *see* Antietam, Battle of
Shenandoah Valley campaign 16, 99
Sheridan, Philip 99
Sheridan's Ride; *see* Sheridan, Philip
Sherman, William T. 112–14,
  142, 249
  and Anthony Toomer Porter 63,
    76–7, 81 n.62, 193, 200–1, 216
    n.52, 253
  and William Porcher DuBose 16–17,
    100, 101, 218, 258
Shi, Victoria (Tori) xix
Shoup, Francis Asbury 221, 224,
  238 n.28
Shrewsbury, George 195–6
Sickles, Daniel 117
Silliman, Molly I. xx
Simkins, William Stewart 48
slave chapels 11, 68, 147, 248, 259
slavery x, xiii, 28 n.24, 112, 114–17,
  249, 259, 263 n.7, 263 n.10
  by another name 127
  and Anthony Toomer Porter 14–15,
    62–3, 65–7, 194, 196–7, 210, 256
  and Christian churches xi, 3–13,
    66, 152–3
  and Episcopal Church of North
    America 7–8, 18, 26 n.12,
    141, 248
  and Episcopal Church of South
    Carolina 139–41, 149
  and Peter Fayssoux Stevens 42–5,
    55, 56 n.7, 58 n.32
  and William Porcher DuBose 21,
    22, 35 n.80, 141, 235
smallpox 75
Smith, Keith W. xx
Smith, Samuel Porcher 48
Smyrna (Delaware) 152
Society for the Propagation of the Gospel
  in Foreign Parts (SPG) 28 n.24
Socrates 243 n.69
The Soteriology of the New Testament
  (book) 229–30, 241 n.59
South Carolina 225
  and the antebellum era 3, 4, 6–13,
    61, 85, 185, 247
  and the Civil War 14, 53, 72, 74,
    89, 90, 95, 112, 193, 249, 256
  and the Episcopal Church of South
    Carolina x, xi, xiv, xvii, xviii,
    68, 140, 142, 147, 160, 163
    n.35, 169, 201, 221–3, 251, 258,
    259, 264 n.15
  and the Reconstruction era xvii,
    113, 115, 119, 120, 125, 127,
    141, 200, 220
  and Redemption 127
  and the Reformed Episcopal
    Church 179, 181, 184, 252
South Carolina Constitutional
  Convention of 1865 115–17
South Carolina Constitutional
  Convention of 1868 119–20
South Carolina General
  Assembly 61, 72
*South Carolina Historical
  Magazine* xx
South Carolina Historical Society xx
South Carolina Legislature; *see* South
  Carolina General Assembly
South Carolina Low Country xi, 26
  n.10, 51, 62, 68, 75, 85, 100,

122–4, 133 n.41, 134 n.47, 148, 156, 179, 180, 218, 248, 252–3, 257, 260
South Carolina Military Academy; *see* The Citadel
South Carolina militia 71
South Carolina Railroad 147
South Carolina State House 126
South Carolina Up Country 23 n.1, 38–40, 115, 122, 172, 133 n.41, 218, 257, 260
South Carolina Upstate; *see* South Carolina Up Country
South Caroliniana Library xx
South Mountain, Battle of; *see* Boonsboro Gap, Battle of
Southern Confederacy; *see* Confederate States of America (CSA)
Spartanburg County (South Carolina) Public Libraries xx
Special Field Order Number 15 112, 113, 128 n.4
Special Jurisdiction of the South; *see* Special Missionary District of the South
Special Missionary District of the South 178, 180
Spong, Jack x
Spotsylvania Court House, Battle of 16, 98
Star of the West (ship) 13, 48–50, 59 n.50, 89
state rights 117
Steinecke, Brad xix
Stephens, Alexander xvi
Stevens, Anne (Ann) 37
Stevens, Annie 40
Stevens, Barnard 37
Stevens, Clement Hoffman 37, 60 n.72
Stevens, Clement William 37–8, 56 n.7
Stevens, Harriett Rebecca Palmer 181, 185
Stevens, Helen 37
Stevens, Helen (Nell) 40
Stevens, Henry Kennedy 37, 60 n.72

Stevens Iron Brigade 50
Stevens, James 37
Stevens, Martha 37
Stevens, Mary 37
Stevens, Mary Singletary Capers 40, 53, 57 n.15
Stevens, Peter Fayssoux: and Anthony Toomer Porter 41
background of xi, xiv–xv, xvi–xvii, xviii, xix, 3–4, 12–17, 37–45, 55 n.5, 247
and the Civil War 13–14, 45–55, 60 n.72, 140
death and legacy of 184–6
and the Episcopal Church of South Carolina 19, 33 n.64, 51, 140, 144, 145, 149, 160, 167 n.78, 169–77, 210, 251–2, 256, 261
and the freed people 19–20, 124, 160, 169–70, 173–5, 178, 185–6, 204, 208, 210, 236, 251–3, 260, 261
photographs of 42, 52, 171, 183
postwar career of 19–20, 111, 127, 169–87 n.5, 251–3, 258–9
and the Reformed Episcopal Church (REC) 19–20, 174–87 n.5, 203, 251, 252
and slavery defense 42–5
and William Porcher DuBose 16, 83, 90, 94, 95, 174–5, 188 n.22, 221
Stevens, Sarah 23 n.1, 37–9
Stevens, Thaddeus 118
Stevens, William D. 181
Stokes, Karen xx
Stoney, Tom 87
Stono Rebellion of 1739 10
Strange, Thomas 7–8
Sullivan's Island (South Carolina) 46, 54, 73, 74
Summerville (South Carolina) 51, 204
Sweetwater Sabre Club 134 n.47

Tallahassee (Florida)   37, 38
Ten Epochs of Church History (multivolume work)   230
tenancy   122
Tennessee   97, 114, 118, 221, 223, 258
Texas   38, 39, 118, 254
Thirteenth Amendment   112, 116, 117, 249
Thirty-ninth Congress   118
Thomas, Albert Sidney   x, 140, 143–4, 156–7
Thomas, Lorenzo   48
Tilden, Samuel J.   126, 135 n.57
Tillinghast, Richard   238–9 n.29
Tillman, Benjamin Ryan "Pitchfork Ben"   134 n.47
Toomer, Esther Ann; *see* Porter, Esther Ann Toomer
Tractarianism   152, 173
Tracts for the Times (publications)   152
Trelease, Allen W.   260
Trenholm, Gr. A.   146, 198
Trinity Church (Chicago, Illinois)   153
Trinity Church (Columbus, Georgia)   221
Trinity Church (Washington, DC)   153
Trinity Episcopal Church (Abbeville, South Carolina)   124, 218–21, 258–61
Trinity Episcopal Church (Columbia, South Carolina)   142
Trinity Episcopal Church (Pinopolis, South Carolina)   17; *see also* Black Oak Parish
  and Loren B. Mead   xviii
  and Peter Fayssoux Stevens   x, xi, xviii, 54, 170, 171
Trinity Reformed Episcopal Church   178
Trumbull, Lyman   117
Turi, Matthew   xx
Turner, Nat   5, 10
Turning Points in My Life (book)   228, 229, 231, 233, 241 n.55, 256
25th South Carolina Regiment   75, 100–1

Union army; *see* Army of the United States
Union Episcopal Church   147
United States of America   91
United States Arsenal   200, 253–4
United States Military Academy; *see* West Point
Unity in the Faith (book)   231
University of Alabama   222
University of North Carolina at Chapel Hill   xx
University of Oxford   152
University of the South   xv, xviii, xx
  and Anthony Toomer Porter   205–6, 254–5
  formation of   221–5
  and William Porcher DuBose   xv, xviii, 15, 21, 22, 124, 163 n.35, 174, 201–2, 226–7, 229, 231, 235, 236, 238 n.29, 241 n.55, 258–60
University of South Carolina Press   xx
University of Vermont   147
University of Virginia   16, 87, 93
Updike, Tessa   xx

Vermont   18
Vesey, Denmark   10, 39
Vicksburg (Mississippi)   96–8
Virginia   16, 52–4, 74, 90, 98, 100, 114, 119, 250
Virginia Theological Seminary   x
Virginia-North Carolina border   62

Waccamaw (South Carolina)   68, 145
Waddell (Dr.)   260
Wade, Benjamin   114
Wade, Francis   xvi–xvii
Walker, C. B.   218
Wallace, Cranmore   147
War of 1812   91, 92
Wardlaw, Judge   219
Warren, Julie   xx
Washington, DC   xii, 46, 72, 153, 197, 200, 206
Washington Light Infantry   15, 73–5, 208–9

Washington Monument   208
Washington Square   208
Wateree Creek (South Carolina)   85
Watt School; *see* Porter Gaud School
Weed, Edwin   231
West Point   52
Whilden, John H.   49
White House   197
white supremacy   24 n.2, 117, 120, 125, 133 n.46, 134 n.47, 157, 172, 220–1, 235, 247, 250, 255, 256
Wilderness, Battles of the   16, 98
William & Mary, College of   12
William R. Laurie University Archives and Special Collections   xx
Willington (school)   260
Wilmer, Richard Hooker   140, 206
Wilmington (Delaware)   153
Wilmington (North Carolina)   95
Wilson, Noriate   152
Wilson Special Collections Library   xx

Winnsboro (Winnsborough) (South Carolina)   14, 15, 17, 65, 85, 86, 94, 100, 101, 217, 218, 257, 258
Winyah Bay (South Carolina)   63, 68, 69
Wise, Barbara (Babs)   xix
Wise, Ben   xix
Wood, A. E.   81 n.62
Woodford, Stewart L.   179

Yale University   85
Yeadon, Richard   94
yellow fever   7, 21, 75, 199
Yerger, Maria Louise; *see* DuBose, Maria Louise Yerger
Yorkville Line (railroad)   40
Young Men's Christian Association   154

Zeitler, Courtnay   xx
Zouave Cadets   49

ABOUT THE AUTHORS

Loren B. Mead (1930–2018) devoted his career to strengthening religious institutions. A native of Florence, South Carolina, he received a bachelor's degree from the University of the South and was elected to Phi Beta Kappa. He also earned a master's degree from the University of South Carolina and an M.Div. degree from Virginia Theological Seminary. Later, he pursued additional graduate studies at the University of North Carolina at Chapel Hill (city and regional planning) and the University of Maine (behavioral sciences). He was ordained deacon in 1955 and priest in 1956. In 1967, he served as fellow of the College of Preachers. Rev. Mead received honorary degrees from the University of the South, Virginia Theological Seminary, Berkeley Divinity School at Yale, and the Episcopal Divinity School. In 1999, he was named the fifth recipient of the Henry Knox Sherrill Medal for Outstanding Service to the Episcopal Church.

Rev. Mead pioneered the use of social-science research methods to study how faith organizations work, particularly local congregations. Beginning in 1969, he directed Project Test Pattern (PTP), a national initiative of the Episcopal Church generally concerned with evangelization but more specifically with revitalizing parishes. In 1974, using the lessons that he learned from PTP, Rev. Mead founded the Alban Institute in Washington, DC, a research, consulting, and publishing nonprofit organization working across lines of denomination and faith. He worked with nonprofit organizations, seminaries, and church agencies around the world, including in Australia, Germany, and South Africa. When he stepped down from its presidency in 1994, the Alban Institute had 8,500 members and was recognized as a leading force in the life of the contemporary church. Rev. Mead continued to consult, write, and teach until the final years of his life.

He published four best-selling books: *The Once and Future Church* (1991); *Transforming Congregations for the Future* (1994); *Five Challenges for the Once and Future Church* (1996); and *Financial Meltdown in the Mainline?* (1998). His first book, *New Hope for Congregations* (1972), and the last published during his lifetime, *The Parish is the Issue* (2015), dealt with the need to strengthen congregations. His work was informed by his previous experiences serving as a parish minister in Pinopolis, South Carolina, and Chapel Hill, North Carolina, from 1955 until 1969.

Born and reared in the segregated South, Rev. Mead worked for racial justice and reconciliation throughout his career. In addition to marching with a delegation of white pastors to support Dr. Martin Luther King Jr. following the death of Medgar Evers, he played a leading role in desegregating Chapel Hill, North Carolina. Always interested in issues of race within the church, Rev. Mead was working on *Fulfill Thy Ministry* until shortly before his death on May 5, 2018. Recognizing that he would not complete the work, he passed the project to his nephew. "I grew up in a church in which nobody believed that Black people and white people ought to be in the same church or community," Rev. Mead once recalled in an interview. "But sitting in those pews, I learned that we should be."

J. Michael Martinez teaches at Georgia Gwinnett College in Lawrenceville, Georgia. Visit him online at www.jmichaelmartinez.com.